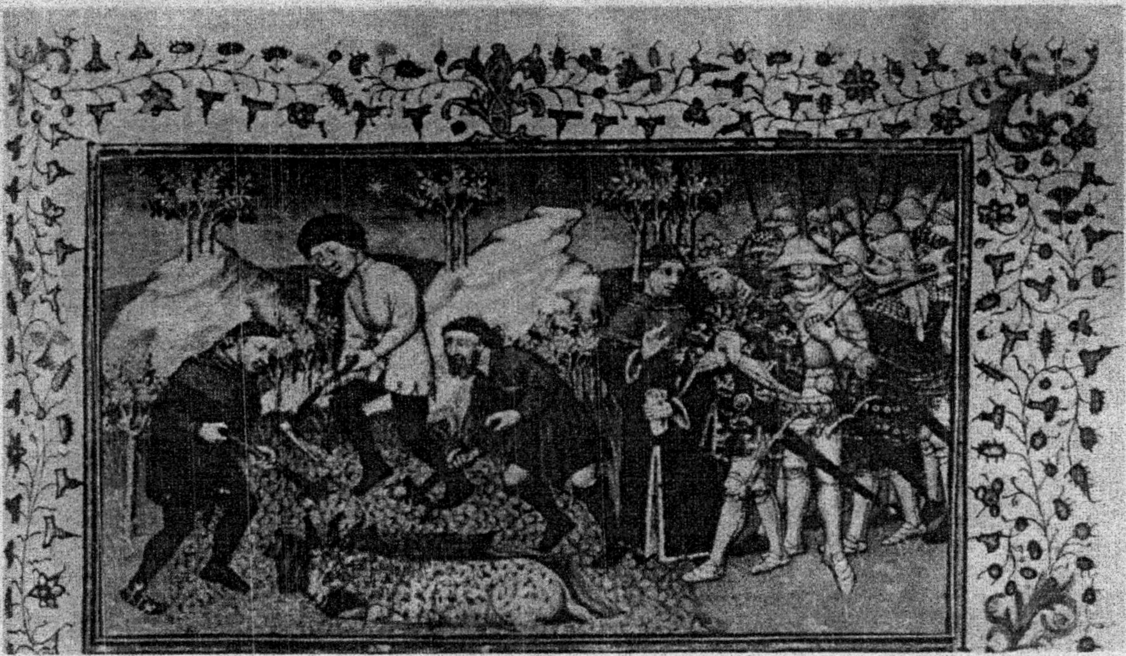

Comēnt le Roy alixādre ploura de pitie quil ont de son cheual
Buciffal qui se mouroit

TABLE OF CONTENTS

THE

INVASION OF INDIA

BY ALEXANDER THE GREAT

AS DESCRIBED BY

ARRIAN Q·CURTIUS DIODOROS PLUTARCH AND JUSTIN

BEING TRANSLATIONS OF SUCH PORTIONS OF THE WORKS OF THESE
AND OTHER CLASSICAL AUTHORS AS DESCRIBE ALEXANDER'S
CAMPAIGNS IN AFGHANISTAN THE PANJÂB SINDH
GEDROSIA AND KARMANIA
WITH AN INTRODUCTION CONTAINING A LIFE OF ALEXANDER
COPIOUS NOTES ILLUSTRATIONS MAPS AND INDICES

BY

J W M'CRINDLE M·A M·R·A·S F·R·S·G·S

LATE PRINCIPAL OF THE GOVERNMENT COLLEGE PATNA AND FELLOW OF
THE CALCUTTA UNIVERSITY
MEMBER OF THE GENERAL COUNCIL OF THE UNIVERSITY OF EDINBURGH

Westminster

ARCHIBALD CONSTABLE AND COMPANY

14 PARLIAMENT STREET S·W

MDCCCXCIII

LIST OF ILLUSTRATIONS

MAPS

PREFACE

En inventant l'histoire, la Grèce inventa le jugement
du monde, et, dans ce jugement, l'arrêt de la Grèce fut
sans appel. A celui dont la Grèce n'a pas parlé, l'oubli,
c'est-à-dire le néant. A celui dont la Grèce se souvient,
la gloire, c'est-à-dire la vie.—*Discours de M. Ernest
Renan du 5 Mai* 1892.

THIS work is the fifth of a series which may be entitled
Ancient India as described by the Classical Writers, since
it was projected to supply annotated translations of all
the accounts of India which have descended to us from
classical antiquity. The volumes which have already
appeared contain the fragments of the *Indika* of Ktêsias
the Knidian, and of the *Indika* of Megasthenês, the *Indika*
of Arrian, the *Periplous of the Erythraian Sea* by an unknown author, and Ptolemy's *Geography of India and the
other countries of Eastern Asia*. A sixth work containing
translations of the chapters in Strabo's *Geography* which
describe *India and Ariana*, is in preparation, and will
complete the series. I cannot at present say whether
this work will appear as a separate publication, or is to be
included in a volume containing new and revised editions
of the three *Indikas* mentioned above, which are now
nearly out of print as are also the other two works of the
series.

In the present work I have translated and annotated all the earliest and most authentic records which have been preserved of the Macedonian invasion of India under Alexander the Great. The notes do not touch on points either of grammar or of textual criticism, but are mainly designed to illustrate the statements advanced in the narratives. When short, they accompany the text as footnotes, and when of such a length as would too much encumber the ·pages, they have been placed together in an appendix by themselves. Such notes again as refer to *persons* have been placed, whether short or long, in a second appendix, which I have designated a *Biographical Appendix*.

In preparing the translations and notes I have consulted a great many works, of which the following may be specified as those which I found most useful :—

Droysen's *Geschichte Alexanders des grossen.*
Williams's *Life of Alexander.*
Sainte-Croix's *Examen Critique des Anciens Historiens d'Alexandre le Grand.*
C. Müller's *collection of the remaining fragments of the Historians of Alexander the Great.*
Thirlwall's *History of Greece*, vols. vi. and vii.
Grote's *History of Greece*, vol. xii.
Duncker's *History of Antiquity*, vol. iv., which treats of India exclusively.
Talboys Wheeler's *History of India.*
Le Clerc's *Criticism upon Curtius*, prefixed to Rooke's Translation of Arrian's *Anabasis.*
Lassen's *Indische Alterthumskunde.*
General Sir A. Cunningham's *Geography of Ancient India.*
V. de Saint-Martin's *Étude sur la Géographie Grecque et Latine de l'Inde*, and his *Mémoire Analytique sur la carte de l'Asie Centrale et de l'Inde.*

Rennell's *Memoir of a Map of Hindoostan.*

Bunbury's *History of Ancient Geography.*

Abbott's *Gradus ad Aornon.*

Journal Asiatique. Serie VIII.

Journal of the Royal Asiatic Society. New series.

Mahaffy's *Alexander's Empire* and his *Greek Life and Thought from the Age of Alexander to the Roman Conquest.*

Professor Freeman's *Essay on Alexander the Great.*

General Chesney's *Lecture on the Indian Campaign of Alexander.*

Wesseling's Latin Translation of Diodôros.

Translations of Curtius by Digby, Pratt, and Vaugelas respectively.

The Notes to the Elzevir edition of Curtius.

Chinnock's Translation of Arrian's *Anabasis of Alexander* and Notes thereto.

Chaussard's Translation of Arrian into French.

Moberly's *Alexander the Great in the Punjaub,* from Arrian. Book V.

Burton's *Sindh.*

Weber's *Die Griechen in Indien.*

Dr. Bellew's *Ethnography of Afghanistan.*

Sir W. W. Hunter's and Professor Max Müller's Works on India.

The translations are strictly literal, but though such will, I trust, be found to give, without crudeness of diction, a faithful reflex not only of the sense, but also of the spirit, force, fluency, and perspicuity of the original compositions. I have at all events spared no pains to combine in the translations the two merits of being at once literal and idiomatic in expression.

In translating Arrian I adopted the text of Sintenis

(2nd edition, Berlin, 1863); and with regard to Curtius, I found the work entitled *Alexander in India*, edited by Heitland and Raven, very serviceable, containing, as it does, exactly that portion of Curtius which it was my purpose to translate. Both the works referred to contain valuable *prolegomena* and notes, to which I must here acknowledge my obligations.

The Introduction consists of two parts. In the first, I have pointed out the sources whence our knowledge of the history of Alexander has been derived, and discussed their title to credibility; while in the second, I have sketched Alexander's career, and added a very brief summary of the events that followed his death till the wars for the division of his empire were finally composed.

In the transcription of Greek proper names I have followed as hitherto the method introduced by Grote, which scholars have now generally adopted. A vindication of the method which, to my thinking, is unanswerable, has appeared in the preface to Professor Freeman's *History of Sicily*, a work which the author unfortunately has not lived to complete.

The most noticeable change resulting from this method is the substitution of *K* for *C* in the spelling of Greek names. This should be borne in mind by those who may have occasion to consult either the Biographical Appendix or the General Index. I may further note that in transcribing Sanskrit or other Indian names I have in all cases used the circumflex to distinguish the long â, which is sounded as *a* in *fall*, from the short *a*, which is sounded as *u* in *dumb*. In Sanskrit and its derivative dialects this short vowel (अ) is never written unless it begin a word, for it is supposed to be inherent in every consonant. The letter *s'* with the acute accent represents the palatal sibilant (श) which is sounded like *sh*.

Two maps accompany the work, the larger of which shows the entire line of the route which Alexander followed in the course of his Asiatic expedition, while the smaller shows more distinctly that part of his route which lay through the northern parts of Afghânistân and the Country of the Five Rivers. For both I consulted the latest and most authoritative maps, both British and German, in which these routes have been laid down, and I found them in pretty close agreement, except with regard to that part of the route which is traced in the smaller map. Here I have generally followed the sketch map of the Panjâb which is given in General Cunningham's *Ancient Geography of India*, but have ventured to differ from him with regard to the position of the Rock Aornos, of Alexander's bridge over the Indus, of Sangala, and of the Oxydrakai, whom I have placed, as in Sir E. H. Bunbury's map, to the south of the Malloi.

The frontispiece to the volume, reproduced from a fifteenth-century French MS. of the Life of Alexander, may, it is hoped, appeal to many as a quaint rendering of a widely " popular " incident.

I cannot conclude without expressing my great obligations to Mr. Archibald Constable, by whose firm this work is published, for all the trouble he has taken in connection with its passage through the press, and especially with the preparation of the illustrations. I have also to thank Dr. Burgess for supplying the photograph from which the As'ôka inscription on page 373 has been reproduced, and for sundry valuable suggestions besides.   J. W. M'C.

9 WESTHALL GARDENS,
   EDINBURGH, 1892.

INTRODUCTION

"Of the life of Alexander we have five consecutive narratives, besides numerous allusions and fragments scattered up and down various Greek and Latin writers. . . . Unluckily, among all the five there is not a single contemporary chronicler. . . . The value of all, it is clear, must depend upon the faithfulness with which they represent the earlier writings which they had before them, and upon the amount of critical power which they may have brought to bear upon their examination. Unluckily again, among all the five, one only has any claim to the name of a critic. Arrian alone seems to have had at once the will and the power to exercise a discreet judgment upon the statements of those who went before him. Diodôros we believe to be perfectly honest, but he is, at the same time, impenetrably stupid. Plutarch, as he himself tells us, does not write history, but lives; his object is rather to gather anecdotes, to point a moral, than to give a formal narrative of political and military events. Justin is a feeble and careless epitomizer. Quintus Curtius is, in our eyes, little better than a romance writer; he is the only one of the five whom we should suspect of any wilful departure from the truth."—From *Historical Essays*, by Professor Freeman, 2d series, third edition, pp. 183, 184.

INTRODUCTION

THE invasion of India by Alexander the Great, like the first voyage of Columbus to America, was the means of opening up a new world to the knowledge of mankind. Before the great conqueror visited that remote and sequestered country, which was then thought to lie at the utmost ends of the earth, nothing was known regarding it beyond a few vague particulars mentioned by Herodotos, and such grains of truth as could be sifted from the mass of fictions which formed the staple of the treatise on India written by Ktêsias of Knidos. A comparison of this work with the *Indika* of Megasthenes, which was written after the invasion, will show how entirely all real knowledge of the country was due to that event. It may even, we think, be asserted that had that invasion not taken place, the knowledge of India among the nations of the West would not have advanced much beyond where Ktêsias left it, until the maritime passage to the East by the Cape of Good Hope had been discovered.

It was early in the year 326 B.C. that Alexander, fresh from the conquest of the fierce tribes of northern Afghânistân, led his army over into the plains of India by a bridge of boats, with which he had spanned the Indus a little below its junction with the Kabul river.[1] He remained in the country not more than twenty months all told, yet

---

[1] With the exception of Alexander, all the great conquerors who have crossed the Indus to invade India have sprung from provinces towards Tartary and Northern Persia.

in that brief space he reduced the Panjâb as far as the Satlej, and the whole of the spacious valley of the lower Indus, downwards to the ocean itself. He would even have penetrated to the Ganges had his army consented to follow him, and, in the opinion of Sandrokottos, would have succeeded in adding to his empire the vast regions through which that river flows. The rapidity with which he achieved his actual conquests in the country appears all the more surprising when we take into account that at every stage of his advance he encountered a most determined resistance. The people were not only of a most martial temperament, but were at the same time inured to arms; and had they but been united and led by such a capable commander as Pôros, the Macedonian army was doomed to utter destruction. Alexander, with all his matchless strategy, could not have averted such a catastrophe; for what is the record of his Indian campaigns? We find that the toughest of all his battles was that which he fought on the banks of the Hydaspes against Pôros; that he had hot work in overcoming the resistance of the Kathaians before the walls of Sangala; that he was wounded near to death in his assault upon the Mallian stronghold; and that in the valley of the Indus he could only overpower the opposition instigated by the Brahmans by means of wholesale massacres and executions. It may hence be safely inferred that if Alexander had found India united in arms to withstand his aggression, the star of his good fortune would have culminated with his passage of the Indus. But he found, on the contrary, the political condition of the country when he entered it eminently favourable to his designs. The regions of the Indus and its great tributary streams were then divided into separate states—some under kingly and others under republican governments, but all alike prevented by their mutual jealousies and feuds from acting in concert against a common enemy, and therefore all the more easy to overcome. Alexander, in pursuance of his usual policy, sought to secure the permanence of his Indian conquests by founding cities,[1] which he strongly fortified and garrisoned with large bodies of troops to overawe and hold in subjection the tribes in their neighbourhood. The system of government also which he established was the same as that which he had provided for his other subject provinces, the civil administration being entrusted to native chiefs, while the executive and military authority was wielded by Macedonian officers.

The Asiatic nations in general submissively acquiesced in the new order of things, and after a time found no reason to regret the old order which it had superseded. Under their Hellenic masters they enjoyed a greater measure of freedom than they had ever before known; commerce was promoted, wealth increased, the administration of justice improved, and altogether they reached a higher level of culture, both intellectual and moral, than they could possibly have attained under a continuance of Persian supremacy.

India did not participate to any great extent in these advantages. Her people were too proud and warlike to brook long the burden and reproach of foreign thraldom, and within a few years after the Conqueror's death they completely freed themselves from the yoke he imposed, and were thereafter ruled by their native princes. The Greek occupation having thus proved so transient, had little more effect in shaping the future course of the national destinies than a casual raid of Scottish borderers into Cumberland in the old days could have had in shaping the general course of English history.[2]

[1] According to Plutarch, seventy Asiatic cities at the least owed their origin to Alexander. Of those, forty can still be traced. Grote thinks the number is probably exaggerated, and disparages their importance.

[2] In saying this, I do not forget that the Græco-Baktrian kings at one time extended their sway in India even far beyond the parts conquered by Alexander; but this cannot be regarded as having resulted from his invasion. It might have equally happened had his invasion been as mythical as the Indian expeditions of Dionysos and Heraklês. Nor do I by any means overlook the effects produced by Greek ideas on the Indian mind—effects which can be traced in a variety of spheres, such as religion, poetry, philosophy, science, architecture, and the plastic arts. On this subject Professor A. Weber read a very learned paper, entitled "Die Griechen in Indien," before the Prussian Academy of Sciences in July

By this disruption of her relations with the rest of
Alexander's empire, India fell back into her former isolation from all the outside world, and for more than fifteen
or sixteen centuries afterwards the western nations knew
as little of her internal condition as they knew till lately
of the interior of the Dark Continent.   The invasion was,
however, by no means fruitless of some good results.   As
has been already indicated, it drew aside the veil which
had till then shrouded India from the observation of the
rest of the world, and it thus widened the horizon of
knowledge.   It is fortunate that what then became known
of India was not left for its preservation at the mercy of
mere oral tradition, but was committed to the safer custody
of writing.   Not a few of Alexander's officers and companions were men of high attainments in literature and
science, and some of their number composed memoirs of
his wars, in the course of which they recorded their im-
pressions of India and the races by which they found it
inhabited.[1]   These reports, even in the fragmentary state
in which they have come down to us, have proved of inestimable value to scholars engaged in the investigation of Indian
antiquity—a task which the sad deficiency of Sanskrit
literature in history and chronology has rendered one of
no ordinary difficulty.   Strabo, we must however note,
stigmatized the authors referred to as being in general a
set of liars, of whom only a few managed now and then
to stammer out some words of truth.   This sweeping
censure is, however, a most egregious calumny.   It may
indeed be admitted that their descriptions are not uni-

1890. It is a paper which well deserves
to be translated into our language.
Scholars now rather incline to believe
that, whatever may be the exact degree of the indebtedness of India to
Greece, the ancient civilization of
India was much less original and self-
contained than it was at one time
supposed to be.

[1] Patroklês, who held an important
command in the East under Seleukos
Nikatôr and his son Antiochos I.,
stated, in a work (now lost) which

included a description of India, that
while the army of Alexander took
but a very hasty view of everything
(in India), Alexander himself took a
more exact one, causing the whole
country to be described by men well
acquainted with it.   This description,
Patroklês says, was put into his
hands by Xenoklês the Treasurer.
On this subject Humboldt thus
writes: "The Macedonian campaign,
which opened so large and beautiful
a portion of the earth to the influence

formly free from error or exaggeration, and may even be tainted by some intermixture of fiction, but on the whole they wrote in good faith—a fact which even Strabo himself practically admits by frequently citing their authority for his statements. If one or two of them are to some extent liable to the censure, it must be remembered that Ptolemy, Aristoboulos, Nearchos, Megasthenes, and others of them, are writers of unimpeachable veracity.

It is to be regretted that the works in which these writers recorded their Indian experiences have all, without exception, perished. We know, however, the main substance of their contents from the histories of Alexander, written several centuries after his death by the authors we have here translated, as well as from Strabo, Pliny, Ailianos, Athênaios, Orosius, and others.

The following is a list of the writers on India who visited the country either with Alexander, or not many years after his death, or who were at least his contemporaries :—

1. Ptolemy, the son of Lagos, who became king of Egypt.

2. Aristoboulos of Potidaia, or, as it was called afterwards, Kassandreia.

3. Nearchos, a Kretan by birth, but settled at Amphipolis, admiral of the fleet.

4. Onêsikritos of Astypalaia, or, as some say, of Aegina, pilot of the fleet.

5. Eumenês of Kardia, Alexander's secretary, who kept the *Ephemerides* or Court Journal. His countryman, Hieronymos, in his work on Alexander's successors, made a few references to the campaigns of the Conqueror.

6. Chares of Mitylene, wrote anecdotes of Alexander's private life.

of one sole highly-gifted race, may therefore certainly be regarded in the strictest sense of the word as a *scientific* expedition, and, moreover, as the first in which a conqueror had surrounded himself with men learned in all departments of science, as naturalists, geometricians, historians, philosophers, and artists."

7. Kallisthenes of Olynthos, Aristotle's kinsman, author of an account of Alexander's Asiatic expedition.
8. Kleitarchos (Clitarchus), son of Deinôn of Rhodes, author of a life of Alexander.
9. Androsthenes of Thasos, a naval officer, author of a Paraplous.
10. Polykleitos of Larissa, author of a history of Alexander, full of geographical details.
11. Kyrsilos of Pharsalos, who wrote of the exploits of Alexander.
12. Anaximenes of Lampsakos, author of a history of Alexander.
13. Diognêtos, who, with Baitôn, measured and recorded the distances of Alexander's marches.
14. Archelaös, a geographer, supposed to have accompanied Alexander's expedition.
15. Amyntas, author of a work on Alexander's *Stathmoi*, *i.e.* stages or halting-places.
16. Patroklês, a writer on geography.
17. Megasthenês, friend of Seleukos Nikator, and his ambassador at the Court of Sandrokottos, king of Palibothra, composed an *Indika*.
18. Dêïmachos, ambassador at the same court in the days of the son and successor of Sandrokottos, author of a work on India in two books.
19. Diodotos of Erythrai, who, like Eumenês, kept Alexander's Court Journal, and may possibly have been in India.

Five consecutive narratives of Alexander's Indian campaigns, compiled several centuries after his death from the works of the writers enumerated, who were either witnesses of the events they described, or living at the time of their occurrence, have descended to our times, and are respectively contained in the following productions :—

1. The Anabasis of Alexander, by Arrian of Nikomêdeia.

2. The History of Alexander the Great, by Quintus Curtius Rufus.
3. The Life of Alexander, in Plutarch's Parallel Lives.
4. The History of Diodôros the Sicilian.
5. The Book of Macedonian History, compiled from the Universal History of Trogus Pompeius, by Justinus Frontinus.

ARRIAN

Arrian, who is universally allowed to be by far the best of all Alexander's historians, was at once a philosopher, a statesman, a military commander, an expert in the tactics of war, and an accomplished writer. He was born towards the end of the first century of our aera at Nikomêdeia (now Ismiknid or Ismid), the capital of Bithynia, situated near the head of a deep bay at the south-eastern end of the Propontis or Sea of Marmora. He became a disciple of the Stoic philosopher Epiktêtos (much in the same way as Xenophon attached himself to Sôkrates), and gave to the world an abstract of his master's lectures, together with an *Encheiridion* or manual of his philosophy—a work which was long and widely popular. Under the Emperor Hadrian he was appointed in A.D. 132 prefect of Kappadokia. He had not long filled this office when a large body of wild Alan horsemen made one of their formidable raids into his province. They had hitherto proved irresistible, but on this occasion they were completely foiled by the skilful strategy and tactics of Arrian, who expelled them from his borders before they had secured any plunder. In Rome he was preferred to various high offices, and under Antoninus Pius was raised to the consulship. In his later years he retired to his native city, where he occupied himself in composing treatises on a considerable variety of subjects, but chiefly on history and geography. He died at an advanced age in the reign of the Emperor Marcus Aurelius.

His account of Alexander's Asiatic expedition was

followed by a treatise on India called the *Indika*. The first part of this work, which gives a description of India and its people, was based chiefly on the *Indika* of Megasthenes; and the second part, which narrates the famous voyage of Nearchos from the mouth of the Indus to the head of the Persian Gulf, was based on a journal kept by Nearchos himself. The work is but a supplement to his history. He speaks himself with noble pride of this great work. "This I do assert," he says, "that this historical record of Alexander's deeds is, and has been from my youth up, in place to me of native land, family, and honours of state; and so I do not regard myself as unworthy to take rank among the foremost writers in the Greek language, if Alexander be forsooth among the foremost in arms." "Quel délire de l'amour propre!" here exclaims Sainte-Croix. His merits as an author are thus well stated by a writer in Smith's *Classical Dictionary*: "This great work (the *Anabasis*) reminds the reader of Xenophon's *Anabasis*, not only by its title, but also by the ease and clearness of its style. . . . Great as his merits thus are as an historian, they are yet surpassed by his excellences as an historical critic. His *Anabasis* is based upon the most trustworthy historians among the contemporaries of Alexander. . . . One of the great merits of the work is the clearness and distinctness with which he describes all military movements and operations, the drawing up of the armies for battle, and the conduct of battles and sieges."

Q. CURTIUS RUFUS

Nothing is known with any certainty respecting either the life of this historian or the time at which he lived. Niebuhr makes him contemporary with Septimius Severus, but most critics with Vespasian. Zumpt again, who, like some other eminent scholars, identifies him with the rhetorician Q. Curtius Rufus, of whom Suetonius wrote a life now lost, places him as early as Augustus.[1] The style in which his history is written certainly shows him to have been a consummate master of rhetoric. He was particularly given to adorning his narrative with speeches and public harangues, and these, as Zumpt observes, are marked with a degree of power and effectiveness which scarcely anything in that species of writing can surpass. It may also be said that his style for elegance does not fall much short of the perfection of Cicero himself. It has of course its faults, and in these can be traced the incipient degeneracy of the Latin language, such as the introduction of poetical diction into prose, the ambition of expressing everything pointedly and strikingly, not to mention certain deviations from strict grammatical propriety.

The materials of his narrative were drawn chiefly from Ptolemy, who accompanied Alexander into India, from Kleitarchos their contemporary, and from Timagenes, who flourished in the reign of Augustus, and wrote an excellent history of Alexander and his successors. While the sources whence he derived his information were thus good on the whole, he was himself deficient in the knowledge of military tactics, geography, chronology, astronomy, and especially in historical criticism, and he is therefore as an historical authority far inferior to Arrian. But in perusing his "pictured pages" the reader takes but little note of his errors and inconsistencies, being fascinated with his graceful and glowing narrative, interspersed as it is with brilliant orations, sage maxims, sound moral reflections, vivid descriptions of life and manners, and beautiful estimates of character. It is not surprising that with such merits Curtius has been one of the most popular of the classical authors. In spite of all his sins, for which he has so often been pilloried by the censors of literary morals, his history of Alexander has been the delight and

---

[1] The editors of *Alexander in India*, however, say that this rhetorician must have flourished early under Claudius, who reigned from A.D. 41 to 54. They add that the Latin of Curtius agrees well with this view, which would place him between Velleius and Petronius.

admiration of not a few of the greatest of European scholars. He seems to have taken Livy as his model, as Arrian took Xenophon for his. His work consisted originally of ten books, but the first two are lost, and in some of the others considerable gaps occur. The French translation of Curtius by Vaugelas, who devoted thirty years of his life to the task, is so remarkable for its elegance that it has been pronounced to be as inimitable as Alexander himself was invincible. It is not, however, a very close version.

PLUTARCH

There are but few works in the wide circle of literature which have afforded so much instruction and entertainment to the world as Plutarch's *Parallel Lives of the Famous Men of Greece and Rome*. These *Lives*, which are forty-six in number, are arranged in pairs, and each pair contains the *life* of a Greek and a Roman, followed, though not always, by a comparison drawn between the two. Alexander the Great and Caesar are ranked together, but no comparison follows. In his introduction to the *life* of the former, Plutarch explains his method as a biographer. "We do not," he says, "give the actions in full detail and with a scrupulous exactness, but rather in a short summary, since we are not writing *histories*, but *lives*. It is not always in the most distinguished achievements that men's vices or virtues may be best discerned, but often an action of but little note—a short saying or a jest—may mark a person's real character more than the greatest sieges or the most important battles." His *Lives*, therefore, while useful to the writer of history, must be used with care, since they are not intended as materials for history. His narrative of Alexander's progress through India has one or two passages which show this indifference to historical accuracy, as when, for instance, he states that the soldiers of Alexander refused to pass the Ganges when they saw the opposite bank covered with the army of the

King of the Praisians.[1]   His account of the battle with
Pôros is, however, excellent, and all the more interesting,
because, as he tells us, he obtained the particulars from
Alexander's own letters.[2]

Plutarch was a native of Chairôneia, a town in Boiôtia.
The date of his birth is unknown, but may be fixed
towards the middle of the first century of our aera.   He
visited Italy, and lectured on philosophy in some of its
cities.   For some time he lived in Rome, where, it is said,
but on doubtful authority, that he was promoted to high
offices of state, and became tutor to the Emperor Trajan.
The later years of his life he spent at Chairôneia, where
he discharged various magisterial offices and held a priest-
hood.   The date of his death, like that of his birth, is
unknown, but it is clear that he lived to an advanced age.
Besides the *Lives*, he published other writings, mostly
essays, having some resemblance to those of Bacon.
They are sixty in number, and are called collectively
Moralia, though some of them are of an historical character.   Two of them are orations *About the Fortune or
Virtue of Alexander*.   His style is somewhat difficult, at
times cumbrous and involved, and somewhat deficient in
that grace and perspicuity for which the works of the
Attic writers are noted.   His writings are all the more
valuable from their supplying a deficiency of the Greek
historians, whose works are filled with the records of war
and politics, while giving us but little insight into men's
private lives and their social surroundings.

DIODOROS THE SICILIAN

Diodôros was born at Agyrium, a city in the interior
of Sicily, and was a contemporary of Julius Caesar and
the Emperor Augustus.   It was the great ambition of his

---

[1] The author of the *Periplous* of
the Erythraian Sea also conducts
Alexander to the Ganges.   So too
does Lucan—*Pharsalia*, x. 33.

[2] Sainte-Croix and Professor Freeman both express strong doubts of
the authenticity of Alexander's letters
quoted by several writers.

life to write an universal history, and having this in view he travelled over a great part of Europe and Asia in order to acquire a more accurate knowledge of countries and nations than could be obtained from merely reading books. In Rome, where a far greater number of the ancient documents which he required to consult had been collected than were to be found elsewhere, he resided for a considerable time. He spent thirty years in the composition of his work, to which he gave the name of *Bibliothêkê*, which indicated that it formed quite *a library* in itself, embracing, as it did, the history of all ages and all countries. It consisted of forty books, which he divided into three great sections : 1st, the mythical period previous to the Trojan war ; 2d, the period thence to the death of Alexander the Great ; 3d, the period from Alexander to the beginning of Caesar's Gallic wars. Considerable portions of the *Bibliothêkê* are lost, but all the books relating to the period with which we are concerned are still extant.

Diodôros constructed his narrative upon the plan of annals, placing the events of each year side by side without regard to their intrinsic connection. The value of the work is greatly impaired by the author's evident want of critical discernment ; he mixes up history with fiction, shows frequently that he has misunderstood his authorities, and advances statements which are mutually contradictory. His style is, however, pleasing, having the merits of simplicity and clearness. In his second book he gives a description of India epitomized from Megasthenes. His account of Alexander's career in India records some interesting particulars of which we should otherwise have remained ignorant. He seems to have drawn largely from the same sources as Curtius.

JUSTINUS FRONTINUS

Justin, in the preface to his work entitled *De Historiis Philippicis*, informs us that it was "a kind of anthology"

—*veluti florum corpusculum*—extracted from the forty-four volumes published by Pompeius Trogus on Philippic (*i.e.* Macedonian) history. As these volumes included histories of nearly all the countries with which the Macedonian sovereigns had transactions, they embraced such a very wide field that they were regarded as a cyclopaedia of general history. Justin remarks that while many authors regard it as an arduous task to write no more than the history of one king or one state, we cannot but think that Pompeius had the daring of Hercules in attacking the whole world, seeing that in his books are contained the *res gestae* of all ages, kings, nations, and peoples. He then states that he had occupied his leisure while in Rome by selecting those passages of Trogus which seemed most worthy of being generally known, and passing over such as he took to be neither particularly interesting nor instructive. He has been much, but unjustly, blamed for his omissions, seeing that his only object in writing was to compile a work of elegant historical extracts. By so doing he has rescued from oblivion many facts not elsewhere recorded. From the extracts relating to India we gather more information about Sandrokottos (Chandragupta) than from any other classical source. Trogus Pompeius belonged, we know, to the age of Augustus, but it is uncertain when Justin lived. As the earliest writer by whom he is mentioned is St. Jerome, his date cannot be later than the beginning of the fifth century of our aera.

THE LIFE OF ALEXANDER THE GREAT

Alexander III., King of Macedonia, surnamed the Great, was born at Pella in the year 356 B.C. He was the son of Philip II. and Olympias, who belonged to the royal race of Epeiros, which claimed to be descended from Achilles, the hero of the *Iliad.* The education of the prince was in the outset entrusted to Lysimachos, an Akarnanian, and to his mother's kinsman Leonidas, a man of an austere character, who inured his pupil to Spartan-like habits of hard exercise and simple fare. In his thirteenth year he was placed under the immediate tuition of Aristotle, who acquired a life-long influence over the mind and character of his pupil. It may

FIG. 1.—LYSIMACHOS.   FIG. 2.—ARISTOTLE.

be supposed that the eager love of discovery which conspicuously distinguished Alexander from ordinary conquerors was in a great measure inspired and stimulated by the precepts of his master. In his sixteenth year he was entrusted, during his father's absence on a foreign expedition, with the regency of Macedonia ; and two years later, at the battle of Chaironeia, which was won chiefly through his impetuous valour, he displayed for the first time his incomparable genius for war. This victory made the Macedonian King supreme in Greece, and at a convention which met soon afterwards at his summons, and which was attended by deputies from all the Grecian states except Sparta, he was appointed to command the national forces and to conduct an expedition against Persia to avenge the invasions of Mardonios and Xerxes. He was actively engaged in preparing for this great contest when he fell by the hand of an assassin. Alexander succeeded (336 B.C.) not only to his sovereignty, but also to his supremacy in the affairs of Greece. He found himself, immediately on his accession, beset on all sides with most formidable opponents. Attalos, who was in Asia with a considerable force under his command, aspired to the throne ; the Greeks, instigated by the passionate eloquence of Demosthenes, attempted to liberate themselves from Macedonian dictation, and the barbarians of the north threatened his hereditary dominions with invasion. The youthful monarch was equal to the emergency. He at once seized Attalos and put him to death. Then suddenly marching southwards, he suppressed by skilful diplomacy the incipient rebellion of the Greek states. In the next place he turned his arms northwards, and, after much severe fighting, subjugated the barbarous tribes which lay between the frontiers of his kingdom and the Danube. Finally, he quelled in blood and desolation the revolt of Thebes, which had been prompted by a false rumour of his death. Having thus in a single year made himself a more powerful monarch than his father had ever been, he directed all his energies to complete the arrangements for the Persian expedition. The whole force which he collected for this purpose amounted to little more than 30,000 foot and 4500 horse.

The empire which this comparatively insignificant force was destined to attack and overthrow was the greatest which the world had as yet seen, and had already subsisted for two hundred years. It had been founded by Cyrus the Great, and extended by his successors till it embraced all Asia from the shores of the Aegean and the Levant to the regions of the Jaxartes and the Indus. It was divided by the great belt of desert, which stretches almost continuously from the Persian Gulf to the Sea of Aral, into two great sections which differed widely both in their physical aspect and the character of their inhabitants. The eastern tribes living amid mountains and deserts were rude, but distinguished for their hardihood, their love of independence, and their martial prowess. The western Asiatics, on the other hand, who inhabited those fair and fertile countries which had been the earliest seats of civilisation, were singularly deficient in these qualities. Enervated by ease and the affluence of luxuries, they offered but a feeble resistance to Alexander, and bent their necks submissively to his yoke. He had quite a different experience when he came into conflict with the tribes of the Oxus, Jaxartes, and Indus. They resisted him with the utmost spirit and determination, rose against him even after defeat, and succeeded in inflicting a signal disaster on his arms.

The system by which the vast empire was governed may be described as a rigid monarchy. It was divided by Darius Hystaspes into twenty provinces, a number which was afterwards much augmented probably by the subdivision of the larger ones. The government of each was committed to a satrap [1] whose powers were almost despotic. He collected the revenues, from which, besides defraying the expenses of his own administration, he was obliged to remit a fixed amount of annual tribute to the royal treasury. The Indian satrapy, which probably included Baktria and was limited to the regions west of the Indus, paid the largest tribute, which, as we learn from Herodotos, amounted to the immense sum of 360 talents of gold dust.

The king who filled the throne at the time of the invasion was Darius Kodomannos, who had some reputation for personal courage and some other virtues which might have adorned his reign had it been fated to be peaceful. He was, however, like Louis XVI. of France, quite destitute of the skill and nerve required for piloting the vessel of the state in stormy times. The empire long before his accession had been falling into decay. Insurrections were for ever breaking out. Some of the provinces, though nominally subject, were practically independent, while in others the satraps both claimed and exercised the right of transmitting their authority by hereditary succession. What saved it from dissolution was, not so much the strength of the government, as the reluctance of the leading men, through their distrust of each other's good faith, to enter into combinations against it. It was another symptom of its weakness, that the king in his wars trusted far more to the Greek

---

[1] In Persian, *Kshatrapa*.

troops in his pay than to his native levies and their leaders. Neither the Greeks nor the Persians had lost sight of the fact that at Kounaxa the victory had been won for Cyrus by the Greek mercenaries.

Alexander having completed his preparations, and appointed Antipater to act as regent of Macedonia during his absence, crossed over the Hellespont into Asia in the spring of 334 B.C. His army, though numerically insignificant when compared with the magnitude of the enterprise which lay before it, proved nevertheless, from the physical superiority, courage, and daring of the men, combined with the perfection of their organisation and discipline, and the consummate skill of their leader, more than a match for any force, however numerous, which was brought into the field against it. We may here quote a passage from Thirlwall, in which he describes the composition, organisation, and equipment of this heroic little army which performed the greatest deeds recorded in military annals :

" The main body, the phalanx—or quadruple phalanx, as it was sometimes called, to mark that it was formed of four divisions, each bearing the same name—presented a mass of 18,000 men, which was distributed, at least by Alexander, into six brigades of 3000 each, formidable in its aspect, and on ground suited to its operations, irresistible in its attacks. The phalangite soldier wore the usual defensive armour of the Greek heavy infantry—helmet, breast-plate, and greaves : and almost the whole front of his person was covered with the long shield called the aspis. His weapons were a sword long enough to enable a man in the second rank to reach an enemy who had come to close quarters with the comrade who stood before him, and the celebrated spear, known by the Macedonian name, sarissa, four-and-twenty feet long. The sarissa, when couched, projected eighteen feet in front of the soldier : and the space between the ranks was such that those of the second rank were fifteen, those of the third twelve, those of the fourth nine, those of the fifth six, and those of the sixth three feet in advance of the first line : so that the man at the head of the file was guarded on each side by the points of six spears. The ordinary depth of the phalanx was of sixteen ranks. The men who stood too far behind to use their sarissas, and who therefore kept them raised until they advanced to fill a vacant place, still added to the pressure of the mass. As the efficacy of the phalanx depended on its compactness, and this again on the uniformity of its movements, the greatest care was taken to select the best soldiers for the foremost and hindmost ranks—the frames, as it were, of the engine. The bulk and core of the phalanx consisted of Macedonians; but it was composed in part of foreign troops. These were no doubt Greeks. But the northern Illyrians, Paeonians, Agrianians, and Thracians, who were skilled in the use of missiles, furnished bowmen, dartsmen, and slingers : probably according to the proportion which the master of tactics deemed the most eligible, about half the number of the phalanx. To these was added another class of infantry, peculiar in some respects to the Macedonian army, though the invention belonged to Iphicrates. They were called Hypaspists, because, like the phalangites, they carried the long shield : but their spears were shorter, their swords longer, their armour lighter. They were thus prepared for more rapid movements, and did not so much depend on the nature of the ground. They formed a corps of about 6000 men. The cavalry was similarly distinguished into three classes by its arms, accoutrements, and mode of warfare. Its main strength consisted in 1500 Macedonian and as many Thessalian horse. But the rider and his horse were cased in armour, and his weapons seem to have corresponded to those of the heavy infantry. The light cavalry, chiefly used for skirmishing and pursuit, and in part armed with the sarissa, was drawn from the Thracians and Paeonians, and was about the third of the number of the heavy horse. A smaller body of Greek cavalry probably stood in nearly the same relation to the other two divisions, as the Hypaspists to the heavy and light infantry. To the Hypaspists belonged the royal foot bodyguard, the Agêma, or royal escort, and the Argyraspides, so called from the silver ornaments with which their long shields were enriched. But the precise relation in which these bodies stood to each other does not appear very distinctly from the descriptions of the ancients. The royal horseguard was composed of eight Macedonian squadrons, filled with the sons of the best families. The numbers of each are not ascertained, but they seem in all not much to have exceeded or fallen short of a thousand."

From this description of the Macedonian army, it may easily be imagined what a formidable aspect its main arm —the phalanx of panoplied infantry—would present to the enemy. Polybios informs us that the Roman officers who were present in the battle of Kynoskephalai, and then saw the phalanx for the first time, told him that in all their experience of war they had never seen anything so terrible. The phalanx, however, as that historian points out, could only operate effectively on level and open ground—was quite unfit for rapid advance and rough terrain, and useless if its ranks were broken. It was thus helpless in face of an active enemy unless well supported by cavalry and light troops. This explains why Alexander attached so much importance to his cavalry. In point of fact he owed none of his victories to the phalanx ; his cavalry, rapid in its evolutions and charging with resistless impetuosity, gained them all. In addition to the troops which have been particularised in the extract, there was one kind organised by Alexander called *dimachai*, intermediate between cavalry and infantry, being designed to fight on horseback or on foot as circumstances required. His artillery formed a very useful part of his equipment. The *balistai* and *katapeltai* of which it consisted threw stones and darts to the distance of 300 yards, and was frequently employed with great effect.

As he foresaw that in the course of his expedition he was likely to penetrate to regions either imperfectly or altogether unknown, he entertained on his staff men of literary and scientific requirements to write his deeds, and describe those countries and nations to which he might carry his arms.

He first came into conflict with the Persians on the banks of the Granîkos, a small river, which, flowing from Mount Ida through the Trojan plain, enters the Propontis to the west of Kyzikos. Their army, which consisted of 20,000 horse, and an equal number of Greek mercenaries, was commanded by several satraps who were assisted by the counsels of Memnon the Rhodian, the ablest general in the service of Darius. The Persians were drawn up in line along the right bank of the stream, while their mercenaries were posted on a range of heights that rose

in the rear.   Alexander drew up his forces on the opposite
bank in the order which he adopted in all his great
battles.   Thus the phalanx formed his centre ; he
commanded himself the extreme right, and the officer
in whom he had most confidence the extreme left.   To
either wing were attached such brigades of the phalanx
as circumstances seemed to require.   The Persians having
observed where Alexander was posted, strengthened their
left wing with dense squadrons of their best cavalry,
anticipating that this part of their line would be exposed
to the first fury of the onset led by himself in person.
They judged aright.   Alexander having sent a detachment of cavalry across the stream, followed with other
cavalry and a portion of the phalanx.   The Persians
made a gallant resistance, but were soon beaten.   Their
darts and scimitars were no match for the tough cornel
of the Macedonian spears.   Their ranks first broke where
Alexander himself in the hottest of the fight was dealing
death . and wounds around him.   A blow which was
descending on his own head, and which if delivered would
have proved fatal, was intercepted by Kleitos, who cut off
the arm of the assailant, scimitar and all.   The field was
won before either the phalanx on the one side, or the
Greek mercenaries on the other, could come into action.
The Macedonians, after returning from a short pursuit,
closed around the mercenaries and cut them down, all but
2000 who were made prisoners and sent in chains to
Macedonia.   The number of the Persians slain was about
1000 against only 115 on the other side.

Alexander did not, like most other conquerors after a
victory, plunder the surrounding country, but regarding
Asia as already his own, treated the inhabitants as subjects
whose interests he was bound to protect and promote.
Neither did he at once advance into the interior, but,
acting by a rule of strategy which he was always careful
to observe, resolved to make his rear secure.   He therefore first reduced all the western provinces of the empire
which Darius after the defeat of his satraps had placed

under the supreme authority of Memnon the Rhodian.
Memnon was a formidable antagonist, both from his skill
in war, and from his having a powerful fleet at his
command, which gave him the dominion of the sea, and
enabled him to threaten at will the shores of Greece and
Macedonia.

Alexander marched from the battle-field to Ilion, and
advanced thence southward through the beautiful regions
of Ionia and the other maritime states, which, in striking
contrast to their present blighted condition, were then at
the height of prosperity—adorned with numerous rich
and splendid cities, which vied with each other in all the
arts of refinement.   The terror of his name preceded him,
and these cities one after another, including even Sardis,
the western capital, which was strongly fortified, threw
open their gates to admit him.   Milêtos, however, and
Halikarnassos, being supported by the Persian fleet,
refused to surrender, and did not fall into his hands until
each had been for some time besieged.   After the fall of
Halikarnassos, the rest of Karia, of which it was the
capital, submitted, and then the operations of the first
year of the war were brought to a close by the reduction
of all Lykia.   In this province he gave his army some
rest.

The next campaign opened with the conquest of
Pamphylia, after which Alexander turned his march away
from the coast with a view to invade Phrygia, which lay
to the north beyond the lofty range of Tauros.   It was
now the depth of winter, but Alexander in defiance of all
obstacles—frost and snow, torrents and precipices, and the
resistance of the fierce Pisidian mountaineers—forced his
way into the Phrygian plains.   This passage of the Tauros
at such a season was an achievement not unworthy to
rank with the more celebrated passage of the Alps made
by Hannibal about a century later.   After he had cleared
the defiles, a march of five days brought him to Kelainai,
the capital of the greater Phrygia, which was pleasantly
situated where the river Marsyas joins the Maeander, and

was embellished with a palace and a royal park. Alexander, deeming its acropolis to be impregnable, made terms with the inhabitants, and then advanced to the ancient capital called Gordion, after Gordios, the father of the celebrated Midas, the first king of the country. Here was the complicated knot to which the prophecy was attached that whoever untied it should be Lord of Asia. It was tied on a rope of bark which fastened the yoke to the pole of the wagon on which Midas had been carried into the city on the day when the people chose him as their king. Alexander either undid the knot or cut it through with his sword.

On the return of spring he moved forward to Ankyra (now Angora), and there had the satisfaction to receive the submission of the Paphlagonians, who at that time were a very powerful nation. Being thus free to move southwards without leaving an enemy in his rear, he entered Kappadokia, and having overrun it without encountering any serious opposition, he recrossed the Tauros by a pass that admitted him into the fertile plains of Eastern Kilikia. The capital of this province was Tarsos, a flourishing seat of commerce, art, and learning, built on both banks of the river Kydnos, which was navigable to the sea. This important city fell without resistance into Alexander's hands, the satrap having fled at the tidings of his approach. Here, however, he nearly lost his life, having caught a violent fever by throwing himself when heated into the waters of the Kydnos, which ran cold with the snows of Mount Tauros. After his recovery he sent Parmeniôn eastward to occupy the passes leading into Syria, called the Syrian Gates, and marched himself in the opposite direction to reduce the hill-tribes of Western Kilikia. In the meantime Darius, advancing from the East, had crossed the Euphrates and the Syrian desert at the head of an army not less numerous than that with which Napoleon invaded Russia, and was lying encamped on a wide plain suitable for his cavalry within a two days' march of the Syrian Gates. Here he

waited for some time ready to fall upon the Macedonian
troops and crush them with the overwhelming superiority
of his numbers when they debouched from the defile.
When he despaired of their coming, he marched into
Kilikia through a pass known as the Amanian Gates and
encamped on the banks of the Pinaros which flows
through the plain of Issos to the sea. He thus placed
himself in a trap where he was hemmed in by the mountains and the sea in a narrow plain not more than a mile
and a half in width. Alexander meanwhile had passed
through the other gates into the Syrian plain when he
learned to his astonishment that Darius was now in his
rear. He at once retraced his steps, and by midnight
regained the pass, where from one of its summits he
beheld the Persian watchfires gleaming far and wide over
the plain of Issos. At daybreak he marched down the
pass, and on reaching the open part of the plain made the
usual disposition of his forces, Parmeniôn commanding the
left, and himself the right wing. Darius had drawn up
his line, which extended from the mountains to the sea,
along the northern bank of the river Pinaros. In the
centre, which confronted the dreaded Macedonian phalanx,
he had posted a body of 30,000 heavy-armed Greek
mercenaries.

Alexander began the action by dislodging a detachment of the enemy which had been posted at the base of
the mountains and threatened his rear. Finding the
Persians did not advance, he crossed the river and charged
their left wing with such impetuosity that he broke their
ranks and swept them from the field irretrievably dis-
comfited. He then wheeled round and brought timely
succour to his phalanx, which the Greek mercenaries of
Darius were driving back with disordered ranks to the
river. The struggle now became desperate, for these
mercenaries, bitterly resenting the state of political degradation to which the Macedonians had reduced their
compatriots in southern Greece, now fought against them
with all the fury that the passions of hate and rivalry

could inspire. They were nevertheless driven back, and the tide of battle surged up towards the state chariot itself, on which Darius was mounted in the centre of his line. The pusillanimous monarch no sooner perceived that his person was in danger than he ordered his charioteer to turn the heads of his horses for flight. This decided the fortunes of the day; it was the signal of his defeat, and his troops, on seeing it, at once broke from their ranks and fled from the field. The cavalry even, which on the extreme right had victory almost within their grasp, yielded to the general panic, and helped to swell the crowd of fugitives. As the narrowness of the plain allowed but very little room for escape, the vanquished were massacred in myriads. Darius escaped across the Euphrates, but his treasures and his family, consisting of his mother, wife, and children, fell into Alexander's hands, who treated these illustrious captives with all the kindness and courtesy which were due alike to their misfortunes and their exalted rank.

He did not pursue Darius, and about two years passed away before he again met him in battle. His victory had left Syria and Egypt open to his arms, and these countries had to be reduced and the power of Persia effectually crushed at sea before he could advance with safety into the heart of the empire. He therefore marched southward to Phoenicia, the seaports of which supplied the Persians with most of their war-galleys. Parmeniôn he sent forward with a small detachment to seize Damascus, where Darius, before his defeat, had deposited his treasures. The city surrendered without resistance, and a vast and varied spoil fell into the hands of the Macedonians. The cities along the Syrian coast submitted in like manner to Alexander himself, all but Tyre, which sent him a golden crown, but refused to admit him within her gates. For this temerity the city of merchant princes paid a dreadful penalty. Alexander, having captured it after a seven months' siege, burned it to the ground, and most of the inhabitants he either slew or sold into slavery. This is considered to have been the greatest of all Alexander's military achievements. Tyre had hitherto been deemed impregnable. It was built on an island separated from the mainland by a channel of the sea half a mile in width; its walls, which were of great solidity, rose to an immense height, and its navy gave it the command of the sea. The inhabitants, moreover, were expert in arms, and defended themselves with such spirit and obstinacy that Alexander found himself unable to overcome their resistance, until he obtained from Cyprus and Sidon a fleet superior to their own. He had also to construct a causeway through the channel to enable him to bring his engines close up to the walls, and this was a work of vast labour and difficulty. His merciless treatment of the vanquished darkly overshadows the glory of this memorable exploit.

Palestine, with the adjoining districts, next submitted to the Conqueror. Gaza alone, like Tyre, closed its gates against him. This city, which stood not far from the sea, towards the edge of the desert which separates Syria from Egypt, was strongly fortified, and held out for two months. Alexander took it by storm, slaughtered the garrison, and then set out for Egypt. A seven days' march through the desert brought him to Pelusium. The Egyptians, who smarted under the bondage of Persia, like the Israelites of old under their own, hailed his advent as that of a deliverer, and gladly submitted to his rule.

Alexander proceeded as far southward as Memphis and the Pyramids, and then embarking on the western or Kanopic branch of the Nile, sailed down to Lake Mareôtis, and landed on the narrow sandy isthmus by which that lake is separated from the sea. This neck of land was faced on the north by the island of Pharos, a long ridge of rock which sheltered it from all the violence of the ocean. Alexander, discerning with his keen eye all the advantages of such a position for commerce, at once founded on the isthmus the city of Alexandria, which, as he anticipated, soon became the great centre of trade between the eastern and western worlds. His next object was to consult the oracle of Jupiter Ammon, which was said to have been visited by Heraklês and Perseus, from both of whom he claimed to be descended. He therefore marched along the coast for about 200 miles to Paraitonion, which lay at the western extremity of Egypt. On the way he was met by deputies from Kyrênê, who brought him valuable presents, and invited him to visit their city. From Paraitonion he marched southward through the Libyan desert, and, after some days, reached the large and beautiful oasis where, embosomed amid thick woods, rose the temple of Ammon and the palace of his priests. On consulting the oracle he obtained answers, about the nature of which he stated nothing further than that they were satisfactory. He then returned across the desert to Memphis, where he settled the future government of Egypt, and ordered justice to be dispensed according to the ancient laws of the country. From Memphis he directed his march to Syria, and on reaching Tyre, remained there for some time. While he was in Egypt he had been visited by Hegelochos, his admiral, who reported that the Persians had been dispossessed of the islands which they had acquired in the Aegean ; that their fleet had been dissipated, and that all their leaders were prisoners except Pharnabazos, the successor of Memnon, who had died somewhat suddenly while Alexander was in Phrygia.

Alexander was now, therefore, the undisputed master of all the countries west of the Euphrates, and could with complete security turn his arms eastward to bring his contest with Persia to a final issue. Darius, on the other hand, who, in the interval between his defeat and the fall of Tyre, had twice sent an embassy to the Conqueror to sue for peace and the ransom of his family, on terms which, though most tempting, had been haughtily refused, was mustering all his forces to encounter the storm of war which would sooner or later burst from the clouds that hung ominously on his western horizon. The army he now raised was far stronger numerically than that with which he had fought at Issos, and, as it was drawn chiefly from the east, consisted of the best troops in his empire.

FIG. 3.—SEAL OF DARIUS.

He led it from Babylon across the Tigris, and marching northward along the eastern bank of that river, reached the plains of northern Assyria, which afforded ample space for the evolutions of his numerous cavalry. Here he encamped on a wide plain between the Tigris and the mountains of Kurdistan, near a village called Gaugamela.

Alexander, having remained at Tyre until his preparations were completed, started from that city after midsummer in the year 331 B.C. On crossing the Euphrates at the fords of Thapsakos, he learned where Darius was, and at once accelerated his march to find him. He passed the Tigris, which had been left unguarded, and advancing southward for a few days, came in sight of the Persian host, which he found already drawn up in line prepared for action. It is said that Parmeniôn, alarmed by the immense array of the hostile ranks, came at a late hour to the king's tent and proposed a night attack, and that Alexander's answer was that it would be a base thing to steal a victory. His forces amounted only to 40,000 infantry and 7000 horse, yet he was so confident of success that on the morning of the decisive day his sleep was deeper and longer than usual.

In its main features, the battle that followed was but a repetition of the day of Issos. Alexander again

commanded the right wing and Parmeniôn the left.   Again
Darius posted himself in the centre of his line, and again
the Greek mercenaries confronted the Macedonian phalanx.
Again Alexander, at the head of the Companion cavalry,
made havoc of the troops which guarded the royal standard ;
and again Darius, terror-struck at his near approach,
ignominiously fled from the field.   His flight gave once
more the signal of defeat, and that too, as at Issos, just
at the time when his cavalry on the right had made the
position of Parmeniôn most critical.[1]   Alexander was recalled from the pursuit of Darius, whom he was eagerly
bent on capturing, by a messenger sent by Parmeniôn
pressing for instant aid.   He at once turned back.   On
his way he met the Persian and Parthian cavalry and the
Indian troops now in full retreat.   A combat close and
hot followed.   The fugitives were for the most part
killed, but sold their lives dearly.   On returning to the
field Alexander found that his left wing was no longer
in distress, but putting the enemy to rout, and he therefore started once more in pursuit of Darius.   The fugitive
escaped, however, to Ekbatana, the capital in former
days of the Median kings.

Accounts differ as to the numbers that were killed in
this battle.   Arrian says, absurdly enough, that 300,000
of the Persians were slain, and a greater number taken
prisoners.   Diodôros reduces the amount to 90,000, and
Curtius to 40,000.   The loss again on Alexander's side
is reckoned by Arrian at 100, by Curtius at 300, and by
Diodôros at 500.[2]

---

[1] The Macedonian line in this part
of the field being broken, some of the
Indians and of the Persian cavalry
burst through the gap and fought
their way to the enemy's baggage,
where a desperate conflict ensued.—
Arrian, iii. 14.

[2] General Chesney, commenting
lately on these numbers, remarks
that "numbers without discipline are,
after a certain point, worse than useless, the men only get in each others'
way.   This was especially the case in
the battles of old times fought at close
quarters."   "The biographers of Sir
Charles Napier," he continues, "have
made a great point of the circumstance that at the battle of Meani the
British force of less than 3000 men
was opposed by 40,000 of the enemy
who fought desperately for several
hours.   Now, the whole British loss
in killed and wounded was under 300,
so that, assuming every wound to
have been inflicted by a separate
sword or bullet, it follows that out of

Alexander pursued the fugitive troops as far as Arbêla
—the place which has given its name to the battle, though
it was sixty miles distant from the field whereon it was
fought.   Here he found the baggage of Darius, and having
enriched himself with its spoils, he advanced southward to
Babylon.   This great capital, which once gave law to all
the nations of the East, had under the rule of the Achaimenids gradually declined both in wealth and importance.
Its inhabitants, like the Egyptians, detested their Persian
masters, who oppressed them and persecuted their religion.
They issued therefore from their gates in a joyful procession to welcome the victor and present him with gifts.   His
first acts on entering the city were well calculated to make
a favourable impression on their minds.   He ordered the
temple of Belus to be rebuilt, honoured that deity with a
public sacrifice according to the Chaldaean ritual, and restored to his priests the immense revenues with which
they had been endowed by the Assyrian kings.[1]

Alexander thus found himself the master of a more
spacious empire than any the world had yet seen.   No
king or conqueror had ever before stood on such a giddy

the 40,000 desperate fighters, 39,700
contributed nothing to the fighting."
In another passage he points out that
an ancient battle was in some respects
a much more formidable thing than a
modern one.   In the battle of old
days the absence of noise, except the
words of command, the tramp of men,
and the clashing of armour, above all
the closeness of one's adversary, must
have been of a kind to try the nerves
much more than the rattle of musketry,
the crashing of shells, and the thunder
of the artillery in a modern battle.
What we shall never get back to is
hand-to-hand fighting at close quarters.
It was this that made a battle so decisive in olden days, and caused the
tremendous slaughter that used to
be the fate of the beaten side.   An
ancient battle was really a very short
affair.   After the marshalling of the
troops and the preliminary skirmishing of the cavalry and the archery
practice of the light troops, in which
a good deal of time would be taken
up, the business must have been decided in a very few minutes when
once the infantry actually engaged.
The fact is that when two bodies of
men meet with sword or spear, a
prolonged contest is from the nature
of the case impossible.   In modern
warfare when a battle is lost, a large
part of the defeated army is already
at a distance and gets off unharmed.
But there was no escape for the man
in armour, and when he turned his
back his shield was no defence.

[1] "Against Phoenicians, Egyptians,
Babylonians, Alexander had no mission of vengeance; he might rather
call on them to help him against the
common foe. . . .   If the gods of
Attica had been wronged and insulted
(by the Persians) so had the gods of
Memphis and Babylon".—Prof. Freeman, *Historical Essays*, ii. pp. 202,
203.

pinnacle of power. As he had made his way to this supreme height before he had yet reached those years or experienced those vicissitudes of fortune which have a sobering effect on the mind, it is not surprising that, as in the case of Napoleon, whose genius was at many points in close touch with his own, and who, at a like early age, had amazed the world with his deeds of arms, unbounded success tended to deteriorate his character. He is found henceforth becoming more arrogant and despotic, more suspicious, and avid of flattery, while less tolerant of advice or remonstrance, and less capable of controlling the violence of his passions. The simple style of living in which he had been brought up seemed no longer to please him, and he began to assume all the pomp and splendour with which an oriental despot loves to surround himself,[1] an innovation in his habits which deeply mortified the pride of the Macedonians. It may be urged in his defence that he may have made the change less from any real inclination than from the politic motive of conciliating his new subjects by conforming to their tastes and habits.

Before leaving Babylon he settled the affairs of Assyria and its dependencies in accordance with a principle on which he generally acted, committing the civil administration to a native ruler, but leaving the command of the forces and the collection of the revenue in the hands of Macedonian officers. He then marched eastward, and in twenty days reached Sousa, the favourite capital of the Persian kings. Rich as Babylon was, its treasures were as nothing compared with those which had been here accumulated. The sums contained in the treasury amounted to 40,000 talents of uncoined gold and silver, and 9000 talents of coined gold, and there was other booty besides of immense value, including the spoils which Xerxes had carried off from Greece—the recovery

---

[1] "From this unhappy time all the worst failings of Alexander become more strongly developed. . . . Impetuosity and self-exaltation now grew upon him till he could bear neither restraint nor opposition."—Prof. Freeman, *Historical Essays*, ii. p. 206.

of which gratified beyond measure the patriotic feelings of the army.

From Sousa Alexander took the road to Persepolis, the ancient capital of the Persians, a rich and splendid city lying to the south-east of Sousa, in the beautiful vale of Persis which was fertilised by the streams descending from Mount Zagros, the Mêdos, and the Araxês.[1] On his route he passed through the hill-country of the Ouxians, which like that of the Pisidians, was occupied by warlike and predatory tribes. These mountaineers were nominally subject to Persia, but they nevertheless at one of their defiles exacted toll even from the Great King himself whenever he passed through their country in going between his two capitals. They beset this defile with the whole of their effective force to levy the customary tribute from Alexander, who payed them what he called their dues in the form of a crushing defeat.[2] He then plundered their villages, and, having received their submission, pressed forward by way of the formidable pass called the Persian Gates.[3] Here the satrap Ariobarzanes, at the head of more than 40,000 men, tried but in vain to arrest his progress. Alexander, with his usual skill and courage forced the position, and meeting with no further resistance reached Persepolis, where no defence was attempted. He not only permitted his soldiers to plunder this ancient capital, but, if we may believe the story, with which Dryden's Ode has made us familiar, set fire with his own hands in a drunken revel to the royal palace, a structure of supreme magnificence, as its ruins, which are still to be seen, attest. It is more probable, however, that he burned it from motives of policy, partly to show the Persians how absolutely he was now their master, and partly to avenge Greece for the destruction of her temples by Xerxes. In the royal treasury he found the vast sum of 120,000 talents,

[1] The Mêdos is now the *Polvar* and the Araxes the Bund-Amir.

[2] Kinneir places the Ouxian passes to the north-west of *Bebehan*.

[3] The narrow defile near *Kaleh Safed* (the white fort), some fifty miles to the north-west of Shiraz.

which falls little short of thirty million pounds of our
money.   As it was now mid-winter he here gave his
army some respite from their toils.   He gave himself,
however, no rest, but led a detachment to Pasargadai,
the primitive seat of the Achaimenids, which ·contained an
august monument, the tomb of Cyrus, which still exists,
and a rich treasury which he plundered.[1]   He next
assailed the Mardians, and marching over ice and snow,
reduced their mountain fastnesses and compelled their
submission.

In the spring of 330 B.C. he resumed the pursuit of
Darius, who was still at Ekbatana making vain efforts
to raise another army.   The fallen monarch, on hearing
that the enemy was again moving against him and had
reached Media, fled eastward hoping to find protection
and safety in the far remote province of Baktria, of
which his kinsman Bessos was the satrap.   The capital
which he had left was the summer residence of the
Persian kings, and was noted for the enormous strength
of its citadel.   Alexander therefore ordered Parmeniôn
to transport thither, as to a place of peculiar security,
the treasures which had been seized at the other capitals,
and to confide their custody to a strong guard of Macedonian soldiers.[2]   This done, he set out with a light
detachment of troops in the hope of overtaking the
fugitive king before he passed through the Kaspian
Gates.   At Rhagai, which was a day's rapid march from
that pass, he learned that Darius had escaped beyond it,
and he therefore halted for five days to recruit his
troops.   On renewing the pursuit and reaching the open
country beyond the gates, he learned that the Persian
officers who were escorting their sovereign had conspired

[1] Curzon thinks that Pasargadai lay
to the north-east of Persepolis at a
distance of some thirty miles. For a
discussion regarding their ruins and
the tomb of Cyrus see his great work
on Persia just published, vol. ii. pp.
70-92.

[2] The release of these enormous
treasure-hoards produced such effects
as resulted in recent times from the
discoveries of gold in California and
Australia.   The prices of all commo-
dities were greatly enhanced, and
prosperity advanced by leaps and
bounds.

against him and deprived him of his liberty. Greatly fearing now lest the traitors had some deadlier purpose in view, he made incredible exertions to overtake them, and he came up with them on the fourth day—but all too late. The conspirators, among whom was Bessos, finding that the pursuit was gaining upon them, mortally wounded the hapless king, who breathed his last before Alexander reached him. " Such," says Arrian, " was the end of Darius, who as a warrior was singularly remiss and injudicious. In other respects his character is blameless, either because he was just by nature, or because he had no opportunity of displaying the contrary, as his accession and the Macedonian invasion were simultaneous. It was not in his power, therefore, to oppress his subjects, as his danger was greater than theirs. His reign was one unbroken series of disasters, and he was at last treacherously assassinated by his most intimate connections. At his death he was about fifty years old." Alexander sent his body into Persia with orders that it should be buried with all due honours in the royal sepulchre. Bessos escaped into his own satrapy where he assumed the upright tiara, the distinguishing emblem of Persian royalty, and took the name of Artaxerxes.

Alexander now halted at Hekatompylos,[1] a place which received this Greek name from its being the centre where many roads met, and which became in after times the capital of the Parthian kings. Being joined here by the rest of his army, he prepared to invade Hyrkania, from which he was separated by the chain of mountains now called the Elburz. As the passes were beset by robber-tribes, he divided his army into three bodies. The most numerous division crossed the mountains under his own command by the shortest and most difficult roads. Krateros made a circuit to the left through the country of the Tapeirians (Taburistan), while the third division

---

[1] Perhaps Damaghan, but its position is very uncertain. According to Apollodoros it was 1260 stadia beyond the Kaspian Gates, but according to Pliny only 133 miles. See Curzon's *Persia*, i. p. 287.

under Erigyios took the royal road which led westward from Hekatompylos to Zadrakarta.[1] The divisions on emerging from the defiles united, and encamped near the last named place, which was the Hyrkanian capital. Hither came to Alexander with three of his sons the aged Artabazos, accompanied by the Tapeirian satrap and by deputies from the Greek mercenaries of Darius. Artabazos was received with distinguished honour, both because of his high rank and the fidelity he had shown to Darius, whom he had accompanied in his flight. The satrap was confirmed in his government, but the deputies were sternly told that as the mercenaries had violated the duty which they owed to their country, they must submit themselves unreservedly to the judgment of the king. Alexander then attacked the Mardians who inhabited the lofty mountains to the north-west of the Kaspian Gates. They submitted after a slight resistance, and were ordered to obey the Tapeirian satrap.

Alexander's next object was to crush Bessos and possess himself of all the eastern provinces as far as the borders of India. He therefore marched eastward towards Baktria, and having traversed the northern part of Parthia, reached Sousia, a city of Areia (now Sous, near Meshed, the present capital of Khorasan). Satibarzanes, the satrap of that province, and one of the conspirators against Darius, met him here, and having tendered his submission, was confirmed in his government, and dismissed with an escort of Macedonian horsemen to his capital, Artakoana. Alexander then resumed his march towards Baktria, but was arrested on the way by receiving word that Satibarzanes had revolted in favour of Bessos, armed the Areians, and slain his Macedonian escort. He therefore at once altered his route, and by the promptitude of his appearance confounded the plans of the satrap, who fled and was deserted by most of his troops. Artakoana was captured by Krateros after a short siege. This city stood in a plain of exceptional fertility at a point where all the roads

[1] *Sari*, according to Droysen.

from the north to the south, and from the west to the
east, united, and Alexander, discerning the incomparable
advantages of its position, whether for war or commerce,
founded in its neighbourhood a new city in which he
planted a Macedonian colony. He called it Alexandreia,
and as it still exists as Herat, it will be seen how well
grounded was its founder's belief in the strategetical and
commercial importance of its site.

Alexander, after suppressing this revolt, instead of
resuming his march to Baktria, moved forward to Prophthasia (now Furrah), the capital of Drangiana (Seistan), of
which Barsaentes, another of the accomplices in the murder
of Darius, was satrap. This traitor was seized and executed. Here an event occurred which has left a dark
stain on the character of Alexander. He was led to
suspect that a conspiracy had been formed against his life
by some of his principal officers, and among others by
the son of Parmeniôn, Philôtas, who held the most coveted
post in the army, that of commander of the Companion
Cavalry. It is certain that he was not an accomplice in
the plot; but as he had been informed of its existence,
and failed to give the king any warning of his danger, he
was accused before the Macedonian army and condemned
to death. He confessed under torture that his father,
Parmeniôn, had formed a design against the king's life, and
that he had himself joined the recent plot, lest his father,
who was now an old man, might, before the plot was ripe,
be snatched away by death from his command at Ekbatana, which placed the vast treasures deposited there at
his disposal. This confession, wrung by torture when its
agonies became insupportable, and obviously framed to
meet the wishes of the questioners, was no proof of the
guilt either of the father or the son. Parmeniôn was, nevertheless, on this worthless evidence condemned to death,
and Alexander, whom he had so faithfully served, took
care that the sentence should be executed before the news
of his son's death, which he might seek to avenge, could
reach his ears. Many other Macedonians were also at

this time tried and put to death.   Alexander's confidence
in his friends was thus much shaken ; and instead of
entrusting as formerly the command of the Companion
Cavalry to one individual, he divided that body into two
regiments, giving the command of one to Kleitos, and of
the other to Hêphaistiôn.

From Prophthasia he proceeded southwards into the
fertile plains along the Etymander (R. Helmund), then
inhabited by a peaceful tribe called the Ariaspians, who
had received from Cyrus the title of *Euergetai*—that is,
benefactors, because they had assisted him at a time when
he had been reduced to great straits.   Alexander spent
two months in their dominions, probably awaiting the
arrival of reinforcements from Ekbatana.   During this
interval Dêmetrios, a member of the king's bodyguard,
was arrested on suspicion of his having been implicated
with Philôtas in the recent plot, and his office was bestowed
on Ptolemy, the son of Lagos, for whom this promotion
opened the way to a royal destiny.   Alexander before
resuming his march appointed a governor over the Euergetai, but rewarded their hospitality by augmenting their
territory and confirming them in the enjoyment of their
political privileges.

He left this country about mid-winter, and ascending
the valley of the Etymander penetrated into Arachosia, a
province which stretched eastward to the Indus.   As he
advanced northward by Kandahar the snow lay deep on
the ground, and the soldiers suffered severely both from
hunger and cold.   About this time he heard that the
Areians had again revolted at the instigation of Satibarzanes, who had entered their province at the head of 2000
horse, and he immediately sent a detachment under Erigyios to quell the insurgents.   Continuing meanwhile his
own advance, he arrived at the foot of the colossal
mountain-barrier, the chain of Paropanisos, which separates
Kabul from Baktria.   Here in a commanding position,
near the village of Charikar, which stands in the rich and
beautiful valley of Koh-Daman, he founded yet another

Alexandreia (called by way of distinction Alexandreia of the Paropamisadai, or Alexandria apud Caucasum), and planted it with Macedonian colonists. According to Strabo he wintered in this neighbourhood, but Arrian leads us to suppose that he departed as soon as he had founded the city. He crossed the mountains, as some think, by the Bamiân Pass, the most western of the four routes which give access from the Koh-Daman to the regions of the Upper Oxus. It is likelier, however, that he ascended by the more direct route along the course of the Panjshir river. The army again suffered on the way from the severity of the cold, and still more from the scarcity of provisions. According to Aristoboulos nothing grew on these hills but terebinth trees and the herb called silphium, on which the flocks and herds of the mountaineers pastured. This march, which terminated at Adrapsa, occupied fifteen days.

The Macedonians had now reached a fertile country ; but as Bessos had ordered it to be ravaged, they found a wide barrier of desolation opposed to their further advance. The barrier was interposed in vain. Alexander resolutely pressed forward, and Bessos and his associates fled at his approach, and, crossing the Oxus, retired into Sogdiana. Aornos and Baktra, the two principal cities of the Baktrian satrapy, surrendered without resistance, and the satrapy itself was soon afterwards reduced. At Baktra Erigyios, who had succeeded in quelling the Areian revolt, rejoined the army. Alexander having appointed Artabazos satrap of his new conquest, marched to the Oxus in pursuit of Bessos, and came upon that river at the point where Kijil now stands. There it was about three-quarters of a mile in breadth, and the current was found to be both deep and rapid. The passage, which occupied five days, was made on floats, supported by skins stuffed with straw, and rendered watertight. The army had no sooner gained the right bank than messengers arrived from two of the leading adherents of Bessos — Spitamenes, the satrap of Sogdiana, and Dataphernes—promising to surrender

Bessos, who was already their prisoner, if Alexander would send a small force to their support. The king assented, and sent Ptolemy forward to receive the traitor from their hands. They gave him up, and he was conducted with a rope round his neck into the presence of the king, who ordered him to be scourged and then conveyed to Zariaspa (which some identify with Baktra), there to await his final doom.

The army next marched forward to Marakanda, now Samarkand, then merely the capital of the Sogdian satrapy, but destined to be in aftertimes the capital of the vast empire founded by Timour. It stood in the valley of the Polytimêtos (R. Kohik), a region of such exuberant fertility and beauty that it figures in Persian poetry as one of the four paradises of the world. Alexander remained for some time in this pleasant neighbourhood to remount his cavalry and otherwise recruit his forces. He then advanced to the river Jaxartes, which formed the boundary between the Persian empire and the barbarous Skythian tribes, and which the Greeks confounded with the Tanais or Don. The country was protected against the inroads of these warlike tribes by a line of fortified towns, of which the largest and strongest, Cyropolis, had been founded, as its name imports, by Cyrus. Alexander captured all these fortresses and manned them with small Macedonian garrisons; and to curb the Skythians still more effectually, founded on the banks of the Jaxartes, near where Khojent now stands, still another Alexandreia, which the Greeks for distinction's sake called *Eschatê*, or "the Extreme." In the midst of this undertaking, he was interrupted by the sudden outbreak of a widespread rebellion instigated by Spitamenes and his confederates. Taking immediate and energetic steps for its suppression, he in a few days recovered the seven towns; and then crossing the Jaxartes, defeated the Skythians, who with a view to aid the insurgents had mustered in great force on its right bank. After this victory he received tidings of the first serious disaster that had befallen his arms. He had sent a large force to operate against Spitamenes, who was at the time besieging the Macedonian garrison which held Marakanda. On learning that this force was approaching, the rebel chief retired down the Polytimêtos to Bokhara, and thence to the vast desert which stretches from Sogd to the Sea of Aral. Here he was joined by a large body of Skythian horsemen, and thus reinforced turned upon his pursuers, drove them back from the edge of the desert, which they had just entered, into the valley whence they had emerged, and there, amid the woody ravines of the Polytimetos, cut them to pieces almost to a man. Encouraged by this success, he returned to Marakanda and renewed the siege of its citadel, but on learning that Alexander was rapidly returning from the Jaxartes, he retraced his steps towards the desert, and reached it before the enemy overtook him. The course of the pursuit led Alexander to the scene of the late disaster. His first care was to bury the slain, and he then avenged their death by ravaging with fire and sword, in all its length and breadth, the lovely valley of the Polytimetos. He showed no mercy, but slaughtered all who fell into his hands, soldier and citizen alike. This is certainly, as Thirlwall remarks, one of the acts of his life for which it is most difficult to find an excuse.

As the year (329 B.C.) was now drawing to a close, he recrossed the Oxus and returned to Zariaspa (Baktra ?), where he spent the winter. Sentence was here pronounced upon Bessos, who was mutilated and then sent to Ekbatana for execution. Alexander's European forces, as the narrative has shown, were constantly undergoing diminution, not only by losses in the field, but also by his leaving Macedonian veterans to garrison important strongholds, or to form the nucleus of the population of the cities he founded. He therefore from time to time sent requisitions for recruits to Macedonia and Greece, and as these were adequately met the fighting quality of his troops was always maintained at the same high level. During his stay at Baktra a great number of such recruits arrived, and filled up the large gap which the late disaster had made in his ranks.   There came thither also ambassadors from the King of the Skythians, bringing presents and the offer of a marriage alliance, which was declined. The King of the Khorasmians, moreover, whose dominions, according to his own account, bordered on the land of the Kolchians and the Amazons, came in person and offered his services to Alexander should he wish to subdue the nations to the north and west of the Kaspian Sea. Alexander, however, being now anxious to enter India, declined his offers for the present.

The accounts of his next two campaigns are confused, and not always mutually consistent.   According to Curtius, when he moved from Zariaspa, he crossed the river Ochos (now the Aksou), and came to a city called Marginia, probably the *Marginan* of our times.   Arrian, however, makes no mention of this expedition.   The Baktrians were still imperfectly subjugated, and the Sogdians, notwithstanding the severe chastisement they had received, were again up in arms against his authority. He therefore left Krateros to deal with the former, while he marched in person against Marakanda.   On his way thither he performed another of his marvellous achievements, the capture of a fortress perched on the summit of a steep, lofty, and strongly fortified rock, held by a powerful garrison, and deemed to be impregnable.   He captured it, nevertheless.   Within this stronghold Oxyartes, a Baktrian chief, had for safety deposited his wife and daughters.   Roxana, the eldest daughter, was, next to the wife of Darius, the most beautiful of all Asiatic women, and Alexander was so captivated with her charms that he did not hesitate to make her his wife.

Spitamenes, meanwhile, assisted by the Massagetai, one of the Skythian tribes that ranged over the Khorasmian desert, made a devastating irruption into Baktria, and though he was in the end repulsed by Krateros, escaped into the desert beyond the reach of pursuit. Fearing he might renew his attack in some other quarter,

Alexander hastened to Marakanda to settle the province and provide for its security against future hostile incursions. To this end he directed a number of new towns to be founded and planted with Macedonian, Greek, and native colonists. In the course of this expedition he came to the Royal Park at Bazaria (perhaps Bokhara), and while hunting within its precincts killed a lion of extraordinary size with his own hand.

On his return to Marakanda a tragic incident occurred —his murder of Kleitos, from whom he had received some provocation in the course of a drunken revel. As he was tenderly attached to Kleitos, who was the brother of his nurse, and had saved his life at the Granîkos, his remorse for this frenzied deed knew no bounds at the time, and gave him many bitter moments in his after life.

His next expedition led him towards the western frontier of the province, where he reduced the district called Xenippa, which lay on the skirts of the Noura mountains—a range that runs from east to west about ten miles north of Bokhara. As Spitamenes was supposed to be in the desert not far off, he left Koinos in that part of the country with orders to capture that audacious rebel, while he himself withdrew to Nautaka, where he intended to pass the winter. This place was situated in a fertile oasis between Samarkand and the Oxus, and must have occupied the site of Kurshee or Kesh, noted afterwards as the birthplace of Timour. Spitamenes, meanwhile, attacked Koinos, but was defeated after a severe struggle, and driven back into the desert. His Skythian confederates, fearing their own country might be invaded, cut off his head and sent it to Alexander ; and so perished the most active, bold, and persevering antagonist that he had as yet encountered in Asia, one of the few who resolutely and to the last scorned to bend his neck to a foreign yoke.

With the first return of spring (B.C. 327) he moved from his winter quarters to invade the Paraitakai, who, as their name indicates, inhabited a mountainous district, and were, some think, a branch of the widespread Takka tribe, the name of which appears in Taxila, which designated a great capital it possessed in India. In the country of the Paraitakai, which lay to the east of Baktria and Sogdiana, there was another great rock fortress, which, like the Sogdian, was deemed impregnable. It was the main stronghold of a chief called Khorienês, who, after holding out for some time, was persuaded by Oxyartes to cast himself on the generosity of the great conqueror, a quality of which he had himself a very satisfactory experience. Khorienês therefore surrendered, and was rewarded by being confirmed in his government. Alexander after this success proceeded to Baktra in order to make preparation for his expedition into India, but left Krateros to reduce such of the tribes as still held out for independence. At Baktra another tragedy was enacted. The court pages, at the instigation of one of their number, called Hermolaos, who had been subjected to some degrading punishment, conspired against the king, who narrowly escaped assassination. The pages, who all belonged to families of high rank, were tortured to extract confessions of their guilt, and were then stoned to death by the Macedonians. The confessions indicated, it is said, that Kallisthenes, a literary man attached to the court who had been permitted, on the recommendation of his kinsman Aristotle, to accompany the expedition, not only knew of the existence of the plot, but had encouraged the pages to persist in their design. He had rendered himself obnoxious to the king by the freedom with which he expressed his opinions and by his opposition to the Persian fashions introduced into the court, and his doom was sealed. Accounts differ as to the time and mode of his death. According to Ptolemy he was tortured and then crucified, but Aristoboulos and Chares agree in stating that he was carried about in chains and died at last of disease in India.

The summer had set in when Alexander set out from Baktra on his Indian expedition. He crossed the chain of Paropamisos in ten days, and halted at the Alexandreia

which he had founded at their base to settle the affairs of
that city and the surrounding district.   The narrative of
his campaigns, from the time he left this place till he led
his army into Karmania, after its disastrous march through
the burning sands of the Gedrosian desert, is given in full
detail in the translations which form the body of this
work.   His march, which on his emerging from the desert
lay through the beautiful and fertile province of Karmania,
resembled a festive procession, and the licence in which
he permitted his soldiers to indulge was meant no less to
obliterate the memory of their terrible sufferings in the
desert than to celebrate according to Bacchic fashion and
example the conquest of India.

In Karmania, Alexander received intelligence that
Philip, who had been left in command of all the country
west of the Indus had been slain in a mutiny by the Greek
mercenaries under his command, but that the Macedonian
troops had quelled the mutiny and put the assassins to
death.   He did not at the time appoint any successor to
Philip, but empowered Eudêmos and Taxiles to take
temporary charge of the affairs of the satrapy.   Before
he left Karmania he was rejoined by Krateros who brought
in safety the division of the army which he had led from
the Indus by way of Arachôsia, Drangiana, and the
Karmanian desert.   Nearchos also visited his camp, which
at the time was a five days' journey distant from the sea,
and communicated the welcome news that the fleet had
arrived in safety at the mouth of the Persian Gulf.   The
admiral was instructed to continue the voyage by sailing
up the Gulf to the mouth of the Tigris, while Hephaistiôn
was put in command of the main army with orders to
proceed to Sousa along the maritime parts of Persis and
Sousiana.   The king himself with a small division took
the upper road which led to that capital through Pasargadai and Persepolis.   In Persis things had not gone well
in his absence.   The satrap whom he had appointed was
dead, and his office had been usurped by Orxines, a Persian
of great wealth and high rank, against whom many acts of

violence and oppression were charged. He found also that the tomb of Cyrus had been desecrated and plundered, and this outrage excited his violent indignation, since he looked upon that conqueror as the founder of the vast empire which was now his own. He could not discover the perpetrators, but had to content himself with ordering the violated sepulchre to be properly restored. On reaching Persepolis he investigated the charges against Orxines, and finding them proved, put him to death, and gave his satrapy to Peukestas, one of the commanders of his bodyguard.

In Persis the health of Kalanos, the Indian gymnosophist, who, at Alexander's request, had abjured the ascetic life and followed him from India, began to fail, and, as he chose rather to die than suffer the infirmities of age, he announced that it was his intention to burn himself. The king attempted to dissuade him, but finding that he was inexorably bent on self-destruction, ordered a funeral pyre to be prepared for him, and all the arrangements connected with his cremation to be superintended by Ptolemy. On the day appointed the devotee ascended the pyre and perished in its flames, exhibiting throughout a serene fortitude and self-possession which greatly astonished the Macedonians who attended in throngs to witness this strange spectacle. Strabo makes Pasargadai to be the scene of this incident, but Diodôros, Sousa, and with more probability, since we know that Nearchos was an eye-witness of the burning.

Alexander reached Sousa in the beginning of the year 324 B.C., and remained there for a considerable time, regulating the affairs of his new dominions. One of his great objects was to fuse together as far as was practicable his European with his Asiatic subjects ; and to this end he assigned to some eighty of his generals Asiatic wives, giving with each an ample dowry. He took himself a second wife, Barsinê, called sometimes Stateira, the eldest daughter of Darius, and, it is said, also a third, Parysatis, the daughter of Ochos, one of the predecessors of Darius.

About 10,000 Macedonians followed the example of their superiors, and all who did so received presents from their royal master. Carrying out this object in another form, he enrolled a large number of Asiatics among his European troops. These new schemes were so bitterly resented by the better class of his Macedonian veterans that they rose against him in a mutiny which he had no little difficulty in quelling. About 10,000 of these veterans were dismissed, and they returned to Europe under the command of Krateros. Towards the close of the year he went to Ekbatana, and there he lost his chief favourite Hêphaistiôn, who succumbed to an attack of fever. His grief at this bereavement knew no bounds, and showed itself in acts which seem copied from those wherewith Achilles demonstrated his passionate sense of the loss of his beloved Patroklos. From Ekbatana he marched back towards Babylon, and was met on the way by ambassadors from all parts of the known world, who came to do homage to the greatest of all kings and conquerors, and also by a deputation of Chaldaean priests who warned him of danger if at that time he should enter Babylon. He entered it nevertheless, though with gloomy forebodings, early in the spring of 323 B.C. As this city was the best point of communication between the eastern and western parts of his dominions, he had selected it to be the capital of his vast empire, and accordingly took measures immediately on his return for the improvement of its internal condition, for the drainage of the swampy lands in its neighbourhood which rendered its climate unhealthy, and also for removing obstacles to the safe and easy navigation of the great river by which it communicated with the sea.

His ambition being still, however, unsated, he meditated fresh conquests, which, if effected, would have made him master of the world from the shores of the Atlantic to the Eastern Ocean. But his end was now drawing near. The climate of Babylon was malarious, and as his spirits were depressed both by his loss of Hêphaistiôn and by superstitious fears, he was less able to withstand its malignant influences. He caught a fever, and having aggravated its virulence by indulging in convivial excesses, was cut off in June 323 B.C. at the age of thirty-three, and after he had reigned for nearly thirteen years. "So passed from the earth," says Bishop Thirlwall, "one of the greatest of her sons: great above most for what he was in himself, and not, as many who have borne the title, for what was given him to effect. Great, not merely in the vast compass and the persevering ardour of his ambition . . . but in the course which his ambition took, in the collateral aims which ennobled and purified it, so that it almost grew into one with the highest of which man is capable, the desire of knowledge and the love of good. In a word, great as one of the benefactors of his kind. . . . It may be truly asserted that his was the first of the great monarchies founded in Asia that opened a prospect of progressive improvement, and not of continual degradation, to its subjects : it was the first that contained any element of moral and intellectual progress." This estimate, high as it is, appears to be just and sober, and to hold a due balance between the extravagant eulogiums and the damnatory criticisms of other writers such as Mitford, Williams, and Droysen on the one hand, and Niebuhr, Sainte-Croix, and Grote on the other, who all alike allowed their ethical and political proclivities to bias their judgment.

FIG. 4.—ALEXANDER THE GREAT.

Alexander was dignified both in his appearance and in his demeanour. He was not above the ordinary height, but his frame was well built and extremely muscular. "He was very handsome in person," says Arrian, "devoted to exertion, of an active mind and a most heroic courage, tenacious of honour, ever ready to meet dangers, indifferent to the pleasures of the body, and strictly observant of his religious duties." Plutarch tells us that the statues of Alexander which most resembled him were those of Lysippos, who alone had his permission to represent him in marble, and who best hit off the turn of his head, which leaned a little to one side.[1] He adds that he was of a fair complexion, with a tinge of red in his face and upon his breast, and that his breath and whole person were so fragrant that they perfumed his under garments. In another passage, describing Alexander's habits, the same author says that he was very temperate in eating, and that he was not so much addicted to wine as he was thought to be. What gave rise to this opinion was his practice of spending a great deal of time at table. The time, however, was passed rather in talking than drinking, every cup introducing some long discussion. Besides, he never sat long at table except when he had abundance of leisure. There was always a magnificence at his table, and the expense rose with his fortune till it came to the fixed sum of 10,000 drachms for each entertainment. As in his dying moments he had given orders that his body should be conveyed to Ammôn in the Libyan oasis, it was embalmed, and after more than two years had been spent in making preparations for its removal, it was conveyed with vast pomp in a car of wondrous magnificence to Egypt, where it was entombed first at Memphis, and afterwards, by the authority of Ptolemy,[2] at Alexandreia, the greatest of all the cities which he had founded and called after his name.

Alexander was so prematurely cut off, and was besides so much occupied before his death with organising fresh expeditions, both maritime and military, that he had no time to improve or complete the measures which he had initiated for promoting the fusion and securing the permanent unification of the multifarious races comprised in his empire. Had he been vouchsafed a longer term of life, it seems probable that he would have succeeded

[1] " Edicto vetuit ne quis se praeter Apellem Pingeret, aut alius Lysippo duceret aera Fortis Alexandri vultum simulantia."—*Horace.*

[2] Pausanias, however, says that it was Philadelphos who brought the body to Alexandreia.

in welding so firmly together all the parts of his dominions that centuries might have elapsed before they became again disintegrated; but the dissensions which speedily broke out between his great captains, originating in their ambition to rule with independent authority, shattered his empire and embroiled it in wars which lasted for nearly half a century.

Soon after his death Perdikkas, to whom in his last moments he had given his signet-ring, was appointed to conduct the government on behalf of the royal family, which was held to consist of Arrhidaios, the king's half-brother, a man of weak intellect and character, and Queen Roxana, who a few months after her husband's death gave birth to a son who received the name of Alexander Aigos. The satrapies were then divided among the leading generals. Perdikkas soon began to use his position for the furtherance of his own selfish designs, and having secured the support of Eumenês, attempted to crush his colleagues and assume all power to himself. He marched first into Egypt against Ptolemy, but on the banks of the Nile he was defeated and slain in a mutiny of his own men 321 B.C. Tidings soon afterwards reached the army that Krateros had been defeated and slain in fighting against Eumenês while marching to assist Ptolemy. The office of regent was upon this offered to Ptolemy, who declined its acceptance, as he held that the satrapies should become independent kingdoms. The army then conferred that office, along with the tutelage of the royal family, on Antipater of Macedonia, who had crossed over into Asia to oppose Perdikkas. A new partition of the provinces, which did not differ much from the former, was then made at a place in Upper Syria called Triparadeisos. Under this arrangement Ptolemy held Egypt; Lysimachos, Thrace; Antigonos, Phrygia or Central Asia Minor; Seleukos, Babylon; Antigenes, Sousiana; Peukestas, Persia; Peithôn, son of Krateros, Media; Nearchos, Pamphylia and Lycia; Arrhidaios, Hellespontine Phrygia; Antipater and Polysperchon, Macedonia and Greece.

Eumenês still held the satrapy at first assigned to him—that
of Kappadokia, Paphlagonia, and Pontos—and was now the
leader of those who had been the adherents of Perdikkas.
He was supported by Alketas, the brother of Perdikkas,
Peukestas, Attalos, Antigenes, and by the influence of
Olympias, the mother of Alexander. Besides Perdikkas
and Krateros, two other great generals had by this time
disappeared from the scene—Meleager, who had been cut
off by Perdikkas, and Leonnatos, who had been slain in
the Lamian war.

Antigonos was appointed by Antipater to conduct the
war against Eumenês, and after many fluctuations of
fortune at last captured him and put him to death.
This happened early in the year 316 B.C. The fortunes
of Alexander's empire were then left at the disposal of
five men — Antigonos, Lysimachos, Ptolemy, Seleukos,
and Kassander, the son of Antipater, who had died in
the year 319 B.C. The ambition and ever-increasing
power of Antigonos soon led his colleagues to form a
coalition against him, and a long series of hostilities
followed. In the end Antigonos and his son Dêmêtrios,
surnamed Poliorkêtês, were defeated by the confederates
in the battle of Ipsos in 301 B.C. Antigonos fell on the
field of battle, and the greater part of his dominions fell
to the share of Seleukos, whose cavalry and elephants had
been chiefly instrumental in winning the victory. He
received as his reward a great part of Asia Minor as well
as the whole of Syria from the Euphrates to the Mediterranean. Ptolemy obtained Phoenicia and Hollow Syria,
but these provinces afterwards gave rise to frequent wars
between succeeding kings of Egypt and Syria. A war
in later times broke out between Seleukos and Lysimachos,
in which the latter was slain in 281 B.C. His kingdom
of Thrace was afterwards merged in that of Macedonia.
Thus the empire of Alexander, after a period of incessant
wars continued for upwards of forty years, was divided
between the powerful monarchs of Macedonia, Egypt,
and Syria.

The successors of Seleukos were unable to retain hold
of their remote eastern dependencies.   About the middle
of the third century B.C. Theodotos or Diodotos, the

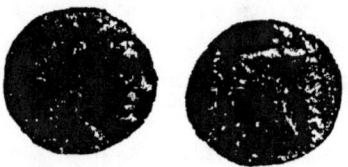

FIG. 5.—DIODOTOS.

governor of Baktra, revolted from his grandson Antiochos
II. and made Baktra an independent kingom.   Not long
afterwards As'ôka, the grandson of Chandragupta, as we
learn from one of his own inscriptions,[1] sent missionaries
to the kings of the West to proclaim to them and to their
subjects the doctrines of Buddhism.   The kings named
in the inscription are Antiyoka (Antiochos II., king of
Syria), Turamaya (Ptolemy III., Euergetes, king of Egypt),
Antigona (Antigonas Gonatas, king of Macedonia), Maga
(Magas, king of Kyrênê).   About the year 212 B.C.
Antiochos III., surnamed the Great, marched eastward to

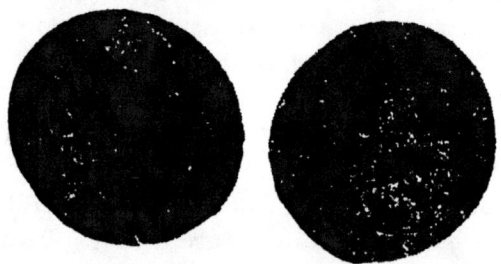

FIG. 6.—ANTIOCHOS THE GREAT.

recover Parthia and Baktria which had both revolted from
the second Antiochos.   He was, however, unable, even after
a war which lasted for some years, to effect the subju-
gation of these kingdoms, and accordingly concluded a
treaty with them in which he recognised their independence.

[1] See Note L*I* in Appendix.

With the assistance of the Baktrian sovereign Euthydêmos, who founded the greatness of the Baktrian monarchy, he made an expedition into India, where he renewed the alliance with that country which had been formed in the

FIG. 7.—EUTHYDÊMOS.

days of Sandrokottos. From Sophagasenos,[1] the chief of the Indian kings, he obtained a large supply of elephants, and then returned to Syria by the route through Arachôsia in the year 205 B.C.

[1] This name, transliterates the Sanskrit *Subhagasena*, which was not a personal name but an official title. See Lassen, *Ind. Alt.* II. p. 273.

ARRIAN

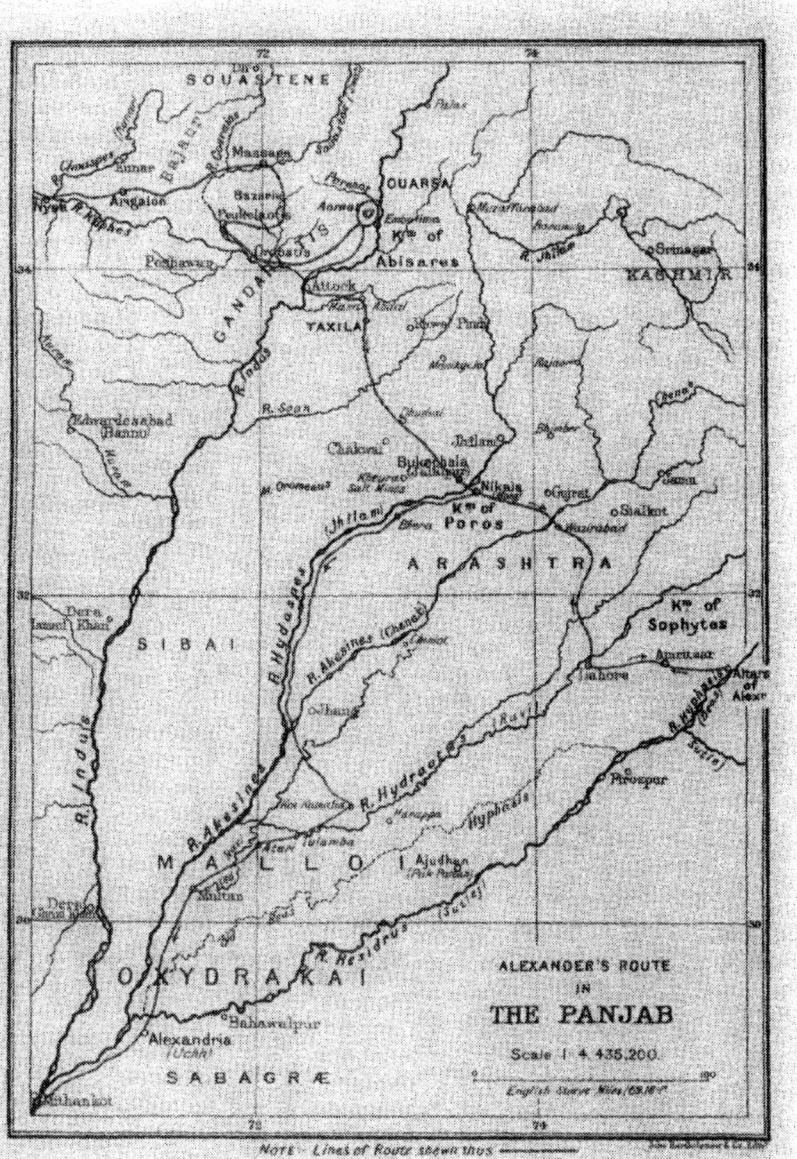

ALEXANDER'S ROUTE
IN
THE PANJAB

Scale 1 : 4.435.200.

English Statute Miles 69.16

NOTE — Lines of Route shewn thus ——————

ARRIAN'S ANABASIS

FOURTH BOOK

Chapter XXII.—Alexander crosses the Indian Kaukasos to invade India and advances to the river Kôphên

AFTER capturing the Rock of Choriênês, Alexander went himself to Baktra, but despatched Krateros with 600 of the Companion Cavalry [1] and a force of infantry, consisting of his own brigade with that of Polysperchôn and Attalos and that of Alketas, against Katanês and Austanês the only chiefs now left in the country of the Paraitakênai [2] who still held out against him. In the battle which ensued Krateros after a severe struggle proved victorious. Katanês fell in the action, while Austanês was made prisoner and brought to Alexander. Of the barbarians who had followed them to the field, there were slain 120 horsemen and about 1500 foot. Krateros after

[1] The Companion Cavalry, called sometimes simply the Companions, were the Royal Horse Guards, a body which at the beginning of the campaign consisted of 1500 men, all scions of the noblest families of Macedonia and Thessaly. In the course of the war their numbers were augmented perhaps to 5000, as Mützell conjectures.

[2] The Parai-tak-ênai possessed part of the mountainous country between the upper courses of the Oxus and the Jaxartes. They were perhaps one in race with the Takkas of India, who had a great and flourishing capital, Taxila (*i.e.* Takkasila, the Rock of the Takkas), situated between the Indus and Upper Hydaspes. The first part of their name *Parai* represents perhaps the Sanskrit *parvata*, a hill, or *pahâr* (a hill) of the common dialect. A tribe of the same name occupied a mountainous part of Media (Herod. i. 101), and another is located by Isidoros of Charax between Drangiana and Arachosia. Another form of the name is Paraitakai (Arrian, iii. 19; Strabo, xvi. 736; Stephanos Byz.)

the victory led his troops also to Baktra. While Alexander was here the tragic incident in his history, the affair of Kallisthenês and the pages, occurred.

When spring was now past,[1] he led his army from Baktra to invade the Indians, leaving Amyntas in the land of the Baktrians with 3500 horse and 10,000 foot. In ten days he crossed the Kaukasos [2] and arrived at the city of Alexandreia [3] which he had founded in the land of the Parapamisadai [4] when he first marched to Baktra. The ruler whom he had then set over the city he dismissed from his office because he thought he had not discharged its duties well. He recruited the population of Alexandreia with fresh settlers from the surrounding district, and also with such of his soldiers as were unfit for further service.[5] He then ordered Nikanor, one of the Companions, to take charge of the city itself and regulate its affairs, but he appointed Tyriaspes satrap of the land of the

[1] The spring of 327 B.C.

[2] Kaukasos here denotes the lofty mountain range, now called the Central Hindu Kush, which forms the northern frontier of Kâbul. Its native designation was Parapamisos, or, as Ptolemy more correctly transliterates it, Paropanisos. Till Alexander's time these mountains were altogether unknown to the Greeks. The officers of his army who wrote accounts of his Asiatic expedition sometimes considered them to be a continuation of the Tauros, and sometimes of the Kaukasos. Arrian, who regarded them as an extension of the former range, says that the Macedonian soldiers called them Kaukasos to flatter Alexander, as if, when he had crossed them to enter Baktria, he had carried his victorious arms beyond Kaukasos. The Greeks of those days, it must be observed, had no definite knowledge of the mountains to which that name was properly applicable, but vaguely conceived them to be the loftiest and the remotest to be found in the eastern parts of the world. The pass by which Alexander recrossed the Paropanisos was most probably the Kushan or Ghorbund Pass.

[3] See Note A, Alexandreia under Kaukasos.

[4] The tribes collectively designated Parapamisadai were, according to Ptolemy (who calls them Paropanisadai), the five following : — The Bôlitai, Aristophyloi, Parsioi, Parsyêtai, and Ambautai. They lived along the spurs of the Hindu Kush, chiefly along its southern and eastern sides. They thus occupied the whole of Kabulistân, and part of Afghânistân. The Bôlitai were probably the people of Kâbul, a city which, no doubt, represents that which Ptolemy calls Karoura (Kaboura ?) or Ortospana.

[5] The colonies which Alexander planted in the countries he overran were of a military character, designed to secure the permanence, cohesion, and ultimate unification of his conquests. The war-worn soldiers whom he made colonists were condemned to perpetual exile, as may be gathered from the fate which overtook the colonists who of their own accord left Baktra and attempted to return to Greece. They were treated as deserters, and were all put to death.

Parapamisadai and the rest of the country as far as the river Kôphên.[1]   Having reached the city of Nikaia[2] and sacrificed to the goddess Athêna, he despatched a herald to Taxilês[3] and the chiefs on this side of the river Indus, directing them to meet him where it was most convenient for each.   Taxilês accordingly and the other chiefs did meet him and brought him such presents as are most esteemed by the Indians.   They offered also to give him the elephants which they had with them amounting in number to five-and-twenty.

Having here divided his army, he despatched Hêphaistiôn and Perdikkas with the brigades of Gorgias, Kleitos,[4] and Meleager, half of the companion cavalry, and the whole of the mercenary cavalry, to the land of Peukelaôtis[5] and the river Indus.[6]   He ordered them either to seize by force whatever places lay on their route or to accept their submission if they capitulated, and when they came to the Indus to make whatever preparations were necessary for the transport of the army across that river.

[1] This is the Kâbul river, called otherwise by the classical writers the *Kôphês*, except by Ptolemy, who calls it the *Kôa*. Its name in Sanskrit is the *Kubhâ*.

[2] See Note B.

[3] Taxilês. His distinctive name, as we learn from Curtius (viii. 14), was Omphis. Diodôros (xvii. 86) less accurately calls him Môphis, and says that Alexander changed his name to Taxiles. This is, however, a mistake, for Taxiles was a territorial title which each sovereign of Taxila assumed on his accession to power. Indian princes are generally designated in the classics by their territorial or dynastic titles. The father of Omphis died about the time Alexander was making his preparations to invade India.

[4] Kleitos had been killed before the army left Baktra, but his brigade continued to bear his name even after his death.

[5] Peukelaôtis designated both a district and its capital city. The name is a transliteration of Pukkalaoti, which is the Pali form of the Sanskrit Pushkalavati, the name by which the ancient capital of Gândhâra was known. General Cunningham has fixed its position at the two large towns of Parang and Chârsada, which form part of Hashtnagar, or *eight cities*, that are seated close together on the eastern bank of the Landaî or lower Swât river. The position thus indicated is nearly seventeen miles to the northwest of Peshâwar. The city was in early times a great emporium of commerce. Ptolemy, who with the author of the Periplûs of the Erythraian sea, calls it Proklaïs, has correctly located it on the eastern bank of the river of Souastênê, *i.e.* the river of Swât. Wilson, however, and Abbott take Pekhely (or Pakholi) in the neighbourhood of Peshâwar to be the modern representative of the old Gândhârian capital (*v.* Cunningham's *Anc. Geog. of India*, pp. 49-51).

[6] The route assigned to this division lay along the course of the Kâbul river and through the Khaiber Pass to Peukelaôtis, which was situated where, or near where, Hasht-nagar on the river Landaï now stands.

They were accompanied on their march by Taxilês and the other chiefs. On reaching the river Indus they began to carry out the instructions which they had received from Alexander. One of the chiefs, however, Astês, a prince of the land of Peukelaôtis, revolted, but perished in the attempt, besides involving in ruin the city to which he had fled for refuge, which the troops under Hêphaistiôn captured in thirty days. Astês himself fell, and Sanggaios,[1] who had some time before fled from Astês and deserted to Taxilês, a circumstance which guaranteed his fidelity to Alexander, was appointed governor of the city.

Chapter XXIII.—Alexander wars against the Aspasians

Alexander took command in person of the other division of the army, consisting of the hypaspists,[2] all the companion cavalry except what was with Hêphaistiôn, the brigades of infantry called the foot-companions, the archers, the Agrianians, and the horse lancers, and advanced into the country of the Aspasians and Gouraians and Assakênians.[3] The route which he followed[4]

---

[1] This name is perhaps a transliteration of the Sanskrit *Sanjaya*, which means *victor*. A Shinwâri tribe called *Sangu* is found inhabiting a part of the Nangrihar district west of the Khaiber Pass.

[2] The hypaspists, so called because they carried the round shield called *aspis*, while the hoplites carried the oblong shield called *hoplon*, formed a body of about 3000 men at the outset of the war, but were perhaps augmented to double that number during its progress. They were not so heavily armed as the hoplites, and were therefore more rapid in their movements. The foot companions were another distinguished corps of guards. The Agrianians, who made excellent light-armed troops, were a Paionian people whose country adjoined the sources of the river Strymôn.

[3] Aspasioi and Assakênoi. See Note C.

[4] Strabo (xv. 697) states the reasons which led Alexander to select the northern route to the Indus in preference to the southern. "Alexander was informed," he says, "that the mountainous and northern parts were the most habitable and fertile, but that the southern part was either without water or liable to be overflowed by rivers at one time, or entirely burnt up at another, more fit to be the haunts of wild beasts than the dwellings of men. He resolved therefore to master first that part of India which had been well spoken of, considering at the same time that the rivers which it was necessary to pass, and which flowed transversely through the country which he proposed to attack, would be crossed with more facility

was hilly and rugged, and lay along the course of the
river called the Khôês,[1] which he had difficulty in crossing.   This done he ordered the mass of the infantry to
follow leisurely, while he rode rapidly forward, taking
with him the whole of his cavalry, besides 800 Macedonian foot soldiers, whom he mounted on horseback
with their infantry shields ; for he had been informed
that the barbarians inhabiting those parts had fled for
refuge to their native mountains, and to such of their
cities as were strongly fortified.   When he proceeded to
attack the first city of this kind that came in his way, he
found men drawn up before it in battle order, and on
these he fell at once, just as he was, put them to rout,
and shut them up within the gates.   He was wounded,
however, in the shoulder by a dart which penetrated
through his breast-plate, but not severely, for the breast-
plate prevented the weapon from going right through his
shoulder.   Ptolemy, the son of Lagos, and Leonnatos were
also wounded.

He then encamped near the city on the side where he
thought the wall was weakest.   Next day, as soon as

towards their sources." The districts
through which he passed are now
called Kafiristan, Chittral, Swât, and
the Yusufzai country.   It is more
difficult to trace in this than in any
other of his campaigns the course of
his movements, and to identify with
certainty the various strongholds which
he attacked.   The country through
which he passed is but little known
even at the present day, and, as Bunbury remarks, a glance at the labyrinth
of mountains and valleys, which occupy
the whole space in question in the
best modern maps, will sufficiently .
show how utterly bewildering they
must have been to the officers of
Alexander, who neither used maps
nor the compass, and were incapable
of the simplest geographical observations.   The time occupied by Alexander in marching from the foot of
Kaukasos to the Indus was about a
year.   Like Napoleon, he kept the
field even in winter, though in these
parts the cold at that season is intense.

[1] Khôês.   This is the first river
Alexander would reach after he had
left his encampment near the junction
of the Panjshîr with the Kôphên,
which appears to have been the place
where he divided his army.   It cannot
have been, as Lassen thought, the
Kamah or Kunâr, but is rather the
stream formed by the junction of the
Alishang and the Alinghar, which
joins the Kôphên on the left in the
neighbourhood of Mandrour above
Jalâlâbâd.   The Alinghar river, as
we learn from Masson, is called also
the *Kow*.   The Kôa of Ptolemy
must not be confounded with the
Khôês of the text, for that author
in describing the Kôa says that it
receives a tributary from the Paropanisadai, and that after being joined
by the Souastos (the river of Swât)
it falls into the Indus.   The Kôa is
therefore probably the Kôphên after
its reception of the Kamah or Kunâr
river.

there was light, the Macedonians attacked the outer of
the two walls by which the city was encompassed, and as
it was but rudely constructed they captured it without
difficulty.   At the inner wall, however, the barbarians
made some resistance ; but when the ladders were applied, and the defenders were galled with darts wherever
they turned, they no longer stood their ground, but
issued from the city through the gates and made for the
hills.   Some of them perished in the flight, while such
as were taken alive were to a man put to death by the
Macedonians, who were enraged against them for having
wounded Alexander.   Most of them, however, made good
their escape to the mountains, which lay at no great
distance from the city.   Alexander razed it to the
ground, and then marched forward to another city called
Andaka, which surrendered on capitulation.   When the
place had thus fallen into his hands he left Krateros in
these parts, with the other infantry officers, to take by
force whatever other cities refused voluntary submission,
and to settle the affairs of the surrounding district in the
best way existing circumstances would permit, while he
himself advanced to the river Euaspla,[1] where the chief
of the Aspasians was.

Chapter XXIV.—Operations against the Aspasians

In this expedition Alexander took with him the
hypaspists, the archers, the Agrianians, the brigade of
Koinos and Attalos, the cavalry guard, about four squadrons
of the other companion cavalry, and one half of the
mounted archers.   After a long march he reached, on

---

[1] Euaspla R. This name, which, so
far as I know, occurs only in Arrian,
has not been satisfactorily explained.
It designated, no doubt, the river
which Aristotle, Strabo, and Curtius
call the Choaspes, and which the best
authorities identify with the Kamah
or Kunâr, a river which rivals the
Kôphên itself in the volume of its
waters and the length of its course.
It rises at the foot of the plateau of
Pamîr, not far from the sources of the
Oxus, and joins the Kôphên at some
distance below Jalâlâbâd.   Strabo
says that the Choaspes traverses
Bandobênê (Badakshan) and Gand-
arîtis after having passed near the
towns of Plêgêrion and Gorydalê.

the second day, the city of the Aspasian chief.[1] The barbarians on hearing of his approach set fire to their city and fled to the mountains. But Alexander's men followed close at the heels of the fugitives, as far as the mountains, and made a great slaughter of the barbarians before they could escape to rough and difficult ground.

During the pursuit Ptolemy, the son of Lagos, descried the chief of the Indians of that country standing at the time on a small eminence, with some of his shield-bearing guards around him, and, although his own following was much smaller, he nevertheless continued the chase, being still on horseback. When the ascent, however, became so difficult that his charger could no longer mount it at a good pace, he left him there, and handing him over to one of the hypaspists to lead, he proceeded on foot, just as he was, to come up with the Indian. The latter on seeing that Ptolemy was now near at hand, turned round to face him, as did also his shield-bearing guards. The Indian, closing with his adversary, struck him on the breast with a long spear which pierced his cuirass, but the cuirass broke all the force of the blow. Ptolemy, on the other hand, smote the Indian right through the thigh, laid him prone at his feet, and stripped him of his arms. When his men saw their leader lying dead they left the place, but the other Indians, when they saw on looking from the mountains that the dead body of their chief was being carried off by the enemy, were filled with grief and rage, and rushing down to the small eminence fought for the recovery of the corpse with the utmost determination; for by this time Alexander also was on the eminence, and had brought with him the infantry soldiers, who had now alighted from their horses. This reinforcement falling upon the Indians succeeded after a hard struggle in driving them off to the mountains and securing the possession of the dead body.

Alexander then crossed the mountains, and came to a

[1] The capital of this chief was probably Gorys on the Choaspes.

city at their base, named Arigaion.[1]   He found that the
inhabitants had burned the place and taken to flight.
Here Krateros, with his staff and the troops under his
command, rejoined him, after having fully carried out all the
orders given by the king.   As the city seemed to occupy
a very advantageous site, he commanded Krateros to
fortify it strongly, and people it with as many natives of
the neighbourhood as should consent to make it their
home, together with any soldiers found unfit for further
service.   He then marched to a place where, as he had
ascertained, most of the barbarians of that part of the
country had taken refuge, and on reaching a certain
mountain encamped at its base.

Meanwhile Ptolemy, the son of Lagos, who had been
sent out by Alexander to procure forage, and had gone
with a few followers a considerable distance in advance
to reconnoitre the enemy, came back to Alexander to
report that he had seen more fires where the barbarians
were posted than in Alexander's camp.   Alexander, without
believing that the fires were so numerous, was still convinced that a host of barbarians had mustered together
from the surrounding country, and therefore leaving a
part of his army where it was encamped in proximity to
the mountain, he took with him such a force as the
reports led him to think would be adequate, and when
the fires were near in view, he divided it into three parts.
The command of one part he gave to Leonnatos, an
officer of the bodyguard, placing under him the brigade
of Attalos, along with that of Balakros.   The command
of the second division he gave to Ptolemy, the son of
Lagos.   It consisted of a third of the royal hypaspists,

[1] Arigaion.   This place, which
was situated to the east of the
Choaspes, is perhaps now represented
by Naoghi, a village in the province
of Bajore.   Ritter identified it with
Bajore or Bagawar, the capital of this
province.   The mountains to which
the inhabitants fled for refuge may
perhaps, as V. de Saint-Martin suggests, be those which Justin (xii. 7)
calls Daedali, whereto he says Alexander led his troops after the Bacchanalian revelry with which they had
been indulged at Nysa.   There is no
mention elsewhere of Arigaion, unless
it be the " Argacum urbem " of the
Itiner. Alex. 105.   It is taken by
Schneider to be the Acadira of
Curtius.

together with the brigade of Philippos and Philôtas, two companies of archers, each a thousand strong, the Agrianians, and half of the horsemen. The third division Alexander led in person against the position occupied by the main body of the barbarians.

Chapter XXV.—Defeat of the Aspasians—The Assakenians and Gouraians attacked

When they saw the Macedonians advancing against them they came down from the high ground which they had occupied into the plain below, confident in their numbers, and despising the Macedonians for the smallness of theirs. A sharp conflict followed, but Alexander without much trouble gained the victory. Ptolemy did not draw up his men in line upon the plain, but since the barbarians were posted on a small hill, he formed his battalions into column, and led them up the hill on the side where it was most assailable. He did not surround the entire circuit of the hill, but left an opening for the barbarians by which to escape if they meant flight. With these men also the conflict was sharp, not only from the difficult nature of the ground, but also because the Indians were of a different mettle from the other barbarians there, and were by far the stoutest warriors in that neighbourhood ; but brave as they were they were driven from the hill by the Macedonians. The men of the third division under Leonnatos were equally successful, as they also routed those with whom they engaged. Ptolemy states that the men taken prisoners were in all above 40,000, and that there were also captured more than 230,000 oxen, from which Alexander chose out the best—those which he thought superior to the others both for beauty and size—with a view to send them to Macedonia to be employed in agriculture.

He marched thence to invade the country of the Assakenians, for they were reported to have under arms

F

and ready for battle an army of 20,000 cavalry and more than 30,000 infantry, besides 30 elephants. Krateros had now completed the work of fortifying the city which he had been left to plant with colonists, and rejoined Alexander with the heavy armed troops and the engines which it might be necessary to employ in besieging towns. Alexander himself then proceeded to attack the Assakenians, taking with him the companion cavalry, the horse archers, the brigade of Koinos and Polysperchon, and the thousand Agrianians and the archers. He passed through the country of the Gouraians, where he had to cross the Gouraios,[1] the river named after that country. The passage was difficult on account of the depth and swiftness of the stream, and also because the stones at the bottom were so smooth and round that the men on stepping on them were apt to stumble. When the barbarians saw Alexander approaching they had not the courage to encounter him in the open field with their collective forces, but dispersed to their several cities, which they resolved to defend to the last extremity.

Chapter XXVI.—Siege of Massaga

Alexander marched first to attack Massaga,[2] which was the greatest city in those parts. When he was now approaching the walls, the barbarians, supported by a body of Indian mercenaries brought from a distance, and no less than 7000 strong, sallied out with a run against the Macedonians when they observed them preparing to encamp. Alexander thus saw that the battle would be

[1] The Gouraios is the river Pañjkora, which unites with the river of Swât to form the Landaï, a large affluent of the Kâbul river. It appears under the name of the *Gauri* in the sixth book of the *Mahâbhârata*, where it is mentioned along with the Suvâstu (the Swât river) and the Kampanâ. It owes its name to the *Ghori*, a great and wide-spread tribe, branches of which are still to be found on the Pañjkora, and also on both sides of the Kâbul River where it is joined by the Landaï. It formed the boundary between the Gouraians and the Assakênians.

[2] Mazaga. See Note D.

fought close to the city, whereas he wished the enemy to be drawn away to a distance from the walls, so that, if they were defeated, as he was certain they would be, they might have less chance of escaping with their lives by a short flight into the city. Alexander therefore ordered the Macedonians to fall back to a little hill which was about seven stadia distant from the place where he had meant to encamp. This gave the enemy fresh courage as they thought the Macedonians had already given way before them, and so they charged them at a running pace and without any observance of order. But when once their arrows began to reach his men, Alexander immediately wheeled round at a signal agreed on and led the phalanx at a running pace to fall upon them. But his horse-lancers and the Agrianians and the archers darted forward, and were the first to come into conflict with the barbarians, while he was leading the phalanx in regular order into action. The Indians were confounded by this unexpected attack, and no sooner found themselves involved in a hand-to-hand encounter than they gave way and fled back to the city. About 200 of them were killed, and the rest were shut up within the walls. Alexander brought up the phalanx against the fortifications, but was wounded in the ankle, though not severely, by an arrow shot from the battlements. The next day he brought up the military engines, and without much difficulty battered down a part of the wall. But when the Macedonians attempted to force their way through the breach which had been made, the Indians repelled all their attacks with so much spirit that Alexander was obliged for that day to draw off his forces. On the morrow the Macedonians renewed their assault with even greater vigour, and a wooden tower was brought up against the wall from which the archers shot at the Indians, while missiles were discharged against them from engines. They were thus driven back to a good distance, but still their assailants were after all unable to force their way within the walls.

On the third day Alexander led the phalanx once more

to the assault, and causing a bridge to be thrown from an engine over to that part of the wall which had been battered down, by that gangway he led the hypaspists over to the breach—the same men who by a similar expedient had enabled him to capture Tyre. The bridge, however, broke down under the great throng which was pushing forward with eager haste, and the Macedonians fell with it. The barbarians on the walls, seeing what had happened, began amid loud cheering to ply the Macedonians with stones and arrows and whatever missiles they had ready at hand or could at the moment snatch up, while others sallying out from posterns in the wall between the towers, struck them at close quarters before they could extricate themselves from the confusion caused by the accident.

Chapter XXVII.—Massaga taken by storm—Ora and Bazira besieged

Alexander then sent Alketas with his brigade to take up the wounded and recall to the camp the active combatants. On the fourth day another gangway on a different engine was despatched by him against the wall.

Now the Indians, as long as the chief of that place was still living, continued with great vigour to maintain the defence, but when he was struck by a missile from an engine and was killed by the blow, while some of themselves had fallen in the uninterrupted siege, and most of them were wounded and disabled for fighting, they sent a herald to treat with Alexander. To him it was always a pleasure to save the lives of brave men, and he came to an agreement with the Indian mercenaries to the effect that they should change their side and take service in his ranks. Upon this they left the city, arms in hand, and encamped by themselves on a small hill which faced the camp of the Macedonians. But as they had no wish to take up arms against their own countrymen, they resolved to arise by night and make off with all speed to their homes. When Alexander was informed of this he surrounded the hill that same night with all his troops, and having thus intercepted the Indians in the midst of their flight, cut them to pieces. The city now stripped of its defenders he took by storm, and captured the mother and daughter of Assakênos.[1] Alexander lost in the siege from first to last five-and-twenty of his men in all.

He then despatched Koinos to Bazira,[2] convinced that the inhabitants would capitulate on learning that Massaga had been captured. He, moreover, sent Attalos, Alketas, and Dêmêtrios, the captain of cavalry, to another city, Ora, instructing them to draw a rampart round it, and to invest it until his own arrival. The inhabitants of this place sallied out against the troops under Alketas, but the Macedonians had no great difficulty in routing them, and driving them back within the walls of the city. As regards Koinos, matters did not go well with him at Bazira, for as it stood on a very lofty eminence, and was strongly fortified in every quarter, the people trusted to the strength of their position and made no proposals about surrendering.

Alexander, on learning this, set out for Bazira, but as he knew that some of the barbarians of the neighbouring country were going to steal unobserved into the city of Ora, having been sent by Abisares[3] for this very purpose, he directed his march first to that city. He then sent orders to Koinos to fortify some strong position as a basis of operations against the city of the Bazirians, and to leave in it a sufficient garrison to prevent the inhabitants from

[1] Alexander seems to have treated these mercenaries with less than his usual generosity towards brave enemies. Plutarch reprobates his slaughter of them as a foul blot on his military fame. The attack upon the city after it had capitulated on terms admits of no justification.

[2] See Note E.

[3] Abisares. Arrian in a subsequent passage calls this chief King of the Mountaineer Indians. His name shows that he ruled over Abhisâra, that region of mountain-girt valleys, now called Hazâra, which lies between the Indus and the upper Hydaspes. In Hazâra the ancient name of the country seems to be preserved. It has been supposed, but less reasonably, that the district was so called from the great number of its petty chiefs, hazâra being the numeral for a thousand (in Persian). Abisares was a very powerful prince, and it is supposed with reason that Kâshmîr was subject to his sway.

going into the country around for provisions without fear of danger. He was then to join Alexander with the remainder of his troops. When the men of Bazira saw Koinos departing with the bulk of his troops they regarded the Macedonians who remained, as contemptible antagonists, and sallied out into the plain to attack them. A sharp conflict ensued in which 500 of the barbarians were slain, and upwards of 70 taken prisoners. The rest fled together into the city and were more rigorously than ever debarred all access to the country by the garrison of the fort. The siege of Ora did not cost Alexander much labour, for he captured the place at the first assault, and got possession of all the elephants which had been left therein.

Chapter XXVIII.—Bazira captured—Alexander marches to the rock Aornos

When the inhabitants of Bazira heard that Ora had fallen, they regarded their case as desperate, and at the dead of night fled from their city to the Rock, as all the other barbarians were doing, for, having left their cities, they were fleeing to the rock in that land called Aornos;[1] for this is a mighty mass of rock in that part of the country, and a report is current concerning it that even Heraklês, the son of Zeus, had found it to be impregnable. Now whether the Theban, or the Tyrian, or the Egyptian Heraklês penetrated so far as to the Indians[2] I can neither

---

[1] Aornos. See Note F.

[2] "Heraklês," says Herodotos (ii. 43, 44), "is one of the ancient gods of the Egyptians, and, as they say themselves, it was 17,000 years before the reign of Amasis, when the number of their gods was increased from eight to twelve, of whom Heraklês was accounted one. And being desirous of obtaining certain information from whatever source I could, I sailed to Tyre in Phoenicia, where, as I had been informed, there was a temple dedicated to Heraklês." The name of the Egyptian Heraklês was Dsona or Chôn, or, according to Pausanias, Makeris, and that of the Tyrian was Melkart. These were more ancient than the Theban Heraklês, the son of Zeus and Alkmênê. The Indian Heraklês, called Dorsanes, who, according to Arrian, was the father of Pandaia, has been identified with S'iva, but also with Balarâma, the eighth avatâr of Vishnu. Diodôros (ii. 39) ascribes to him the building of

positively affirm nor deny, but I incline to think that he did not penetrate so far; for we know how common it is for men when speaking of things that are difficult to magnify the difficulty by declaring that it would

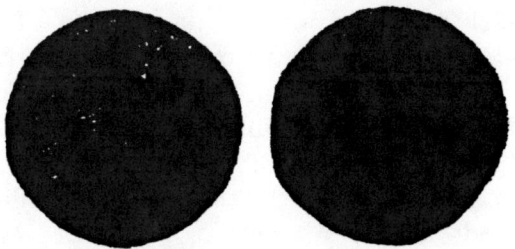

FIG. 8.—THE TYRIAN HERAKLÊS.

baffle even Heraklês himself. And in the case of this rock my own conviction is that Heraklês was mentioned to make the story of its capture all the more wonderful. The rock is said to have had a circuit of about 200 stadia, and at its lowest elevation a height of eleven stadia.[1] It was ascended by a single path cut by the hand of man, yet difficult. On the summit of the rock there was, it is also said, plenty of pure water which gushed out from a copious spring. There was timber besides, and as much good arable land as required for its cultivation the labour of a thousand men.

Alexander on learning these particulars was seized with an ardent desire to capture this mountain also, the story current about Heraklês not being the least of the incentives. With this in view he made Ora and Massaga strongholds for bridling the districts around them, and at the same time strengthened the defences of Bazira. The division under Hêphaistiôn and Perdikkas fortified for him

the walls and of the palace of Pali-bothra (now Pâtnâ). Arrian in the second book of this work (c. 16) distinguishes the Tyrian Heraklês from the Egyptian and Argive or Theban. The latter, he says, lived about the time of Oidipous, son of Laios.

[1] The Olympic stadium, which was the chief Greek measure for itinerary distances, was equal to 600 Greek feet, 625 Roman feet, and 606 feet 9 inches English. The stadium of this length was the only one in use before the third century of our aera.

another city called Orobatis [1] in which they left a garrison and then marched on to the river Indus. On reaching it they began preparing a bridge to span the Indus in accordance with Alexander's orders.

Alexander now appointed Nikanor, one of the companions, satrap of the country on this side of the Indus, [2] and then first marched himself towards that river and received the submission of the city of Peukelaôtis which lay not far from the Indus. He placed in it a garrison of Macedonian soldiers under the command of Philippos, and then occupied himself in reducing other towns—some small ones—situated near the river Indus. [3] He was accompanied on this occasion by Kôphaios and Assagetês the local chiefs. [4] On reaching Embolima, [5] a city close

[1] The site of Orobatis must be sought for in the district west of Peukelaôtis, through which Hêphaistiôn advanced on his way to the Indus. The position and name of Arabutt, a village in this locality where ruins exist, plainly show its identity with the Orobatis of the text. It is situated on the left bank of the Landaï, and is near Naoshera. It is probably the Oroppa of the Ravenna geographer.

[2] Nikanor was succeeded in this office by Philippos, who was placed in command of the garrison of Peukelaôtis.

[3] Peukelaôtis, as has been stated, stood on the Landaï at a distance of seventeen miles north-west from Peshâwar. Alexander after the fall of Bazira moved westwards toward that river, judging it expedient before attacking the Rock to reduce all the yet unconquered region west of the Indus. He took Peukelaôtis, and then directed his march eastward till he approached the embouchure of the Kôphên, whence turning northwards he advanced up the right bank of the Indus till he reached Embolima, about eight miles distant from Aornos, and as high up the river as an army could go.

[4] Kôphaios, to judge from his name and from what is here stated, must have been the ruler of the valley of the lower Kôphên or Kâbul river.

Hence it is unlikely, as some have supposed, that the dominions of Taxilês lay partly in the country west of the Indus. I find nothing anywhere in the classical writers lending countenance to such a supposition. The name of Assagetes is probably a transliteration into Greek of the Sanskrit Aśvajit, "gaining horses by conquest."

[5] Ritter taking Embolima to be a word of Greek origin, equivalent in meaning to ἐκβολή, "the mouth of a river," thought that this place lay opposite to Attak, in the angle of land where the Kôphên discharges into the Indus, and was thus led to identify Aornos with the hill in that locality on which the fort of Raja Hodi stands. Embolima appears, however, to be rather a combination of two native names, Amb and Balimah. Amb is the name of a fort, now in ruins, from which runs the ordinary path up to the summit of Mahâban. It crowns a position of remarkable strength, which faces Derbend, a small town on the opposite side of the Indus. Not far westward from this fort, and on the same spur of the Mahâban, there is another fort also in ruins, which preserves to this day in the tradition of the inhabitants the name of Balimah. It is in accordance with Indian custom thus to combine into one the names of two neighbouring places.

adjoining the rock of Aornos,[1] he there left Krateros with a part of the army to gather into the city as much corn as possible and all other requisites for a long stay, that the Macedonians having this place as the basis of their operations might, during a protracted siege, wear out the defenders of the rock by famine, should it fail to be captured at the first assault. He himself then advanced to the rock, taking with him the archers, the Agrianians, the brigade of Koinos, the lightest and best-armed men selected from the remainder of the phalanx, 200 of the companion cavalry, and 100 horse-archers. At the end of the day's march he encamped on what he took to be a convenient site. The next day he advanced a little nearer to the Rock, and again encamped.

Chapter XXIX.—Siege of Aornos

Some men thereupon who belonged to the neighbourhood came to him, and after proffering their submission undertook to guide him to the most assailable part of the rock, that from which it would not be difficult to capture the place. With these men he sent Ptolemy, the son of Lagos, a member of the bodyguard, leading the Agrianians and the other light-armed troops and the selected hypaspists, and directed him, on securing the position, to hold it with a strong guard and to signal to him when he had occupied it. Ptolemy, who followed a route which proved rough and otherwise difficult to traverse, succeeded in occupying the position without being perceived by the barbarians.[2]

[1] See Note F, Aornos.

[2] "All this account," says Abbott, who takes Aornos to be Mount Mahâban, "will answer well for the Mahâban, which is a mountain-table about five miles in length at summit, scarped on the east by tremendous precipices from which descends one large spur down upon the Indus between Sitana and Amb. The mountain spur being comparatively easy of ascent would not probably be contested by the natives, who would concentrate their power to oppose the Macedonians as they climbed the precipitous fall of the main summit. The great extent of the mountain, covered as it is with pine forest, would enable Ptolemy, under the guidance of natives, to gain any distant point of the summit without observation."

The whole circuit of this he fortified with a palisade and a trench, and then raised a beacon on the mountain from which the flame was likely to be seen by Alexander. Alexander did see it, and next day moved forward with his army, but as the barbarians obstructed his progress he could do nothing more on account of the difficult nature of the ground. When the barbarians perceived that Alexander had found an attack to be impracticable, they turned round, and in full force fell upon Ptolemy's men. Between these and the Macedonians hard fighting ensued, the Indians making strenuous efforts to destroy the palisade by tearing up the stakes, and Ptolemy to guard and maintain his position. The barbarians were worsted in the skirmish and when night began to fall withdrew.

From the Indian deserters Alexander selected one who knew the country and could otherwise be trusted, and sent him by night to Ptolemy with a letter importing that when he himself assailed the rock, Ptolemy should no longer content himself with defending his position but should fall upon the barbarians on the mountain, so that the Indians, being attacked in front and rear, might be perplexed how to act. Alexander, starting at daybreak from his camp, led his army by the route followed by Ptolemy when he went up unobserved, being convinced that if he forced a passage that way, and effected a junction with Ptolemy's men, the work still before him would not then be difficult; and so it turned out; for up to mid-day there continued to be hard fighting between the Indians and the Macedonians—the latter forcing their way up the ascent, while the former plied them with missiles as they ascended. But as the Macedonians did not slacken their efforts, ascending the one after the other, while those in advance paused to rest, they gained with much pain and toil the summit of the pass early in the afternoon, and joined Ptolemy's men. His troops being now all united, Alexander put them again in motion and led them against the rock itself; but to get close up to it was not yet practicable.   So came this day to its end.

Next day at dawn he ordered the soldiers to cut a hundred stakes per man.   When the stakes had been cut he began piling them up towards the rock (beginning from the crown of the hill on which the camp had been pitched) to form a great mound, whence he thought it would be possible for arrows and for missiles shot from engines to reach the defenders.   Every one took part in the work helping to advance the mound.   Alexander himself was present to superintend, commending those that were intent on getting the work done, and chastising any one that at the moment was idling.

Chapter XXX.—Capture of Aornos—Advance to the Indus

The army by the first day's work extended the mound the length of a stadium, and on the following day the slingers by slinging stones at the Indians from the mound just constructed, and the bolts shot at them from the engines, drove them back whenever they sallied out to attack the men engaged upon the mound.   The work of piling it up thus went on for three days, without intermission, when on the fourth day a few Macedonians forced their way to a small hill which was on a level with the rock, and occupied its crest.   Alexander without ever resting drove the mound towards the hill which the handful of men had occupied, his object being to join the two together.

But the Indians terror-struck both by the unheard-of audacity of the Macedonians in forcing their way to the hill, and also by seeing that this position was now connected with the mound, abstained from further resistance, and, sending their herald to Alexander, professed they were willing to surrender the rock if he granted them terms of capitulation.   But the purpose they had in view was to consume the day in spinning out negotiations, and to disperse by night to their several homes. When Alexander saw this he allowed them to start off as well as to withdraw the sentinels from the whole circle of outposts. He did not himself stir until they began their retreat, but, when they did so, he took with him 700 of the body-guards and the hypaspists and scaled the rock at the point abandoned by the enemy. He was himself the first to reach the top, the Macedonians ascending after him pulling one another up, some at one place and some at another. Then at a preconcerted signal they turned upon the retreating barbarians and slew many of them in the flight, besides so terrifying some others that in retreating they flung themselves down the precipices, and were in consequence dashed to death. Alexander thus became master of the rock which had baffled Heraklês himself. He sacrificed upon it and built a fort, giving the command of its garrison to Sisikottos,[1] who long before had in Baktra deserted from the Indians to Bessos, but after Alexander had conquered the Baktrian land served in his army, and showed himself a man worthy of all confidence.

He then set out from the rock and invaded the land of the Assakênians,[2] for he had been apprised that the brother of Assakênos, with the elephants and a host of the barbarians from the adjoining country, had fled for refuge to the mountains of that land. On reaching Dyrta[3] he found there were no inhabitants either in the city itself or the surrounding district. So next day he sent out Nearchos and Antiochos, commanders of the hypaspists, the former with the light-armed Agrianians, and the latter

---

[1] His name seems a transliteration of *S'as'igupta*, " protected by the moon."

[2] That is the eastern part of their country. He had already reduced the western and the capital Massaga.

[3] On descending the Mahâban by its northern or western spurs, Alexander would have found himself in the valleys of Chumla and Buner. The fugitives from the rock would no doubt flee for shelter to these valleys or the mountains by which they were enclosed. Dyrta probably lay to the north of Mahâban, near the point where the Indus issues from the mountains. Court's opinion that Dyrta was a place so far remote from the rock as Dir, which lies beyond the Pañjkora river, seems altogether improbable. Yet it is adopted by Lassen, though the regions in which Dir is situated had already been subdued.

with his own regiment and other two regiments besides. They were despatched to examine the nature of the localities, and to capture, if possible, some of the barbarians who might give information about the state of matters in the country, and particularly about the elephants, as he was very anxious to know where they were.

He himself now marched towards the river Indus, and the army going on before made a road for him, without which there would have been no means of passing through that part of the country.[1] He there captured a few of the barbarians, from whom he learned that the Indians of the country had fled away for refuge to Abisarês,[2] but had left their elephants there at pasture near the river Indus. He ordered these men to show him the way to the elephants. Now many of the Indians are elephant hunters,[3] and men of this class found favour with him and were kept in his retinue, and on this occasion he went with them in pursuit of the elephants. Two of these animals were killed in the chase by throwing themselves down a steep place, but the others on being caught suffered drivers to mount them, and were added to the army. He was further fortunate in finding serviceable timber[4] along the river, and this was cut for him by the army and employed in building boats. These were taken down the river Indus to the bridge which a

---

[1] " This road," says Abbott, " was probably the path leading amongst precipices above and along the torrent of the Burindu, a river which, after watering the valleys of Buner and Chumla, flows into the Indus above Amb. The path even now is very difficult. This would have brought Alexander back to Amb." On this route probably lay the pass which the chief called Eryx by Curtius and Aphrikes by Diodôros attempted, but unsuccessfully, to defend against Alexander. The river Burindu above mentioned may be identified with the *Parenos* of the Greek writers.

[2] In doing so they had of course to cross over to the left bank of the Indus.

[3] Arrian in his *Indika* (c. 14) has described the mode of elephant hunting practised by the Indians. It is still in vogue.

[4] Abbott points out that at Amb large quantities of drift timber are yearly arrested at an eddy near Derbend. It is probable, he thinks, that the pine forest in those days descended lower down the river than it does at present. At one time forests of fine sisoo, mulberry, and willow timber grew along both banks of the Indus at that part of its course.

good while before this Hêphaistiôn and Perdikkas had constructed.[1]

[1] The bridge in all probability spanned the Indus near Attak, which stands on a steep and lofty part of the left bank about two miles below the junction of the Kâbul and Indus. The width of the latter river at the fortress of Attak is, according to Lieutenant Wood who measured it, 286 yards. A little lower down where the channel is usually spanned by a bridge of boats it varies, as stated by Vigne, from 80 to 120 yards. According to Cunningham, the bridge was made higher up the river, at Ohind. From Alexander's campaign north of the Kâbul river, General Chesney (in a lecture at Simla) hints that a *moral* may be drawn':—"We have been accustomed," he says, "to consider the country north of the Kâbul river as virtually impregnable. The march of Alexander's army is a practical proof to the contrary, and although he was not burdened with artillery, and had apparently only mule transport, yet the Greek soldiers all marched in heavy armour, which must have added greatly to the difficulties of warfare among those mountains. There is an obvious moral to be drawn by us from these incidents."

FIFTH BOOK

Chapter I.—Alexander at Nysa

IN the country traversed by Alexander between the Kôphên and the river Indus, they say that besides the cities already mentioned, there stood also the city of Nysa,[1] which owed its foundation to Dionysos, and that Dionysos founded it when he conquered the Indians, whoever this Dionysos in reality was, and when or whencesoever he made his expedition against the Indians; for I have no means of deciding whether the Theban Dionysos setting out either from Thebes or the Lydian Tmôlos[2] marched with an army against the Indians, passing through a great many warlike nations unknown to the Greeks of those days, but without subjugating any of them by force of arms except only the Indian nations; all I know is, that one is not called on to sift minutely the legends of antiquity concerning the gods; for things that are not credible, if one reasons as to their consistency with the course of nature, do not seem to be incredible altogether if one takes the divine agency into account.

When Alexander came to Nysa, the Nysaians sent out to him their president, whose name was Akouphis,[3] and along with him thirty deputies of their most eminent citizens, to entreat him to spare the city for the sake of

---

[1] See Note G, Nysa.

[2] Mount Tmôlos, as we learn from Virgil, Ovid, and Pliny, was famous for its vines. It was therefore considered to be a favourite haunt of the wine-god.

[3] As the Greek φ represents the *bh* of Sanskrit, his name would be *Akubhi*.

the god. The deputies, it is said, on entering Alexander's tent found him sitting in his armour, covered with dust from his journey, wearing his helmet and grasping his spear. They fell to the ground in amazement at the sight, and remained for a long time silent. But when Alexander had bidden them rise and to be of good courage, then Akouphis taking up speech thus addressed him.

"The Nysaians entreat you, O King! to permit them to be still free and to be governed by their own laws from reverence towards Dionysos; for when Dionysos after conquering the Indian nation was returning to the shores of Greece he founded with his war-worn soldiers, who were also his bacchanals, this very city to be a memorial to posterity of his wanderings and his victory, just as you have founded yourself an Alexandreia near Kaukasos, and another Alexandreia in the land of the Egyptians, not to speak of many others, some of which you have already founded, while others will follow in the course of time, just as your achievements exceed in number those displayed by Dionysos. Now Dionysos called our city Nysa, and our land the Nysaian, after the name of his nurse Nysa; and he besides gave to the mountain which lies near the city the name of Mêros, because according to the legend he grew, before his birth, in the thigh of Zeus. And from his time forth we inhabit Nysa as a free city, and are governed by our own laws, and are a well-ordered community. But that Dionysos was our founder, take this as a proof, that ivy which grows nowhere else in the land of the Indians, grows with us."[1]

Chapter II.—Alexander permits the Nysaians to retain their Autonomy—Visits Mount Mêros

It gratified Alexander to hear all this, for he was desirous that the legends concerning the wanderings of

[1] Ivy abounds, however, in Hazâra as well as in some other parts of India.

Dionysos should be believed, as well as that Nysa owed
its foundation to Dionysos, since he had himself reached
the place to which that deity had come, and meant to
penetrate farther than he; for the Macedonians, he
thought, would not refuse to share his toils if he advanced
with an ambition to rival the exploits of Dionysos. He
therefore confirmed the inhabitants of Nysa in the enjoyment of their freedom and their own laws; and when he
enquired about their laws, he praised them because the
government of their state was in the hands of the
aristocracy. He moreover requested them to send with
him 300 of their horsemen, together with 100 of their
best men selected from the governing body, which consisted of 300 members. He then asked Akouphis, whom
he appointed governor of the Nysaian land, to make the
selection. When Akouphis heard this, he is said to have
smiled at the request, and when Alexander asked him
why he laughed, to have replied, " How, O King! can a
single city if deprived of a hundred of its best men continue to be well-governed ? But if you have the welfare
of the Nysaians at heart, take with you the 300 horsemen,
or, if you wish, even more; but instead of the hundred of
our best men you have asked me to select, take with you
twice that number of our worst men, so that on your
returning hither you may find the city as well governed
as it is now." By these words he persuaded Alexander,
who thought he spoke sensibly, and who ordered him to
send the horsemen without again asking for the hundred
men who were to have been selected, or even for others
to supply their place. He requested Akouphis, however,
to send him his son and his daughter's son to attend him
on his expedition.

Alexander felt a strong desire to see the place where
the Nysaians boasted to have certain memorials of Dionysos. So he went, it is said, to Mount Mêros with the
companion cavalry and the body of foot-guards, and
found that the mountain abounded with ivy and laurel
and umbrageous groves of all manner of trees, and that

G

it had also chases supplied with game of every description. The Macedonians, to whom the sight of the ivy was particularly welcome, as it was the first they had seen for a long time (there being no ivy in the land of the Indians, even where they have the vine), are said to have set themselves at once to weave ivy chaplets, and, accoutred as they were, to have crowned themselves with these, chanting the while hymns to Dionysos and invoking the god by his different names.[1]   Alexander, they say, offered while there sacrifice to Dionysos and feasted with his friends. Some even go so far as to allege, if any one cares to believe such things, that many of his courtiers, Macedonians of no mean rank, while invoking Dionysos, and wreathed with ivy crowns, were seized with the inspiration of the god, raised in his honour shouts of Evoi, and revelled like Bacchanals celebrating the orgies.

Chapter III.—How Eratosthenes views the legends concerning Heraklês and Dionysos—Alexander crosses the Indus

Any one who hears these stories is free to believe them or disbelieve them as he chooses. For my own part, I do not altogether agree with Eratosthenes the Kyrênian, who says that all these references to the deity were circulated by the Macedonians in connection with the deeds of Alexander, to gratify his pride by grossly exaggerating their importance. For, to take an instance, he says that the Macedonians, on seeing a cavern among the Paropamisadai, and either hearing some local legend about it, or inventing one themselves, spread a report that this was beyond doubt the cave in which Promêtheus had been bound, and to which the eagle resorted to prey upon his vitals, until Heraklês, coming that way, slew the

---

[1] His other names were Bacchos, Iacchos, Lyaios, Lênaios, Evios, Bromios, and among the Romans Liber also.

eagle and freed Promêtheus from his bonds.[1]   And again, he says that the Macedonians transferred the name of Mount Kaukasos from Pontos to the eastern parts of the world and the land of the Paropamisadai adjacent to India (for they called Mount Paropamisos, Kaukasos), to enhance the glory of Alexander as if he had passed over Kaukasos.   And again, he says that when the Macedonians saw in India itself oxen marked with a brand in the form of a club, they took this as a proof that Heraklês had gone as far as the Indians.   Eratosthenes has likewise no belief in similar stories about the wanderings of Dionysos.   Whether or not the accounts about them are true, I cannot decide, and so leave them.

When Alexander arrived at the river Indus he found a bridge already made over it by Hêphaistiôn, and two thirty-oared galleys, besides a great many small boats. He found also a present which had been sent by Taxilês the Indian, consisting of 200 talents of silver, 3000 oxen fattened for the shambles, 10,000 sheep or more, and 30 elephants.   The same prince had also sent to his assistance a force of 700 horsemen, and these brought word that Taxilês surrendered into his hands his capital Taxila, the greatest of all the cities between the river Indus and the Hydaspês.   Alexander there offered sacrifices to the gods to whom it was his custom to sacrifice, and entertained his army with gymnastic and equestrian contests

[1] Arrian writes to the same effect in his *Indika*, c. 5: "When the Greeks noticed a cave in the dominions of the Paropamisadai, they asserted that it was the cave of Promêtheus the Titan, in which he had been suspended for stealing the fire:" At the distance of thirty-four miles from Birikot, a place near the river Swât, is Daityapûr, now called Daiti-Kalli, said to have been built by one of the Daityas, *i.e. enemies of the gods*, such as were the Titans of the Greeks. In the hill adjacent is a vast cavern which, as Abbott has suggested, the companions of Alexander may have taken to be the cave frequented by the eagle which preyed upon the vitals of Promêtheus the Titan.   At Bamiân, which lies on one of the routes from Kâbul to Baktria, there are some very notable caves, one of which, some think, must have been that which the Greeks took to be the cave of Promêtheus.   But Alexander does not appear to have selected the Bamiân route either in crossing or recrossing the Kaukasos.   The mountains of the real Kaukasos were the loftiest known to the Greeks before Alexander's time, and hence to have crossed them was regarded as a transcendent achievement.

on the banks of the river. The sacrifices proved to be favourable for his undertaking the passage.

Chapter IV.—General description of the Indus and of the people of India

That the Indus is the greatest of all the rivers of Asia, except the Ganges, which is itself an Indian river ; that its sources lie on this side of the Paropamisos or Kaukasos ;[1] that it falls into the great sea which washes the shores of India towards the south wind ; that it has two mouths, both of which outlets abound with shallows, like the five mouths of the Ister ; and that it forms a delta in the land of the Indians closely resembling the Egyptian Delta, and that this is called in the Indian tongue Pâtâla,[2] let this be my description of the Indus, setting forth those facts which can least be disputed, since the Hydaspês and the Akesinês and the Hydraôtês and the Hyphasis, which are also Indian rivers, are considerably larger than any other rivers in Asia, but are smaller, I may even say much smaller, than the Indus, just as also the Indus itself is smaller than the Ganges. Indeed, Ktêsias (if any one thinks him a proper authority) states

[1] Arrian, like other ancient writers, supposed that the Indus had its sources in those mountains from which it emerges into the plains some sixty miles above Attak. It is now known that it rises in Tibet on a lofty Himalayan peak, Mount Kailâsa, famous in Hindu fable as the residence of S'iva and the Paradise of Kuvera, and that before it issues into the plains it has nearly run the half of its course of about 1800 miles. The number of its mouths has varied from time to time. Ptolemy, the geographer, gives it seven.

[2] Pâtâla in Sanskrit mythology denotes *the underworld*—the abode of snakes and demons—to which the sun at the close of day seems to descend. It was, therefore, Ritter says, the name applied by the Brah-mans to all the provinces in India that lay towards sunset. Cunningham, however, suggests that Pâtali, a Sanskrit word meaning *the trumpet-flower* (*bignonia suaveolens*) may have given its name to the Delta "in allusion," he says, "to the 'trumpet' shape of the province included between the eastern and western branches of the mouth of the Indus, as the two branches as they approach the sea curve outwards like the mouth of a trumpet." But could the idea of such a resemblance have occurred to the minds of the Indians unless maps were in use among them? For a better etymology see Note U. It has been conclusively proved that Haidarâbâd is the modern representative of the ancient Pâtâla.

that where the Indus is narrowest its banks are 40 stadia apart, and where broadest 100 stadia, while its ordinary breadth is the mean between these two distances.[1]

This river Indus Alexander began to cross at daybreak with his army to enter the country of the Indians. Concerning this people I have, in this present work, described neither under what laws they live, nor what strange animals their country produces, nor in what number and variety fish and water-monsters are bred in the Indus, the Hydaspês, the Ganges, and other Indian rivers. Nor have I described the ants which dig up gold for them, nor its guardians the griffins,[2] nor other stories invented rather to amuse than to convey a knowledge of facts, since there was no one to expose the falsehood of any absurd stories told about the Indians. However, Alexander and those who served in his army did expose the falsehood of most of them, although some even of these very men invented lies of their own. They proved also, in contradiction of the common belief, that the Indians were goldless, those tribes at least, and they were many, which Alexander visited with his army ; and that they were not at all luxurious in their style of living, while they were of so great a stature [3] that they were amongst the tallest men in Asia, being five cubits in height, or nearly so. They were blacker than any other men except the Aethiopians,[4] while in the art of war they were far superior to the other nations by which Asia was at that time inhabited. For

[1] The Indus after receiving the united streams of the great Panjâb rivers is increased in breadth from 600 to 2000 feet. Its breadth is therefore grossly exaggerated here unless the extent to which its inundations spread beyond its banks enters into the account.

[2] See Note H.

[3] The Afghans and Rajputs are still noted for their great stature.

[4] The Greek geographers derived the name of the Aethiopians from αἴθω, I burn, and ὤψ, the visage, and applied it to all the sun-burnt, dark-complexioned races south of Egypt. As the Aethiopic language is, however, purely Semitic, the name, if indigenous, must also be Semitic, since, as Salt states, the Abyssinians to this day call themselves Itiopjawan. Herodotus (vii. 70) speaks of Asiatic Aethiopians. These served in the army which Darius led into Greece, and were marshalled with the Indians, and did not at all differ from the others in appearance, but only in their language and in their hair, which was straight, while that of the Aethiopians of Libya (Africa) was woolly.

I cannot make any proper comparison between the Indians and the race of ancient Persians, who, under the command of Cyrus, the son of Kambyses, wrested the supremacy of Asia from the Medes, and added to their empire other nations, some by conquest and others by voluntary submission; for the Persians of those days were but a poor people, inhabiting a rugged country and approximating closely in the austerity of their laws and usages to the Spartan discipline.[1]　Then with regard to the discomfiture of the Persians in the Skythian land, I cannot with certainty conjecture to what cause it was attributable, whether to the difficult nature of the country into which they were led, or to some other mistake made by Cyrus, or whether it was that the Persians were inferior in the art of war to those Skythians whose territories they invaded.[2]

Chapter V.—The rivers and mountains of Asia

However, I shall treat of the Indians in a separate work,[3] in which I shall set down whatever seems to be most credible in the reports supplied by those who accompanied Alexander in his expedition, and by Nearchos who made a voyage round the Great Sea which adjoins the Indians.　I shall then add the accounts of the country which were compiled by Megasthenes and Eratosthenês, who are both writers of standard authority.

---

[1] The Persians were originally the inhabitants of that poor and insignificant province called Persis, which was included between the Persian Gulf in the south and Mêdia in the north, and which stretched eastward from Susiana (Elam) to the deserts of Karmania. The great empire won by their arms, extended from the Mediterranean to the Jaxartes and Indus. Xenophon says that the Persians in early times led a life of penury and hard toil, as they inhabited a rugged country which they cultivated with their own hands (*Kyrop.* vii. 5, 67).

[2] Cyrus is said to have perished in this expedition against the Skythians, who lived beyond the Jaxartes, and were led by Queen Tomyris. The account of this expedition, given by Herodotos in the closing chapters of his first book, is examined at length by Duncker in the sixth volume of his *History of Antiquity*, pp. 112-124. Xenophon represents Cyrus as dying in peace at an advanced age.

[3] Called the *Indika*, written in the Ionic dialect, and based chiefly on the works (now lost) of Megasthenes and Nearchos.

I shall describe the customs of the Indians and the remarkable animals which their country is said to produce, and also the voyage which was made by Nearchos in the outer sea.[1] In the meantime it will suffice if I content myself with describing only what seems requisite to make the account of Alexander's operations clearly intelligible. Mount Tauros divides Asia, beginning from Mykalê, the mountain which lies opposite to the island of Samos ; then forming the boundary of the country of the Pamphylians and Kilikians, it stretches onwards to Armenia. From the Armenians it passes into Mêdia, and runs through the country of the Parthians and the Khorasmians. Reaching Baktria it there unites with Mount Parapamisos, which the Macedonians of Alexander's army called the Kaukasos, for the purpose, it is said, of magnifying the deeds of Alexander, for it could thus be said that he had carried his victorious arms even beyond the Kaukasos. It is possible, however, that this mountain range may be a continuation of that other Kaukasos which is in Skythia, in the same way as it is a continuation of the Tauric range. For this reason I have before this occasionally called this range Kaukasos, and in future I mean to call it so. This Kaukasos extends as far as the great Indian Ocean in the direction of the east.[2] All the important rivers of Asia accordingly rise either in Mount Tauros or Mount Kaukasos, and shape their courses some to the north, and others to the south. Those which run northward discharge their waters either into the Maiôtic Lake, or into the Hyrkanian Sea, which is in reality a gulf of the Great Sea.[3] The rivers which run southward are the

[1] The Indian Ocean and Persian Gulf, in contrast to the interior sea or Mediterranean.

[2] By the Indian Ocean (called immediately afterwards the Great Sea) is meant here the Bay of Bengal and the ocean beyond, then unknown, which extended to the shores of China. By the Kaukasos, which extended to this eastern ocean, is meant the vast Himâlayan range.

[3] Regarding the Maiôtic Lake, now generally called the Sea of Azof, the ancients entertained very hazy and inaccurate notions. They supposed it to be situated in the remotest regions of the earth (Aisch. *Prom.* 427), and to be almost equal in size to the Euxine (Herod. iv. 86). Arrian, who might have known better, seems here to have adopted the crude notion current in Alexander's time

Euphrates, Tigris, Indus, Hydaspês, Akesines, Hydraôtes, and Hyphasis, together with the rivers between these and the Ganges. All these either enter the sea, or, like the Euphrates, disappear among the swamps which receive their waters.

Chapter VI.—Position and boundaries of India and how its plains may have been formed

If anyone takes this view of Asia, that it is divided by the Tauros and the Kaukasos from west to east, then he finds that it is formed by the Tauros itself into two great sections, one of which lies towards the south and the south wind, and the other towards the north and the north wind. The southern section is divided into four parts, of which, according to Eratosthenês, India is the largest, this being also the opinion of Megasthenes who resided with Siburtios the satrap of Arakhôsia, and who tells us that he frequently visited Sandrakottos the king of the Indians.[1] They say that the smallest part is that which is bounded by the river Euphrates, and which extends to our own inland sea, while the other two parts which lie between the river Euphrates and the Indus will scarcely bear comparison with India even if both were taken together. They also say that India is bounded towards the east and the east wind as far as the south by the Great Sea, and towards the north by Mount Kaukasos, as far as its junction with the Tauros, while the river Indus cuts it off from other countries towards the west and the north-west wind as far as the Great Sea. The larger portion of India is a plain, and this, as they conjecture, has been formed from the alluvial deposits of

that the Jaxartes (which they confounded with the Tanais or Don) entered by one arm the Hyrkanian or Kaspian Sea, and by another the Maiôtic Lake. The Kaspian itself was taken to be a gulf of the Great Eastern Ocean. Herodotos, however, is guiltless of this geographical heresy.

[1] This does not mean that Megasthenes was sent on frequent embassies to Sandrakottos, but that during his embassy he had frequent interviews with him. The former interpretation, however, finds its advocates.

the rivers, just as in other countries plains which are not far off from the sea are generally formations of their respective rivers, a fact which explains why the names of such countries were applied of old to their rivers. There is, for instance, in the country of Asia the plain of the Hermos, a river which rises in the mountain of Mother Dindymênê, and on its way to the sea flows past the Aiolian city of Smyrna. There is again another Lydian plain, called that of the Kaÿstros, which is a Lydian river, and another plain in Mysia, that of the Kaïkos, and another in Karia, that of the Maiandros, which extends as far as the Ionian city of Milêtos. In the case of Egypt again, the two historians, Herodotos, and Hêkataios (or at any rate the author of the work on Egypt, if he was other than Hêkataios) agree in declaring that in the same way Egypt was the gift of its river,[1] and clear proofs have been adduced by Herodotos in support of this view, so that even the country itself got perhaps its name from the river, for that in early times Aigyptos was the name of the river which the Egyptians and other nations now call the Nile the words of Homer sufficiently prove, since he says[2] that Menelaös anchored his ships at the mouth of the river Aigyptos. Now if the rivers we have mentioned, which are of no great size, can each of them separately form in its course to the sea a large tract of new country, by carrying down silt and slime from the upland districts in which they have their sources, there can be no good reason for doubting that India is mostly a plain which has been formed by the alluvial deposits of its rivers.[3] For if the Hermos and the Kaÿstros and the Kaïkos and the Maiandros and the other rivers of

---

[1] See Herodotos, ii. 5. Diodôros applies to Lower Egypt the epithet ποταμόχωστος, i.e. deposited by the river.

[2] See Odyssey, iv. 477, 581.

[3] Modern science confirms this theory. Thus Sir W. Hunter in his Brief History of the Indian People, says: "In order to understand the Indian plains we must have a clear idea of the part played by these great rivers; for the rivers first create the land, then fertilize it, and finally distribute its produce. The plains were in many parts upheaved by volcanic action, or deposited in an aqueous aera long before man appeared on the earth."

Asia which fall into the inland sea were united, they could not be compared in volume of water with one of the Indian rivers, and much less with the Ganges, which is the greatest of them all, and with which neither the volume of the Egyptian Nile, nor the Istros (Danube) which flows through Europe, can be for a moment compared. Nay, the whole of those rivers if combined into one would not be equal to the Indus, which is already a large river where it issues from its springs, and which after receiving as tributaries fifteen rivers,[1] all greater than those of Asia, enters the sea still retaining its own name. Let these remarks which I have made about the country of the Indians suffice for the present, while I reserve all other particulars for my description of India.

Chapter VII.—The bridging of rivers

In what manner Alexander made his bridge over the Indus neither Aristoboulos nor Ptolemy, the authorities whom I chiefly follow, have given any account; nor can I decide for certain whether the passage was bridged with boats, as was the Hellespont by Xerxes and as were the Bosporos and the Istros by Darius,[2] or whether the bridge he made over the river was one continuous piece of work. I incline, however, to think that the bridge must have been made of boats,[3] for neither would the depth of the river have admitted the construction of an ordinary kind of bridge, nor could a work so vast and difficult have been executed in so short a time. But if the passage was bridged with boats I cannot decide whether the vessels being fastened together with cables and anchored in a row sufficed to form a bridge as did those by which, as Herodotos the Halikarnassian says, the Hellespont was joined, or whether the method was that which is used by the Romans in bridging the Istros and the Keltic Rhine,[4]

---

[1] Arrian has named these in his *Indika*, c. 4.

[2] See Herod. vii. 33-36; iv. 83, 97, 133-141.

[3] Diodôros says the passage was made by a bridge of boats.

[4] There is a Rhenos in Italy—the Reno, a tributary of the Po, from

and by which they bridged the Euphrates and the Tigris as often as necessity required. Since, however, the Romans, as far as my knowledge goes, have found that the bridging of rivers by boats is the most expeditious method of crossing them, I think it worth a description here. The vessels at a preconcerted signal are let go from their moorings and rowed down stream not prow but stern foremost. The current of course carries them downward, but a small pinnace furnished with oars holds them back till they settle into their appointed place. Then baskets of wicker work, pyramid-shaped and filled with rough stones, are lowered into the river from the prow of each vessel to make it hold fast against the force of the current. As soon as one of those vessels has been held fast another is in the same way anchored with its prow against the stream as far from the first as is commensurate with their bearing the strain of what is put upon them. On both of them beams of wood are rapidly laid lengthwise, and on these again planks are placed crosswise to bind them together. In this manner the work proceeds through all the vessels which are required for bridging the passage. At each end of the structure firmly fixed railed gangways are thrown forward to the shore so that horses and beasts of burden may with the greater safety enter upon it. These gangways serve at the same time to bind the bridge to the shore. In a short time the whole is completed amid great noise and bustle, though discipline is by no means lost sight of as the work proceeds. In each vessel the occasional exhortations of the overseers and their rebukes of negligence neither prevent orders from being heard nor the work from being quickly executed.

which the great Rhine is distinguished as the Keltic. The famous bridge made by Caesar over the latter river is described in his *De Bello Gallico*, iv. 17.

Chapter VIII.—Alexander arrives at Taxila—Receives an embassy from Abisares and advances to the Hydaspês

This method has been practised by the Romans from of old, but how Alexander bridged the river Indus I cannot say, for even those who served in his army are silent on the matter. But the bridge was made, I should think, as nearly as possible in the way described, or if it was otherwise contrived let it be so.

When Alexander had crossed to the other side of the Indus he again offered sacrifice according to his custom. Then marching away from the Indus he arrived at Taxila,[1] a great and flourishing city, the greatest indeed of all the cities which lay between the river Indus and the Hydaspês. Taxilês, the governor of the city, and the Indians who belonged to it received him in a friendly manner, and he therefore added as much of the adjacent country to their territory as they requested. While he was there Abisarês, the king of the Indians of the hill-country, sent him an embassy which included his own brother and other grandees of his court. Envoys came also from Doxarês, the chief of the province, and those like the others brought presents. Here again in Taxila Alexander offered his customary sacrifices and celebrated a gymnastic and equestrian contest. Having appointed Philip, the son of Makhatas, satrap of the Indians of that district, he left a garrison in Taxila and those soldiers who were invalided, and then moved on towards the river Hydaspês—for he had learned that Pôros with the whole of his army lay on the other side of that river resolved either to prevent him from making the passage or to attack him when crossing.[2]

---

[1] See Note I, Taxila.

[2] We learn from Curtius that Alexander, before taking hostile action against Pôros, demanded from him through an envoy called Cleochares that he should pay tribute and come to meet him on the frontiers of his dominions. To this Pôros replied that in compliance with the second request he would meet Alexander at the place appointed, but would attend in arms. Alexander was perhaps justified by the laws of war in exacting submission from the tribes west of the Indus, since these had been subject to Darius, whom he had over-

Upon learning this Alexander sent back Koinos, the son of Polemokratês, to the river Indus with orders to cut in pieces all the boats that had been constructed for the passage of the Indus and to bring them to the river Hydaspês. In accordance with these orders the smaller boats were cut each into two sections and the thirty-oared galleys into three, and the sections were then transported on waggons to the banks of the Hydaspês. There the boats were reconstructed, and appeared as a flotilla upon that river. Alexander then taking the forces which he had with him when he arrived at Taxila and 5000 of the Indians commanded by Taxilês and the chiefs of that country advanced towards the Hydaspês.[1]

thrown, and to whose rights he had succeeded, but the tribes of the Panjâb, those at least that lay to the east of the Hydaspês, had never, so far as is known, been under Persian domination, and hence his invasion, according to modern ideas, was altogether indefensible. He could, however, justify himself on the ground of the principles held by the Greeks of his day, who considered that their superiority in wisdom and virtue to the rest of mankind gave them a natural right to attack, plunder, and enslave all barbarians except such only as were protected by a special treaty. Such a view, repugnant as it seems to every principle of justice, was held nevertheless by Aristotle, who no doubt impressed it on the mind of his illustrious pupil. Hence Alexander, in attacking Pôros, was not conscious, like Caesar, when he invaded Britain, of perpetrating an unwarrantable aggression for which some kind of an excuse had to be trumped up.

[1] The Hydaspês, now the Jhilam, is called by the natives of Kâs'mîr, where it rises, the Bedasta, which is but a slightly altered form of its Sanskrit name, the Vitastâ, which means "wide-spread." In Ptolemy's geography it appears as the Bidaspês —a form nearer the original than Hydaspês. It is mentioned in one of the hymns of the Rig - Veda, along with other great Indian rivers:

"Receive favourably this my hymn, O Gangâ, Yamunâ, Sarasvatî, S'utudrî, Parashni ; hear O Marudvridhâ, with the Asiknî and Vitastâ, and thou Arjîkîyâ with the Sushômâ." In advancing from the Indus at Attak to the Hydaspês, Alexander followed the Râjapatha, that is, the king's highway, called by Megasthenes the ὁδὸς βασιληίη. It is the route which has been taken by all foreign conquerors who have penetrated into India by the valley of the Kôphês. Elphinstone, who followed this route in returning from Kâbul, describes it thus : "The whole of our journey across the track between the Indus and Hydaspês was about 160 miles ; for which space the country is among the strongest I have ever seen. The difficulty of our passage across it was increased by heavy rain. While in the hilly country our road sometimes lay through the beds of torrents" (Mission to Kâbul, p. 78). In another passage (p. 80) he says : "I was greatly struck with the difference between the banks of this river ; the left bank had all the characteristics of the plains of India. The right bank, on the contrary, was formed by the end of the range of the Salt Hills, and had an air of extreme ruggedness and wildness that must inspire a fearful presentiment of the country he was entering into the mind of a traveller from the East." General

Chapter IX.—Alexander on reaching the Hydaspês finds
Pôros prepared to dispute its passage

Alexander encamped on the banks of the river,[1] and
Pôros was seen on the opposite side, with all his army
and his array of elephants around him.[2] Against the
place where he saw Alexander had encamped, he
remained himself to guard the passage, but he sent
detachments of his men, each commanded by a captain,
to guard all parts of the river where it could be easily
forded, as he was resolved to prevent the Macedonians
from effecting a landing. When Alexander saw this, he
thought it expedient to move his army from place to
place, so that Pôros might be at a loss to discover his real
intentions. For this purpose he divided his army into
many parts, and some of the troops he led himself in
different directions, sometimes to ravage the enemy's
country, and sometimes to find out where he could most
easily ford the river. He placed various commanders at
various times over different divisions of his army, and
despatched them also in different directions. At the
same time he caused provisions to be conveyed to the
camp from all parts of the country on this side of the
river, to impress Pôros with the conviction that he
intended to remain where he was near the bank, till
the waters of the river subsided in winter, and afforded
him a large choice of passages. As the boats were
constantly plying up and down the stream, and the

Chesney, in the lecture already cited,
thus remarks on the advance of Alexander to the Hydaspês : " What is
remarkable about this part of the
advance is that it was not made direct
on Jhelum, as would appear natural.
True, that line is over what would be
a very difficult country, as any traveller
by the existing road knows. Still it
would be the easiest line; nevertheless it appears certain that Alexander
took a more southerly line, and
threading his way through the intri-

cate ravines of the upper part of the
Salt range, and leaving Tilla and
Rhotas on his left, penetrated that
range by the gorge through which
runs the Bhundar river, and struck
the river Jhelum at Jalâlpûr, about
thirty miles below Jhelum."

[1] See Note I, Site of Alexander's
camp on the Hydaspês.

[2] The Greeks, for the first time,
saw elephants used in war at the
battle of Arbela.

skins were being filled with hay, while all the bank was lined, here with horse and there with foot, all this prevented Pôros from resting and concentrating his preparations at any one point selected in preference to any other as the best for defending the passage. At this time of the year besides, all the Indian rivers were swollen and flowing with turbid and rapid currents, for the sun is then wont to turn towards the summer tropic.[1] At this season incessant rains deluge the soil of India, and the snows of the Kaukasos then melting flood the numerous rivers to which they give birth. In winter they again subside and become small and clear, and in many places fordable, with the exception of the Indus and the Ganges, and perhaps some one or two others. The Hydaspês at all events does become fordable.

Chapter X.—Alexander's devices to deceive Pôros and steal the passage of the river

Alexander therefore publicly announced that he would remain where he was throughout that season of the year if his passage was for the present to be obstructed, but he continued as before waiting in ambush to see whether he could anywhere rapidly steal a passage to the other side without being observed. He clearly saw that it was impossible for him to cross where Pôros himself had encamped near the bank of the Hydaspês, not only because he had so many elephants, but also because his large army arrayed for battle, and splendidly accoutred, was ready to attack his troops the moment they

[1] Arrian, in the nineteenth chapter of this book, states that the battle with Pôros was fought in the Archonship of Hêgemôn at Athens, in the month of Mounychiôn, *i.e.* between the 18th of April and 18th of May, 326 B.C. Here, however, according to the reading of all the MSS., he makes the battle take place *after* the solstice of June 21st, μετὰ τροπάς. Editors remove the difficulty by substituting κατά for μετά, and I have translated accordingly. As the rainy season, however, does not set in till near the end of June, and it had set in, as Strabo informs us, during the march to the Hydaspês, the later date has probability in its favour.

landed. He foresaw besides that his horses would refuse to mount the opposite bank, where the elephants would at once encounter them, and by their very aspect and their roaring would terrify them outright; nor did he think that even before they gained the shore they would remain upon the inflated hides during the passage; but that on seeing the elephants even at a distance off, they would become frantic and leap into the water. He resolved therefore to steal the passage, and to do this in the following way. Leading out by night the greater part of his cavalry along the river bank in different directions, he ordered them to set up a loud clamour, raise the war-shout,[1] and fill the shores with every kind of noise, as if they were really preparing to attempt the passage. Pôros marched meanwhile along the opposite bank, in the direction of the noise, having his elephants with him, and Alexander gradually accustomed him to lead out his men in this way in opposition. When this had been done repeatedly, and the men did nothing more than make a great noise and shout the war-cry, Pôros no longer made any counter-movement when the cavalry issued out from the camp, but remained within his own lines, his spies being, however, posted at numerous points along the bank. When Alexander had thus quieted the suspicions of Pôros about his nocturnal attempts, he devised the following stratagem.

Chapter XI.—Arrangements made by Alexander for crossing the Hydaspês unobserved

There was a bluff ascending from the bank of the Hydaspês at a point where the river made a remarkable bend, and this was densely covered with all sorts of trees. Over against it lay an island in the river overspread with jungle, an untrodden and solitary place. Perceiving that this island directly faced the bluff, and that both places

---

[1] Enyalios, an epithet of the war-god.

were wooded and adapted to screen his attempt to cross the river, he decided to take his army over this way. Now the bluff and the island were 150 stadia distant from the great camp.[1] But along the whole of the bank he had posted running sentries[2] at a proper distance for keeping each other in sight, and readily transmitting along the line any orders that might be received from any quarter. In every direction, moreover, shouts were raised by night, and fires were burnt for many nights together. But when he had made up his mind to attempt the passage, the preparations for crossing were made in the camp without any concealment. In the camp Krateros had been left with his own division of the cavalry, and the Arakhosian and Parapamisadan horsemen, together with the brigades of the Macedonian phalanx commanded by Alketas and Polysperchon and the contingent of 5000 men under the chiefs of the hither Indians. He had ordered Krateros not to attempt to cross the river before Pôros moved off against them, or before learning that he was flying from the field, and that they were victorious. "If, however," said he, "Pôros with one part of his army advances against me while he

---

[1] Curtius mentions that near the bluff there was a deep hollow or ravine which sufficed to screen both the infantry and the cavalry, and on this Cunningham remarks: "There is a ravine to the north of Jalâlpûr which exactly suits the descriptions of the historians. This ravine is the bed of the Kandar Nala, which has a course of six miles from its source down to Jalâlpûr, where it is lost in a waste of sand. Up this ravine there has always been a passable, but difficult road towards Jhelum. From the head of the Kandar this road proceeds for three miles in a northerly direction down another ravine called the Kasi, which then turns suddenly to the east for six and a half miles, and then again one and a half mile to the south, where it joins the river Jhelum immediately below Dilâwar, the whole distance from Jalâlpûr being exactly seventeen miles." These seventeen miles are about the equivalent of the 150 stadia given by Arrian as the distance from the great camp to the bluff.

[2] "Arrian," says Cunningham, "records that Alexander placed running sentries along the bank of the river at such distances that they could see each other and communicate his orders. Now, I believe that this operation could not be carried out in the face of an observant enemy along any part of the river bank, excepting only that one part which lies between Jalâlpûr and Dilâwar. In all other parts the west bank is open and exposed, but in this part alone the wooded and rocky hills slope down to the river and offer sufficient cover for the concealment of single sentries."
—*Geog. of Anc. India*, pp. 170, 171.

leaves the other part and his elephants in his camp, then please to remain where you are ; but if Pôros takes all his elephants with him, and a portion of the rest of his army is left behind in the camp, then do you cross the river with all possible speed ; for," added he, " it is the elephants only which make it impossible for the horses to land on the other bank. The rest of the army can cross over without difficulty."

Chapter XII.—Alexander crosses the Hydaspês

Such were the instructions given to Krateros ; but half-way between the island and the main camp in which he had been left, there were posted Meleager, Attalos and Gorgias, with the mercenary cavalry and infantry, who had received orders to cross to the other side in detachments, into which their ranks were to be separated as soon as they saw the Indians fairly engaged in battle. He then selected to be taken under his own command the corps of body-guards called Companions, the regiments of cavalry under Hêphaistiôn, Perdikkas and Dêmêtrios, also the Baktrian, Sogdian, and Skythian cavalry, and the Daan horse-archers, and from the phalanx of infantry the hypaspists, the brigade of Kleitos and Koinos, and the archers and the Agrianians, and with these troops he marched with secrecy, keeping at a considerable distance from the bank that he might not be seen to be moving towards the island and the bluff, from which he intended to cross over to the other side. There in the night the skins, which had long before been provided for the purpose, were stuffed with hay, and securely stitched up. During the night a violent storm of rain came on, whereby his preparations and the attempt at crossing were not betrayed to the enemy by the rattle of arms and the shouting of orders, since the thunder and rain drowned all other sounds. Most of the boats which he had ordered to be cut into sections had been conveyed to this place, and when secretly pieced together again were hidden away in the woods along with the thirty-oared galleys. Towards daybreak the wind had died down and the rain ceased. The rest of the army then crossed over in the direction of the island, the cavalry mounted on the skin pontoon rafts, and as many of the foot-soldiers as the boats could hold embarked in them. They so proceeded, that they were not seen by the sentries posted by Pôros till they had passed beyond the island, and were not far from the bank.

Chapter XIII.—Incidents of the passage of the river

Alexander himself embarked on a thirty-oared galley, and went over accompanied by Ptolemy, Perdikkas, and Lysimachos, his body-guards, and by Seleukos, one of the companions, who was afterwards king, and by one half of the hypaspists, the other half being on board of the other galleys of like size. As soon as the soldiers had passed beyond the island, they steered for the bank, being now full in view of the enemy, whose sentinels on seeing their approach galloped off at the utmost speed of each man's horse to carry the tidings to Pôros. Meanwhile Alexander was himself the first to disembark, and taking the horsemen who had been conveyed over in his own and the other thirty-oared galleys, he at once formed them into line as they kept landing, for the cavalry had orders to be the first to disembark. At the head of these duly marshalled he moved forward. Owing, however, to his ignorance of the locality he had unawares landed not on the mainland, but upon an island, the great size of which prevented it all the more from being recognised as an island. It was separated from the mainland by a branch of the river in which the water was shallow; but the violent storm of rain which had lasted the most of the night had so swollen the stream that the horsemen could not find the ford, and he feared that the latter part of the passage would be as laborious as the first. When

at last the ford was found he led his men through it with
difficulty ; for the water where deepest reached higher
than the breasts of the foot soldiers, and as for the horses
their heads only were above the river.   When he had
crossed this piece of water also, he selected the mounted
corps of body-guards, and the best men from the other
squadrons of cavalry, and brought them from column
into line upon the right wing.[1]   Then in front of all the
cavalry he posted the horse archers, and next in line to
the cavalry and in front of all the infantry the royal
hypaspists commanded by Seleukos.   Next to these
again he placed the royal foot guards, and then the
other hypaspists, each in what happened to be the order
of his precedence for the time being.   At each extremity
of the phalanx were posted the archers and the Agrianians
and the javelin men.

*Chapter XIV.—Skirmish with the son of Pôros at the
landing-place*

Alexander having made these dispositions, ordered the
infantry, which numbered nearly 6000 men, to follow
him at the ordinary marching pace and in regular order,
for when he saw that he was superior in cavalry, he took
with himself only the horsemen, about 5000 in number,
and led them forward at a rapid pace.   Taurôn, the
captain of the archers, he ordered to hasten forward
with his men to give support to the cavalry.   He
had come to the conclusion that if Pôros engaged him
with all his troops he would either, without difficulty,
overpower him by charging with his cavalry, or would
remain on the defensive till the infantry came up during

---

[1] With Alexander's passage of the
Hydaspês may be compared Hannibal's passage of the Rhone made
upwards of a century later.   The
Carthaginian general, whose education
included a knowledge of Greek, was
no doubt familiar with the history of
Alexander's wars, and from knowing
how the Hydaspês was crossed may
have laid his plans for crossing the
Rhone.   *v.* Livy, xxi. 26-28 ; Polyb.
iii. 45, 46.

the action, or that if the Indians, terrified by the marvellous audacity of his passage of the river, should take to flight, he would be able to pursue them closely, and the slaughter being thus all the greater there would not be left much more work for him to do.

Aristoboulos says that the son of Pôros arrived with about 60 chariots before Alexander made the final passage from the large island, and that he could have hindered Alexander from landing (for he made the passage with difficulty even when no one opposed him), if the Indians had but leaped down from their chariots and fallen upon those who first stepped on shore. The prince, however, passed by with his chariots, and allowed Alexander to accomplish the passage in complete safety. Against these Indians Alexander, he says, despatched his horse archers, who easily put them to a rout which was by no means bloodless. Other writers say that while the troops were landing an encounter took place between the Indians who had come with the son of Pôros and Alexander at the head of his cavalry, and that as the son of Pôros had come with a superior force Alexander himself was wounded by the Indian prince, and that his favourite horse Boukephalas was killed, having been wounded, like his master, by the son of Pôros. But Ptolemy, the son of Lagos, with whom I agree, gives a different account, for he states, like the others, that Pôros sent off his son, but not in command of merely 60 chariots; and indeed it is not at all likely that Pôros, on learning from the scouts that either Alexander himself, or, at all events, a part of his army, had made the passage of the Hydaspês, would have sent his own son with no more than 60 chariots, which, considered as a reconnoitring party, would have been too numerous, and not rapid in retreat, but considered as meant to repel such of the enemy as had not yet crossed the river, and to attack those who had already landed, an altogether inadequate force. He says that the son of Pôros arrived at the head of 2000 men and 120 chariots, and that Alexander had made even the final passage from the island before the prince appeared upon the scene.

Chapter XV.—The arrangements made by Pôros for the conflict

Ptolemy states further that Alexander at first despatched against the prince the horse archers, and led the cavalry himself, under the belief that Pôros was advancing against him with the whole of his army, and that this was a body of advanced cavalry thrown forward by Pôros. But when he discovered what the real strength of the Indians was he then briskly charged them with what cavalry he had with him. When they noticed that Alexander himself and his body of cavalry did not charge them in an extended line, but by squadrons, their ranks gave way, and 400 of their horsemen fell, and among them the son of Pôros. Their chariots, moreover, were captured, horses and all, for they proved heavy in the retreat and useless in the action itself, by having stuck fast in the clay. When the horsemen who had escaped from this rout reported one after another to Pôros that Alexander himself had crossed the river with the strongest division of his army, and that his son had been slain in the fight, he was still at a loss what to determine, for the division which had been left with Krateros in the great camp right opposite to his own position appeared to be undertaking the passage, but he at last decided to march with all his forces against Alexander and fight it out with the strongest division of the Macedonians led by the king in person. He nevertheless left there in his camp a few of the elephants and a small force to deter the cavalry under the command of Krateros from landing. He then took all his cavalry, 4000 strong, all his chariots, 300 in number, 200 of his elephants, and 30,000 efficient infantry, and marched against Alexander. When he found a place where he saw there was

no clay, but that the ground from its sandy nature was
all flat and firm, and suited for the movements of cavalry
whether charging or falling back, he then drew up his
army in order of battle,[1] posting his elephants in the
front line at intervals of at least 100 feet, so as to have
his elephants ranged in front before the whole body of
his infantry, and so to spread terror at all points among
Alexander's cavalry.   He took it for certain besides that
none of the enemy would have the audacity to push in
at the intervals between the elephants—not the cavalry,
since their horses would be terrified by these animals, and
much less the infantry, since they would be checked in
front by his heavy-armed foot soldiers falling upon them,
and trampled down when the elephants wheeled round
upon them.   Behind these he drew up his infantry,
which did not close up in one line with the elephants,
but formed a second line in their rear, so that the
regiments were only partly pushed forward into the
intervals.   He had also troops of infantry posted on the
wings beyond the elephants, and on both sides of the
infantry the cavalry had been drawn up, and in front of
it the chariots.

Chapter XVI.—The plan of attack adopted by Alexander

In this manner had Pôros arranged his troops.   As
soon as Alexander perceived that the Indians had been
drawn up in battle order he made his cavalry halt, that
he might get in hand each regiment of the infantry as it
came up ; and even when the phalanx by a rapid march
had effected a junction with the cavalry he still did not
at once marshal its ranks and lead it into action, and
thus expose the men, while tired and out of breath, to
the barbarians, who were quite fresh, but he gave them
time, while he rode round their ranks, to rest until they

[1] Here, or in the immediate neighbourhood, was fought, in 1849, the
battle of Chilianwála.   On this occasion the inferiority of the British commander as a strategist to Alexander
was signally manifested.

could recover themselves. When he had observed how the Indians were arranged he made up his mind not to advance against the centre, in front of which the elephants had been posted, while the intervals between them had been filled with compact masses of infantry, for he feared lest Pôros should reap the advantage which he had calculated on deriving from that arrangement. But as he was superior in cavalry he took the greater part of that force, and marched along towards the left wing of the enemy to make his attack in this quarter.[1] Koinos he sent at the head of his own regiment of horse and that of Dêmêtrios to the right, and ordered him, when the barbarians on seeing what a dense mass of cavalry was opposed to them, should be riding along to encounter it, to hang close upon their rear.[2] The command of the phalanx of infantry he committed to Seleukos, Antigenês, and Taurôn, who received orders not to take part in the action till they saw that the phalanx of infantry and the cavalry of the enemy were thrown into disorder by the cavalry under his own command.

When the Indians were now within reach of his missiles he despatched against their left wing the horse archers, who were 1000 strong, to throw the enemy in that part of the field into confusion with storms of arrows and charges of their horses. He marched rapidly for-

[1] The left wing of the Indian army was flanked by the river.

[2] This passage, as interpreted by Droysen, Thirlwall, and indeed as generally understood, intimates that Alexander ordered Koinos to station himself opposite *the enemy's* right, and not on the *Macedonian* extreme right. Thus Moberly, who holds the general view, remarks (*Alexander in the Punjaub*, p. 61):—"Coenus was ordered to station himself opposite the enemy's right; then, in case of Porus withdrawing all his cavalry from the right, in order to meet Alexander's attack on the left, Coenus was to pass from one wing to the other, apparently in front of the Macedonian line, and to attack the Indian cavalry in the rear as soon as, in advancing to meet Alexander, they had got some little distance from their supports. . . . Distance can be got over quickly by cavalry." Köchly and Rüstow, however, in their *History of the Greek Military System*, advocate a different view. "Alexander," they say, "must have sent Koinos to the extreme right wing with the order, that if the cavalry broke from the line against himself (Alexander) he was to fall upon their rear. Had he been detached to oppose the right wing of Pôros he would have been too far off to support Alexander's front attack by an attack on the enemy's rear." This seems the preferable view.

ward himself with the companion cavalry against the l wing of the barbarians, making haste to attack th... cavalry in a state of disorder while they were still in column, and before they could deploy into line.

Chapter XVII.—Description of the battle of the Hydaspês—Defeat of Pôros

The Indians meanwhile had collected their horsemen from every quarter, and were riding forward to repulse Alexander's onset, when Koinos, in accordance with his orders, appeared with his cavalry upon their rear. Seeing this the Indians had to make their cavalry face both to front and rear—the largest and best part to oppose Alexander, and the remainder to wheel round against Koinos and his squadrons. This therefore at once threw their ranks into confusion, and disconcerted their plan of operations; and Alexander, seeing that now was his opportunity while their cavalry was in the very act of forming to front and rear, fell upon those opposed to him with such vigour that the Indians, unable to withstand the charge of his cavalry, broke from their ranks, and fled for shelter to the elephants as to a friendly wall.[1] Upon this the drivers of the elephants urged these animals forward against the cavalry; but the Macedonian phalanx itself now met them face to face, and threw darts at the men on the elephants, and from one side and the other struck the elephants themselves as they stood around

[1] " To meet the double assault (of Alexander and Coenus) they resorted to one of those changes of front in which Indian cavalry are often so surprisingly rapid—facing partly to the front and partly to the rear. Yet Alexander was beforehand with them; and his renewed charge threw them into utter confusion before they could fully assume their new formation. Flying along the front of their own infantry, they took refuge in the spaces left between every two elephants, and (as it would seem in the absence, from Arrian's account, of the full details) passed as soon as possible through the intervals of the foot regiments, so as to be for the moment quite outside the battle. As soon as they were out of the way the Indian elephants were sent on, supported by the infantry, but were at once met face to face by the Macedonian phalanx."—*v.* Moberly's *Alexander in the Punjaub*, Introd. p. 12.

them. This kind of warfare was different from any of which they had experience in former contests, for the huge beasts charged the ranks of the infantry, and wherever they turned went crushing through the Macedonian phalanx though in close formation ; while the horsemen of the Indians, on seeing that the infantry was now engaged in the action, again wheeled round and charged the cavalry. But Alexander's men, being far superior in personal strength and military discipline, again routed them, and again drove them back upon the elephants, and cooped them up among them. Meanwhile the whole of Alexander's cavalry had now been gathered into one battalion, not in consequence of an order, but from being thrown together in the course of the struggle, and wherever they fell upon the ranks of the Indians they made great carnage before parting from them. The elephants being now cooped up within a narrow space, did no less damage to their friends than to their foes, trampling them under their hoofs as they wheeled and pushed about. There resulted in consequence a great slaughter of the cavalry, cooped up as it was in a narrow space around the elephants. Many of the elephant drivers, moreover, had been shot down, and of the elephants themselves some had been wounded, while others, both from exhaustion and the loss of their mahouts, no longer kept to their own side in the conflict, but, as if driven frantic by their sufferings, attacked friend and foe quite indiscriminately, pushed them, trampled them down, and killed them in all manner of ways. But the Macedonians, who had a wide and open field, and could therefore operate as they thought best, gave way when the elephants charged, and when they retreated followed at their heels and plied them with darts ; whereas the Indians, who were in the midst of the animals, suffered far more the effects of their rage. When the elephants, however, became quite exhausted, and their attacks were no longer made with vigour, they fell back like ships backing water, and merely kept trumpeting as they retreated with their faces to the enemy. Then did Alexander surround with his cavalry the whole of the enemy's line, and signal that the infantry, with their shields linked together so as to give the utmost compactness to their ranks, should advance in phalanx. By this means the cavalry of the Indians was, with a few exceptions, cut to pieces in the action. Such also was the fate of the infantry, since the Macedonians were now pressing upon them from every side. Upon this all turned to flight wherever a gap could be found in the cordon of Alexander's cavalry.

Chapter XVIII.—Sequel of the battle and surrender of Pôros

Meanwhile Krateros and all the other officers of Alexander's army, who had been left behind on the opposite bank of the Hydaspês, crossed the river when they perceived that Alexander was winning a splendid victory. These men, being fresh, were employed in the pursuit, instead of Alexander's exhausted troops, and they made no less a slaughter of the Indians in the retreat than had been made in the engagement.

The loss of the Indians in killed fell little short of 20,000 infantry and 3000 cavalry, and all their chariots were broken to pieces.[1] Two sons of Pôros fell in the battle, and also Spitakês,[2] the chief of the Indians of that district. The drivers of the elephants and of the chariots were also slain and the cavalry officers and the generals in the army of Pôros all . . .[3] The elephants, moreover, that escaped destruction in the field were all captured. On Alexander's side there fell about 80 of the 6000 infantry who had taken part in the first attack, 10 of the

[1] Diodôros gives the number of Indians killed at upwards of 12,000, and of the captured at more than 9000, besides 80 elephants.

[2] The Spitakês here mentioned as one of the slain is probably the same as Pittacus, who is recorded by Polyainos to have had an encounter with Alexander during the march of the latter from Taxila to the Hydaspês, as Droysen and Thirlwall agree in thinking.

[3] The hiatus is supposed to have contained the number of officers killed.

horse archers who first began the action, 20 of the companion cavalry, and 200 of the other cavalry.[1]

When Pôros, who had nobly discharged his duties throughout the battle, performing the part not only of a general, but also that of a gallant soldier, saw the slaughter of his cavalry and some of his elephants lying dead, and others wandering about sad and sullen without their drivers, while the greater part of his infantry had been killed, he did not, after the manner of Darius, the great king, abandon the field and show his men the first example of flight, but, on the contrary, fought on as long as he saw any Indians maintaining the contest in a united body ; but he wheeled round on being wounded in the right shoulder, where only he was unprotected by armour in the battle. All the rest of his person was rendered shot-proof by his coat of mail, which was remarkable for its strength and the closeness with which it fitted his person, as could afterwards be observed by those who saw him. When he found himself wounded he turned his elephant round and began to retire. Alexander, perceiving that he was a great man and valiant in fight, was anxious to save his life, and for this purpose sent to him first of all Taxilês the Indian. Taxilês, who was on horseback, approached as near the elephant which carried Pôros as seemed safe, and entreated him, since it was no longer possible for him to flee, to stop his elephant and listen to the message he brought from Alexander. But Pôros, on finding that the speaker was his old enemy Taxilês, turned round and prepared to smite him with his javelin ; and he would probably have killed him had not Taxilês instantly put his horse to the gallop and got beyond the reach of Pôros. But not even for this act did Alexander feel any resentment against Pôros, but sent to him messenger after messenger, and last of all Meroês, an Indian, as he had learned that Pôros and this

[1] This death-roll evidently greatly under-estimates the loss on Alexander's side. Diodôros says that there fell of the Macedonians 280 cavalry and more than 700 infantry.

Meroês were old friends. As soon as Pôros heard the message which Meroês now brought just at a time when he was overpowered by thirst, he made his elephant halt and dismounted. Then, when he had taken a draught of water and felt revived, he requested Meroês to conduct him without delay to Alexander.[1]

Chapter XIX.—Alexander makes Pôros his firm friend and ally—Founds two cities—Death of his famous horse Boukephalas

He was then conducted to Alexander, who, on learning that Meroês was approaching with him, rode forward in front of his line with a few of the Companions to meet him. Then reining in his horse he beheld with admiration the handsome person and majestic stature of Pôros, which somewhat exceeded five cubits. He saw, too, with wonder that he did not seem to be broken and abased in spirit, but that he advanced to meet him as a brave man would meet another brave man after gallantly contending with another king in defence of his kingdom. Then Alexander, who was the first to speak, requested Pôros to say how he wished to be treated. The report goes that Pôros said in reply, " Treat me, O Alexander ! as befits a king ; " and that Alexander, being pleased with his answer, replied, " For mine own sake, O Pôros ! thou shalt be so treated, but do thou, in thine own behalf, ask for whatever boon thou pleasest," to which Pôros replied that in what he had asked everything was included. Alexander was more delighted than ever with this rejoinder, and not only appointed Pôros to govern his own Indians, but added to his original territory another of still greater extent. Alexander thus treated this brave man

[1] Pôros was the first sovereign that Alexander had captured on the field of battle. Curtius and Diodôros relate somewhat differently from Arrian the story of his capture, representing him to have been protected to the last by his faithful elephant.

as befitted a king, and he consequently found him in all respects faithful and devoted to his interests. Such, then, was the result of the battle in which Alexander fought against Pôros[1] and the Indians of the other side of the Hydaspês in the month of Mounychion of the year when Hêgemôn was archon in Athens.[2]

Alexander founded two cities, one on the battlefield, and the other at the point whence he had started to cross the river Hydaspês. The former he called Nikaia in honour of his victory over the Indians, and the other Boukephala[3] in memory of his horse Boukephalas, which died there, not from being wounded by any one, but from toil and old age, for he was about thirty years old,[4] and had heretofore undergone many toils and dangers along with Alexander. This Boukephalas was never mounted by any one except Alexander only, for he disdained all other riders. He was of an uncommon size and of generous mettle. He had by way of a distinguishing mark the head of an ox impressed upon him, and some say that from this circumstance he got his name. But others say that though he was black, he had on his forehead a white mark which bore a close resemblance to the brow of an ox. In the country of the Ouxians this horse disappeared from Alexander, who sent a proclamation through the land that he would kill all the Ouxians if

[1] See Note R, Battle with Pôros.

[2] Diodôros says the battle occurred while Chremes was archon at Athens.

[3] Nikaia most probably occupied the site of the modern town of Mong, near the left bank. Nothing is known of its history. With respect to its sister city Boukephala, the ancient writers are not in agreement. Plutarch places it on the left or eastern bank of the Hydaspês, for he says that Boukephalas was killed in the battle, and that the city was built where he fell and was buried. According, however, to Strabo, Arrian, and Diodôros, it stood on the west bank; but while Strabo places it at the point where the troops embarked, Arrian places it farther down the stream on the site of

the great camp at Jalâlpûr. It became a great emporium of commerce, as we find from the Periplûs of the Erythraian Sea, c. 47. In the Peutinger Tables it is called Alexandria Bucefalos.

[4] "Schmieder says that Alexander could not have broken in the horse before he was sixteen years old. But since at this time he was in his twenty-ninth year he would have had him thirteen years. Consequently the horse must have been at least seventeen years old when he acquired him. Can any one believe this? Yet Plutarch also states that the horse was thirty years old at his death."— Chinnock's Anabasis of Alexander, p. 296, note 4.

they did not bring him his horse, and brought back he was immediately after the proclamation had been issued [1]—so great was Alexander's attachment to his favourite, and so great was the fear of Alexander which prevailed among the barbarians. Let so much honour be paid by me to this Boukephalas for Alexander's sake.

Chapter XX.—Alexander conquers the Glausai, receives embassies from Abisarês and other chiefs, and crosses the Akesinês

When Alexander had duly honoured with splendid obsequies those who had been slain in the battle, he offered to the gods in acknowledgment of his victory the customary sacrifices, and celebrated athletic and equestrian contests on the bank of the river Hydaspês, at the place where he first crossed with his army. He then left Krateros behind with a part of the army to build and fortify the cities which he was founding there, while he advanced himself against the Indians whose country lay next to the dominions of Pôros. Aristoboulos says that the name of the nation was the Glaukanikoi, but Ptolemy calls them the Glausai.[2] By which of the names it was called I take to be a matter of no consequence. Alexander invaded their country with the half of the companion cavalry, picked men from each phalanx of the infantry, all the horse-archers, the Agrianians, and the other archers. The people everywhere surrendered on terms of capitula-

[1] This incident is referred by Plutarch to Hyrkania, and by Curtius to the land of the Mardians. The Ouxioi lived on the borders of Persis, between that province and Sousiana.

[2] Alexander, according to Diodôros, halted to recruit his army for thirty days in the dominions of Pôros. He then advanced northwards with a part of his army to the fertile and populous regions that lay in the south of Kâs'mîr (the Bhimber and Bajaur districts) between the upper courses of the Hydaspês and the Akesinês and Chenâb. The name of the inhabitants, *Glausai* or *Glaukantkoi*, has been identified by V. de Saint-Martin with that of the Kalaka, a tribe mentioned in the *Varâha Sanhita*, a work of the sixth century of our aera. In the *Mahâbhârata* the name is written *Kalaja*, and in the Rajput Chronicles *Kalacha*, a form which justifies the Greek *Glausai*. The second part of the longer name, *antka*, means a troop or army in Sanskrit.—v. Saint-Martin's *Etude*, pp. 102, 103.

tion.   In this manner he took seven-and-thirty cities, the smallest of which contained not fewer than 5000 inhabitants, while many contained upwards of 10,000.   He took also a great many villages which were not less populous than the towns ; and this country he gave to Pôros to rule,[1] and between him and Taxilês he effected a reconciliation.   He then sent Taxilês home to his capital.

At this time envoys came from Abisarês to say that their king surrendered himself and his whole realm to Alexander.[2]   Yet before the battle in which Alexander had defeated Pôros, Abisarês was ready with his army to fight on the side of Pôros.   But he now sent his brother along with the other envoys to Alexander, taking with them money and forty elephants as a present.   Envoys also arrived from the independent Indians, and from another Indian ruler called Pôros.[3]   Alexander ordered Abisarês to come to him as quickly as possible, threatening that if he did not come he would see him and his army arriving where he would not rejoice to see them.

At this time Phratophernes, the satrap of Parthia and Hyrkania, at the head of the Thracians who had been left with him came to Alexander.   There came also envoys from Sisikottos, the satrap of the Assakênians, reporting that these people had slain their governor and revolted from Alexander.   Against these he sent Philippos and Tyriaspês to quell the insurrection and restore tranquillity and order to the province.

Alexander himself advanced towards the river Akesinês.[4]   This is the only Indian river of which Ptolemy,

[1] Conf. Strabo, XV. i. 3.   "Other writers affirm that the Macedonians conquered nine nations situated between the Hydaspês and the Hypanis (Beas), and obtained possession of 500 cities, not one of which was less than Kos Meropis, and that Alexander, after having conquered all this country, delivered it up to Pôros."

[2] This was a second embassy. An earlier is mentioned in Chapter VIII. of this book.

[3] Strabo (XV. i. p. 699) says this Pôros was a nephew of the Pôros whom Alexander had defeated, and that his country was called Gandaris. The Gandarai were a widely extended people, occupying a district stretching from the upper part of the Panjâb to the west of the Indus as far as Qandahar. They are the Gandhâra of Sanskrit.

[4] The Akesinês, now the Chenâb, is called in the Vedic Hymns the *Asikni, i.e.* "dark-coloured." It was called also, and more commonly,

the son of Lagos, has mentioned the size. He state:
where Alexander crossed it with his army in boat
on inflated hides the current was so rapid that the v
dashed with foam and fury against the large and jagged
rocks with which the channel was bestrewn. He informs
us also that it was 15 stadia in breadth ; and while the
passage was easy for those who crossed upon inflated
hides, not a few of those who were carried in boats perished in the waters, as many of the boats were dashed to
pieces by striking against the rocks. From this description we may fairly conclude, if we institute a comparison,
that the size of the river Indus has been pretty correctly
stated by those who take it to have an average breadth of
40 stadia, while, where narrowest and of course deepest,
it contracts to a breadth of 15 stadia, which I take to be
its actual breadth in many parts of its course, for I conclude that Alexander selected a part of the Akesinês
where the passage was widest, and where the current
would consequently be slower than elsewhere.

*Chapter XXI.—Pursuit after Pôros, nephew of the great
Pôros—Conquest of the country between the Akesinês
and the Hydraôtês—Passage of the latter river*

After crossing the river he left Koinos there upon the
bank with his own brigade, and ordered him to superintend the passage of the river by those troops which had
been left behind to collect corn and other supplies from
the part of India which was now under his authority.
Pôros he sent home to his capital with orders to select
the best fighting men of the Indians, and to muster all

Chandrabhâgâ, which, being trans-
literated into Greek, becomes Sandro-
phagos. This word suggested to the
soldiers of Alexander another of bad
omen, *Ale-xandrophagos*, which means
devourer of Alexander, and hence
they adopted its other name, perhaps
on account of the disaster which befell

the Macedonian fleet at the turbulent
junction of this river with the Hydaspês. In Ptolemy's *Geography* it is
called Sandabala by an obvious error
for Sandabaga. The Akesinês, though
joined by the other great Panjâb
rivers, retained its name until it fell
into the Indus.

I

the elephants he possessed, and to rejoin him with these. He resolved to pursue in person the other Pôros—the bad one—with the lightest troops in his army, for word had been brought that he had fled from the country of which he was the ruler ; for, while hostilities still subsisted between Alexander and the other Porôs, this Pôros had sent envoys to Alexander offering to surrender into his hands both his person and the country over which he ruled, but this more from enmity to Pôros than friendliness to Alexander. On learning therefore that Pôros had not only been set at liberty, but had his kingdom restored to him, and that too with a large accession of territory, he was overcome with fear, not so much of Alexander as of his namesake Pôros, and fled from his country, taking with him as many fighting men as he could persuade to accompany him in his flight.

Alexander, while marching to overtake him, arrived at the Hydraôtês—another Indian river, not less in breadth than the Akesinês, but not so rapid.[1] Over all the country which he overran he planted garrisons in the most suitable places, so that the troops under Krateros and Koinos might, while scouring it far and near for forage, traverse it in safety to join him. He then despatched Hêphaistiôn with a force comprising two divisions of infantry, his own regiment of cavalry and that of Dêmêtrios, and one-half of the archers, into the country of that Pôros who had revolted. He received orders to hand over the country to the other Pôros, and when he had reduced all the independent Indian tribes bordering on the banks

---

[1] The Hydraôtês is called by Strabo (XV. i. 21) the Hyarôtis, and in Ptolemy's *Geography* the Adris or Rhouadis. It is now the *Râvî*, which is an abridged form of its Sanskrit name, the Airâvatî. It passes the city of Lahore, and joins the Chenâb about 30 miles *above* Multân. In former times, however, the junction occurred 15 miles *below* that city. In Ptolemy's *Geography* the Rhouadis is erroneously made to join the Hydas- pês, or, as Ptolemy calls it, the Bidaspês. Arrian in his *Indika* (c. 4) describes the Hydraôtês as rising in the country of the Kambistholoi, and after receiving the Hyphasis among the Astrybai, and the Saranges from the Kêkeans (the Sekaya of Sanskrit), and the Neudros from the Attakênoi, falling into the Akesinês. The Hyphasis does not, however, join the Hydraôtês.

of the Hydraôtês, to place these also under the rule of Pôros. He himself then crossed the river Hydraôtês, where he met with none of the difficulties which had attended the passage of the Akesinês. When he was advancing into the country beyond the Hydraôtês he found most of the natives willing to surrender on capitulation, while some met him in arms, and others were captured when attempting to escape and reduced to submission.

Chapter XXII.—Alexander marches against the Kathaians —Takes Pimprama, and lays siege to Sangala

Alexander meanwhile had learned that the Kathaians[1] and other tribes of independent Indians[2] were preparing to meet him in battle if he invaded their country, and were inviting the neighbouring tribes, which were independent like themselves, to coöperate with them. He learned also that the city near which they meant to engage him was strongly fortified, and was called Sangala.[3] The Kathaians themselves enjoyed the highest reputation for courage and skill in the art of war, and the same warlike spirit characterised the Oxydrakai, another Indian race, and the Malloi, who were also an Indian race, for when shortly before this time Pôros and Abisarês had marched against them with their armies, and had besides stirred up many of the independent Indians against them, they were obliged, as it turned out, to retreat without accomplishing anything at all adequate to the scale of their preparations.

Alexander, on receiving this intelligence, marched rapidly against the Kathaians, and on the second day after he had left the river Hydraôtês arrived at a city

---

[1] *v.* Note L, Kathaians.
[2] The expression *independent* shows that the Greeks were cognisant of the Indian village system. Each of its rural units they took to be an independent republic.
[3] *v.* Note M, Sangala.

named Pimprama, belonging to an Indian race called the Adraïstai,[1] which surrendered on terms of capitulation. Alexander gave his troops rest the next day, and on the third day advanced to Sangala, where the Kathaians and the neighbouring tribes that had joined them were mustered before the city, and drawn up in battle-order on a low hill, which was not on all sides precipitous. They lay encamped behind their waggons, which, by encircling the hill in three rows, protected the camp with a triple barricade. Alexander, on perceiving the great number of the barbarians, and the nature of the position they occupied, drew up his army in the order which seemed best suited to the circumstances, and at once despatched against them the horse-archers just as they were, with orders to ride along and shoot at the Indians from a distance, so as not only to prevent them from making a sortie before his own dispositions should be completed, but to wound them within their stronghold even before the battle began. Upon his right wing he posted the corps of horseguards and the cavalry regiment of Kleitos, next to these the hypaspists, and then the Agrianians. The left wing he assigned to Perdikkas, who commanded his own cavalry regiment and the battalions of the footguards. The archers he formed into two bodies, and placed them upon each wing. While he was making these dispositions the infantry and cavalry which formed the rearguard arrived upon the field. This cavalry he divided in two parts, and led one to each wing, and with the infantry that had arrived he closed up the ranks of the phalanx more densely. Then he took the cavalry which had been drawn up on the right and advanced against the waggons ranged on the left wing

[1] The Adraïstai appear to be the people called in the *Periplûs of the Erythraean Sea*, the Aratrioi. Lassen identifies them with the Aratta of the *Mahâbhârata*. Diodôros calls them the Adrêstai, and Orosius in his *History* (iii. 19) the Adrestae. Their capital, Pimprama, has not as yet been identified with certainty, but V. de Saint-Martin suggests that it may be represented by *Bhîranah*, a place eight leagues distant from Lahore towards the south-east. The same author thinks that the *Adrastae* are very probably the *Aïrâvatâ* or *Raïvâtaka* of Sanskrit.

of the Indians, where the position seemed easier to assault, and where the waggons were not so closely packed together.

Chapter XXIII.—Alexander drives the Kathaians into Sangala, which he invests on every side

But when the Indians, instead of sallying out from behind their waggons to attack the cavalry as it advanced, mounted upon them, and began to shoot from the top of them, Alexander saw that this was not work for cavalry, and so, having dismounted, he led on foot the phalanx of infantry against them. The Macedonians found no difficulty in driving the Indians from the first row of waggons, but on the other hand the Indians, having formed in line in front of the second row, were able to force back their assailants with greater ease, standing as they did more compactly together, and in a narrower circle, while the Macedonians had less room in which to operate against them. At this time they quietly drew back the waggons of the first row, and through the gaps each man, as he found an opportunity, assailed the enemy in an irregular way.[1] Yet even from these waggons they were forcibly driven by the phalanx of infantry, and even at the third row they no longer held ground, but fled with all the haste they could into the city and shut themselves up within its gates. Alexander that same day encamped with his infantry around the city, as far at least as the phalanx enabled him to surround it, for the wall was of such great extent that his camp did not completely environ it. Opposite the part where the gap was left, and where also was a lake not far from the walls, he posted the cavalry all round the lake, as he knew it not to be deep, and at the same time anticipated that the Indians, terrified by their previous defeat, would abandon

---

[1] Chinnock notes that Caesar's troops were assailed in a similar manner by the Helvetians. — *v.* Caesar's *De Bello Gallico*, i. 26.

the city during the night. The event showed he had conjectured aright, for about the second watch the most of
them dropped down from the wall and came upon the
outposts of the cavalry. The foremost of them were cut
to pieces by the sentinels, but those in the rear, perceiving
that the lake was guarded all round, withdrew into the
city. Alexander now encompassed the city with a double
stockade, except where the lake shut it in, and around
the lake he posted guards to keep still stricter watch. He
resolved also to bring up the military engines against the
place for battering down the walls. Some deserters, however, came to him from the city and informed him that
the Indians intended that very night to escape from the
city by way of the lake where the gap occurred in the
stockade. So at that point he stationed Ptolemy, the
son of Lagos, with three divisions of the hypaspists, each
1000 strong, all the Agrianians, and a single line of
archers, and pointed out to him the particular spot where
the barbarians, as he conjectured, were likeliest to attempt
forcing their passage. " And now," said he, " when thou
perceivest the barbarians forcing their way at this point,
do thou with the army arrest their advance, and order the
trumpets to sound the signal ; and do you, sirs," he added,
turning to the officers, " as soon as the signal is given,
each of you with your men in battle-order, hasten towards
the noise wherever the trumpet summons you. I shall
not myself stand idly by away from the broil."

*Chapter XXIV.—Alexander captures Sangala, razes it to
the ground, and advances to the river Hyphasis*

Such were the directions he gave, and Ptolemy in that
place collected as many as he could of the waggons which
the enemy had left behind in their first flight, and placed
them athwart so that the fugitives might imagine there
were many obstacles to their escaping by night. He
ordered the stakes, which had been cut but not fixed in

the ground, to be formed into stockades at different points between the lake and the wall. All this was done by the soldiers during the night. But when it was now about the fourth watch the barbarians, in accordance with the information Alexander had received, opened the gates which fronted the lake and rushed towards it at full speed. They did not, however, escape the vigilance either of the picquets posted there, or of Ptolemy who lay behind ready to support them ; and just then the trumpeters gave him the signal, and he advanced against the barbarians with his troops which were under arms and drawn up ready for action. The waggons, moreover, as well as the stockade, which had been constructed between the wall and the lake, impeded the fugitives ; and as soon as the trumpet sounded the alarm Ptolemy with his men fell upon them and killed them, one after another, as they slunk out from the waggons. Upon this the Indians fled back once more to the city for refuge, and as many as 500 of them were slain in the retreat.

Meanwhile Pôros also arrived, bringing with him the remainder of his elephants and a force of 5000 Indians, and the military engines which had been constructed by Alexander were now being brought up to the wall. But the Macedonians, before any part of it was battered down, took the city by storm, having undermined the wall, which was of brick, and planted ladders against it all round. In the capture 17,000 of the Indians were slaughtered, and more than 70,000 were captured, together with 300 waggons and 500 horsemen.[1] The loss in Alexander's army during all the siege was somewhat under 100 killed, but the proportion of the wounded to the number killed was higher than usual, for there were 1200 wounded, including some officers, and among these Lysimachos, a member of the body-guard.

Alexander having buried the dead according to custom, sent Eumenês, his secretary, in command of 300

[1] Curtius gives the loss of the Kathaians at 8000 killed. Arrian's numbers here seem to be greatly exaggerated.

horsemen to the two cities which had revolted along with Sangala, to tell those who held them that Sangala had been captured, and that Alexander would not at all deal hardly with them if they remained where they were and received

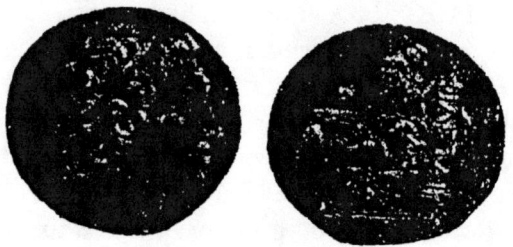

FIG. 9.—EUMENÊS.

him in a friendly way, for that none of the independent Indians who had voluntarily surrendered themselves had received any ill-treatment at his hands. But they had already learned that Sangala had been stormed by Alexander, and being terrified by the news had left the cities and were in flight. When Alexander was informed of their flight he hastened after them, but as they had a long start of him most of them baffled his efforts to overtake them. Those, however, who were left behind in the retreat when their strength failed were taken by the troops and slaughtered to the number of about 500. As he gave up the design of pursuing the fugitives any farther, he drew back to Sangala and razed the city to the ground. The land belonging to it he made over to those Indians who had formerly been independent, but who had voluntarily submitted to him. He then sent Pôros with his own forces to the cities which had submitted to introduce garrisons within them, but he himself with his army advanced to the river Hyphasis[1] to conquer the Indians

[1] The Hyphasis, now the Beäs or Beias, is variously called by the classical writers the Bibasis, the Hypasis, and the Hypanis. Its Sanskrit name is the *Vipâsâ*, which means "uncorded," and it is said to have been so called because it *destroyed the cord* with which one of the Indian sages intended to hang himself. It joins the Satlej (not the Hydraôtês, as Arrian says in his *Indika*), and the united stream is called in Sanskrit the S'atadru, *i.e.* "flowing in a hundred channels." It marked the limit of Alexander's advance eastward. In his time it flowed in a different

who dwelt beyond it. Nor did there appear to him any end of the war as long as an enemy remained to be encountered.

Chapter XXV.—Alexander finding the army unwilling to advance beyond the Hyphasis, convokes his officers and addresses them on the subject

It was reported that the country beyond the Hyphasis was exceedingly fertile, and that the inhabitants were good agriculturists, brave in war, and living under an excellent system of internal government ; for the multitude was governed by the aristocracy, who exercised their authority with justice and moderation. It was also reported that the people there had a greater number of elephants than the other Indians, and that those were of superior size and courage. This information only whetted Alexander's eagerness to advance farther, but the Macedonians now began to lose heart when they saw the king raising up without end toils upon toils and dangers upon dangers. The army, therefore, began to hold conferences at which the more moderate men bewailed their condition, while others positively asserted that they would follow no farther though Alexander himself should lead the way. When this came to Alexander's knowledge he convoked the officers in command of brigades, before the disorder and despondency should

channel, one by which it reached the Chenâb about 40 miles above Uchh. Curtius and Diodôros inform us that Alexander before reaching this river had entered the dominions of King Sôphites, who submitted without resistance, and was therefore left in possession of his sovereignty. Another chief (called Phêgeus by Diodôros, but more correctly Phegelas by Curtius), whose dominions adjoined the Hyphasis, entertained Alexander and his army for two days. By this time he had been rejoined by Hêphaistiôn, who had been conducting operations elsewhere, and he then proceeded to the bank of the river. The country beyond it Arrian represents as exceedingly fertile, whereas in Curtius and Diodôros we read how Alexander was informed that a desert lay beyond it which would occupy a journey of eleven days. Arrian's statement holds true of the northern districts beyond the river, and the other statement of the southern districts. Thirlwall, following the latter statement, takes it that Alexander reached the Satlej after it had received the Hyphasis, but this is a very questionable view.

be further developed among the soldiers, and he thus addressed them :

"On seeing that you, O Macedonians and allies! no longer follow me into dangers with your wonted alacrity, I have summoned you to this assembly that I may either persuade you to go farther, or be persuaded by you to turn back. If you have reason to complain of past labours, and of me your leader, I need say no more. But if by those labours you have acquired Ionia,[1] and the Hellespont with the two Phrygias, Kappadokia, Paphlagonia, Lydia, Karia, Lykia, and Pamphylia, as well as Phoenikia and Egypt, together with Hellenic Lybia, part of Arabia, Hollow Syria, Mesopotamia, Babylon, Sousiana, Persis, and Media, and all the provinces governed by the Medes and Persians, not to mention other states which were never subject to them ; if in addition we have conquered the regions beyond the Kaspian Gates, those beyond Kaukasos, the Tanais[2] also, and the country beyond, Baktria, Hyrkania, and the Hyrkanian Sea ; if we have driven the Skythians back into their deserts, and if besides, the Indus, Hydaspês, Akesinês, and Hydraôtês flow through territories that are ours, why should you hesitate to pass the Hyphasis also and add the tribes beyond it to your Macedonian conquests? Are you afraid there are other barbarians who may yet successfully resist you, although of those we have already met some have willingly submitted, others have been captured in flight, while others have left us their deserted country to be distributed either to our allies or to those who have voluntarily submitted to us."

[1] The name of Ion, the eponymous ancestor of the Ionians, had originally the digamma, and hence was written as Ivon. The Hebrew transcription of this digammated form is *Javan*, the name by which *Greece* is designated in the Bible. The Sanskrit transcription is *Yavana*, the name applied in Indian works to Ionians or Greeks and foreigners generally.

[2] The Tanais is properly the Don, but Alexander meant by it the Jaxartes, which formed the eastern boundary of the Persian empire, and which he had crossed to attack the nomadic Skythians, who had made threatening demonstrations against him on the right or northern bank (*v.* the 16th and 17th chapters of the fourth book).

Chapter XXVI.—Continuation of Alexander's Speech

" For my part, I think that to a man of spirit there is no other aim and end of his labours except the labours themselves, provided they be such as lead him to the performance of glorious deeds. But if any one wishes to know the limits of the present warfare, let him understand that the river Ganges and the Eastern Sea are now at no great distance off. This sea, I am confident, is connected with the Hyrkanian Sea, because the Great Ocean flows round the whole earth.[1] I shall besides prove to the Macedonians and their allies that the Indian Gulf is connected with the Persian, and the Hyrkanian Sea with the Indian Gulf. From the Persian Gulf our fleet will sail round to Lybia as far as the Pillars of Heraklês.[2] From these pillars all the interior of Lybia becomes ours, and thus all Asia shall belong to us,[3] and the boundaries of our empire in that direction will coincide with those which the deity has made the boundaries of the earth.

[1] It was a prevalent belief in antiquity that the Kaspian or Hyrkanian Sea was a gulf of the great ocean which encircles the earth, and not an inland sea.

[2] Arrian (vii. 1) says : " When Alexander reached Pasargadai and Persepolis he conceived an ardent desire to sail down the Euphrates and Tigres to the Persian sea, and survey their mouths. . . . Some writers have stated that he had in contemplation a voyage round the greater portion of Arabia, the land of the Aethiopians, Lybia, and Numidia beyond Mount Atlas to Gadeira (Cadiz) inward into the Mediterranean." One of the writers referred to is Plutarch, who says (*Alexander*, c. 68): " Nearchos joined him (Alexander) here (at the capital of Gedrosia), and he was so much delighted with the account of his voyage that he formed a design to sail in person from the Euphrates with a great fleet, circle the coast of Arabia and Africa, and enter the Mediter-ranean by the Pillars of Hercules." Herodotos (iv. 42) says that Nekô, king of the Egyptians, sent certain Phoenicians in ships with orders to sail back through the Pillars of Hercules into the Northern Sea (the Mediterranean that is), and so to return to Egypt. The pillars designated the twin rocks which guard the entrance to the Mediterranean at the eastern extremity of the Straits of Gibraltar, the one on the European side being called *Kalpê*, and that on the African side, where now stands the citadel of Ceuta, *Abila* or *Abyla. v.* Pliny (iii. prooem.): " Proximis autem faucibus utrimque impositi montes coercent claustra, Abyla Africae, Europae Calpe, laborum Herculis metae, quam ob causam indigenae columnas ejus dei vocant."

[3] Arrian (iii. 30) informs us that in the opinion of some the Nile formed the boundary of Asia, but he writes here as if Lybia or Northern Africa were part of Asia.

But, if we now turn back, many warlike nations extending beyond the Hyphasis to the Eastern Sea, and many others lying northwards between these and Hyrkania, to say nothing of their neighbours the Skythian tribes, will be left behind us unconquered, so that if we turn back there is cause to fear lest the conquered nations, as yet wavering in their fidelity, may be instigated to revolt by those who are still independent. Our many labours will in that case be all completely thrown away, or we must enter on a new round of toils and dangers. But persevere, O Macedonians and allies! glory crowns the deeds of those who expose themselves to toils and dangers. Life, signalised by deeds of valour, is delightful, and so is death, if we leave behind us an immortal name. Know ye not that it was not by staying at home in Tiryns [1] or Argos, or even in Peloponnêsos or Thebes, that our ancestor was exalted to such glory, that from being a man he became, or was thought to be, a god. Nor were the labours few even of Dionysos, who ranks as a god far. above Heraklês. But we have advanced beyond Nysa, and the rock Aornos, which proved impregnable to Heraklês, is in our possession. Add, then, the rest of Asia to our present acquisitions—the smaller part of it to the greater. Could we ourselves, think you, have achieved any great and memorable deeds if, sitting down at home in Macedonia, we had been content without exertion merely to preserve our own country, by repelling the attacks of the neighbouring Thracians, Illyrians, and Triballians, or those Greeks whose disposition to us is unfriendly ?

"If, indeed, while leading you, I had myself shrunk from the toils and dangers to which you were exposed, you would not without good reason be dispirited in prospect of undertaking fresh enterprises, seeing that while you alone shared the toils, it was for others you procured

[1] The Macedonian kings claimed to be descended from Heraklês, who resided for some time at Tiryns, one of the most ancient cities in Greece, situated near Argos, and, like Argos, famous for its Cyclopean walls.

the rewards.   But our labours are in common; I, equally with you, share in the dangers, and the rewards become the public property.   For the land is yours, and you are its satraps; and among you the greater part of its treasures has already been distributed.   And when all Asia is subdued then, by heaven, I will not merely satisfy, but exceed every man's hopes and wishes.   Such of you as wish to return home I shall send back to your own country, or even myself will lead you back.   But those who remain here I will make objects of envy to those who go back."

Chapter XXVII.—Koinos, replying to Alexander, states the grievances of the army

When Alexander had spoken to this and the like effect, a long silence followed, because those present neither dared to speak freely in opposition to the king, nor yet wished to assent to what he proposed.   Alexander again and again requested that any one who wished should speak, even if his views differed from those which he had himself expressed.   But the silence was unbroken for a long time, till at last Koinos, the son of Polemokratês, summoned up courage and spoke to this effect:

"Forasmuch as you do not wish, O king! to rule Macedonians by constraint, but say that you will lead them by persuasion, or suffering yourself to be persuaded by them, will not have recourse to compulsion, I intend to speak, not on behalf of myself and fellow-officers who have been honoured above the other soldiers, and have most of us received splendid rewards of our labours, and from having been highly exalted above others are more zealous than others to serve you in all things, but in behalf of the great body of the army.   Yet on behalf of this army I intend not to say what may be agreeable to the men, but what I think will be conducive to your present interests and safest for the future.   I feel bound

by my age not to conceal what appears to be the best
course to follow ; bound by the high authority conferred
on me by yourself, and bound also by the unhesitating
boldness which I have hitherto exhibited in all enterprises
of danger.   The more I look to the number and magnitude of the exploits performed under your command by
us who set out with you from home, the more does it
seem to me expedient to place some limit to our toils
and dangers.   For you see yourself how many Macedonians
and Greeks started with you, and how few of us are left.
From our ranks you sent away home from Baktra the
Thessalians [1] as soon as you saw they had no stomach
for further toils, and in this you acted wisely.   Of the
other Greeks, some have been settled in the cities founded
by you, where all of them are not willing residents ;
others still share our toils and dangers.   They and the
Macedonian army have lost some of their numbers in
the fields of battle ; others have been disabled by wounds ;
others have been left behind in different parts of Asia,
but the majority have perished by disease.   A few only
out of many survive, and these few possessed no longer
of the same bodily strength as before, while their spirits
are still more depressed.[2]   All those, whose parents are
still living, have a yearning to see them—a yearning
to see their wives and children—a yearning to see were
it but their native land itself—a desire pardonable in
men who would return home in great splendour derived
from your munificence, and raised from humble to high
rank, and from indigence to wealth.   Seek not, therefore,
to lead them against their inclinations, for you will not
find them the same men in the face of dangers, if they
enter without heart into their contests with the enemy.

[1] " Alexander," says Arrian (iii.
19), "on reaching Ekbatana, sent
back to the sea the Thessalian cavalry
and the other Grecian allies, paying
them the full amount of the stipulated
hire, and giving them besides a donative of 2000 talents."   Was Baktra a
slip of memory on the part of Koinos ?

[2] The drenching rains to which
the Macedonian soldiers were continually exposed during their march
from Taxila to the Hyphasis must
have had a considerable effect in ex-
hausting their strength and depressing
their spirits.

But do you also, if it agree with your wishes, return home with us, see your mother once more, settle the affairs of the Greeks, and carry to the house of your fathers those your great and numerous victories. Then having so done, form, if you so wish, a fresh expedition against these same tribes of eastern Indians, or, if you prefer, against the shores of the Euxine Sea, or against Karchêdon,[1] and the parts of Lybia beyond the Karchê-donians. It will then be your part to unfold your purpose, and then other Macedonians and other Greeks will follow you—young men full of vigour instead of old men worn out with toils—men for whom war, through their inexperience of it, has no immediate terrors, and eager to set out from the hope of future rewards. They will also naturally follow you with the greater alacrity, from seeing that the companions of your former toils and dangers have returned home wealthy instead of poor, and raised to high distinction from their original obscurity. Moderation, in the midst of success, is, O king ! the noblest of virtues, for though, at the head of so brave an army, you have nothing to dread from mortal foes, yet the visitations of the deity cannot be foreseen, and man cannot, therefore, guard against them."

Chapter XXVIII.—Alexander mortified by the refusal of his army to advance, secludes himself in his tent, but in the end resolves to return

When Koinos had concluded his address, those present are said to have signified their approval of what he said by loud applause, while many by their streaming tears showed still more expressively their aversion to encounter further dangers, and how welcome to them was the idea of returning. But Alexander, who resented the freedom

[1] Karchêdon is Carthage. The name is said to be a corruption of *Kereth-Hadeshoth* or *Carth-hadtha*, *i.e.* "new city," in contra-distinction to Utica, which either signifies in Phoenician "old city," or is derived, as Olshausen, thinks, from a root signifying "a colony."

with which Koinos had spoken, and the hesitation displayed by the other generals, broke up the conference ; but next day while his wrath was still hot he summoned the same men again, and told them that he was going forward himself, but would not force any of the Macedonians to accompany him against their wishes, for he would find men ready to follow their king of their own free will. But those who wished to go away were free to go home, and might tell their friends there that they had returned, and left their king in the midst of his enemies. It is said that with these words he withdrew into his tent, and did not admit any of his companions to see him on that day, nor even till the third day after, waiting to see whether a change of mood, such as often takes place in an assemblage of soldiers, would manifest itself among the Macedonians and the allies, and make them readier to yield to his persuasions. But when a deep silence again reigned throughout the camp, and the soldiers were evidently offended by his wrath without their minds being changed by it, he began none the less, as Ptolemy, the son of Lagos, states, to offer there sacrifice for the passage of the river ; but when on sacrificing he found the omens were against him, he then assembled the oldest of the Companions, and especially his intimate friends among them, and as everything indicated that to return was his most expedient course he intimated to the army that he had resolved to march back.

Chapter XXIX.—Alexander erects altars on the banks of the Hyphasis to mark the limits of his advance, recrosses the Hydraôtês and Akesinês and regains the Hydaspês

Then they shouted, as a mixed multitude would shout when rejoicing, and many of them shed tears. Some of them even approached the royal pavilion, and invoked many blessings on Alexander, because by them and them only did he permit himself to be vanquished. He then divided the army into brigades, which he ordered to prepare twelve altars[1] to equal in height the highest military towers, and to exceed them in point of breadth, to serve as thankofferings to the gods who had led him so far as a conqueror, and also as a memorial of his own labours. When the altars had been constructed, he offered sacrifice upon them with the customary rites, and celebrated a gymnastic and equestrian contest. Having thereafter committed all the country west of the river Hyphasis to the government of Pôros, he marched back to the Hydraôtês. After crossing this river, he retraced his steps to the Akesinês, and on arriving there found the city which he had ordered Hêphaistiôn to fortify completely built.[2] Herein he settled as many of the inhabitants of the neighbourhood as were willing to make it their domicile, and such also of the mercenary soldiers as were now unfit for further service. He then began to make preparations for the downward voyage to the Great Sea.

At this time Arsakês,[3] ruler of the country adjoining the dominions of Abisarês, together with the brother of Abisarês and his other relatives, came to him, bringing presents such as the Indians consider the most valuable, and some thirty elephants sent by Abisarês. They represented that Abisarês was prevented from coming in person by illness—a statement which the ambassadors sent by Alexander to Abisarês corroborated. Alexander, readily believing that such was the case, made Abisarês satrap of his own dominions, and moreover placed Arsakês under his jurisdiction. Having then fixed the amount which was to be paid as tribute, he again offered sacrifice near

---

[1] See Note N, Alexander's altars on the Hyphasis.

[2] "This city," says Lassen, "lay probably where Wazîrâbâd now stands. Here the great road to the Hydaspês parts into two, one leading to Jalâlpûr, and the other to Jhelam. It is the sixth of the Alexandreias mentioned in Stephanos Byz." *v. Ind. Alt.* ii. 165, n. The Chenab here has a width of about a mile and a half.

[3] Arsakês, to judge from his name and what is here said of him, was probably the king of Uras'a. This district, the Arsa of Ptolemy, the W-la-shi of Hwen Thsiang, and now Rash in Dantâwar, included all the hill country between the Indus and Kas'mîr as far south as Attak.

the river Akesinês. He then recrossed that river, and reached the Hydaspês where he employed his army in repairing the damage caused by the rains to the cities of Nikaia and Boukephala, and set the other affairs of the country in order.

SIXTH BOOK

Chapter I.—Alexander mistakes the Indus for the upper Nile—Prepares to sail down stream to the sea

WHEN Alexander had got ready upon the banks of the Hydaspês a large number of thirty-oared galleys, and others of one bank and a half of oars, besides numerous horse transports and every other requisite for the easy conveyance of an army by river, he resolved to sail down the Hydaspês [1] to the Great Sea. As he had before this seen crocodiles in the river Indus, and in no other river but the Nile only, and had besides seen beans of the same species as those which Egypt produces [2] growing near the banks of the Akesinês, and as he had heard that this river falls into the Indus, he was led to think that he had discovered the sources of the Nile. His idea was that this river rose somewhere among the Indians and pursued its course through a vast tract of desert country, where it lost

[1] *v.* Strabo (XV. i. 29). Between the Hydaspês and Akesinês . . . is the forest in the neighbourhood of the Emodoi mountains, in which Alexander cut down a large quantity of fir, pine, cedar, and a variety of other trees fit for shipbuilding, and brought the timber down the Hydaspês. With this he constructed a fleet on the Hydaspês near the cities which he built on each side of the river where he had crossed it and conquered Pôros. "The timber," says Sir A. Burnes, "of which the boats of the Panjâb are constructed is chiefly floated down *by the Hydaspês* from the Indian Caucasus, which most satisfactorily explains the selection of its banks by Alexander in preference to the other rivers." Bunbury, citing this passage, adds: "The navigation of the Indus itself for a considerable part of its course below Attock is so dangerous on account of rapids as to render it wholly unsuitable for the descent of a flotilla such as that of Alexander."

[2] This is the *nelumbum speciosum*, or Cyathus Smithii, the sacred Egyptian or Pythagorean bean. The use of its fruit was forbidden to the Egyptian priests (*v.* Herod. ii. 37).

the name of the Indus, and that from the time when it
began to flow through the inhabited parts of the world it
was called the Nile both by the Aithiopians, who lived
there and by the Egyptians, just as Homer also changed
its name, calling it the river Egypt after Egypt, the
country where at last it discharges itself into the Inner
Sea.[1] Accordingly when he was writing to his mother
Olympias about the country of the Indians, he mentioned,
it is said, among other things that he thought he had discovered the sources of the Nile, actually basing on such
slight and comtemptible evidence his judgements respecting questions of so much importance. When, however,
he investigated. with special care the facts relating to the
river Indus, he ascertained from the natives that the
Hydaspês unites with the Akesinês, and the Akesinês with
the Indus, to which the other two rivers lose both their
waters and their names. He learned further that the
Indus discharges itself into the Great Sea by two mouths,
and that it has no connection with the Egyptian country.
He is said to have then deleted what he had written
about the Nile in the letter to his mother, and as he had
set his mind on sailing down the rivers to the Great Sea
he ordered a fleet for this purpose to be prepared for him.
Adequate crews for the vessels were supplied by the
Phoenicians, Cyprians, Karians, and Egyptians who accompanied the army.

---

[1] " It is remarkable to see how in
this respect the geographical information of the Greeks seems to have
retrograded since the time of Herodotus. No allusion is found to the
voyage of Scylax related by that
historian, while the just conclusions
derived from it by Herodotus had
fallen into the same oblivion. But
absurd as was this identification (of
the Indus with the Nile), the general
resemblance between these rivers,
which are constantly brought into
comparison by the Greek geographers
(Strabo, XV. p. 692, etc.), is certainly
such as to justify their observations.
The resemblance of the lower valley
of the Indus from the time it has
received the waters of the Panjab
with Egypt is dwelt upon by modern
travellers. One description (says
Mr. Elphinstone) might serve for
both. A smooth and fertile plain is
bounded on one side by mountains,
and on the other by a desert. It is
divided by a large river, which forms
a Delta as it approaches the sea, and
annually inundates and enriches the
country near its banks. The climate
of both is hot and dry, and rain is of
rare occurrence in either country."—
v. Bunbury's *Hist. of Anc. Geo.* p.
510.

Chapter II.—Description of the voyage down the Hydaspês

At this time Koinos, who was one of Alexander's most faithful companions, took ill and died, and his master buried him with all the magnificence circumstances allowed. He then assembled the Companions and all the ambassadors of the Indians who had come to him, and in their presence appointed Pôros king of all the Indian territories already subjugated—seven nations in all, containing more than 2000 cities. He then made the following distribution of his army. He took in the ships along with himself all the hypaspists, and the archers, and the Agrianians, and the corps of horse-guards.[1] Krateros commanding a division of the infantry and cavalry, conducted it along the right bank of the Hydaspês, while Hêphaistiôn on the opposite bank advanced in command of the largest and best division of the army, to which the elephants, now about 200 in number, were attached. These generals were instructed to march with all possible speed to where the palace of Sôpeithês[2] was situated. Philippos, the

[1] Arrian in the 19th chapter of the *Indika* states that the number of men conveyed in the fleet was 8000, and that the whole strength of his army was 120,000 soldiers, including those whom he brought from the shores of the Mediterranean, as well as recruits drawn from various barbarous tribes armed in their own fashion. In the preceding chapter he gives a list of the great officers whom Alexander appointed to be in temporary command of the triremes. Of these, thirty-three in number, twenty-four were Macedonians, eight were Greeks, and one a Persian. Seleukos is the only officer of note whose name does not appear in this list.

[2] Diodôros and Curtius, as has been pointed out (in Note M), place the dominions of Sôpeithês between the upper Hydraôtês and the Hyphasis, but here we find them transferred to a more western position. Strabo was unable to decide where they lay. "Some writers (he says) place Kathaia and the country of Sôpeithês, one of the monarchs, in the tract between the rivers (Hydaspês and Akesinês); some on the other side of the Akesinês and of the Hyarotis, on the confines of the territory of the other Pôros, the nephew of Pôros who was taken prisoner by Alexander, and call the country subject to him Gandaris. . . . It is said that in the territory of Sôpeithês there is a mountain composed of fossil salt sufficient for the whole of India. Valuable mines, also, both of gold and silver, are situated, it is said, not far off among other mountains, according to the testimony of Gorgos the miner." Strabo then describes (as do also Diodôros and Curtius) the fight between a lion and four dogs which Sôpeithês exhibited to Alexander. To account for the discrepancy in these statements one is almost tempted

satrap of the province lying west of the Indus in the direction of the Baktrians, received orders to follow them with his troops after an interval of three days, but the cavalry of the Nysaians he now sent back to Nysa. The command of the whole naval squadron was entrusted to Nearchos, while the pilot of Alexander's own ship was Onêsikritos, who, in the narrative which he composed about the wars of Alexander, among his other lies, described himself as the commander of the fleet, although he was in reality only a pilot. According to Ptolemy, the son of Lagos, whose authority I principally follow, the ships numbered collectively eighty thirty-oared galleys, but the whole fleet, including the horse-transports and the small craft and other river boats consisting of those that formerly plied on the rivers and those recently built for the present service, did not fall much short of 2000.[1]

Chapter III.—Description of the voyage down the Hydaspês continued

When all the preparations had been completed, the army at break of day began to embark. Alexander him-

to believe that as there were two princes of the name of Pôros, each ruling dominions of his own, so there were also two chiefs of the name of Sôpeithês or (as Curtius more correctly transcribes it) Sôphytês. General Cunningham would identify *Gandaris* with the present district of *Gundul-bâr* or *Gundurbâr*, and fixes the capital of Sôphytês on the western bank of the Hydaspês at *Old Bhira*, a place near Ahmedabad, with a very extensive mound of ruins, and distant from Nikaia (now Mong) three days by water. His rule must have extended westward to the Indus, since the mountain of rock-salt which Strabo includes in his territory can only refer to the salt range (the Mount Oromenus of Pliny, xxxi. 39) which extends from the Indus to the Hydaspês. The transcription of the name *Sôphytês* will be found discussed elsewhere.

[1] Arrian in his *Indika*, where he apparently follows Nearchos instead of Ptolemy as here, gives the whole number of ships at only 800, including both ships of war and transports. Schmieder and some other editors would correct this to 1800, but it seems more probable, Bunbury thinks, that the basis of the two calculations was different. Ptolemy, he says, distinctly includes the ordinary river boats which would doubtless have been collected in large numbers to assist in transporting so great an army and its supplies ; while the terms of Nearchos would seem to imply only ships of war or regular transports. Krüger would correct the 2000 of the text to 1000, which is the number of the vessels as given by Diodôros and Curtius. The fleet began the downward voyage at the end of October 326 B.C.

self sacrificed according to custom both to the gods and to the river Akesinês as the seers directed. After he had embarked he poured a libation into the river, from his station on the prow, out of a golden bowl, and invoked not only the Hydaspês, but also the Akesinês, as he had learned that the Akesinês was the greatest of all the confluents of the Hydaspês, and that their point of junction was not far off. He invoked likewise the Indus, into which the Akesinês · falls after receiving the Hydaspês. He further poured out libations to his ancestor Heraklês, and to Ammôn[1] and every other god to whom it was his custom to sacrifice, and then he ordered the signal for starting on the voyage to be given by sound of trumpet. The fleet as soon as the signal sounded began the voyage in due order, for directions had been given at what distances the luggage-boats, the horse-transports, and the war-galleys should keep apart from each other to prevent collisions which would be inevitable if the ships sailed at random down the channel. Even the fast sailers were not allowed to break rank by out-distancing the others. The noise caused by the rowing was great beyond all precedent, proceeding as it did from a vast number of boats being rowed simultaneously, and swelled by the shouts of the officers directing the rowing to begin or to stop, commingled with the shouts of the rowers, which rung like the war-cry when they joined together in keeping time to the dashing of the oars. The banks, moreover, being in many places higher than the ships, and compressing the sound within a narrow compass, sent the echoes, greatly increased by the compression itself, flying to and fro between them. The ravines also which occasionally opened on the river on either of its shores served further to swell the din by reverberating amid their solitudes the

[1] Alexander deduced his pedigree from Ammôn, just as the legend traced the pedigree of Heraklês and Perseus to Zeus. He accordingly made an expedition to the oasis in the Libyan desert where Ammôn had his oracle for the purpose of more certainly learning his origin. His mother, Olympias, according to Plutarch, used to complain that Alexander was for ever embroiling her with Juno.

thuds of the oars. The appearance of the war-horses on the decks of the transports struck the barbarians, who saw them through the lattice work, with such wonder and astonishment, that the throng which lined the shores to witness the departure of the fleet accompanied it to a great distance, for in the country of the Indians horses had never before been seen on shipboard, nor was there any tradition to the effect that the Indian expedition of Dionysos was of a naval character. Those Indians also who had already submitted to Alexander, as soon as they heard the shouts of the rowers and the dashing of the oars, ran down to the edge of the river and followed the fleet, singing their wild native chaunts, for the Indians have been peculiarly distinguished among the nations as lovers of dance and song, ever since Dionysos and his attendant Bacchanals made their festive progress through the realms of India.[1]

Chapter IV.—Alexander accelerates his voyage to frustrate the plans of the Malloi and Oxydrakai, and reaches the turbulent confluence of the Hydaspês and Akesinês

Alexander sailing thus,[2] halted on the third day at the place where he had ordered Hêphaistiôn and Krateros to pitch their camps right opposite each other, each on his own side of the river.[3] Having waited here for two days until Philippos arrived with the rest of the army, he sent that general forward with the detachment he had brought with him to the river Akesinês, with orders to continue his march along the banks of that river. He also sent Krateros and Hêphaistiôn off again with instructions how they were to conduct the march. He himself continued

[1] "The Indians (says Arrian in his *Indika*, c. 7) worship the other gods, and especially Dionysos, with cymbals and drums, which he had taught them to use. He taught them also the Satyric dance, called by the Greeks *Kordax*.

[2] See Note O, Voyage down the Hydaspês and Akesinês to the Indus.

[3] This halting-place was at Bhira or Bheda, if Cunningham is right in fixing the capital of Sôphytês in its neighbourhood.

his voyage down the river Hydaspês, which was found throughout the passage to be nowhere less than twenty stadia in breadth. Mooring his boats wherever he could on the banks, he subjected the Indians who lived near the Hydaspês to his authority, some having surrendered on terms of capitulation, and such as resorted to arms, having been subdued by force. He then sailed rapidly to the country of the Malloi and Oxydrakai, because he had ascertained that they were the most numerous and warlike of all the Indian tribes in those parts, and news had reached him that they had conveyed their children, and their wives for safety into their strongest cities, and that they meant themselves to give him a hostile reception. He in consequence prosecuted the voyage with still greater speed, so that he might attack them before they had settled their plans, and while their preparations were still incomplete and they were in a state of confusion and alarm. On the fifth day after he had started from the place where he had halted, and been joined by Krateros and Hêphaistiôn, he reached the junction of the Hydaspês and Akesinês. Where these rivers unite the one river formed from them is very narrow, and not only is the current swift from the narrowness of the channel, but the waters whirl round in monstrous eddies, curl up in great billows, and dash so violently that the roar of the surge is distinctly heard by those who are still a great distance off. All this had been previously reported by the natives to Alexander, and he had repeated the information to the soldiers ; but, notwithstanding, when the army in approaching the confluence caught the roar of the stream, the sailors simultaneously suspended the action of the oars, not at any order from the boatswains, who had become mute from astonishment, but because they were stunned with terror by the thundering noise.[1]

[1] Diodôros carelessly represents these rapids as occurring at the confluence of the two rivers with the Indus. The dangers of their navigation seem to have been exaggerated by the ancient writers, though their accounts have some foundation in fact. Sir A. Burnes, the first European known to have visited the spot, says there are no eddies and no rocks,

*Chapter V.—Dangers encountered by the fleet at the con-
fluence—Plan of the operations which followed—
Voyage down the Akesinês*

When they were not far from the meeting of the rivers,
the pilots enjoined the rowers to put all their strength to
the oars to clear the rapids, so that the vessels might not
be caught and capsized in the eddies, but by the exertions
of the rowers might overcome the whirling of the waters.
The merchant vessels accordingly, if they happened to be
whirled round by the current, suffered no damage from
the eddy, beyond the alarm caused to the men on board,
for these vessels, being of a round form, were kept upright
by the current itself, and settled into the proper course.
But the ships of war did not escape so unscathed from the
eddying stream, for, owing to their length, they were not
upheaved in the same way as the others on the seething
surges, and if they had two banks of oars, the lower oars
were not raised much above the level of the water.   When
the broad sides, therefore, of these vessels were exposed
to the eddying current, their oars, if not lifted in proper
time, were caught by the water and the blades snapped
asunder.   Many of the ships were thus damaged, and two
which fell foul of each other sunk with the greater part of
their crews.   But when the river began to widen out, the
current was no longer so rapid and dangerous, and the
impetuosity of the eddies diminished.   Alexander therefore brought his fleet to moorings on the right bank where
there was a protection from the strength of the current
and a roadstead for the ships.   Here was also a headland
projecting into the river which afforded facilities for col-
lecting the wrecks and whatever living freight they brought.

nor is the channel confined, while
the ancient character is only supported by the noise of the confluence,
which is greater than that of any of
the other rivers.   The boatmen of
the locality, however, still regard the
passage as a perilous one during the
season when the river is swollen (v.
Travels, i. p. 109).   Thirlwall thinks
the principal obstructions have been
worn away.   According to Curtius,
Alexander's own ship was here in
imminent danger of being wrecked.

He saved the survivors; and when he had repaired the damaged craft, ordered Nearchos to sail downward till he reached the confines of the nation called the Malloi. He made himself an inroad into the territories of the barbarians who refused their submission,[1] and prevented them sending succours to the Malloi. He then rejoined the fleet.

Hêphaistiôn, Krateros, and Philippos had there already united their forces. He then transported to the other side of the river Hydaspês the elephants, the brigade of Polysperchôn, the archers, and Philippos with the troops under his command, and appointed Krateros to conduct this expedition. Nearchos he despatched in command of the fleet, and instructed him to start on the voyage three days before the departure of the army. The rest of his forces he divided into three parts. Hêphaistiôn was directed to set out five days in advance, so that if any of the enemy fled forward before the division commanded by the king in person they might be captured, when endeavouring to escape in that direction, by falling into Hêphaistiôn's hands. He gave also a part of the army to Ptolemy, the son of Lagos, with orders to follow him three days later, so that such of the enemy as fled backward from his own troops might fall into the hands of those under Ptolemy.[2] The detachment that marched in advance he ordered to wait until he himself should come up at the confluence of the Akesinês and Hydraôtês,[3] where Krateros and Ptolemy had orders to join him with their divisions.

[1] These barbarians were probably the Sibi (v. Diodôros, xvii. 96).

[2] Hêphaistiôn by this arrangement would beset the banks of the Hydraôtês, Ptolemy those of the Akesinês. The former probably marched to the Hydraôtês by way of Shorkote, which Cunningham thinks may be the Sôrianê of Stephanos Byz.

[3] The Hydaspês loses its name as well as its waters to the Akesinês. The junction of the latter with the Hydraôtês (Râvi) occurs at present at a point more than thirty miles above Multân, but in Alexander's time it occurred some miles below that city.

Chapter VI.—Alexander invades the territories of the Malloi

Alexander selected for his own division the hypaspists, the archers, the Agrianians, the corps of foot-guards under Peithôn, all the horse-archers, and the half of the companion cavalry, and led them through a waterless tract of country against the Malloi,[1] a race of independent Indians. On the first day he encamped near a small stream which was twenty stadia distant from the river Akesinês. Having dined there and allowed the army a short time for repose, he ordered every man to fill whatever vessel he had with water. He then marched during the remainder of the day and all night a distance of about 400 stadia, and with the dawn arrived before a city to which many of the Malloi had fled for refuge. As they never imagined that Alexander would come to attack them through the waterless desert, most of them were abroad in the fields, and without their arms ; and just as it was manifest that he led his forces by this route because of the difficulties it presented, so did it appear to the enemy past belief that he would conduct an army by a way so perilous. He thus fell upon them unexpectedly, and slew most of them without their even turning to offer resistance, since they were unarmed. The rest he shut up within the city, and as the phalanx of infantry had not yet arrived, he posted the cavalry in a cordon round the wall, thus making it serve for a stockade. No sooner, however, did the infantry come up than he despatched Perdikkas with his own cavalry regiment and that of Kleitos, together with the Agrianians, to another city of the Malloi, into which many of the Indians of that district had fled for refuge. He was enjoined to blockade the men in the city, but not to attempt to storm the place until his own arrival, so that no one might escape and carry the news of Alexander's approach to the other barbarians. He then

[1] See Note P, The Malloi and Oxydrakai.

made an assault upon the wall, which the barbarians abandoned on seeing it could no longer hold out, since many had been killed during the siege, and others disabled for fighting by reason of their wounds. They fled into the citadel, which, being seated on a commanding height and difficult of access, they continued to defend for some time. As the Macedonians, however, vigorously pressed the attack at all points, while Alexander himself was seen everywhere urging forward the work, the citadel was stormed, and all the men who had fled to it for refuge were put to the sword to the number of 2000.[1]

Perdikkas meanwhile reached the city whither he had been sent, but on learning that the inhabitants had not long before fled from it, he rode away at full gallop on the track of the fugitives, while the light troops followed him on foot as fast as they could. Some of the fugitives he overtook and killed, but such as had been too quick for him made their escape to the river marshes.[2]

[1] General Cunningham has identified this place with Kot-Kamâlia, a small but ancient town situated on an isolated mound on the right or northern bank of the Râvi, marking the extreme limit of the river's fluctuations on that side. The small rivulet on which Alexander encamped at the end of his first march he believes to be the lower course of the Ayek river which rises in the outer range of hills and flows past Syâlkot towards Sâkala, below which the bed is still traceable for some distance. It appears again, he says, eighteen miles to the east of Jhang, and is finally lost about two miles to the east of Shorkot. Now somewhere between these two points Alexander must have crossed the Ayek, as the desert country which he afterwards traversed lies immediately beyond it. If he had marched to the south he would have arrived at Shorkot, but he would not have encountered any desert, as his route would have been over the Khâdar, or low-lying lands in the valley of the Chenâb. A march of forty-six miles in a southerly direction would have carried him also right up to the bank of the Hydraôtês or Râvi, a point which Alexander only reached after another night's march. As this march lasted from the first watch until daylight, it cannot have been less than eighteen or twenty miles, which agrees exactly with the distance of the Râvi opposite Tulamba from Kot-Kamâlia. The direction of Alexander's march must therefore have been to the south-east; first to the Ayek river, and thence across the hard, clayey, and waterless tract called Sandar-bâr, that is the bâr, a desert of the Sandar and Chandra river. Thus the position of the rivulet, the description of the desolate country, and the distance of the city from the confluence of the rivers, all agree in fixing the site of the fortress assaulted by Alexander with Kot-Kamâlia. — Anc. Geog. of India, pp. 208-210.

[2] The city to which Perdikkas was sent in advance of Alexander, Cunningham has identified with Harapa. "The mention of marshes (he says) shows that it must have been near the Râvi, and, as Perdikkas was sent in advance of Alexander, it must also have been beyond Kot-

Chapter VII.—Siege and capture of several Mallian strongholds

Alexander having dined and allowed his troops to rest till the first watch of the night, began to march forward, and having travelled a great distance in the night, arrived at the river Hydraôtês at daybreak. There he learned that many of the Malloi had already crossed to the other bank, but he fell upon others who were in the act of crossing and slew many of them during the passage. He crossed the river along with them, just as he was, and by the same ford. He then closely pursued the fugitives who had outstripped him in their retreat. Many of these he slew and he captured others, but most of them escaped to a position of great natural strength which was also strongly fortified.[1] But when the infantry came up with him, Alexander sent Peithôn with his own brigade and two squadrons of cavalry against the fugitives. This detachment attacked the stronghold, captured it at the first assault, and made slaves of all who had fled into it, except, of course, those who had fallen in the attack.

Kamâlia, that is to the east or south-east of it. Now this is exactly the position of Harapa, which is situated sixteen miles to the east-south-east of Kot-Kamâlia, and on the opposite high bank of the Râvi. There are also several marshes in the low ground in its immediate vicinity." Cunningham then gives a description of Harapa as it now exists. He had encamped at the place on three different occasions. It had been visited previously and described both by Burnes and Masson. Its ruined mound forms an irregular square of half a mile on each side, or two miles in circuit (*Anc. Geog. of India*, pp. 210, 211). It seems to me a serious objection to this identification that Kot-Kamâlia and Harapa (Harup, in Ainsworth's large map) lie on *opposite* sides of the Râvi, while Arrian's narrative leads us to suppose that they both lay to the west of that river. No mention is made of Perdikkas crossing it, and had the fortress he attacked lain beyond it, he could easily have intercepted the inhabitants in their flight to the marshes of the river.

[1] Cunningham identifies this well-fortified position with Tulamba. "A whole night's march (he says) of eight or nine hours could not have been less than twenty-five miles, which is the exact distance of the Râvi opposite Tulamba from Kot-Kamâlia." It was defended by brick walls and enormous mounds of earthen ramparts. Tulamba lies on the high road to Multân, to which, as the capital of the Malloi, Alexander was marching.

Then Peithôn and his men, their task fulfilled, returned to the camp.

Alexander himself next led his army against a certain city of the Brachmans,[1] because he had learned that many of the Malloi had fled thither for refuge. On reaching it he led the phalanx in compact ranks against all parts of the wall. The inhabitants, on finding the walls undermined, and that they were themselves obliged to retire before the storm of missiles, left the walls and fled to the citadel, and began to defend themselves from thence. But as a few Macedonians had rushed in along with them, they rallied, and turning round in a body upon the pursuers, drove some from the citadel and killed twenty-five of them in their retreat. Upon this Alexander ordered his men to apply the scaling ladders to the citadel on all its sides, and to undermine its walls; and when an undermined tower had fallen and a breach had been made in the wall between two towers, thus exposing the citadel to attack in that quarter, Alexander was seen to be the first man to scale and lay hold of the wall. Upon seeing this, the rest of the Macedonians for very shame ascended the wall at various points, and quickly had the citadel in their hands. Some of the Indians set fire to their houses, in which they were caught and killed, but most part fell

---

[1] The Brachmans, as is well known, formed a religious caste, and were not a distinct race or tribe. Their city Cunningham has identified with the old ruined town and fort of Atâri, which is situated twenty miles to the west-south-west of Tulamba and on the high road to Multân, from which it is thirty-four miles distant. The remains consist of a strong citadel 750 feet square and 35 feet high. On two of its sides are to be found the remains of the old town. Of its history there is not even a tradition, but the large size of its bricks shows that it must be a place of considerable antiquity. The name of the old city is quite unknown, Atâri being merely that of the adjacent village, which is of recent origin.

Curtius states that Alexander went completely round the citadel in a boat, and Cunningham thinks this is probable enough, as its ditch could be filled at pleasure with water from the Râvi. Curtius must, however, be romancing when he says that the three greatest rivers in India except the Ganges (Indus, Hydaspês, and Akesinês) joined their waters to form a ditch round the castle (v. *Anc. Geog. of India*, pp. 228-230). The mention of a special city of the Brachmans, Lassen observes, shows that but few priests lived in this part of the country, and that they had established themselves in particular cities to protect themselves against those people by whom they were held in but small esteem.

fighting. About 5000 in all were killed, and, as they were men of spirit, a few only were taken prisoners.

Chapter VIII.—Alexander defeats the Malloi at the Hydraôtês

He remained there one day to give his army rest, and next day he moved forward to attack the rest of the Malloi. He found their cities abandoned, and ascertained that the inhabitants had fled into the desert. There he again allowed the army a day's rest, and next day sent Peithôn and Dêmêtrios, the cavalry commander, back to the river with their own troops, and as many battalions of light-armed infantry as the nature of the work required. He directed them to march along the edge of the river, and if they came upon any of those who had fled for refuge to the jungle, of which there were numerous patches along the river-bank, to put them all to death unless they voluntarily surrendered. The troops under these two officers captured many of the fugitives in these jungles and killed them.

He marched himself against the largest city of the Malloi, to which he was informed many men from their other cities had fled for safety. The Indians, however, abandoned this place also when they heard that Alexander was approaching. They then crossed the Hydraôtês, and with a view to obstruct Alexander's passage, remained drawn up in order of battle upon the banks, because they were very steep. On learning this, he took all the cavalry which he had with him, and marched to that part of the Hydraôtês where he had been told the Malloi were posted; and the infantry were directed to follow after him. When he came to the river and descried the enemy drawn up on the opposite bank, he plunged at once, just as he was after the march, into the ford, with the cavalry only. When the enemy saw Alexander now in the middle of the stream they withdrew in haste, but yet in good order, from the bank, and Alexander pursued them with the cavalry only. But when the Indians perceived he had nothing but a party of horse with him, they faced round and fought stoutly, being about 50,000 in number. Alexander, perceiving that their phalanx was very compact, and his own infantry not on the ground, rode along all round them, and sometimes charged their ranks, but not at close quarters. Meanwhile the Agrianians and other battalions of light-armed infantry, which consisted of picked men, arrived on the field along with the archers, while the phalanx of infantry was showing in sight at no great distance off. As they were threatened at once with so many dangers, the Indians wheeled round, and with headlong speed fled to the strongest of all the cities that lay near.[1] Alexander killed many of them in the pursuit, while those who escaped to the city were shut up within its walls. At first, therefore, he surrounded the place with his horsemen as soon as they came up from the march. But when the infantry arrived he encamped around the wall on every side for the remainder of this day—a time too short for making an assault, to say nothing of the great fatigue his army had undergone, the infantry from their long march, and the cavalry by the continuous pursuit, and especially by the passage of the river.

Chapter IX.—Alexander assails the chief stronghold of the Malloi, scales the wall of the citadel, into which he leaps down though alone

On the following day, dividing his army into two parts, he himself assaulted the wall at the head of one division, while Perdikkas led forward the other. Upon this the Indians, without waiting to receive the attack of the Macedonians, abandoned the walls and fled for refuge to the citadel. Alexander and his troops therefore burst open a small gate, and entered the city long before the

---

[1] See Note Q, The capital of the Malloi.

others. But Perdikkas and the troops under his command entered it much later, having found it no easy work to surmount the walls. The most of them, in fact, had neglected to bring scaling ladders, for when they saw the wall left without defenders they took it for granted that the city had actually been captured. But when it became clear that the enemy was still in possession of the citadel, and that many of them were drawn up in front of it to repel attack, the Macedonians endeavoured to force their way into it, some by sapping the walls, and others by applying the scaling ladders wherever that was practicable. Alexander, thinking that the Macedonians who carried the ladders were loitering too much, snatched one from the man who carried it, placed it against the wall, and began to ascend, cowering the while under his shield. The next to follow was Peukestas, who carried the sacred shield which Alexander had taken from the temple of the Ilian Athênâ, and which he used to keep with him and have carried before him in all his battles.[1] Next to him Leonnatos, an officer of the bodyguard, ascended by the same ladder; and by a different ladder Abreas, one of those soldiers who for superior merit drew double pay[2] and allowances. The king was now near the coping of the wall, and resting his shield against it, was pushing some of the Indians within the fort, and had cleared the parapet by killing others with his sword. The hypaspists, now alarmed beyond measure for the king's safety, pushed each other in their haste up the same ladder and broke it, so that those who were already mounting it fell down and made the ascent impracticable for others.

Alexander, while standing on the wall, was then assailed on every side from the adjacent towers, for none of the Indians had the courage to come near him. He

---

[1] Arrian (i. 11) relates that Alexander, after crossing the Hellespont, proceeded to Ilion, where, after sacrificing to the Trojan Athênê, he placed his own armour in the temple of that goddess, and took away in exchange some of the consecrated arms which had been preserved from the time of the Trojan war.

[2] Called in Greek a *dimoiritês* in Latin a *duplicarius*.

was assailed also by men in the city, who threw darts at him from no great distance off, for it so happened that a mound of earth had been thrown up in that quarter close to the wall.   Alexander was, moreover, a conspicuous object both by the splendour of his arms[1] and the astonishing audacity he displayed.   He then perceived that if he remained where he was, he would be exposed to danger without being able to achieve anything noteworthy, but if he leaped down into the citadel he might perhaps by this very act paralyse the Indians with terror, and if he did not, but necessarily incurred danger, he would in that case not die ignobly, but after performing great deeds worth being remembered by the men of after times. Having so resolved, he leaped down from the wall into the citadel.   Then, supporting himself against the wall, he slew with his sword some who assailed him at close quarters, and in particular the governor of the Indians, who had rushed upon him too boldly.   Against another Indian whom he saw approaching, he hurled a stone to check his advance, and another he similarly repelled.   If any one came within nearer reach, he again used his sword.   The barbarians had then no further wish to approach him, but standing around assailed him from all quarters with whatever missiles they carried or could lay their hands on.

Chapter X. —Alexander is dangerously wounded within the citadel

At this crisis Peukestas, and Abreas the dimoirite, and after them Leonnatos, the only men who succeeded in

---

[1] Alexander's dress and arms on the day of Arbêla are thus described by Plutarch: "He wore a short tunic of the Sicilian fashion, girt close round him, over a linen breastplate strongly quilted; his helmet, surmounted by the white plume, was of polished steel, the work of Theophilos; the gorget was of the same metal, and set with precious stones; the sword, his favourite weapon in battle, was a present from a Cyprian king, and not to be excelled for lightness or temper; but his belt, deeply embossed with massive figures, was the most superb part of his armour; it was a gift from the Rhodians, on which old Helikôn had exerted all his skill. If we add to these the shield, lance, and light greaves, we may form a fair idea of his appearance in battle."

reaching the top of the wall before the ladder broke, leaped down and began fighting in front of the king. But there Abreas fell, pierced in the forehead by an arrow. Alexander himself was also struck by one which pierced through his cuirass into his chest above the pap, so that, as Ptolemy says, air gurgled from the wound along with the blood. But sorely wounded as he was, he continued to defend himself as long as his blood was still warm. Since much blood, however, kept gushing out with every breath he drew, a dizziness and faintness seized him, and he fell where he stood in a collapse upon his shield. Peukestas then bestrode him where he fell, holding up in front of him the sacred shield which had been taken from Ilion, while Leonnatos protected him from side attacks. But both these men were severely wounded, and Alexander was now on the point of swooning away from the loss of blood. As for the Macedonians, they were at a loss how to make their way into the citadel, because those who had seen Alexander shot at upon the wall and then leap down inside it had broken down the ladders up which they were rushing in all haste, dreading lest their king, in recklessly exposing himself to danger, should come by some hurt. In their perplexity they devised various plans for ascending the wall. It was made of earth, and so some drove pegs into it, and swinging themselves up by means of these, scrambled with difficulty to the top. Others ascended by mounting one upon the other. The man who first reached the top flung himself headlong from the wall into the city, and was followed by the others. There, when they saw the king fallen prostrate, they all raised loud lamentations and outcries of grief. And now around his fallen form a desperate struggle ensued, one Macedonian after another holding his shield in front of him. In the meantime, some of the soldiers · having shattered the bar by which the gate in the wall between the towers was secured, made their way into the city a few at a time, and others, when they saw that a rift was made in the gate, put their shoulders under it, and having then pushed it into the space within the wall, opened an entrance into the citadel in that quarter.

Chapter XI.—Dangerous nature of Alexander's wound—Arrian refutes some current fictions relating to this accident

Upon this some began to kill the Indians, and in the massacre spared none, neither man, woman, nor child. Others bore off the king upon his shield. His condition was very low, and they could not yet tell whether he was likely to survive. Some writers have asserted that Kritodêmos, a physician of Kôs, an Asklêpiad by birth,[1] extracted the weapon from the wound by making an incision where the blow had struck. Other writers, however, say that as no surgeon was present at this terrible crisis, Perdikkas, an officer of the bodyguard, at Alexander's own desire, made an incision into the wound with his sword and removed the weapon. Its removal was followed by such a copious effusion of blood that Alexander again swooned, and the swoon had the effect of staunching the flux. Many fictions also have been recorded by historians concerning this accident, and Fame, receiving them from the original inventors, has preserved them to our own day, nor will she cease to transmit the falsehoods to one generation after another except they be finally suppressed by this history.

The common account, for example, is that this accident befell Alexander among the Oxydrakai, but in fact it occurred among the Malloi an independent Indian nation. The city belonged to the Malloi, and the men who wounded Alexander were Malloi. They had certainly

[1] The descendants of Asklêpios (Aesculapius) were called by the patronymic name *Asklêpiadai*. They were regarded by some as the real descendants of Asklêpios, but by others as a caste of priests who practised the art of medicine, combined with religion. Their principal seats were Kôs and Knidos.

agreed to combine with the Oxydrakai and give battle to
the common enemy, but Alexander had thwarted this
design by his sudden and rapid march through the waterless country, whereby these tribes were prevented from
giving each other mutual help.   To take another instance,
according to the common account, the last battle fought
with Darius (that at which he fled, nor paused in his flight
till he was seized by the soldiers of Bêssos and murdered
at Alexander's approach) took place at Arbêla, just as the
previous battle came off at Issos, and the first cavalry
action at the Granikos.   Now this cavalry action was
really fought at the Granikos, and the next battle with
Darius at Issos.   But Arbêla is distant from the field
where Darius and Alexander had their last battle 600
stadia according to those authors who make the distance
greatest, and 500 stadia according to those who make it
least.   But Ptolemy and Aristoboulos say that the battle
took place at Gaugamêla near the river Boumodos.   Gaugamêla, however, was not a city, but merely a good-sized village,
a place of no distinction, and bearing a name which offends
the ear.   This seems to me the reason why Arbêla, which
was a city, has carried off the glory of the great battle.[1]   But
if we must perforce consider that this battle took place near
Arbêla, though fought at so great a distance off, then we
may as well say that the sea fight at Salamis came off
near the Isthmus of Corinth, and the sea-fight at Arte-
mision in Euboia, near Aigina or Sunium.

With regard again to those who protected Alexander
with their shields in his peril, all agree that Peukestas was
of the number, but with respect to Leonnatos and Abreas
the dimoirite, they are no longer in harmony.   Some say
that Alexander received a blow on his helmet from a
bludgeon and fell down in an access of dizziness, and that

---

[1] Plutarch writes to the same effect:
"The great battle with Darius was
not fought at Arbêla, as most historians
will have it, but at Gaugamêla, which,
in the Persian tongue, is said to
signify *the house of the camel*, so called
because one of the ancient kings,
having escaped his enemies by the
swiftness of his camel, placed her
there, and appointed the revenues of
certain villages for her maintenance."
—*Life of Alexander*, c. 31.

on regaining his feet he was hit by a dart which pierced through his breastplate into his chest. But Ptolemy, the son of Lagos, says that this wound in his chest was the only one he received. I take, however, the following to be the greatest error into which the historians of Alexander have fallen. Some have written that Ptolemy, the son of Lagos, along with Peukestas mounted the ladder together with Alexander; that Ptolemy held his shield over him when he was lying on the ground, and that he thence received the sur-name of Sôtêr.[1] And yet Ptolemy himself has recorded that he was not present at this conflict, but was fight-ing elsewhere against other bar-barians, in command of a different division of the army. Let me mention these facts in digressing from my narrative that the men of

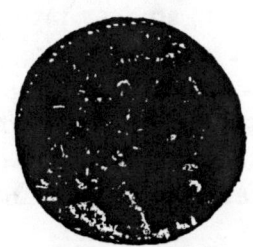

FIG. 10.—PTOLEMY SÔTÊR.

after times may not regard it as a matter of indifference how these great deeds and great sufferings are reported.

Chapter XII.—Distress and anxiety of the army at the prospect of Alexander's death

While Alexander remained at this place to be cured of his wound, the first news which reached the camp whence he had started to attack the Malloi was that he had died of his wound. Then there arose at first a loud lamenta-tion from the whole army, as the mournful tidings spread from man to man. But when their lamentation was ended, they gave way to despondency and anxious doubts about the appointment of a commander to the army, for among

[1] Kleitarchos, who accompanied Alexander to Asia, and wrote a history of the expedition, and Tima-genes, an historian in the reign of Augustus, gave currency to this fiction, which Curtius is at one with Arrian in rejecting. Ptolemy received his title of Sôtêr (saviour) from the Rhodians, whom he had relieved from the attacks of Dêmêtrios Polior-kêtês (*v.* Pausanias, I. viii. 6).

the officers many could advance claims to that dignity which both to Alexander and the Macedonians seemed of equal weight. They were also in fear and doubt how they could be conducted home in safety, surrounded as they were on all hands by warlike nations, some not yet reduced, but likely to fight resolutely for their freedom, while others would to a certainty revolt when relieved from their fear of Alexander. They seemed besides to be just then among impassable rivers, while the whole outlook presented nothing but inextricable difficulties when they wanted their king. But on receiving word that he was still alive, they could hardly think it true, or persuade themselves that he was likely to recover. Even when a letter came from the king himself intimating that he would soon come down to the camp, most of them from the excess of fear which possessed them distrusted the news, for they fancied that the letter was a forgery concocted by his body-guards and generals.

Chapter XIII.—Joy of the army on seeing Alexander after his recovery—His officers rebuke him for his rashness

On coming to know this, Alexander, anxious to prevent any commotions arising in the army, as soon as he could bear the fatigue, had himself conveyed to the banks of the river Hydraôtês, and embarking there, he sailed down the river to reach the camp, at the junction of the Hydraôtês and the Akesinês, where Hêphaistiôn commanded the land forces and Nearchos the fleet. When the vessel which carried the king was now approaching the camp, he ordered the awning to be removed from the poop that he might be visible to all. They were, however, even yet incredulous, supposing that the freight of the vessel was Alexander's dead body, until he neared the bank, when he raised his arm and stretched out his hand to the multitude. Then the men raised a loud cheer, and lifted up their hands, some towards heaven and some towards Alexander himself. Tears even started involuntarily to the eyes of not a few at the unexpected sight. Some of the hypaspists brought him a litter where he was carried ashore from the vessel, but he called for his horse. When he was seen once more on horseback, the whole army greeted him with loud acclamations, which filled with their echoes the shores and all the surrounding hills and dales. On approaching his tent he dismounted that he might be seen walking. Then the soldiers crowded round him, touching some his hands, others his knees, and others nothing but his raiment. Some, satisfied with nothing more than a near view, went away with expressions of admiration. Others again covered him with garlands, and others with the flowers of the clime and the season.

Nearchos says that he was offended with certain of his friends who reproached him for exposing himself to danger when leading the army, for this, they said, was not the duty of a commander, but of a common soldier, and it seems to me that Alexander resented these remarks because he felt their truth, and knew he had laid himself open to censure. Owing, however, to his prowess in fighting and his love of glory, he, like other men who are swayed by some predominant pleasure, yielded to temptation, lacking sufficient force of will to hold aloof from dangers. Nearchos also says that a certain elderly Boiôtian (whose name he does not give) observing that Alexander resented the censures of his friends, and was giving them sour looks, approached him, and in the Boiôtian tongue thus addressed him : " O Alexander, it is for heroes to do great deeds," and then he subjoined an Iambic verse, the purport of which was that he who did any great deed was bound also to suffer.[1] The man, it is said, not only found favour with Alexander, but was admitted afterwards to closer intimacy.

[1] Thirlwall has noted that this line is found in Stobaeus. It is a fragment from one of the lost tragedies of Aeschylus, δράσαντι γάρ τι καὶ παθεῖν ὀφείλεται.

Chapter XIV.—Submission of the Malloi, Oxydrakai, ana others—Voyage down the Hydraôtês and Akesinês to the Indus

At this time envoys came to Alexander from the Malloi who still survived, tendering the submission of the nation ; and from the Oxydrakai came the leading men of their cities and their provincial governors, besides 150 of their most eminent men, entrusted with full powers to conclude a treaty. They brought with them those presents which the Indians consider the choicest, and, like the Malloi, tendered the submission of their nation. Their error in so long delaying to send an embassy was, they said, pardonable, for they were attached more than others to freedom and autonomy, and their freedom they had preserved intact from the time Dionysos came to India until Alexander's arrival. Since, however, Alexander was also, according to current report, of the race of the gods, they were willing, if he so pleased, to receive whatever satrap Alexander might appoint, pay the tribute he chose to impose, and give as many hostages as he required. Upon this he asked for a 1000 men, the flower of the nation, to be retained, if he thought good, as hostages, but, if not, to be employed as auxiliaries until he had finished the war against the other Indians. They selected accordingly 1000 men, their best and tallest, and sent them to him, together with 500 chariots and their charioteers, though these were not demanded. Alexander appointed Philippos as satrap over that nation and over the Malloi who still survived. The hostages he sent back, but he kept the chariots.

When these arrangements had been completed, and many vessels had been built in the interval while his wound was healing, he put on board the fleet 1700 of the cavalry companions, the same number of light-armed troops as before, and about 10,000 infantry, and sailed a short distance down the river Hydraôtês. But when the

Hydraôtês fell into the Akesinês he continued the voyage down the latter river (which in preference to the Hydraôtês gives its name to the united stream) until he reached the junction of the Akesinês with the Indus. For these four vast rivers which are all navigable yield up their waters to the river Indus, but not each of them under its own special name. For the Hydaspês discharges into the Akesinês, and the single stream then forms what is called the Akesinês. But this Akesinês again unites with the Hydraôtês, and after absorbing this river is still the Akesinês. The Akesinês after this receives the Hyphasis,[1] and still keeping its own name falls into the Indus, but after the junction it resigns its name to that river. Hence I am ready to believe that the Indus from this point to where it bifurcates to form the Delta expands to a breadth of 100 stadia or even more in places where it spreads out more like a lake than a river.

Chapter XV.—Appointment of Satraps—Voyage down the Indus to the dominions of Mousikanos, who tenders his submission

There at the confluence of the Akesinês and Indus he waited until Perdikkas arrived with his forces. This general in the course of his march had subjugated the Abastanoi,[2] one of the independent tribes. Meanwhile

---

[1] The Hyphasis is here probably the Satlej, though the application of the name so far down as is here indicated is contrary to Sanskrit usage. Several arms of the Hyphasis may have anciently existed which went to join the Hydraôtês or perhaps the lower Akesinês. Megasthenês was the first who made the existence of the Satlej known. Pliny calls it the Hesydrus, and Ptolemy the Zaradros. The united stream which joins the Indus, called the Panjnad, has before the confluence a width of 1076 yards. The Indus after the confluence is augmented to 2000 yards from 600 yards only above the confluence. From the present confluence to the sea the distance is 490 miles.

[2] The *Abastanoi* are more correctly designated by Diodôros (xvii. 102) the *Sambastai*, under which form of the name the *Ambashtha*, who are mentioned as a people of the Panjâb in the *Mahâbhârata* and elsewhere in Sanskrit literature, can be recognised. It is evident from the text that they were settled on the lower Akesinês. They appear to be the people called by Curtius the *Sabarcae*, and by Orosius *Sabagrae*.

there arrived at the camp other thirty-oared galleys and transport vessels which had been built for him among the Xathroi,[1] another independent tribe of Indians whose submission he had received.   From the Ossadioi[2] also, another independent tribe, came envoys offering the submission of their nation.   Alexander then fixed the confluence of the Akesinês and Indus as the boundary of the satrapy of Philippos, and left with him all the Thracians and as many foot-soldiers as seemed sufficient for the defence of his province.   Then he ordered a city to be founded there at the very confluence of the rivers,[3] hoping it would become a great city and make a name for itself in the world.   He ordered also the construction of dockyards.   At this time the Baktrian Oxyartês, the father of Alexander's wife Roxana, arrived, and on him he bestowed the satrapy of the Parapamisadai after dismissing

---

[1] The Xathroi are the Kshâtri of Sanskrit mentioned in the Laws of Manu as an impure tribe, being of mixed origin.   In Williams's *Sanskrit Dictionary* a *Kshâtri* is defined as "a man of the second (*i.e.* military) caste (by a woman of another caste?)."

[2] V. de Saint-Martin suggests that in the *Ossadioi* we have the Vasâti or Basâti of the *Mahâbhârata*, a people whom Hematchandra in his *Geographical Dictionary* places between the Hydaspês and the Indus, on the plateau of which the Salt Mountains form the southern escarpment.   If the Vasâti were really so placed, it can scarcely be supposed that they would have sent offers of submission to Alexander, who had already passed through their part of the country, and was now marching homeward, leaving them far in his rear.   Cunningham prefers to identify them with the *Yaudheya* or *Ajudhiya*, now the *Johiyas*, who are settled as formerly along the banks of the lower Satlej.   *Assodioi* or Ossadioi seems a pretty close transcription of *Ajudhiya*.

[3] The name of this city is not given by any of the historians, but in all probability it bore the name of its founder.   Its site has generally been referred to the neighbourhood of

Mithânkôt, a town situated on the western bank of the Indus a little below the junction of that river with the united streams of the Panjâb.   V. de Saint-Martin identifies it more precisely with Chuchpûr or Chuchur, an ancient fort standing on the eastern bank of the Indus right opposite Mithânkôt.   This fort bore formerly the names of Askalanda, Askelend, and Sikander, which are but variant forms of Alexandreia.   The great confluence, however, did not anciently take place at Mithânkôt, but at Uchh, an old city lying forty miles to the north-east of the confluence at Mithânkôt.   The place is called by Rashed-ud-din *Askaland-usah*, which, as Cunningham points out, would be an easy corruption of *Alexandria Uchha* or *Ussa*, as the Greeks must have written it.   The word *uchha* means "high" both in Sanskrit and in Hindi, and Uchh seems to owe its name to the fact that it stands on a mound.   "Uchh is chiefly distinguished (says Masson) by the ruins of the former towns, which are very extensive, and attest the pristine prosperity of the locality."   *v.* V. de Saint-Martin, *Etude,* pp. 124, 125 ; Cunningham's *Anc. Geog. of India,* pp. 242-245.

the previous satrap Tyriaspês, who had been reported guilty of irregularities in the exercise of his authority.

Then he transported Krateros, with the bulk of the army and the elephants, to the left side of the river Indus, because the route along that bank of the river seemed easier for an army heavily accoutred, and because the tribes inhabiting those parts were not quite friendly. He sailed himself down to the capital of the Sôgdoi, where he fortified another city, constructed other dockyards, and repaired his damaged vessels. He then appointed Oxy-artês and Peithôn satraps of the country which extended from the confluence of the Indus and Akesinês to the sea, together with the whole sea-board of India.[1]

Krateros he again despatched with the army [through the country of the Arachôtians and Drangians]; while he sailed down himself to the realm of Mousikanos,[2] which was reported to be the most opulent in India, because that sovereign had neither come to surrender himself and his country, nor sent envoys to seek his friendship. He had not even sent presents to show the respect due to a

[1] v. Note R, Alexander in Sindh.

[2] In Strabo (XV. i.) we find several references to the country of Mousi-kanos. These were based on infor-mation supplied by Onesikritos, who expatiates in praise of its fertility, on the virtues of its people, and the good-ness of the laws and government under which they lived. It seems now generally agreed that Alôr, which was anciently and for many ages the metropolis of the rich and powerful kingdom of Upper Sindh, was the capital of Mousikanos. Its ruins were visited by M'Murdo and Lieutenant Wood, and afterwards by General Cunningham, who thus describes their site: "The ruins of Alôr are situated to the south of a gap in the low range of sandstone hills which stretches from Bhakar towards the south for about twenty miles until it is lost in a broad belt of sandhills which bound the Nâra, or old bed of the Indus, on the west. Through this gap a branch of the Indus once flowed, which protected the city on the north-west. To the north-east it was covered by a second branch of the river, which flowed nearly at right angles to the other at a distance of three miles. . . . In A.D. 680 the latter was probably the main stream of the Indus, which had gradually been working to the westward from its original bed in the old Nâra." With regard to the name of the king it appears to be a territorial title, since Curtius designates the people Musicani. Lassen (Ind. Alt. ii. 176) takes this to represent the Sanskrit Mûshika (which means a mouse or a thief), and points out that a part of the Malabar coast was also called the Mûshika kingdom. Saint-Martin thinks that the Mûshika still exist in the great tribe of the Moghsis, which forms the most numerous part of the population of Kach Gandâra, a region bordering on the territories of the ancient Mûsikani (Etude, p. 162).

mighty king, nor had he asked any favour from Alexander. He therefore made the voyage down the river so rapidly that he reached the frontiers of the country of Mousikanos before that prince had even heard that Alexander had started to attack him.   Mousikanos, dismayed by his sudden arrival, hastened to meet him, taking the choicest presents India could offer and all his elephants with him. He offered to surrender both his nation and himself, and acknowledged his error, which was the most effective way with Alexander to obtain from him whatever one wanted. Alexander therefore granted Mousikanos a full pardon on account of his submission and penitence, expressed much admiration of his capital and his realm, and confirmed him in his sovereignty.   Krateros was then ordered to fortify the citadel which protected the capital, and this work was executed while Alexander was still on the spot. A garrison was placed in the fortress, which he thought suitable for keeping the surrounding tribes in subjection.

Chapter XVI.—Campaign against Oxykanos and Sambos

Then he took the archers and the Agrianians and the cavalry which was sailing with him, and marched against the governor of a district in that part of the country whose name was Oxykanos, because he neither came himself nor sent envoys to offer the surrender of himself and his country.[1]   At the first assault he took by storm the two

[1] Curtius calls the subjects of Oxykanos the Praesti, a name which would indicate that they inhabited a level country, since the Sanskrit word of which their name is a transcript—*prastha*—denotes *a tableland* or *a level expanse*.   The name, Saint-Martin thinks, is in Justin altered to *Praesidae*; but Justin, it appears to me, means the Praisioi thereby. Oxykanos is called both by Strabo and Diodôros *Portikanos*, representing perhaps the Sanskrit *Pârtha*, "a prince." It is not easy to determine where his dominions lay. They were not on the Indus, for Alexander left that river to attack them. Cunningham places them to the west of the Indus in the level country around Larkhâna, which, though now close to the Indus, was in Alexander's time about forty miles distant from it. Their capital he identifies with Mahorta, a place about ten miles north-west from Larkhâna, where there are the remains of an ancient fortress on a huge mound, whence perhaps its name *Mâha-urddha*, "very high." Lassen, on the other hand, followed by Saint-Martin, places the country of Oxy-

largest cities under the rule of Oxykanos, in the second of which that chief himself was taken prisoner. The booty he gave to the army, but the elephants he led away and reserved for himself. The other cities in the same country surrendered without attempting resistance wherever he advanced; so much were the minds of all the Indians paralysed with abject terror by Alexander and the success of his arms.

He then advanced against Sambos, whom he had appointed satrap of the Indian mountaineers, and who was reported to have fled on hearing that Mousikanos had been pardoned by Alexander, and was ruling his own land, for he and Mousikanos were on hostile terms. But when Alexander approached the city called Sindimana,[1] which formed the metropolis of the country of Sambos, the gates were thrown open on his arrival, and the members of the household of Sambos with his treasure (of which they had reckoned up the amount) and his elephants went forth to meet him. Sambos, these men informed him, had fled, not from hostility to Alexander, but from fears to which the pardon of Mousikanos had given rise. He captured besides another city,[2] which had at this time revolted, and he put to death all those Brachmans who had instigated the revolt. These Brachmans are the philosophers of the Indians, and of their philosophy, if so it may be called, I shall give an account in my work which describes India.

Chapter XVII.—Mousikanos is captured by Peithôn and executed—Alexander reaches Patala at the apex of the Indus Delta

Meantime he received word that Mousikanos had revolted. Thereupon he despatched the satrap Peithôn,

kanos to the east of the river, and therefore in the vast Mesopotamia (the Prasiane of Pliny) comprised between the old or eastern arm of the Indus and the present channel (*v.* Lassen, *Ind. Alt.* ii. 177; Saint-Martin, *Etude*, p. 165; Cunningham, *Anc. Geog. of India*, pp. 259-262).

[1] See note S, Sindimana.

[2] See Note T, City of the Brachmans, Harmatelia; also Note H*h*, Indian Philosophers.

the son of Agênor, against him with an adequate force, while he marched himself against the cities which had been placed under the rule of Mousikanos. Some of these he razed to the ground after reducing the inhabitants to slavery; into others he introduced garrisons and fortified their citadels. When these operations were finished he returned to the camp and the fleet—whither Mousikanos was conducted, who had been taken prisoner by Peithôn. Alexander ordered the rebel to be taken to his own country and hanged there, together with all those Brachmans who had instigated him to revolt. Then there came to him the ruler of the country of the Patalians, which, as I have stated, consists of the Delta formed by the river Indus, and is larger than the Egyptian Delta. This chief surrendered to him the whole of his land, and entrusted both himself and all his possessions to him. Alexander sent him back to his government with orders to make all due preparations for the reception of his expedition. He then sent away Krateros into Karmania by the route through the Arachôtians and the Sarangians,[1] leading the brigades of Attalos, Meleager, and Antigenês, along with some of the archers and such of the com-

[1] In the 15th chapter of this book Arrian states that Alexander had sent Krateros away by this route after he had left the Sogdian capital (near Bhakar). From this we may infer that Krateros, soon after he set out on his homeward march, had been temporarily recalled by Alexander, who may have found the resistance to his arms more formidable than he had anticipated. Strabo states in one place (XV. ii. 5) that Krateros set out on his march from the Hydaspês and proceeded through the country of the Arachotoi and the Drangai into Karmania, and in another (XV. ii. 11) that he traversed Choarênê and entered Karmania simultaneously with Alexander. Now the former of these routes would have been so needlessly circuitous that it cannot be supposed it was that which Krateros selected. He no doubt marched through Choarênê (the district of Ariana nearest India), to which there was access from India through the Bolan Pass. Before rejoining Alexander he must have encountered formidable difficulties in traversing the great desert of Karman, which occupies the northern part of Karmania, and extends from thence to the confines of Yezd, Khorasân, and Seïstan. "This desert (says Bunbury) is a vast track of the most unmitigated barrenness, and a considerable portion of this interposed between the fertile districts of Murmansheer in Northern Carmania, and the Lake Zarrah in Seïstan must of necessity have been traversed by Craterus with his army. An Afghan army which invaded Persia in 1719 suffered the most dreadful hardships in this waste" (v. his Hist. of Anc. Geog. p. 522, also Droysen's Geschichte Alexanders, p. 454, and Lassen, Ind. Alt. ii. 180).

panions and other Macedonians as he was sending home to Macedonia as unfit for further service. He also sent away the elephants with him. The rest of the army, except that portion which with himself was sailing down to the sea, was placed under the command of Hêphaistiôn. Peithôn, who led the horse-lancers and the Agrianians, he transported to the opposite bank so that he might not be on that side of the river by which Hêphaistiôn was to advance. Peithôn was instructed to put colonists into the cities which had just been fortified, to suppress any insurrection which the Indians might attempt, to introduce settled order among them, and then to join him at Patala.

On the third day after Alexander had started on the voyage, he was informed that the Prince of Patala was fleeing from that city, taking with him most of its inhabitants, and leaving the country deserted. He accordingly accelerated his voyage down the river, and on reaching Patala found that both the city itself and the cultivated lands which lay around it had been deserted by the inhabitants. But he despatched his lightest troops in pursuit of the fugitives, and when some of these had been captured sent them on to their countrymen to bid them take courage and return, for they were free to inhabit their city and cultivate their lands as formerly; and so most of them did return.[1]

---

[1] According to Aristoboulos, as cited by Strabo (XV. i. 17), the voyage down stream from Nikaia on the Hydaspês to Patala occupied ten months. "The Greeks (he says) remained at the Hydaspês while the ships were constructing, and began their voyage not many days before the setting of the Pleiades (late in the autumn of B.C. 326), and were occupied during the whole autumn, winter, and the ensuing spring and summer in sailing down the river, and arrived at Patalênê about the rising of the dog-star (towards the end of summer B.C. 325). The passage down the river lasted ten months." According to Plutarch, Alexander spent seven months in falling down the rivers to the ocean. Sir A. Burnes ascended the Indus up to Lahore in sixty days, a distance of about 1000 miles. He estimated that a boat could drop down from Lahore to the sea in fifteen days, and from Multân in nine days.

*Chapter XVIII.—Alexander orders wells to be dug in the
district round Patala, and sails down the western arm
of the Indus*

After directing Hêphaistiôn to construct a citadel in
Patala, he sent out men into the adjacent country, which
was waterless, to dig wells [1] and make it habitable. Some
of the barbarians in the neighbourhood attacked them,
and, as they fell upon them quite unexpectedly, killed
several of their number, but as the assailants lost many
on their own side, they fled to the desert. The men were
thus able to complete the work they were sent to execute,
especially as Alexander, on learning that they had been
attacked by the barbarians, had sent additional troops to
take part in the work.

Near Patala the stream of the Indus is divided into
two large rivers,[2] both of which retain the name of the
Indus till they enter the sea. Here Alexander set about
the construction of a roadstead and dock, and when some
satisfactory progress had been made with these undertak-
ings, he resolved to sail down to the mouth of the right
arm of the river.[3] To Leonnatos he gave the command
of about 1000 cavalry and 8000 heavy and light infantry,
and despatched him to move down the island of Patala,
holding along the shore in a line with the squadron of
ships. He set out himself on a voyage down the right
arm of the river, taking with him the fastest vessels with
one and a half bank of oars, all the thirty-oared galleys,
and several of the smaller craft. As the Indians of that
region had fled, he had no pilot to direct his course, and
this made the navigation all the more difficult. Then on

---

[1] In the 41st chapter of the *Periplûs of the Erythraian Sea* it is said
that in the regions adjoining the Indus
mouths "there are preserved even to
this very day memorials of the expedition of Alexander, old temples,
foundations of camps, and *large
wells.*"

[2] *v.* Note U, Patala.

[3] This was the northern channel
of the Ghâra, the waters of which,
some centuries after Alexander, found
another channel more to the south,
in the southern Ghâra which joins the
main stream below Lâri Bandar.

the second day after he had started a storm arose, and the gale blowing against the current made deep furrows in the river, and battered the hulls of the vessels so violently that most of his ships were damaged, while some of the thirty-oared galleys were completely wrecked, though the sailors managed to run them on shore before they went all to pieces in the water. Other vessels were therefore constructed ; and Alexander, having despatched the quickest of the light-armed troops some distance into the interior, captured some Indians, whom he employed in piloting his fleet for the rest of the voyage. But when they found themselves where the river expands to the vast breadth of 200 stadia the wind blew strong from the outer sea, and the oars could scarcely be raised in the swell. They therefore again drew toward the shore for refuge, and the fleet was steered by the pilots into the mouth of a canal.

Chapter XIX.—The fleet is damaged by the tide, halts at an island in the Indus, and thence reaches the open sea

While the fleet was at anchor here, a vicissitude to which the Great Sea is subject occurred, for the tide ebbed, and their ships were left on dry ground. This pheno-menon, of which Alexander and his followers had no previous experience, caused them no little alarm, and greater still was their dismay, when in due course of time the tide advanced, and the hulls of the vessels were floated aloft. Those vessels which it found settled in the soft mud were uplifted without damage, and floated again, nothing the worse for the strain; but as for those vessels which had been left on a drier part of the beach, and were not firmly embedded, some on the advance of a massive wave fell foul of each other, while others were dashed upon the strand and shattered in pieces.[1]

[1] Caesar's fleet, it is well known, suffered a similar disaster on the shores of Britain. The tides in the Indus are not felt more than sixty miles from the sea, whence Cunning-ham concludes that Alexander must

Alexander caused these vessels to be repaired as well as circumstances allowed, and despatched men in advance down the river in two boats to explore an island at which the natives informed him he must anchor on his way to the sea. They said that the name of the island was Killouta.[1] When he learned that the island had harbours, was of great extent, and yielded water, he ordered the rest of the fleet to make its way thither, but he himself with the fastest sailing ships advanced beyond the island to see the mouth of the river, and ascertain whether it offered a safe and easy passage out into the open main. When they had proceeded about 200 stadia beyond the island, they descried another which lay out in the sea. Then they returned to the island in the river, and Alexander, having anchored his ships near its extremity, offered sacrifice to those gods to whom, he said, Ammôn had enjoined him to sacrifice. On the following day he sailed down to the other island which lay in the ocean, and approaching close to it also, offered other sacrifices to other gods and in another manner. These sacrifices, like the others, he offered under sanction of an oracle given by Ammôn. He then advanced beyond the mouths of the river Indus, and sailed out into the great main to discover, as he declared, whether any land lay anywhere near in the sea, but, in my opinion, chiefly that it might be said that he had navigated the great outer sea of India. He then sacrificed bulls to the god Pôseidôn, which he threw into the sea; and following up the sacrifice with a libation, he threw the goblet and bowls of gold into the bosom of the deep as thanks-offerings, beseeching the god to conduct in safety the

---

then have reached as far as Bambhra on the Ghâra, which is about fifty miles by water from the sea. The breaking up of the monsoon, which occurs in October, is attended with high winds, intervals of calm, and violent hurricanes.

[1] Plutarch says that Alexander called this island Skilloustis, but others Psiltoukis. It was from this island Nearchos started on his memorable voyage early in October, before the monsoon had subsided. On his reaching the port now called Karachi, the great emporium of the trade of the Indus, he remained there for twenty-four days, and renewed the voyage as soon as the weather permitted.

naval expedition which he intended to despatch under
Nearchos to the Persian Gulf and the mouths of the
Euphrates and Tigris.

*Chapter XX.—Alexander after returning to Patala sails
down the eastern arm of the Indus*

On his return to Patala, he found the citadel fortified,
and Peithôn arrived with his troops after completing the
objects of his expedition. Hêphaistiôn was then ordered
to prepare what was requisite for the fortification of the
harbour, and the construction of a dockyard, for here at
the city of Patala, which stands where the river Indus
bifurcates, he meant to leave behind him a very considerable naval squadron.

He himself sailed down again to the Great Sea by the
other mouth of the Indus,[1] to ascertain by which of the
mouths it was easier to reach the ocean.   The mouths of
the river Indus are about 1800 stadia distant from each
other.[2]   When he was approaching the mouth, he came
to a large lake formed by the river in widening out,
unless, indeed, this watery expanse be due to rivers which
discharge their streams into it from the surrounding
districts, and give it the appearance of a gulf of the sea;[3]

---

[1] The eastern branch of the Indus
is that now called the Phuleli. It
separates from the main channel at
Muttâri, twelve miles above Haidarâbâd, and enters the sea by the Kori
estuary, named by Ptolemy the Loni-
bari mouth. Its bed is now almost
dry except at the time of the inundations, when it assumes the appearance of a great river. At the lower
part of its course it is known as the
Guni. On its east side it receives the
branch of the Indus, which in ancient
times passed Arôr, and is now called
the *Purana darya* or *Old river*.

[2] This exaggerated estimate Arrian
has taken from the Journal of Nearchos. Aristoboulos said that the

distance was 1000 stadia. The truth
is here pretty accurately hit.

[3] "This great lake (says Saint-
Martin) might have been the western
extremity of the Ran of Kachh, a
vast depression which abuts on the
point where the estuary begins, and
which for some months of the year
(from July to October) is inundated
by the waters of several rivers. By
a singular coincidence the terrible
earthquake of 1819 has formed a large
hollow and created a spacious lake
traversed by the Kori, and occupying
probably the same site as the lake
mentioned by Arrian. Brahmanic
tradition, moreover, preserves the
memory of a lake formerly existing

for salt-water fish were now seen in it of larger size than the fish in our sea. Having anchored in the lake, at a place selected by the pilots, he left there most of the soldiers under the command of Leonnatos and all the boats, while he himself with the thirty-oared galleys, and the vessels with one and a half bank of oars passed beyond the mouth of the Indus, and sailing out into the sea by this other route, satisfied himself that the mouth of the Indus on this side was easier to navigate than the other. He then anchored his fleet near the beach, and taking with him some of the cavalry, proceeded along the shore a three days' journey, examining what sort of a country it was for a coasting voyage, and ordering wells to be sunk for supplying sea-farers with water. He then returned to the fleet, and sailed back to Patala. He sent, however, a part of the army to complete the work of digging wells along the shore, with instructions to return to Patala on their completing this service. Sailing down again to the lake, he constructed there another harbour and other docks, and, having left a garrison in the place, he collected sufficient food to supply the army for four months, and made all other necessary preparations for the voyage along the coast.

Chapter XXI.—Alexander crosses the river Arabios and invades the Oreitai

The season of the year was impracticable for navigation from the prevalence of the Etesian winds, which do not blow there as with us from the north, but come as a south wind from the Great Ocean. It was ascertained that from the beginning of winter, that is from the

near the Korî, not far from its em- bouchure. In the *Bhagavata Purâna* translated by Bournouf, we read that ' in the west at the confluence of the Sindhu and the ocean is the vast tank of Nârâyana Saras, which is frequented by the Recluses and the Siddhas.'

. . . A local tradition picked up by M'Murdo refers to the disappear- ance of this lake of old times, and explains the event by a conflagration of the country " (*v. Etude*, pp. 178, 179).

setting of the Pleiades,[1] till the winter solstice, the weather was suitable for making voyages, because the mild breezes which then blow steadily seaward from the land, which is drenched by this time with heavy rains, favour coasting voyages, whether made by oar or by sail. Nearchos, who had been appointed to the command of the fleet, was waiting for the season for coasting, but Alexander set out from Patala, and advanced with the whole of his army to the river Arabios.[2] He then took half of the hypaspists and archers, the infantry brigades called foot companions, the corps of companion cavalry, and a squadron from each division of the other cavalry, and all the horse archers, and turned towards the sea, which lay on the left, not only to dig as many wells as possible for the use of the expedition while coasting those shores, but also to fall suddenly upon the Oreitai (an Indian tribe in those parts which had long been independent), because they had rendered no friendly service either to himself or the army. The command of the troops which he did not take with him was entrusted to Hêphaistiôn. There was settled near the river Arabios another[3] independent tribe called the Arabitai, and, as

---

[1] In Italy the Pleiades set in the beginning of November. The south-west monsoon prevails from April to October. It sets in on the Sindh coast with strong west-south-westerly winds, which cause a heavy swell on the sea. The north-east monsoon, which is favourable for navigation, begins in the Arabian Sea about the middle of October.

[2] The name of this river has various forms, Arabis, Arbis, Artabis, and Artabius. It is now called the Purâli and is the river which, rising in the mountain range called by Ptolemy the Baitian, flows through the present district of Las into the Bay of Sonmi-yâni. It gave its name to the Arabioi, whose territory it divided from that of the Oritai, who were farther west. Curtius states that Alexander reached the eastern boundary of the Arabioi (which may be placed about Karâchi)

in nine days from Patala, and their western boundary formed by the Arabius in five days more. The distance from Haidarâbâd to Karâchi is 114 miles, and from Karâchi to Son-miyâni fifty miles. The average of a day's march was therefore about twelve miles, the same as now in these parts.

[3] The Arabitai are called in the *Indika*, *Arabies*; in Strabo, *Arbies*; in Diodôros, *Ambritai*; in Marcian the geographer, *Arbitoi*; and in Dion. Perieg. *Aribes*. Their territories extended from the western mouth of the Indus to the river Purâli. This people and their neighbours, the Oritai, Cunningham would include within the geographical limits of India, although they have always been beyond its political boundaries during the historical period. They were tributary to Darius Hystaspês, and

these neither thought themselves a match for Alexander, nor yet wished to submit to him, they fled into the desert when they learned that he was marching against them. But Alexander having crossed the Arabios, which was neither broad nor deep, traversed the most of the desert, and found himself by daybreak near the inhabited country. Then leaving orders with the infantry to follow him in regular line, he set forward with the cavalry, which he divided into squadrons, to be spread over a wide extent of the plain, and it was thus he marched into the country of the Oreitai.[1] All who turned to offer resistance were cut down by the cavalry, but many were taken prisoners. He then encamped near a small sheet of water, and on being joined by the troops under Hêphaistiôn still continued his progress, and arrived at the village called Rambakia,[2] which was the largest in the dominions of the Oreitai. He was pleased with the situation, and thought that if he colonised it, it would become a great and prosperous city. He therefore left Hêphaistiôn behind him to carry this scheme into effect.

were still subject to the Persians when the Chinese pilgrim Hwen Thsiang visited their country in the seventh century of our aera.

[1] In the country of the Oreitai is a river called the Aghor, from which, it has been supposed, the people take their name, as thus: Aghoritai, Aoritai, Oritai, or Horatae, as they are called by Curtius. They are the Neoritai of Diodôros. The length of their coast Arrian gives in his *Indika* at 1600 stadia, while Strabo extends it to 1800. The actual length is 100 English miles, somewhere about half of Arrian's estimate taken from Near-chos. The western boundary of the Oritai was marked by Cape Mâlân (the *Malana* of Arrian), which is twenty miles distant from the river Aghor. According to Strabo the Oritai were the people by whose

poisoned arrows Ptolemy was all but mortally wounded.

[2] This name is probably a transcription of the Indian *Râmbâgh*, which designated the place where pilgrims assemble before starting for the Aghor Valley, in which the principal sacred places are connected with the history of Râma, the great hero of the Râmâyana. Cunningham accordingly identifies Râmbâgh with Arrian's Rambakia, and remarks that the occurrence of the name of Râmbâgh at so great a distance to the west of the Indus, and at so early a period as the time of Alexander, shows not only the wide extension of Hindu influence in ancient times, but also the great antiquity of the story of Râma (v. his *Anc. Geog. of India*, pp. 307-310).

Chapter XXII.—Submission of the Oreitai—Description of the Gadrôsian desert

He then took again the half of the hypaspists and Agrianians, and the corps of cavalry and the horse-archers, and marched forward to the frontiers of the Gadrôsoi and the Oreitai, where he was informed his way would lie through a narrow defile before which the combined forces of the Oreitai and the Gadrôsoi were lying encamped, resolved to prevent his passage. They were in fact drawn up there, but when they were apprised of Alexander's approach most of them deserted the posts they were guarding and fled from the pass. Then the leaders of the Oreitai came to him to surrender themselves and their nation. He ordered them to collect the multitude of the Oreïtai, and send them away to their homes, since they were not to be subjected to any bad treatment. Over these people he placed Apollophanês as satrap. Along with him he left Leonnatos, an officer of the body-guard in Ora,[1] in command of all the Agrianians, some of the archers and cavalry, and the rest of the Grecian mercenary infantry and cavalry, and instructed him to remain in the country till the fleet sailed past its shores, to settle a colony in the city, and establish order among the Oreitai, so that they might be readier to pay respect and obedience to the satrap. He himself with the great bulk of the army (for Hêphaistiôn had now rejoined him with his detachment) advanced to the country of the Gadrôsoi[2] by a route mostly desert.

[1] D'Anville and Vincent have assumed that Ora is the *Haur* mentioned by Edrisi as lying on the route from Dîbal, near the mouth of the Indus, to Firûzâbâd in Mekran. Its situation is uncertain, however, as its name does not occur in any recently published account of the country. Ora may perhaps have been in the neighbourhood of Kôkala, mentioned in the *Indika* as situated on the Oreitian coast, probably near Cape Katchari, to the east of the Hingul river, where the fleet was supplied with a fresh stock of provisions. Perhaps it may have here denoted the country of the Oreitai.

[2] Gadrôsia in Arrian denotes the *inland* region which extends from the Oreitai to Karmania. The *maritime* region between the same limits he calls the country of the Ichthyophagoi.

Aristoboulos says that myrrh-trees larger than the common kind grow plentifully in this desert, and that the Phoenicians who followed the army as suttlers collected the drops of myrrh which oozed out in great abundance from the trees (their stems being large and hitherto uncropped), and conveyed away the produce loaded on their beasts of burden. He says also that this desert yields an abundance of odoriferous roots of nard, which the Phoenicians likewise collected ; but much of it was trodden down by the army, and the sweet perfume thus crushed out of it was from its great abundance diffused far and wide over the country.[1] Other kinds of trees are found in the desert, one in particular which had a foliage like that of the laurel, and grew in places washed by the waves of the sea. These trees when the tide ebbed were left in dry ground, but when it returned they looked as if they grew in the sea. The roots of some were always washed by the sea, since they grew in hollows from which the water never receded, and yet trees of this kind were not destroyed by the brine. Some of these trees attained here the great height of 30 cubits. They happened to be at that season in bloom, and their flower closely resembled the white violet,[2] which, however, it far surpassed in the sweetness of its perfume. Another kind of thorny stalk is mentioned, which grew on dry land, and was armed with a thorn so strong that when it got entangled in the dress of some who were riding past, it rather pulled the rider down from his horse than was itself torn away from

The Gedrôsian desert since the days of Alexander has protected Lower Sindh from any attack by the maritime route. The Persian invader has preferred to encounter the dangers and difficulties of the mountain passes of Afghânistân rather than to expose himself to such horrible sufferings in the burning desert as were experienced by the soldiers of Semiramis, Cyrus, and Alexander. The length of the Makrân or Beluchistan coast between the Oreitai and Karmania is given by Arrian at 10,000 stadia and by Strabo at 7000 only. The actual length is 480 English miles, and the time taken by Nearchos in its navigation was twenty days.

[1] A description of this unguent is given by Pliny (N. H. xii. c. 26). He there mentions that a special kind of it was produced in the Gangetic regions. In the 33d chapter of the same book will be found a description of the myrrh-tree and its produce.

[2] Chinnock notes that this was probably the snow-flake.

its stalk. When hares are running past these bushes the thorns are said to fasten themselves in the fur so that the hares are caught like birds with bird-lime or fish with hooks. These thorns were, however, easily cut through with steel, and when severed the stalk yielded juice even more abundant and more acid than what flows from fig-trees in springtime.[1]

Chapter XXIII.—Alexander marching through Gadrôsia endeavours to collect supplies for the fleet

Thence he marched through the country of the Gadrôsoi by a difficult route, on which it was scarcely possible to procure the necessaries of life, and which often failed to yield water for the army. They were besides compelled to march most of the way by night, and at too great a distance from the sea; for Alexander wished to go along the sea-coast, both to see what harbours it had, and to make in the course of his march whatever preparations were possible for the benefit of the fleet, either by making his men dig wells or seek out markets and anchorages. The maritime parts of Gadrôsia were, however, entirely desert. Nevertheless he sent Thoas, the son of Mandradôros, down to the sea with a few horsemen to see if there happened to be any anchorage or water not far from the sea, or anything else that could supply the wants of the fleet. This man on returning reported that he found some fishermen upon the beach living in stifling huts, which had been constructed by heaping up mussel shells, while the roofs were formed of the backbones of fish. He also reported that these fishermen had only scanty supplies of water, obtained with difficulty by their

[1] This, says Sintenis, can be nothing else than a kind of acacia. He points out that Dioscorides (i. 33) applies to this thorn the expression ἀκακία, which Willdenow identifies with the acacia catechu. It grows abundantly in the Bombay and Bengal presidencies, producing a gum employed both as a colouring matter and a medicinal astringent, and known in commerce by the name of cutch.

digging through the shingle, and that what they got was far from sweet.[1]

When Alexander came to a district of the Gadrôsian country where corn was more abundant, he seized it, placed it upon the beasts of burden, and having marked it with his own seal ordered it to be conveyed to the sea. But when he was coming to the halting station nearest the sea, the soldiers paid but little regard to the seal, and even the guards themselves made use of the corn and gave a share of it to such as were most pinched with hunger. Indeed, they were so overcome by their sufferings, that, as reason dictated, they took more account of the impending danger with which they now stood face to face than of the unseen and remote danger of the king's resentment. Alexander, however, forgave the offenders when made aware of the necessity which had prompted their act. He himself scoured the country in search of provisions, and sent Krêtheus the Kallatian[2] with all the supplies he could collect for the use of the army which was sailing round with the fleet. He also ordered the natives to grind all the corn they could collect in the interior districts, and convey it, for sale to the army, along with dates and sheep. He besides sent Telephos, one of the companions, to another locality with a small supply of ground corn.

Chapter XXIV.—Difficulties encountered on the march through Gadrôsia

He then advanced towards the capital of the Gadrôsoi, called Poura,[3] and arrived there in sixty days after he had

---

[1] These people were the Ichthyophagoi of whom Arrian makes frequent mention in his *Indika* when describing the voyage of Nearchos along their coast. His description of their appearance and habits closely agrees with that given by Strabo in his chapter on Ariana.

[2] Kallatis or Kallatia was a large city of Thrace on the coast of the Euxine, colonised from Milêtos. Pliny says its former name was Cerbatis.

[3] *v.* Note V, Alexander's march through Gedrôsia, Poura.

started from Ora. Most of Alexander's historians admit that all the hardships which his army suffered in Asia are not to be compared with the miseries which it here experienced. Nearchos is the only author who says that Alexander did not take that route in ignorance of its difficulty, but that he chose it on learning that no one had as yet traversed it with an army except Semiramis when she fled from India. The natives of the country say that she escaped with only twenty men of all her army, while even Cyrus, the son of Kambyses, escaped with only seven. For Cyrus, they say, did in truth enter this region to invade India, but lost, before reaching it, the greater part of his army from the difficulties which beset his march through the desert. When Alexander heard these accounts he was seized, it is said, with an ambition to outrival both Cyrus and Semiramis. Nearchos says that this motive, added to his desire to be near the coast in order to keep the fleet supplied with provisions, induced him to march by this route; but that the blazing heat and want of water destroyed a great part of the army, and especially the beasts of burden, which perished from the great depth of the sand, and the heat which scorched like fire, while a great many died of thirst. For they met, he says, with lofty ridges of deep sand not hard and compact, but so loose that those who stepped on it sunk down as into mud or rather into untrodden snow. The horses and mules besides suffered still more severely both in ascending and descending the ridges, because the road was not only uneven, but wanted firmness. The great distances also between the stages were most distressing to the army, compelled as it was at times from want of water to make marches above the ordinary length. When they traversed by night all the stage they had to complete and came to water in the morning, their distress was all but entirely relieved. But if as the day advanced they were caught still marching owing to the great length of the stage, then suffer they did, tortured alike by raging heat and thirst unquenchable.

Chapter XXV.—Sufferings of the army in the Gadrôsian desert

The soldiers destroyed many of the beasts of burden of their own accord. For when their provisions ran short they came together and killed most of the horses and mules. They ate the flesh of these animals, which they professed had died of thirst and perished from the heat. No one cared to look very narrowly into the exact nature of what was doing, both because of the prevailing distress and also because all were alike implicated in the same offence. Alexander himself was not unaware of what was going on, but he saw that the remedy for the existing state of things was to pretend ignorance of it rather than permit it as a matter that lay within his cognisance. It was therefore no longer easy to convey the soldiers labouring under sickness, nor others who had fallen behind on the march from exhaustion. This arose not only from the want of beasts of burden, but also because the men themselves took to destroying the waggons when they could no longer drag them forward owing to the deepness of the sand. They had done this even in the early stages of the march, because for the sake of the waggons they had to go not by the shortest roads, but those easiest for carriages. Thus some were left behind on the road from sickness, others from fatigue or the effects of the heat or intolerable thirst, while there were none who could take them forward or remain to tend them in their sickness. For the army marched on apace, and in the anxiety for its safety as a whole the care of individuals was of necessity disregarded. As they generally made their marches by night, some of the men were overcome by sleep on the way, but on awaking afterwards those who still had some strength left followed close on the track of the army, and a few out of many saved their lives by overtaking it. The majority perished in the sand like shipwrecked men at sea.

Another disaster also befell the army which seriously affected the men themselves as well as the horses and the beasts of burden.   For the country of the Gadrôsians, like that of the Indians, is supplied with rains by the Etesian winds; but these rains do not fall on the Gadrôsian plains, but on the mountains to which the clouds are carried by the wind, where they dissolve in rain without passing over the crests of the mountains.   When the army on one occasion lay encamped for the night near a small winter torrent for the sake of its water, the torrent which passes that way about the second watch of the night became swollen by rains which had fallen unperceived by the army, and came rushing down with so great a deluge that it destroyed most of the women and children of the camp-followers, and swept away all the royal baggage and whatever beasts of burden were still left.   The soldiers themselves, after a hard struggle, barely escaped with their lives, and a portion only of their weapons.   Many of them besides came by their death through drinking, for if when jaded by the broiling heat and thirst they fell in with abundance of water, they quaffed it with insatiable avidity till they killed themselves. For this reason Alexander generally pitched his camp not in the immediate vicinity of the watering-places, but some twenty stadia off to prevent the men and beasts from rushing in crowds into the water to the danger of their lives, as well as to prohibit those who had no self-control from polluting the water for the rest of the troops by their stepping into the springs or streams.

Chapter XXVI.—Incidents of the march through Gadrôsia

Here I feel myself bound not to pass over in silence a noble act performed by Alexander, perhaps the noblest in his record, which occurred either in this country or, as some other authors have asserted, still earlier, among the Parapamisadai.   The story is this.   The army was prosecuting its march through the sand under a sun already blazing high because a halt could not be made till water, which lay on the way farther on was reached, and Alexander himself, though distressed with thirst, was nevertheless with pain and difficulty marching on foot at the head of his army, that the soldiers might, as they usually do in a case of the kind, more cheerfully bear their hardships when they saw the misery equalised. But in the meantime some of the light-armed soldiers, starting off from the army, found water collected in the shallow bed of a torrent in a small and impure spring. Having, with difficulty, collected this water they hastened off to Alexander as if they were the bearers of some great boon. As soon as they came near the king they poured the water into a helmet, and offered it to him. He took it and thanked the men who brought it, but at once poured it upon the ground in the sight of all. By this deed the whole army was inspired with fresh vigour to such a degree that one would have imagined that the water poured out by Alexander had supplied a draught to the men all round. This deed I commend above all others, as it exhibits Alexander's power of endurance as well as his wonderful tact in the management of an army.

The army met also with the following adventure in this country. The guides, becoming uncertain of the way, at last declared that they could no longer recognise it, because all its tracks had been obliterated by the sands which the wind blew over them. Amid the deep sands, moreover, which had been everywhere heaped up to a uniform level, nothing rose up from which they could conjecture their path, not even the usual fringe of trees, nor so much as the sure landmark of a hill-crest. Nor had they practised the art of finding their way by observation of the stars by night or of the sun by day, as sailors do by watching one or other of the Bears—the Phoenicians the Lesser Bear, and all other nations the Greater. Alexander, at last perceiving that he should direct his march to the left, rode away forward, taking a small party of horsemen with him.   But when their horses were tired out by the heat, he left most of his escort behind, and rode on with only five men and found the sea. Having scraped away the shingle on the beach, he found water, both fresh and pure, and then went back and brought his whole army to this place.   And for seven days they marched along the sea-coast, and procured water from the beach.   As the guides by this time knew the way, he led his expedition thence into the interior parts.

Chapter XXVII.—Appointment of satraps — Alexander learns that the satrap Philippos had been murdered in India—Punishes satraps who had misgovernea

When he arrived at the capital of the Gadrôsians he then gave his army a rest.   Apollophanês he deposed from his satrapy because he found out that he had utterly disregarded his instructions.   He appointed Thoas to be satrap over the people of this district, but, as he took ill and died, Siburtios received the vacant office.   The same man had also recently been appointed by Alexander satrap of Karmania, but now the government of the Arachotians and Gadrôsians was committed to him, and Tlêpolemos, the son of Pythophanês, got Karmania.   The king was already advancing into Karmania when tidings reached him that Philippos, the satrap of the Indian country, had been plotted against by the mercenaries and treacherously murdered ; but that the Macedonian body-guards of Philippos had put to death his murderers whom they had caught in the very act, and others whom they had afterwards seized.   On learning what had occurred he sent a letter to India addressed to Eudêmos and Taxilês directing them to assume the administration of the province previously governed by Philippos until he could send a satrap to govern it.

When he arrived in Karmania, Krateros joined him,

N

bringing the rest of the army and the elephants.   He
brought also Ordanês, whom he had made prisoner for
revolting and attempting to make a revolution.   Thither
came also Stasanôr, the satrap of the Areians and
Zarangians, accompanied by Pharismanes, the son of
Phrataphernês, the satrap of the Parthyaians and Hyr-
kanians.   There came besides the generals who had been
left with Parmenion over the army in Media, Kleander and
Sitalkês and Hêrakôn, who brought with them the greater
part of their army.   Against Kleander and Sitalkês both
the natives and the soldiers themselves brought many
accusations, as that they had pillaged temples, despoiled
ancient tombs, and perpetrated other outrageous acts of
injustice and tyranny against their subjects.   When these
charges were proved against them, he put them to death,
to make others who might be left as satraps, or governors,
or chiefs of districts, stand in fear of suffering a like
punishment if they violated their duty.   This was the
means which above all others served to keep in due order
and obedience the nations which Alexander had conquered
in war or which had voluntarily submitted to him, numerous as they were, and so far remote from each other,
because under his sceptre the ruled were not allowed to
be unjustly treated by their rulers.   Hêrakôn on this
occasion was acquitted of the charge, but was soon afterwards punished, because he was convicted by the men
of Sousa of having plundered the temple of their
city.   Stasanôr and Phrataphernês in setting out to join
Alexander, took with them a multitude of beasts of
burden and many camels, because they learned that he
was taking the route through the Gadrôsians, and conjectured that his army would suffer, as it actually did.
These men arrived therefore very opportunely, as did also
their camels and their beasts of burden.   For Alexander
distributed all these animals to the officers one by one, to
the squadrons and centuries of the cavalry, and to the
companies of the infantry as far as their number
sufficed.

Chapter XXVIII.—Alexander holds rejoicings in Karmania on account of his Indian victories—List of his body-guards—Nearchos reports to him the safety of the fleet

Some authors have recorded, though I cannot believe what they state, that he made his progress through Karmania stretched at length with his companions on two covered waggons joined together, enjoying the while the music of the flute, and followed by the soldiers crowned with garlands and making holiday. They say also that food and all kinds of good cheer were provided for them along the roads by the Karmanians, and that these things were done by Alexander in imitation of the Bacchic revelry of Dionysos, because it was said of that deity that, after conquering the Indians, he traversed, in this manner, a great part of Asia, and received the name of Thriambos in addition to that of Dionysos, and that for this very reason the splendid processions in honour of victories in war were called *Thriamboi.*[1] But neither Ptolemy, the son of Lagos, nor Aristoboulos has mentioned these doings in their narratives, nor any other writer whose testimony on such subjects it would be safe to trust, and as for myself I have done enough in recording them as unworthy of belief. But in the account I now proceed to offer I follow Aristoboulos. In Karmania Alexander offered sacrifice in thanksgiving to the gods for his victory over the Indians, and the preservation of his army during its march through Gadrôsia. He celebrated also a musical and a gymnastic contest. He then appointed Peukestas to be one of his body-guards, having already resolved to make him the satrap of Persis. He wished him, before his promotion to the satrapy, to experience this honour and mark of confidence for the service he rendered among the Malloi. Up to this time the number of his body-guards was seven—Leonnatos,

[1] In Latin *triumphi.*

the son of Anteas ; Hêphastiôn, the son of Amyntôr ; Lysimachos, the son of Agathoklês ; Aristonous, the son of Peisaios, who were all Pellaians ; Perdikkas, the son of Orontês from Orestis ; Ptolemy, the son of Lagos, and Peithôn, the son of Krateuas, who were both Heordaians —Peukestas, who had held the shield over Alexander, was added to them as an eighth.

At this time Nearchos, having sailed round the coast of Ora and Gadrôsia, and that of the Ichthyophagoi, put into port in the inhabited parts of the Karmanian coast, and going up thence into the interior with a few followers related to Alexander the incidents of the voyage which he had made for him in the outer sea. He was sent down again to sea, to sail round to the land of the Sousians and the outlets of the river Tigris. How he sailed from the river Indus to the Persian Sea and the mouth of the Tigris, I shall describe in a separate work, wherein I shall follow Nearchos himself, as the history which he composed in the Greek language had Alexander for its subject. Perhaps at some future time I shall produce this work if my own inclination and the deity prompt me to the task.

Q. CURTIUS RUFUS

HISTORY OF ALEXANDER THE GREAT, BY Q. CURTIUS RUFUS

EIGHTH BOOK

Chapter IX.—Description of India

ALEXANDER, not to foster repose which naturally sets rumours in circulation, advanced towards India, always adding more to his glory by warfare than by his acts after victory.

India lies almost entirely towards the east,[1] and it is of less extent in breadth than in length.[2] The southern parts rise in hills of considerable elevation.[3] The country is elsewhere level, and hence many famous rivers which rise in Mount Caucasus traverse the plains with languid currents. The Indus is colder than the other rivers, and its waters differ but little in colour from those of the sea. The Ganges, which is the greatest of all rivers in the east, flows down to the south country, and running in a straight bed washes great mountain-chains until a barrier of rocks diverts its course towards the east. Both rivers enter the Red Sea.[4] The Indus wears away its banks, absorbing

[1] That is, to one who, like Alexander, approached it from Central Asia.

[2] Eratosthenes and other ancient writers describe India as of a rhomboidal figure with the Indus on the west, the mountains on the north, and the sea on the east and the south. Curtius follows them here in reckoning its length from west to east.

[3] These are the mountains of the peninsular part of India.

[4] By the Red or Erythraean Sea is meant the Indian Ocean, which included both the Red Sea proper and the Persian Gulf. Curtius here makes the two great Indian rivers flow into the same sea. His conception of the configuration of India perhaps resembled that of Ptolemy, in whose

into its waters great numbers of trees and much of the soil. It is besides obstructed with rocks by which it is frequently beaten back. Where it finds the soil soft and yielding it spreads out into pools and forms islands. The Acesines increases its volume. The Ganges, in running downward to the sea, intercepts the Iomanes,[1] and the two streams dash against each other with great violence. The Ganges in fact presents a rough face to the entrance of its affluent, the waters of which though beaten back in eddies, hold their own.

The Dyardanes is less frequently mentioned, as it flows through the remotest parts of India. But it breeds not only crocodiles, like the Nile, but dolphins also, and various aquatic monsters unknown to other nations.[2] The Ethimanthus, which curves time after time in frequent maeanders, is used up for irrigation by the people on its banks. Hence it contributes to the sea but a small and nameless residue of its waters.[3] The country is every-

map India is so misrepresented that it appears without its peninsula, but with a point (a little below the latitude of Bombay) whence the coast bends at once sharply to the east instead of pursuing its actual course southward to Cape Comorin.

[1] "Iomanes, a clever conjectural insertion due to Hedike. Foss had suspected some such omission, as the old attempt to make the Acesines run into the Ganges by finding some other modern name for it was preposterous" (*Alexander in India*, by Heitland and Raven, p. 90). The Iomanes appears in Ptolemy's *Geography* as the Diamouna — that is the Yamunâ or Jamnâ, the great river which, after passing Delhi, Mathurâ, Agrâ, and other places, joins the Ganges at Allâhâbâd. It rises from hot springs not far westward from the sources of the Ganges. Arrian, who in his *Indika* calls it the Jobares, says that it flows through the country of the Sourasenoi, who possess two great cities, Methora (Mathurâ) and Kleisobara (Krishnapura?). Pliny (vi. 19) states that it passes through the Palibothri to join the Ganges. At its junction

with the Jamnâ, and a third, but imaginary river, the Sarasvatî, the Ganges is called the *Trivênî*, *i.e.* " triple plait," from the intermingling of the three streams.

[2] This river is most probably that which is called the Doanas in Ptolemy's *Geography*, where it designates the Brahmaputra. The Doanas was probably also the Oidanes of Artemidôros, who, according to Strabo (XI. i. 72), described it as a river that bred crocodiles and dolphins, and that flowed into the Ganges. If the first two letters in *Doanas* be transposed, we get almost letter for letter the *Oidanes* of Artemidôros, and we get it again, though not so closely, if we discard *r* from the Dyardanes of Curtius. That these two writers had the same river in view is confirmed by their mentioning the very same animals as bred in its waters.

[3] No satisfactory identification of this river has as yet, so far as I am aware, been proposed. The river called by Arrian (iv. 6) the *Erymandros*, and by Polybios the *Erymanthus*, and now known as the Helmund,

where intersected with many rivers besides these, but they are obscure, their course being too short to bring them into prominent notice. The maritime tracts, however, are most parched up by the north wind. This wind is prevented by the mountain-summits from penetrating to the interior parts, which for this reason are mild and nourish the crops.[1]   But so completely has nature altered the regular changes of the season in these regions that, when other countries are basking under the hot rays of the sun, India is covered with snow ; and on the other hand, when the world elsewhere is frost-bound, India is oppressed with intolerable heat. The reason why nature has thus inverted her order is not apparent ; the sea, at anyrate, by which India is washed does not differ in colour from other seas. It takes its name from King Erythrus, and hence ignorant people believe that its waters are red.[2]

The soil produces flax from which the dress ordinarily

has a name pretty similar, but it does not discharge into the sea. It enters the inland lake called Zarah, in the province of Seistan in Afghanistan. According to Arrian it disappears in the sands.

[1] These statements about the north wind as it affects India have no basis in fact, and those that immediately follow reach the very acme of absurdity. The cold season occurs in India as in Europe during winter, but snow never falls on the plains. During the hot season, however, hailstorms occasionally occur and inflict more or less damage on the crops. I have myself witnessed in Calcutta a thunderstorm accompanied with a descent of hail, commingled with large pieces of ice, and this in one of the hottest months of the year, June or July, I forget which.

[2] Agatharchides, a writer of the second century B.C., begins his work on the Erythraean Sea by inquiring into the origin of its name. On this point four different opinions were held, and of these he adopted that which fathered the name on King Erythrus. He then tells the story of

this king (who was a Persian) as he had learned it from a Persian called Boxos who had settled in Athens. Strabo (xvi. 20) gives a brief summary of this passage, and Pliny (*N. H.* vi. 28) a still briefer. Nearchos, as we learn from Arrian's *Indika* (c. 37), in the course of his memorable voyage put into an island called Oärakta (now Kishm), where the natives showed him the tomb of the first king of the island. They said that his name was Erythrês, and that the sea in those parts was called after him the *Erythraean*. Opinions still differ as to the origin of the name. According to some it was given from the red and purple colouring of the rocks which in some parts border the sea, according to others from the red colour sometimes given to the waters by the sea-weed called Sûph. Fresnel, however, rejecting such views, interprets the name as meaning the sea of the Homêritai, *i.e. Himyar* or *Hhomayr*, or *red men*, whose name and the Arabic word *ahhmar* (red) have the same root. The people here indicated occupied Yemen, and were called *red men* in contrast to the *black men* of

worn by the natives is made.[1]   The tender side of the
barks of trees receives written characters like paper.[2]
The birds can be readily trained to imitate the sounds of
human speech.[3]   The animals except those imported are
unknown among other nations.   The same country yields
fit food for the rhinoceros, but this animal is not
indigenous.[4]   The elephants are more powerful than those

the opposite coast. Others again attribute the name to *Edom* (Idumea), which bordered the Gulf of Akaba, the eastern arm of the Red Sea, at its northern extremity. *Edom* signifies *red*. Further references to this subject will be found in Mela (III. viii. 1), Solinus (c. 36), Dio Cassius (lxviii. 28), and Stephanos Byz. *s.v.* 'Ερυθρά.

[1] As the dress of the natives was made in ancient times as at present, chiefly from cotton, this perhaps may be the substance meant here by flax. The valuable properties of the wool-like product of the cotton plant (*Gossypium herbaceum*, the *Karpâsa* of Sanskrit) were early known, as in one of the hymns of the Rig-veda mention is made of female weavers intertwining the extended thread. "The dress worn by the Indians (says Arrian, citing Nearchos) is made of cotton, a material produced from trees. They wear an under-garment of cotton which reaches below the knee half-way down to the ankles, and also an upper garment which they throw partly over their shoulders, and partly twist in folds round their head" (*Indika*, c. 16). This costume is mentioned in old Sanskrit literature, and is carefully represented in the frescoes on the caves of Ajanta. We learn from the *Periplûs of the Erythraean Sea* that muslin (othonion) was imported into the marts of India from China, and exported thence along with Indian muslin and coarser cotton fabrics to Egypt.

[2] Strabo (XV. i. 67) states on the authority of Nearchos that the Indians wrote letters upon cloth, which was well pressed to make it smooth, but adds that other writers affirmed that the Indians had no knowledge of writing. They were, however, acquainted with writing for some cen-

turies before Alexander's time, but whence they got their alphabet is a question not yet quite settled, though the weight of opinion inclines to assign it a Himyaritic origin. We learn from Pliny (xiii. 21) that paper made from the papyrus plant did not come into common use out of Egypt till the time of Alexander the Great. He then goes on to say that for writing on, the leaves of palm-trees were first used, and then the barks (*libri*) of certain trees. Some of the Egyptian papyrus-rolls are as old as the sixth dynasty.

[3] Nearchos, as we learn from Arrian's *Indika*, c. 15, was taken with surprise when he heard in India parrots talking like human beings. Pliny says (x. 58) that India produces this bird, which is called the *Septagen*, and that it salutes its masters, and pronounces the words it hears. If it fails to do so it is beaten on the head, which is as hard as its bill, with an iron rod, until it repeats the words properly. Ovid (*Amores*, ii. 6) calls the parrot the imitative bird from the Indians of the East. Another Indian bird, the Maina, which in size and appearance somewhat resembles the thrush, can be taught to speak with great distinctness. It is probably the bird which Aelian (*Hist. Anim.* xvi. 3) describes under the name of the *Kerkiôn*.

[4] Here Curtius makes a mistake, for not only is the rhinoceros bred in India, but the Indian species is the largest known, and its flesh was, by the Brahmans, allowed to be eaten, though most other kinds of animal food were interdicted. Ktêsias describes it, but very incorrectly, under the name of the one-horned ass. It is described also in Aelian's *History of Animals* (xvi. 20) in a passage sup-

tamed in Africa, and their size corresponds to their strength.[1] Gold is carried down by several rivers, whose loitering waters glide with slow and gentle currents.[2] The sea casts upon the shores precious stones and pearls, nor has anything contributed more to the opulence of the natives, especially since they spread the community of evil to foreign nations; for these offscourings of the

posed to have been copied from the lost *Indika* of Megasthenes. It is there called the Kartazôn. The fables about the unicorn had their source most probably in the fanciful account Ktêsias has given of the Indian wild ass. Aristotle, referring to it, says briefly: "We have never seen a solid-hoofed animal with two horns, and there are only a few of them that have one horn, as the Indian ass and the oryx." Kosmas Indikopleustes, who, as his surname shows, had visited India, gives in the eleventh book of his *Christian Topography* a description of the rhinoceros, illustrated with a picture of the animal which represents it as somewhat like a horse, with its nose surmounted by a pair of horns slightly curved. We know that the picture is meant to be that of the rhinoceros from the name being attached. Kosmas says that he had only seen the animal from a distance. He has also given a description and picture of the unicorn, an animal which he had never seen, but had delineated from four brazen statues of it which adorned a palace in Aethiopia. A single straight horn of great length is represented as springing up from the top of its head.

[1] Pliny (*Nat. Hist.* viii. 11) notes, like Curtius here, that India produced the largest elephants. He had, however, stated previously (vi. 22) that, according to Onesikritos, the elephants of Taprobane (Ceylon) were larger and more warlike than those of India. Many references to the Indian elphants occur in the classics. Arrian, in the thirteenth and fourteenth chapters of his *Indika*, describes the mode in which they were hunted, and other particulars regarding them. Polybios (v. 84) says that

the African elephants could neither endure the smell nor the trumpeting of their Indian congeners.

[2] Herodotos (iii. 106) says that gold was produced in great abundance in India, some of it washed down by the streams, and some dug out of the earth, but the greater part of it being the ant-gold surreptitiously procured. The heavy tribute levied by Darius on the Indian provinces (chiefly west of the Indus) was paid in gold-dust. We learn, notwithstanding, from Arrian that the companions of Alexander found that the Indian tribes they met with, which were numerous, were destitute of gold. The ant-gold produced in Dardistan seems therefore to have found its way rather to the provinces west of the Indus than to the Panjâb. Strabo (XV. i. 57), quoting Megasthenes, says that the rivers in India bring down gold-dust, a part of which is paid as a tax to the king. By the king is here meant Chandragupta (Sandrokottos), at whose court Megasthenes for some years resided. As the river Sôn, which in his time entered the Ganges at Palibothra (now Patna), was called poetically the *Hiranyavâha—i.e.* "bearing gold,"—we may assume that gold was found in the sands of that river. The grandson of Chandragupta, As'ôka, as is stated in the *Mahavansâ*, sent missionaries to preach Buddhism into the *gold district* of Suvarnabhûmi, a region which Turnour identified with Burma, but which Lassen took to be a maritime district situated somewhere in the west (*v.* his *Ind. Alt.* ii. pp. 236, 237; also i. 237, 238). Strabo (XV. i. 30) says that in the country of Sopeithês there were valuable mines both of gold and silver among the mountains.

boiling sea are valued at the price which fashion sets on coveted luxuries.[1]

The character of the people is here, as elsewhere, formed by the position of their country and its climate. They cover their persons down to the feet with fine muslin, are shod with sandals,[2] and coil round their heads cloths of linen (cotton). They hang precious stones as pendants from their ears, and persons of high social rank, or of great wealth, deck their wrist and upper arm with bracelets of gold. They frequently comb, but seldom cut, the hair of their head. The beard of the chin they never cut at all, but they shave off the hair from the rest of the face, so that it looks polished.[3] The luxury of their kings, or as they call it, their magnificence, is carried to a vicious excess without a parallel in the world.

When the king condescends to show himself in public his attendants carry in their hands silver censers, and perfume with incense all the road by which it is his pleasure to be conveyed. He lolls in a golden palanquin, garnished with pearls, which dangle all round it, and he is robed in fine muslin embroidered with purple and gold.

[1] Pliny, in the latter part of his 37th book, treats of the various kinds of precious stones found in India, and of the uses to which they are there applied. In some of the other books incidental notices of them are also to be met with, while his 9th book is full of details about the pearl. From Strabo (II. iii. 4) we learn that an adventurer, Eudoxos of Kyzikos, who had been sent by Ptolemy Physkôn, king of Egypt, to India, returned thence, bringing back with him some precious stones, some of which the Indians collect from among the pebbles of the river, and others of which they dig out of the earth. In his 15th book he states that India produces precious stones, as crystals, carbuncles of all kinds, and pearls. In Ptolemy's *Geography of India*, and in the *Periplûs of the Eythraean Sea* mention is made of the diamond, beryl, onyx, carnelian, hyacinth, and sapphire as precious stones of India. They mention also various pearl fisheries existing in and near India. Arrian states in his *Indika* (c. 8) that the pearl in India is worth thrice its weight in refined gold, and that it was called in the Indian tongue *Margarita*. This, which is also its classical name, may represent either the Sanskrit *manjari*, or the Persian *marwarîd*.

[2] Arrian, on the authority of Nearchos, states in his *Indika* (c. 16) that the Indians wear shoes of white leather elaborately trimmed, and having thick soles (or heels) to make them look taller.

[3] Strabo notes from Kleitarchos similar statements regarding the treatment of their hair by the Indians (XV. i. 71), and Arrian has noted the Indian practice (which is still in vogue) of dying the beard of a variety of colours.

Behind his palanquin follow men-at-arms and his body-guards, of whom some carry boughs of trees, on which birds are perched trained to interrupt business with their cries.[1]   The palace is adorned with gilded pillars clasped all round by a vine embossed in gold, while silver images of those birds which most charm the eye diversify the workmanship.   The palace is open to all comers even when the king is having his hair combed and dressed. It is then that he gives audience to ambassadors, and administers justice to his subjects.   His slippers being after this taken off, his feet are rubbed with scented ointments. His principal exercise is hunting; amid the vows and songs of his courtesans he shoots the game enclosed within the royal park.   The arrows, which are two cubits long, are discharged with more effort than effect, for though the force of these missiles depends on their light-ness they are loaded with an obnoxious weight.   He rides on horseback when making short journeys, but when bound on a distant expedition he rides in a chariot (howdah) mounted on elephants, and, huge as these animals are, their bodies are covered completely over with trappings of gold.   That no form of shameless profligacy may be wanting, he is accompanied by a long train of courtesans carried in golden palanquins, and this troop holds a separate place in the procession from the queen's retinue, and is as sumptuously ap-pointed.   His food is prepared by women, who also serve him with wine, which is much used by all the Indians.   When the king falls into a drunken sleep his

---

[1] "In the processions at Indian festivals (says Strabo, XV. i. 69) are to be seen wild beasts, as buffaloes, panthers, tame lions, and a multitude of birds of variegated plumage and of fine song." Aelian, in a passage copied most probably from Megasthenes, says that the favourite bird of the king of the Indians (Chandragupta no doubt) was the hoopoe. He carried it on · his wrist, and amused himself with it, and never tired gazing with ad-miration on its exquisite beauty, and the splendour of its plumage. The luxurious mode of life in which the Indian king (Chandragupta) indulged is described by Strabo (XV. i. 55) much in the same terms as by Curtius here. The native writings called *sutras* describe in like manner how the kings at festivals march out on elephants to the sound of all kinds of instruments, amid the scent of perfumes and clouds of frankin-cense.

courtesans carry him away to his bedchamber, invoking the gods of the night in their native hymns.[1]

Amid this corruption of morals who would expect to find the culture of philosophy? Notwithstanding, they have men whom they call philosophers, of whom one class lives in the woods and fields, and is extremely uncouth. These think it glorious to anticipate the hour of destiny, and arrange to have themselves burned alive when age has destroyed their activity, or the failure of health has made life burdensome. They regard death if waited for as a disgrace to their life, and when dissolution is simply the effect of old age funeral honours are denied to the dead body. They think that the fire is polluted unless the pyre receives the body before the breath has yet left it.[2] Those philosophers again who lead a civilised life in cities are said to observe the motions of the heavenly bodies, and to predict future events on scientific principles. These believe that no one accelerates the day of his death who can without fear await its coming.[3]

[1] Strabo adds the significant statement that the king at night is obliged from time to time to change his couch from dread of treachery. The frequency of changes in the succession shows that such a precaution was not unnecessary. If a woman put to death a king when he was drunk, she was rewarded by becoming the wife of his successor. From Athênaios we learn that among the Indians the king might not get drunk. The assertion made by Curtius that the Indians all use much wine is contrary to the testimony of Megasthenes, who said that they use it only on sacrificial occasions. Wine was no doubt imported into the marts of the Malabar coast, but the quantity must have been limited, and could only have been purchased by the rich. The Brahmans of the Ganges, from whom Megasthenes obtained much information, punished indulgence in intoxicating drinks with great severity. The Aryans of the Panjâb were less abstemious, and this led to dissen-sions, and a final rupture between them and their brethren of Iran. The wine used at sacrifices was the fermented juice of the plant called *soma*. When required for drinking it was mixed with milk.

[2] The diversity of views which prevailed in India regarding suicide was noticed by Megasthenes. The book of the law, in case of incapacity, regards it as meritorious, but the Buddhists altogether condemned it. Pliny (vi. 19) says that the Indian sages *always* ended their life by a voluntary death on the funeral pile.

[3] This is a very vague and meagre account of the opinions and practices of the Indian philosophers and ascetics. Other writers are more copious on the subject, as Strabo (XV.), Arrian (*Anab.* vii. 2, 3; *Indika*, 11), Diodôros (ii. 40), Plutarch (*Life of Alexander*, 64, 65). References are made to it by Mela, Suidas, Orosius, Philo, Ambrosius, Aelian, Porphyrius, and others (*v.* Notes W and H*h*).

They regard as gods whatever objects they value, especially trees, to violate which is a capital offence.[1] Their months they make to consist each of fifteen days, but they nevertheless assign to the year its full duration. They mark the divisions of time by the course of the moon, not like most nations when that planet shows a full face, but when she begins to appear horned, and hence, by fixing the duration of a month to correspond with this phase of the moon, they have their months one-half shorter than the months of other people.[2] Many other things have been related of them, but to interrupt with them the progress of the narrative I consider quite out of place.

Chapter X.—Campaign in the regions west of the Indus—Alexander captures Nysa, and visits Mount Merus—Siege of Mazaga, and its surrender

Alexander had no sooner entered India than the chiefs of various tribes came to meet him with proffers of service. He was, they said, the third descendant of Jupiter who had visited their country, and that while Father Bacchus and Hercules were known to them merely by tradition, him they saw present before their eyes. To these he accorded a gracious reception, and intending to employ them as his guides, he bade them to accompany him. But when no more chiefs came to surrender, he despatched Hephaestion and Perdiccas in advance with a part of his army to reduce whatever tribes declined his authority. He ordered them to proceed to the Indus and build boats for transporting the army to the other side of that river. Since many rivers would have to be crossed, they so constructed the vessels that, after being taken to pieces, the sections could be conveyed in waggons, and be again pieced together. He himself, leaving Craterus to follow with the infantry, pressed forward with

[1] Certain trees are still held sacred in India. The pipal, for instance, is thought to be frequented by bhûts, *i.e.* demons. [2] See Note X.

the cavalry and light troops, and falling in with the enemy easily routed them, and chased them into the nearest city. Craterus had now rejoined him, and the king, wishing to strike terror into this people, who had not yet proved the Macedonian arms, gave previous orders that when the fortifications of the city under siege had been burned, not a soul was to be left alive. Now, in riding up to the walls he was wounded by an arrow, but he captured the place, and having massacred all the inhabitants, vented his rage even upon the buildings.[1]

Having conquered this obscure tribe, he moved thence towards the city of Nysa. The camp, it so happened, was pitched under the walls on woody ground, and as the cold at night was more piercing than had ever before been felt, it made the soldiers shiver. But they were fortunate enough to have at hand the means of making a fire, for felling the copses they kindled a flame, and fed it with faggots, so that it seized the tombs of the citizens, which, being made of old cedar wood, spread the fire they had caught in all directions till every tomb was burned down. The barking of dogs was now heard from the town, followed by the clamour of human voices *from the camp*. Thus the citizens discovered that the enemy had arrived, and the Macedonians that they were close to the city.

The king had now drawn out his forces and was assaulting the walls, when some of the defenders risked an engagement. These were, however, overpowered with darts, so that dissensions broke out among the Nysaeans, some advising submission, but others the trial of a battle. Alexander, on discovering that their opinions were divided, instituted a close blockade, but forbade further bloodshed.

After a while they surrendered, unable to endure longer the miseries of a blockade. Their city, so they asserted, was founded by Father Bacchus, and this was in fact its

[1] Arrian says, however, that most of the inhabitants of this city, which belonged to the Aspasians, and was fortified by a double wall, escaped to the mountains.

origin. It was situated at the foot of a mountain which the inhabitants call Meros, whence the Greeks took the license of coining the fable that Father Bacchus had been concealed in the thigh of Jupiter. The king learned from the inhabitants where the mountain lay, and sending provisions on before, climbed to its summit with his whole army.[1] There they saw the ivy-plant and the vine growing in great luxuriance all over the mountain, and perennial waters gushing from its slopes. The juices of the fruits were various and wholesome since the soil favoured the growth of chance-sown seeds, and even the crags were frequently overhung with thickets of laurel and spikenard. I attribute it not to any divine impulse, but to wanton folly, that they wreathed their brows with chaplets of gathered ivy and vine-leaves, and roved at large through the woods like bacchanals; so that, when the folly initiated by a few had, as usually happens, suddenly infected the whole multitude,[2] the slopes and peaks of the mountain rang with the shouts of thousands paying their homage to the guardian divinity of the grove. Nay, they even flung themselves down full length on the greensward, or on heaps of leaves as if peace reigned all around. The king himself, so far from looking askance at this extemporaneous revel, supplied with a liberal hand all kinds of viands for feasting, and kept the army engaged for ten days in celebrating the orgies of Father Bacchus. Who then can deny that even distinguished glory is a boon for which mortals are oftener indebted to fortune than to merit, seeing that when they had abandoned themselves to feasting and were drowsed with wine the enemy had not even the courage to fall upon them, being terrified no less by the uproar and howling made by the revellers than if the shouts of warriors rushing to battle had rung

---

[1] Philostratos (ii. 4) says that Alexander did not ascend the mountain, but, though anxious to do so, contented himself with offering prayers and sacrifices at its base. He was afraid that the Macedonians on seeing the vines would be reminded of home, and have their love of wine revived after being accustomed to do without it.

[2] The Elzevir editor aptly quotes here Tacit. *H.* i. 55 : *Insita mortalibus natura, propere sequi, quae piget inchoare.*

in their ears. The like good fortune afterwards protected them in the presence of their enemies when on returning from the ocean they gave themselves up to drunken festivity.

From Nysa they came to a region called Daedala.[1] The inhabitants had deserted their habitations and fled for safety to the trackless recesses of their mountain forests. He therefore passed on to Acadira, which he found burned, and like Daedala deserted by the flight of the inhabitants. Necessity made him therefore change his plan of operations. For having divided his forces he showed his arms at many points at once, and the inhabitants taken by surprise were overwhelmed with calamities of every kind. Ptolemy took a greater number of cities, and Alexander himself those that were more important. This done, he again drew together his scattered forces. Having next crossed the river Choaspes,[2] he left Coenus to besiege an opulent city—the inhabitants called it Beira[3]—while he himself went on to Mazaga.

Assacanus, its previous sovereign, had lately died, and his mother Cleophis now ruled the city and the realm. An army of 38,000 infantry defended the city which was strongly fortified both by nature and art. For on the

---

[1] Justin (xii. 7) speaks of mountains which he calls *Daedali*, and these Cunningham (p. 52) takes to be Mount *Dantalok*, which is about three miles distant from *Palo-dheri* (or *Pelley*, as General Court calls it), a place forty miles distant from Pashkalavati (Hasht-nagar). In the spoken dialect, he adds, *Dantalok* becomes *Dattalok*, which the Greek *Daidalos* may fairly be taken to represent. I think, however, Alexander had not penetrated so far eastward as this identification implies. It has been taken by Müller to be Arrian's *Andaka* or *Andēla*, which he would therefore alter to *Daidala*. An Indian city called *Daidala* is mentioned by Stephanos Byz., and in Ptolemy's *Geography* another city of the same name is mentioned as belonging to the Kaspeiraioi (or Kash-

mirians), who in Ptolemy's days had extended their rule as far eastward as the regions of the Jamna. Abbot in his *Gradus ad Aornon* seems to identify Daedala with Doodial, and Acadira, which is mentioned immediately after, with Kaldura.

[2] Arrian calls this river the *Euaspla*. It is most probably the Kâmah or Kunâr river. Its name, *Cho-asp-es*, has one of the elements of the name of the people in its neighbourhood, the *Asp-asioi*. The prefix *cho* may, like *eu* or *su*, mean *river*, and Aspa means *a horse*, in Zend.

[3] Beira, it has been supposed, is the *Bazira* of Arrian; but as this has been on adequate grounds identified with Bazâr of the present day, the supposition is untenable. Bazâr lies too far east to suit the requirements.

east, an impetuous mountain-stream with steep banks on both sides barred approach to the city, while to south and west nature, as if designing to form a rampart, had piled up gigantic rocks, at the base of which lay sloughs and yawning chasms hollowed in the course of ages to vast depths, while a ditch of mighty labour drawn from their extremity continued the line of defence. The city was besides surrounded with a wall 35 stadia in circumference which had a basis of stonework supporting a super-structure of unburnt, sun-dried bricks. The brick-work was bound into a solid fabric by means of stones so interposed that the more brittle material rested upon the harder, while moist clay had been used for mortar. Lest, however, the structure should all at once sink, strong beams had been laid upon these, supporting wooden floors which covered the walls and afforded a passage along them.[1]

Alexander while reconnoitring the fortifications, and unable to fix on a plan of attack, since nothing less than a vast mole, necessary for bringing up his engines to the walls, would suffice to fill up the chasms, was wounded from the ramparts by an arrow which chanced to hit him in the calf of the leg. When the barb was extracted, he called for his horse, and without having his wound so much as bandaged, continued with unabated energy to pro-secute the work on hand. But when the injured limb was hanging without support, and the gradual cooling, as the blood dried, aggravated the pain, he is reported to have said that though he was called, as all knew, the son of Jupiter, he felt notwithstanding all the defects of the weak body.[2] He did not, however, return to the camp till he

---

[1] "How this arrangement was to prevent the upper part of the wall from settling down is a mystery as the text stands; and we can only suppose that (a) Curtius has not understood his authorities, or (b) has left out some important steps in the description, or (c) that the text is mutilated so as to conceal his real meaning."—*Alex. in India*, p. 107.

[2] Seneca (*Epistle* 59) puts almost the same words into his mouth : "All swear that I am the son of Jupiter, but this wound proclaims me to be a man." This is perhaps the occasion to which Plutarch refers when he states (*Alex.* 28) that Alexander when shot with an arrow turned in his pain to his attendants, and said: "This blood, my friends, is not the ichor

had viewed every thing and ordered what he wanted to
be done. Accordingly some of the soldiers began, as
directed, to destroy the houses outside the city and to
take from the ruins much material for raising a mole,
while others cast into the hollows large trunks of trees,
branches and all, together with great masses of rock.
When the mole had now been raised to a level with the
surface of the ground, they proceeded to erect towers ; and
so zealously did the soldiers prosecute the works, that
they finished them completely within nine days. These
the king, before his wound had as yet closed, proceeded
to inspect. He commended the troops, and then from
the engines which he had ordered to be propelled a great
storm of missiles was discharged against the defenders on
the ramparts. What had most effect in intimidating the
barbarians was the spectacle of the movable towers, for to
works of that description they were utter strangers.
Those vast fabrics moving without visible aid, they
believed to be propelled by the agency of the gods.[1] It
was impossible, they said, that those javelins for attacking
walls—those ponderous darts hurled from engines could
be within the compass of mortal power. Giving up therefore the defence as hopeless, they withdrew into the
citadel, whence, as nothing but to surrender was open to
the besieged, they sent down envoys to the king to sue
for pardon.[2] This being granted, the queen came with a
great train of noble ladies who poured out libations of
wine from golden bowls. The queen herself, having
placed her son, still a child, at Alexander's knees, obtained
not only pardon, but permission to retain her former
dignity, for she was styled queen, and some have believed

which blest immortals shed "—a
quotation from Homer.

[1] Pratt (ii. 276, n.) notices from
Athenaios that these movable towers
were invented by Dyades, pupil of
Polyeïdes, who accompanied Alexander.

[2] According to Arrian, the besieged
lost heart not from terror of the
engines, but on seeing their commander killed. We read in Caesar
that his engines produced a similar
effect on the minds of the Gauls.
They said that they could not believe
the Romans were warring without the
help of the gods since they were able
to move forward engines of so great a
height and with such celerity (*De Bell.
Gall.* ii. 31).

that this indulgent treatment was accorded rather to the charms of her person than to pity for her misfortunes. At all events she afterwards gave birth to a son who received the name of Alexander, whoever his father may have been.

Chapter XI.—Siege and capture of the Rock Aornis

Polypercon being despatched hence with an army to the city of Nora, defeated the undisciplined multitude which he encountered, and pursuing them within their fortifications compelled them to surrender the place. Into the king's own hands there fell many inconsiderable towns, deserted by their inhabitants who had escaped in time with their arms and seized a rock called Aornis. A report was current that this stronghold had been in vain assaulted by Hercules, who had been compelled by an earthquake to raise the siege. The rock being on all sides steep and rugged, Alexander was at a loss how to proceed, when there came to him an elderly man familiar with the locality accompanied by two sons, offering, if Alexander would make it worth his while, to show him a way of access to the summit. Alexander agreed to give him eighty talents, and, keeping one of his sons as a hostage, sent him to make good his offer. Mullinus (Eumenês ?), the king's secretary, was put in command of the light-armed men, for these, as had been decided, were to climb to the summit by a detour, to prevent their being seen by the enemy.

This rock does not, like most eminences, grow up to its towering top by gradual and easy acclivities, but rises up straight just like the *meta*, which from a wide base tapers off in ascending till it terminates in a sharp pinnacle.[1] The river Indus, here very deep and enclosed

---

[1] Curtius had no doubt here in his eye a passage from Livy, whose picturesque style was his exemplar: "Ipse collis est in modum metae in acutum cacumen a fundo satis lato fastigatus" (B. xxxvii. 27). In the centre of the Roman circus ran lengthways down the course a low wall, at each extremity of which were placed, upon a base, three wooden cylinders of a conical shape which were called *metae*—the goals.

between rugged banks, washes its roots. In another quarter are swamps and craggy ravines; and only by filling up these could an assault upon the stronghold be rendered practicable. A wood which was contiguous the king directed to be cut down. The trees where they fell were stripped of their leaves and branches which would otherwise have proved an impediment to their transport. He himself threw in the first trunk, whereupon followed a loud cheer from the army, a token of its alacrity, no one refusing a labour to which the king was the first to put his hand. Within the seventh day they had filled up the hollows, and then the king directed the archers and the Agrianians to struggle up the steep ascent. He selected besides from his personal staff [1] thirty of the most active among the young men, whom he placed under the command of Charus and Alexander. The latter he reminded of the name which he bore in common with himself.

And at first, because the peril was so palpable, a resolution was passed that the king should not hazard his safety by taking part in the assault.[2] But when the trumpet sounded the signal, the audacious prince at once turned to his body-guards, and bidding them to follow was the first to assail the rock. None of the Macedonians then held back, but all spontaneously left their posts and followed the king. Many perished by a dismal fate, for they fell from the shelving crags and were engulfed in the river which flowed underneath—a piteous sight even for those who were not themselves in danger. But when reminded by the destruction of their comrades what they had to dread for themselves, their pity changed to fear, and they began to lament not for the dead but for themselves.

[1] *Ex sua cohorte*—that is, from the retinue of pages in immediate attendance on the king. From this body officers were selected to fill the highest civil and military posts in the Macedonian state.

[2] Perhaps passed by a council of war or a general assembly of the troops. Philôtas, the son of Parmenion, was condemned to death by the Macedonian army.

And now they had attained a point whence they could not return without disaster unless victorious, for as the barbarians rolled down massive stones upon them while they climbed, such as were struck fell headlong from their insecure and slippery positions.   Alexander and Charus, however, whom the king had sent in advance with the thirty chosen men, reached the summit, and had by this time engaged in a hand-to-hand fight; but since the barbarians discharged their darts from higher ground, the assailants received more wounds than they inflicted.   So then Alexander, mindful alike of his name and his promise, in fighting with more spirit than judgment, fell pierced with many darts.   Charus, seeing him lying dead, made a rush upon the enemy, caring for nothing but revenge.   Many received their death from his spear and others from his sword.   But as he was single-handed against overwhelming odds, he sank lifeless on the body of his friend.[1]

The king, duly affected by the death of these heroic youths and the other soldiers, gave the signal for retiring. It conduced to the safety of the troops that they retreated leisurely, preserving their coolness, and that the barbarians, satisfied with having driven them down hill, did not close on them when they withdrew.   But, though Alexander had resolved to abandon the enterprise, deeming the capture of the rock hopeless, he still made demonstrations of persevering with the siege, for by his orders the avenues were blocked, the towers advanced, and the working parties relieved when tired.   The Indians, on seeing his pertinacity, by way of demonstrating not only their confidence but their triumph, devoted two days and nights to festivity and beating their national music out of their drums.   But on the third night the rattle of the drums ceased to be heard.   Torches, however, which, as the night was dark, the barbarians had lighted

---

[1] The readers of Virgil will be reminded by this episode of that of Euryalus and Nisus.   Curtius indeed seems to me to have borrowed his account of the death-scene from that poet rather than from any historical authority.

to make their flight safer down the precipitous crags, shed their glare over every part of the rocks.

The king learned from Balacrus, who had been sent forward to reconnoitre, that the Indians had fled and abandoned the rock. He thereupon gave a signal that his men should raise a general shout, and he thus struck terror into the fugitives as they were making off in disorder. Then many, as if the enemy were already upon them, flung themselves headlong over the slippery rocks and precipices and perished, while a still greater number, who were hurt, were left to their fate by those who had descended without accident. Although it was the position rather than the enemy he had conquered, the king gave to this success the appearance of a great victory by offering sacrifices and worship to the gods. Upon the rock he erected altars dedicated to Minerva and Victory. To the guides who had shown the way to the light-armed detachment which had been sent to scale the rock he honourably paid the stipulated recompense, even although their performance had fallen short of their promises. The defence of the rock and the country surrounding was entrusted to Sisocostus.

Chapter XII.—Alexander marches to the Indus, crosses it, and is hospitably received by Omphis, King of Taxila

Thence he marched towards Embolima, but on learning that the pass which led thereto was occupied by 20,000 men in arms under Erix,[1] he hurried forward himself with the archers and slingers, leaving the heavy-armed troops under the command of Coenus to advance leisurely. Having dislodged those men who beset the defile, he cleared the passage for the army which followed. The Indians, either from disaffection to their chief or to court the favour of the conqueror, set upon Erix during his flight and killed him. They brought his head and his

---

[1] He is called Aphrikês by Diodôros.

armour to Alexander, who did not punish them for their crime, but to condemn their example gave them no reward.   Having left this pass, he arrived after the sixteenth encampment at the river Indus, where he found that Hephaestion, agreeably to his orders, had made all the necessary preparations for the passage across it.

The sovereign of the territories on the other side was Omphis,[1] who had urged his father to surrender his kingdom to Alexander, and had moreover at his father's death sent envoys to enquire whether it was Alexander's pleasure that he should meanwhile exercise authority or remain in a private capacity till his arrival.   He was permitted to assume the sovereignty, but modestly forbore to exercise its functions.   He had extended to Hephaestion marks of civility, and given corn gratuitously to his soldiers, but he had not gone to join him, from a reluctance to make trial of the good faith of any but Alexander. Accordingly, on Alexander's approach, he went to meet him at the head of an army equipped for the field.   He had even brought his elephants with him, which, posted at short intervals amidst the ranks of the soldiery, appeared to the distant spectator like towers.

Alexander at first thought it was not a friendly but a hostile army that approached, and had already ordered the soldiers to arm themselves, and the cavalry to divide to the wings, and was ready for action.   But the Indian prince, on seeing the mistake of the Macedonians, put his horse to the gallop, leaving orders that no one else was to stir from his place.   Alexander likewise galloped forward, not knowing whether it was an enemy or a friend he had to encounter, but trusting for safety perhaps to his valour, perhaps to the other's good faith.   They met in a friendly spirit, as far as could be gathered from the expression of each one's face, but from the want of an interpreter to converse was impossible.   An interpreter was therefore

---

[1] Diodôros less accurately calls him Môphis.   His name *Ambhi* (in Sanskrit) is found in the Gana-pâtha, a genuine appendix to Pânini's *Gram-*mar (v. *Journal Asiatique,* Series VIII. tome xv. p. 235).   For remarks on the *coined money* which he gave to Alexander, see Note KA.

procured, and then the barbarian prince explained that he had come with his army to meet Alexander that he might at once place at his disposal all the forces of his empire, without waiting to tender his allegiance through deputies. He surrendered, he said, his person and his kingdom to a man who, as he knew, was fighting not more for fame than fearing to incur the reproach of perfidy.

The king, pleased with the simple honesty of the barbarian, gave him his right hand as a pledge of his own good faith, and confirmed him in his sovereignty. The prince had brought with him six-and-fifty elephants, and these he gave to Alexander, with a great many sheep of an extraordinary size, and 3000 bulls of a valuable breed, highly prized by the rulers of the country. When Alexander asked him whether he had more husbandmen or soldiers, he replied that as he was at war with two kings he required more soldiers than field labourers. These kings were Abisares and Porus, but Porus was superior in power and influence. Both of them held sway beyond the river Hydaspes, and had resolved to try the fortune of war whatever invader might come.

Omphis, under Alexander's permission, and according to the usage of the realm, assumed the ensigns of royalty along with the name which his father had borne. His people called him Taxiles, for such was the name which accompanied the sovereignty, on whomsoever it devolved. When, therefore, he had entertained Alexander for three days with lavish hospitality, he showed him on the fourth day what quantity of corn he had supplied to Hephaestion's troops, and then presented him and all his friends with golden crowns, and eighty talents besides of coined silver. Alexander was so exceedingly gratified with this profuse generosity that he not only sent back to Omphis the presents he had given, but added a thousand talents from the spoils which he carried, along with many banqueting vessels of gold and silver, a vast quantity of Persian drapery, and thirty chargers from his own stalls, caparisoned as when ridden by himself.

This liberality, while it bound the barbarian to his interests, gave at the same time the deepest offence to his own friends.   One of them, Meleager, who had taken too much wine at supper, said that he congratulated Alexander on having found in India, if nowhere else, some one worthy of a thousand talents.   The king, who had not forgotten what remorse he had suffered when he killed Clitus for audacity of speech, controlled his temper, but remarked that envious persons were nothing but their own tormentors.

Chapter XIII.—Alexander and Porus confront each other on opposite banks of the Hydaspes

On the following day envoys from Abisares reached the king, and, as they had been instructed, surrendered to him all that their master possessed.   After pledges of good faith had been interchanged, they were sent back to their sovereign.   Alexander, thinking that by the mere prestige of his name Porus also would be induced to surrender, sent Cleochares to tell him in peremptory terms that he must pay tribute and come to meet his sovereign at the very frontiers of his own dominions. Porus answered that he would comply with the second of these demands, and when Alexander entered his realm he would meet him, but come armed for battle.   Alexander had now resolved to cross the Hydaspes, when Barzaentes, who had instigated the Arachosians to revolt, was brought to him in chains, along with thirty captured elephants, an opportune reinforcement against the Indians, since these huge beasts more than the soldiery constituted the hope and main strength of an Indian army.

Samaxus was also brought in chains, the king of a small Indian state, who had espoused the cause of Barzaentes.   Alexander having then put the traitor and his accomplice under custody, and consigned the elephants to the care of Taxiles, advanced till he reached the river

Hydaspes, where on the further bank Porus had encamped to prevent the enemy from landing. In the van of his army he had posted 85 elephants of the greatest size and strength, and behind these 300 chariots and somewhere about 30,000 infantry, among whom were the archers, whose arrows, as already stated, were too ponderous to be readily discharged. He was himself mounted on an elephant which towered above all its fellows, while his armour, embellished with gold and silver, set off his supremely majestic person to great advantage. His courage matched his bodily vigour, and his wisdom was the utmost attainable in a rude community.

The Macedonians were intimidated not only by the appearance of the enemy, but by the magnitude of the river to be crossed, which, spreading out to a width of no less than four stadia in a deep channel which nowhere opened a passage by fords, presented the aspect of a vast sea. Yet its rapidity did not diminish in proportion to its wider diffusion, but it rushed impetuously like a seething torrent compressed into a narrow bed by the closing in of its banks. Besides, at many points the presence of sunken rocks was revealed where the waves were driven back in eddies. The bank presented a still more formidable aspect, for, as far as the eye could see, it was covered with cavalry and infantry, in the midst of which, like so many massive structures, stood the huge elephants, which, being of set purpose provoked by their drivers, distressed the ear with their frightful roars. The enemy and the river both in their front, struck with sudden dismay the hearts of the Macedonians, disposed though they were to entertain good hopes, and knowing from experience against what fearful odds they had ere now contended. They could not believe that boats so unhandy could be steered to the bank or gain it in safety. In the middle of the river were numerous islands to which both the Indians and Macedonians began to swim over, holding their weapons above their heads. Here they would engage in skirmishes, while each king endeavoured from the result of these minor conflicts to gauge the issue of the final struggle.   In the Macedonian army were Symmachus and Nicanor, both young men of noble lineage, distinguished for their hardihood and enterprise, and from the uniform success of their side in whatever they assayed, inspired with a contempt for every kind of danger.   Led by these, a party of the boldest youths, equipped with nothing but lances, swam over to the island when it was occupied by crowds of the enemy.

Armed with audacious courage, the best of all weapons, they slew many of the Indians, and might have retired with glory if temerity when successful could ever keep within bounds.   But while with contempt and pride they waited till succours reached the enemy, they were surrounded by men who had unperceived swum over to the island, and were overthrown by discharges of missiles. Such as escaped the enemy were either swept away by the force of the current or swallowed up in its eddies. This fight exalted the confidence of Porus, who had witnessed from the bank all its vicissitudes.

Alexander, perplexed how to cross the river, at last devised a plan for duping the enemy.   In the river lay an island larger than the rest, wooded and suitable for concealing an ambuscade.   A deep hollow, moreover, which lay not far from the bank in his own occupation, was capable of hiding not only foot-soldiers but mounted cavalry.   To divert, therefore, the attention of the enemy from a place possessing such advantages, he ordered Ptolemy with all his squadrons of horse to ride up and down at a distance from the island in view of the enemy, and now and then to alarm the Indians by shouting, as if he meant to make the passage of the river.[1]   For several days Ptolemy repeated this feint, and thus obliged Porus to concentrate his troops at the point which he pretended to threaten.

---

[1] It was Krateros, however, and not Ptolemy, who was left in charge of the division of the army which faced the camp of Pôros. Curtius has therefore here made a mistake.

The island was now beyond view of the enemy.[1] Alexander then gave orders that his own tent should be pitched on a part of the bank looking the other way, that the guard of honour which usually attended him should be posted before it, and that all the pageantry of royal state should be paraded before the eyes of the enemy on purpose to deceive them.　He besides requested Attalus, who was about his own age, and not unlike him in form and feature, especially when seen from a distance, to wear the royal mantle, and so make it appear as if the king in person was guarding that part of the bank without any intention of crossing the river.　The state of the weather at first hindered, but afterwards favoured, the execution of this design, fortune making even untoward circumstances turn out to his ultimate advantage.　For when the enemy was busy watching the troops under Ptolemy which occupied the bank lower down, and Alexander with the rest of his forces was making ready to cross the river and reach the land over against the island already mentioned, a storm poured down torrents of rain, against which even those under cover could scarcely protect themselves. The soldiers, overcome by the fury of the elements, deserted the boats and ships, and fled back for safety to land, but the din occasioned by their hurry and confusion could not be heard by the enemy amid the roar of the tempest.　All of a sudden the rain then ceased, but clouds so dense overspread the sky that they hid the light, and made it scarcely possible for men conversing together to see each other's faces.

Any other leader but Alexander would have been appalled by the darkness drawn over the face of heaven just when he was starting on a voyage across an unknown river, with the enemy perhaps guarding the very bank to

---

[1] That is, Pôros had been enticed down the bank so far that the island which lay where the passage was really to be made was no longer visible.　Curtius says nothing of the other island on which the Macedonians landed under the erroneous impression that they had gained the bank of the river, and Diodôros is equally silent.

which his men were blindly and imprudently directing their course. But the king deriving glory from danger and regarding the darkness which terrified others as his opportunity, gave the signal that all should embark in silence, and ordered that the galley which carried himself should be the first to be run aground on the other side. The bank, however, towards which they steered was not occupied by the enemy, for Porus was in fact still intently watching Ptolemy only. Hence all the ships made the passage in safety except just one, which stuck on a rock whither it had been driven by the wind. Alexander then ordered the soldiers to take their arms and to fall into their ranks.

Chapter XIV.—Battle with Porus on the left bank of the Hydaspes—Porus being defeated surrenders

He was already in full march at the head of his army, which he had divided into two columns, when the tidings reached Porus that the bank was occupied by a military force, and that the crisis of his fortunes was now imminent. In keeping with the infirmity of our nature, which makes us ever hope the best, he at first indulged the belief that this was his ally Abisares come to help him in the war as had been agreed upon. But soon after, when the sky had become clearer, and showed the ranks to be those of the enemy, he sent 100 chariots and 4000 horse to obstruct their advance. The command of this detachment he gave to his brother Hages.[1] Its main strength lay in the chariots, each of which was drawn by four horses and carried six men, of whom two were shield-bearers, two, archers posted on each side of the chariot, and the other two, charioteers, as well as men-at-arms, for when the fighting was at close-quarters they dropped the reins and hurled dart after dart against the enemy.

But on this particular day these chariots proved to be

---

[1] According to Arrian this force was commanded by the son of Pôros.

scarcely of any service, for the storm of rain, which, as already said, was of extraordinary violence, had made the ground slippery, and unfit for horses to ride over, while the chariots kept sticking in the muddy sloughs formed by the rain, and proved almost immovable from their great weight. Alexander, on the other hand, charged with the utmost vigour, because his troops were lightly armed and unencumbered. The Scythians and Dahae first of all attacked the Indians, and then the king launched Perdiccas with his horse upon their right wing. The fighting had now become hot everywhere, when the drivers of the chariots rode at full speed into the midst of the battle, thinking they could thus most effectively succour their friends. It would be hard to say which side suffered most from this charge, for the Macedonian foot-soldiers, who were exposed to the first shock of the onset, were trampled down, while the charioteers were hurled from their seats, when the chariots in rushing into action jolted over broken and slippery ground. Some again of the horses took fright and precipitated the carriages not only into the sloughs and pools of water, but even into the river itself.

A few which were driven off the field by the darts of the enemy made their way to Porus, who was making most energetic preparations for the contest. As soon as he saw his chariots scattered amid his ranks, and wandering about without their drivers, he distributed his elephants to his friends who were nearest him. Behind them he had posted the infantry and the archers and the men who beat the drums, the instruments which the Indians use instead of trumpets to produce their war music. The rattle of these instruments does not in the least alarm the elephants, their ears, through long familiarity, being deadened to the sound. An image of Hercules was borne in front of the line of infantry, and this acted as the strongest of all incentives to make the soldiers fight well. To desert the bearers of this image was reckoned a disgraceful military offence, and they had even ordained death as a penalty for those who failed to bring it back from the battlefield, for the dread which the Indians had conceived for the god when he was their enemy had been toned down to a feeling of religious awe and veneration.

The sight not only of the huge beasts, but even of Porus himself, made the Macedonians pause for a time, for the beasts, which had been placed at intervals between the armed ranks, presented, when seen from a distance, the appearance of towers, and Porus himself not only surpassed the standard of height to which we conceive the human figure to be limited, but, besides this, the elephant on which he was mounted seemed to add to his proportions, for it towered over all the other elephants even as Porus himself stood taller than other men. Hence Alexander, after attentively viewing the king and the army of the Indians, remarked to those near him, " I see at last a danger that matches my courage. It is at once with wild beasts and men of uncommon mettle that the contest now lies." Then turning to Coenus, " When I," he said, "along with Ptolemy, Perdiccas, and Hephaestion, have fallen upon the enemy's left wing, and you see me in the heat of the conflict, do you then advance the right wing,[1] and charge the enemy when their ranks begin to waver. And you, sirs," he added, turning to Antigenes, Leonnatus, and Tauron, "must bear down upon their centre, and press them hard in front. The formidable length and strength of our pikes will never be so useful as when they are directed against these huge beasts and their drivers. Hurl, then, their riders to the ground, and stab the beasts themselves. Their assistance is not of a kind to be depended on, and they may do their own side more damage than ours, for they are driven against the enemy by constraint, while terror turns them against their own ranks."

Having spoken thus he was the first to put spurs to his horse. And now, as had been arranged, Coenus, upon seeing that Alexander was at close-quarters with

[1] See Note Y, Battle with Pôros.

P

the enemy, threw his cavalry with great fury upon their left wing. The phalanx besides, at the first onset, broke through the centre of the Indians. But Porus ordered his elephants to be driven into action where he had seen cavalry charging his ranks. The slow-footed unwieldy animals, however, were unfitted to cope with the rapid movements of horses, and the barbarians were besides unable to use even their arrows. These weapons were really so long and heavy that the archers could not readily adjust them on the string unless by first resting their bow upon the ground. Then, as the ground was slippery and hindered their efforts, the enemy had time to charge them before they could deliver their blows.

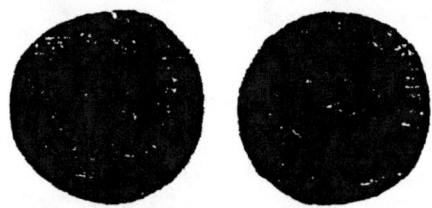

FIG. 11.—INDIAN BOWMAN.

The king's authority was in these circumstances unheeded, and, as usually happens when the ranks are broken, and fear begins to dictate orders more peremptorily than the general himself, as many took the command upon themselves as there were scattered bodies of troops. Some proposed that these bodies should unite, others that they should form separate detachments, some that they should wait to be attacked, others that they should wheel round and charge the enemy in the rear. No common plan of action was after all concerted. Porus, however, with a few friends in whom the sense of honour was stronger than fear, rallied his scattered forces, and marching in front of his line advanced against the enemy with the elephants. These animals inspired great terror, and their strange dissonant cries frightened not only the horses, which shy at everything, but the men also, and disordered the ranks, so that those who just before were victorious began now to look round them for a place to which they could flee. Alexander thereupon despatched against the elephants the lightly-armed Agrianians and the Thracians, troops more serviceable in skirmishing than in close combat. They assailed the elephants and their drivers with a furious storm of missiles, and the phalanx, on seeing the resulting terror and confusion, steadily pressed forward.

Some, however, by pursuing too eagerly, so irritated the animals with wounds that they turned their rage upon them, and they were in consequence trampled to death under their feet, thus warning others to attack them with greater caution. The most dismal of all sights was when the elephants would, with their trunks, grasp the men, arms and all, and hoisting them above their heads, deliver them over into the hands of their drivers. Thus the battle was doubtful, the Macedonians sometimes pursuing and sometimes fleeing from the elephants, so that the struggle was prolonged till the day was far spent. Then they began to hack the feet of the beasts with axes which they had prepared for the purpose, having besides a kind of sword somewhat curved like a scythe, and called a chopper, wherewith they aimed at their trunks. In fact, their fear of the animals led them not only to leave no means untried for killing them, but even for killing them with unheard-of forms of cruelty.

Hence the elephants, being at last spent with wounds, spread havoc among their own ranks, and threw their drivers to the ground, who were then trampled to death by their own beasts. They were therefore driven from the field of battle like a flock of sheep, as they were maddened with terror rather than vicious. Porus, meanwhile, being left in the lurch by the majority of his men, began to hurl from his elephant the darts with which he had beforehand provided himself, and while many were wounded from afar by his shot he was himself exposed as a butt for blows from every quarter. He had already received nine wounds before and behind, and became so faint from the great loss of blood that the darts were dropped rather than flung from his feeble hands. But his elephant, waxing furious though not yet wounded, kept charging the ranks of the enemy until the driver, perceiving the king's condition—his limbs failing him, his weapons dropping from his grasp, and his consciousness almost gone—turned the beast round and fled.

Alexander pursued, but his horse being pierced with many wounds fainted under him, and sank to the ground, laying the king down gently rather than throwing him from his seat.[1] The necessity of changing his horse retarded of course his pursuit. In the meantime the brother of Taxiles, the Indian King whom Alexander had sent on before, advised Porus not to persist in holding out to the last extremity, but to surrender himself to the conqueror.[2] Porus, however, though his strength was exhausted, and his blood nearly spent, yet roused himself at the well-known voice, and said, " I recognise the brother of Taxiles, who gave up his throne and kingdom." Therewith he flung at him the one dart that had not slipped from his grasp, and flung it too with such force that it pierced right through his back to his chest.[3]

[1] Boukephalos was no doubt the horse to which Curtius here refers, but according to some accounts that famous steed was not in the battle. Curtius here follows Chares, as the following passage quoted from this writer by Aulus Gellius (*Noct. Attic.* v. 2) will show : " The horse of King Alexander was both by his head and by his name *Bucephalas* (*i.e.* ox-head). Cares has stated that he was bought for thirteen talents, and presented to King Philip. . . . Regarding this horse it seems worth recording that when caparisoned and armed for battle he would not suffer himself to be mounted by any one but the king. It is also told of this horse that in the Indian war when Alexander, mounted upon him, and performing noble deeds of bravery, had with too little heed for his own safety entangled himself amid a battalion of the enemy, where he was on all sides assailed with darts, his horse was stabbed with deep wounds in the neck and sides. Ready to expire, and drained of nearly all his blood, he nevertheless bore back the king from the midst of his foes at a most rapid pace ; and when he had conveyed him beyond reach of spears, he straightway dropped down, and having no further fear for his master's safety, he breathed his last as if with the consolation of human sensibility. Then King Alexander having gained the victory in this war, built a town on this spot, and in honour of his horse called it Bucephalon."

[2] Arrian says that the first messenger sent was Taxilês himself.

[3] According to Arrian, Taxilês escaped by a hasty flight.

Having roused himself to this last effort of valour, he began to flee faster than before, but his elephant, which had by this time received many wounds, was now, like himself, quite exhausted, so that he stopped the flight, and made head against the pursuers with his remaining infantry.

Alexander had now come up, and knowing how obstinate Porus was, forbade quarter to be given to those who resisted.[1]   The infantry therefore, and Porus himself, were assailed with darts from all points, and as he could no longer bear up against them he began to slip from his elephant.   The Indian driver, thinking the king wished to alight, made the elephant kneel down in the usual manner.   On seeing this the other elephants also knelt down, for they had been trained to lower themselves when the royal elephant did so.   Porus and his men were thus placed entirely at the mercy of the conqueror.   Alexander, supposing that he was dead, ordered his body to be stripped,[2] and men then ran forward to take off his breastplate and robes, when the elephant turned upon them in defence of its master, and lifting him up placed him once more on its back.

Upon this the animal was on all sides overwhelmed with darts, and when it was stabbed to death, Porus was placed upon a waggon.   But the king perceiving him to lift up his eyes, forgot all animosity, and being deeply moved with pity, said to him, " What the plague ! what madness induced you to try the fortune of war with me, of whose exploits you have heard the fame, especially when in Taxiles you had a near example of my clemency to those who submit to me ? "   He answered thus : " Since you propose a question, I shall answer with the freedom which you grant by asking it.   I used to think there was no one braver than myself, for I knew my own strength, but had not yet experienced thine.   The result

[1] Diodôros states, on the contrary, that Alexander checked the slaughter.

[2] This is scarcely probable. The incident is mentioned by no other writer.

of the war has taught me that you are the braver man, but even in ranking next to you, I consider myself to be highly fortunate." Being asked again how he thought the victor should treat him, " in accordance,", he replied, " with the lesson which this day teaches—a day in which you have witnessed how readily prosperity can be blasted."

By giving this admonition he gained more than if he had resorted to entreaty, for Alexander, in consideration of the greatness of his courage which scorned all fear, and which adversity could not break down, extended pity to his misfortunes and honour to his merits.[1] He ordered his wounds to be as carefully attended to as if he had fought in his service, and when he had recovered strength, he admitted him into the number of his friends, and soon after presented him with a larger kingdom than that which he had.[2] And in truth his nature had no more essential or more permanent quality than a high respect for true merit and renown ; but he estimated more candidly and impartially glory in an enemy than in a subject. In fact, he thought that the fabric of his fame might be pulled down by his own people, while it could but receive enhanced lustre the greater those were whom he vanquished.

[1] Curtius has here marred with his rhetoric and moral reflections the simple and dignified answer of Pôros, that he wished to be treated like a king. Lucan similarly has dilated into some twenty lines of rhetoric Caesar's famous words to the boatmen in the storm : "Fear not, you carry Caesar and his fortunes." Plutarch, both in his *Life of Alexander* and in his *De Ira Cohibenda* (c. 9), has stated the reply of Pôros in the same terms as Arrian.

[2] Cicero (*pro Marcello*) extols Alexander in the highest terms for acting thus towards his vanquished enemy ; and Seneca in his *De Clementia* follows in a similar strain.

NINTH BOOK

*Chapter I.—Alexander's speech to his soldiers after the
victory—Abisares.sends him an embassy*

ALEXANDER rejoicing in a victory so memorable, which
led him to believe that the East to its utmost limits had
been opened up to his arms, sacrificed to the sun,[1] and
having also summoned the soldiers to a general meeting,
he praised them for their services, that they might with
the greater alacrity undertake the wars that yet remained.
He pointed out to them that all power of opposition on
the part of the Indians had been quite overthrown in the
battle just fought. What now remained for them was a
noble spoil. The much-rumoured riches of the East
abounded in those very regions, to which their steps
were now bent. The spoils accordingly which they had
taken from the Persians had now become cheap and
common. They were going to fill with pearls, precious
stones, gold, and ivory, not only their private abodes, but
all Macedonia and Greece. The soldiers who coveted
money as well as glory, and who had never known his
promises to fail, on hearing all this, readily placed their
services at his command. He sent them away full of good
hope, and ordered ships to be built in order that when he

---

[1] Philostratos, in his life of Apollonios of Tyana, states that Alexander
dedicated likewise to the sun one of
the elephants of Pôros, the first of
them that deserted to his side, and
which he called *Ajax*, and also the
altars which he reared on the banks
of the Hyphasis to mark the limits of
his advance. As the same author
states that Apollonios saw *Ajax* still
alive at Taxila some 370 years later,
his veracity may be suspected.

had overrun all Asia, he might be able to visit the sea which formed the boundary of the world.

In the neighbouring mountains was abundance of timber fit for building ships, and the men in hewing down the trees came upon serpents of most extraordinary size.[1] There they also found the rhinoceros, an animal rarely met with elsewhere. This is not the name it bears among the Indians, but one given it by the Greeks, who were ignorant of the speech of the country.[2] The king having built two cities, one on each side of the river which he had lately crossed, presented each of the generals with a crown, in addition to a thousand pieces of gold. Others also received rewards in accordance either with the place which they held in his friendship, or the value of the services which they had rendered. Abisares, who had sent envoys to Alexander before the battle with Porus had come off, now sent others to assure him that he was ready to do whatever he commanded, provided only he was not obliged to surrender his person ; for he could neither live, he said, without having the power of a king, nor have that power if he were to be kept in captivity. Alexander bade them tell their master that if he grudged to come to Alexander, Alexander would go to him.

Chapter I. Continued.—Alexander advancing farther into the interior of India, passes through forests and deserts— Crosses the Hydraotes—Besieges and captures Sangala, and enters the kingdom of Sopithes, who receives him with great hospitality and shows him a dog and lion fight

After crossing a river some distance farther on, he advanced into the interior parts of India. The forests there extended over an almost boundless tract of country,

---

[1] See Note Z, Indian Serpents.
[2] The Sanskrit name of the rhin- oceros is *Ganda*, also *Gandaka* and *Gandânga*.

and abounded with umbrageous trees of stateliest growth, that rose to an extraordinary height. Numerous branches, which for size equalled the trunk of ordinary trees, would bend down to the earth, and then shoot straight up again at the point where they bent upward, so that they had more the appearance of a tree growing from its own root than of a bough branching out from its stem.[1] The climate is salubrious, for the dense shade mitigates the violence of the heat, and copious springs supply the land with abundance of water. But here, also, were multitudes of serpents, the scales of which glittered like gold. The poison of these is deadlier than any other, since their bite was wont to prove instantly fatal, until a proper antidote was pointed out by the natives.[2] From thence they passed through deserts to the river Hyarôtis, the banks of which were covered with a dense forest, abounding with trees not elsewhere seen, and filled with wild peacocks.[3] Decamping hence, he came to a town that lay not far off. This he captured by a general attack all round the walls, and having received hostages, imposed a tribute upon the inhabitants.[4] He came next to a great city—great at least for that region—and found it not only encompassed with a wall, but further defended by a morass.[5] The barbarians nevertheless sallied out to give battle,

---

[1] This is the *ficus Indica*, commonly called the banyan-tree, because of the frequent use made of its shelter by traders who dealt in grain, called in India *Banyans*. Strabo (XV. i. 21) describes this tree from Onesikritos, who saw it growing in the country of Mousikanos. Pliny also (*N. H.* xii. 11) describes the tree and its fruit, adding that it grows chiefly in the neighbourhood of the Acesines (*Chenâb*); see also Theophrastos, *De Plantis*, iv. 5, and Arrian's *Indika*, c. 11. Several English poets have made it the subject of their verse— Ben Jonson, Milton, Tickell, and Southey. Its stately stems rise in solemn grandeur like the basaltic pillars of Fingal's Cave, and with the over-arching boughs form a vast and wondrous dome—

"Where as to shame the temples decked By skill of earthly architect, Nature herself, it seems, would raise A minster to her Maker's praise."

[2] Ailianos (*H. A.* xii. 32) says that while the Indians knew the proper antidote against the bites of each kind of serpent, none of the Greek physicians had discovered any such antidote. See Note Z, Indian Serpents.

[3] See Note A*a*, Indian Peacocks.

[4] This must be the town which Arrian calls *Pimprama*, distant a day's march from Sangala. The accounts of the two historians are at variance, however, since Arrian says that the place surrendered without resistance.

[5] This place was Sangala, for which see Note M.

taking their waggons with them, which they fastened together each to each. For weapons of offence some had pikes and others axes, and they were in the habit of leaping nimbly from waggon to waggon if they saw their friends hard pressed and wished to help them. This mode of fighting being quite new to the Macedonians, at first alarmed them,[1] since they were wounded by enemies beyond their reach, but coming afterwards to look with contempt upon a force so undisciplined, they completely surrounded the waggons and began stabbing all the men that offered resistance. The king then commanded the cords which fastened the waggons together to be cut[2] that it might be easier for the soldiers to beset each waggon separately. The enemy after a loss of 8000 men withdrew into the town.[3] Next day the walls were escaladed all round and captured. A few were indebted for their safety to their swiftness of foot. Those who swam across the sheet of water when they saw the city was sacked, carried great consternation to the neighbouring towns, where they reported that an invincible army, one of gods assuredly, had arrived in the country.

Alexander having sent Perdiccas with a body of light troops to ravage the country, and given another detachment to Eumenes to be employed in bringing the barbarians to submission, marched himself with the rest of the army against a strong city within which the inhabitants of some other cities had taken refuge. The citizens sent deputies to appease the king's anger, but continued all the same to make warlike preparations. A dissension, it seems, had arisen among them and divided their counsels, some pre-

[1] Caesar's men were similarly alarmed on seeing for the first time the war chariots of the Britons : *perturbatis nostris novitate pugnae* (*Bell. Gall.* iv. 34). See also Livy, x. 28.

[2] Arrian mentions gaps between the waggons, but does not state that they were fastened together. Vegetius (*De re Militari*, iii. 10), however, observes : " All barbarians fasten their chariots together in a ring in the fashion of a camp, and thus keep themselves safe from surprise during the night."

[3] " It is impossible to compare the numbers given by Curtius and Arrian, as neither gives the total of killed, and the details of the numbers who fell in the separate operations of the siege are not so stated as to admit of comparison " (*Alex. in India*, p. 130).

ferring to submit to the last extremities rather than surrender, others thinking that resistance on their part would
be altogether futile.   But as no consultation was held in
common, those who were bent on surrendering threw open
the gates and admitted the enemy.   Alexander would
have been justified in making the advocates of resistance
feel his displeasure, but he nevertheless pardoned them all
without exception, and after taking hostages marched
forward to the next city.   As the hostages were led in
the van of the army, the defenders on the wall recognised
them to be their own countrymen, and invited them to a
conference.   Here they were prevailed on to surrender,
when they were informed of the king's clemency to the
submissive, and his severity if opposed.   In a similar way
he gained over other towns, and placed them under his
protection.

They entered next the dominions of King Sopithes,[1]
whose nation in the opinion of the barbarians excels
in wisdom, and lives under good laws and customs.
Here they do not acknowledge and rear children
according to the will of the parents, but as the officers
entrusted with the medical inspection of infants may
direct, for if they have remarked anything deformed or
defective in the limbs of a child they order it to be
killed.[2] In contracting marriages they do not seek an
alliance with high birth, but make their choice by the
looks, for beauty in the children is a quality highly
appreciated.

Alexander had brought up his army before the capital
of this nation where Sopithes was himself resident.   The
gates were shut, but as no men-at-arms showed themselves
either on the walls or towers, the Macedonians were in
doubt whether the inhabitants had deserted the city, or
were hiding themselves to fall upon the enemy by surprise.

[1] The better form of the name is
Sôphytes, which properly transliterates the Sanskrit original Saubhutu,
but see Biographical Appendix, s.v.
Sôphytes.

[2] According to Strabo the inspection was made when the child was two
months old. He notices that the practice of widow-burning was known here.

The gate, however, was on a sudden thrown open, and the Indian king with two grown-up sons issued from it to meet Alexander. He was distinguished above all the other barbarians by his tall and handsome figure. His royal robe, which flowed down to his very feet, was all inwrought with gold and purple. His sandals were of gold and studded with precious stones, and even his arms and wrists were curiously adorned with pearls. At his ears he wore pendants of precious stones which from their lustre and magnitude were of an inestimable value. His sceptre too was made of gold and set with beryls,[1] and this he delivered up to Alexander with an expression of his wish that it might bring him good luck, and be accepted as a token that he surrendered into his hands his children and his kingdom.

His country possesses a noble breed of dogs, used for hunting, and said to refrain from barking when they sight their game which is chiefly the lion.[2] Sopithes wishing to show Alexander the strength and mettle of these dogs, caused a very large lion to be placed within an enclosure where four dogs in all were let loose upon him. The dogs at once fastened upon the wild beast, when one of the huntsmen who was accustomed to work of this kind tried to pull away by the leg one of the dogs which with the others had seized the lion, and when the limb would not come away, cut it off with a knife. The dog could not even by this means be forced to let go his hold, and so the man proceeded to cut him in another place, and finding him still clutching the lion as tenaciously as before, he continued cutting away with his knife one part of him after another. The brave dog, however, even in dying kept his fangs fixed in the lion's flesh ; so great is the eagerness for

[1] "The Indians," says Solinus (c. 55), "rub down the beryl into hexagonal forms in order to impart vigour to the dull tameness of the colour by the reflection from the angles. Of the beryl the varieties are manifold." Pliny, from whom Solinus no doubt drew this information, states (xxxvii. 5) that beryls were seldom found elsewhere than in India, and that the Indians had discovered how to make counterfeit gems and especially beryls by staining crystal.

[2] See Note B*b*, Indian Dogs.

hunting which nature has implanted in these animals, as testified by the accounts transmitted to us.

I must observe, however, that I copy from preceding writers more than I myself believe, for I neither wish to guarantee statements of the truth of which I am doubtful, nor yet to suppress what I find recorded. Alexander therefore leaving Sopithes in possession of his kingdom, advanced to the river Hyphasis, where he was rejoined by Hephaestion who had subdued a district situated in a different direction. Phegeus,[1] who was king of the nearest nation, having beforehand ordered his subjects to attend to the cultivation of their fields according to their wont, went forth to meet Alexander with presents and assurances that whatever he commanded he would not fail to perform.

Chapter II.—Alexander obtains information about the Ganges and the strength of the army kept by Agrammes, king of the Prasians—His speech to the soldiers to induce them to advance to the Ganges

The king made a halt of two days with this prince, designing on the third day to cross the river, the passage of which was difficult, not only from its great breadth, but also because its channel was obstructed with rocks. Having therefore requested Phegeus to tell him what he wanted to know, he learned the following particulars: Beyond the river lay extensive deserts which it would take eleven days to traverse.[2] Next came the Ganges, the largest river in all India, the farther bank of which was inhabited by two nations, the Gangaridae and the Prasii,[3] whose king Agrammes[4] kept in the field for

---

[1] The ordinary and correct reading is not *Phegeus*, as in the text from which I translate, but *Phegelas*, which transliterates the Sanskrit *Bhagala*. See Biog. Appendix, *s.v.* Phegelas.

[2] A sandy desert stretches from the southern borders of the Panjâb almost to the Gulf of Kachh. The breadth of this desert from east to west is about 400 miles. In some places it is altogether uninhabited; in others villages and patches of cultivation are found thinly scattered. On the east it gradually gives way to the fertile parts of India.

[3] For Gangaridae see Note *Cc*, and for Prasii, Note *Dd*. The common reading of this name in the editions of Curtius is Pharasii.

[4] The name as given here seems

guarding the approaches to his country 20,000 cavalry and 200,000 infantry, besides 2000 four-horsed chariots, and, what was the most formidable force of all, a troop of elephants which he said ran up to the number of 3000.

All this seemed to the king to be incredible, and he therefore asked Porus, who happened to be in attendance, whether the account was true. He assured Alexander in reply that, as far as the strength of the nation and kingdom was concerned, there was no exaggeration in the reports, but that the present king was not merely a man originally of no distinction, but even of the very meanest condition. His father was in fact a barber, scarcely staving off hunger by his daily earnings, but who, from his being not uncomely in person, had gained the affections of the queen, and was by her influence advanced to too near a place in the confidence of the reigning monarch. Afterwards, however, he treacherously murdered his sovereign ; and then, under the pretence of acting as guardian to the royal children, usurped the supreme authority, and having put the young princes to death begot the present king, who was detested and held cheap by his subjects, as he rather took after his father than conducted himself as the occupant of a throne.

The attestation of Porus to the truth of what he had heard made the king anxious on manifold grounds ; for while he thought contemptuously of the men and elephants that would oppose him, he dreaded the difficult nature of the country that lay before him, and in particular, the impetuous rapidity of the rivers. The task seemed hard indeed, to follow up and unearth men removed almost to the uttermost bounds of the world. On the other hand, his avidity of glory and his insatiable ambition forbade him to think that any place was so far distant or inaccessible as to be beyond his reach. He did indeed sometimes doubt whether the Macedonians who had

less correct than the form in Diod. *Xandrames*, which can be referred to the Indian word *Chandramas*, mean- ing *moon-god*. See Biog. Appendix, s.vv. Xandrames and Sandrokottos.

traversed all those broad lands and grown old in battle-
fields and camps, would be willing to follow him through
obstructing rivers and the many other difficulties which
nature would oppose to their advance. Overflowing and
laden with booty, they would rather, he judged, enjoy
what they had won than wear themselves out in getting
more. They could not of course be of the same mind as
himself, for while he had grasped the conception of a
world-wide empire, and stood as yet but on the threshold
of his labours, they were now worn out with toil, and
longed for the time when, all their dangers being at length
ended, they might enjoy their latest winnings. In the
end ambition carried the day against reason ; and, having
summoned a meeting of the soldiers, he addressed them
very much to this effect :

"I am not ignorant, soldiers, that during these last
days the natives of this country have been spreading all
sorts of rumours designed expressly to work upon your
fears ; but the falsehood of those who invent such lies is
nothing new in your experience. The Persians in this
sort of way sought to terrify you with the gates of Cilicia,
with the plains of Mesopotamia, with the Tigris and
Euphrates, and yet this river you crossed by a ford, and
that by means of a bridge. Fame is never brought to a
clearness in which facts can be seen as they are. They
are all magnified when she transmits them. Even our
own glory, though resting on a solid basis, is more indebted for its greatness to rumour than to reality. Who
but till the other day believed that it was possible for us
to bear the shock of those monstrous beasts that looked
like so many ramparts, or that we could have passed the
Hydaspes, or conquered other difficulties which after all
were more formidable to hear of than they proved
to be in actual experience. By my troth we had long
ago fled from Asia could fables have been able to
scare us.

"Can you suppose that the herds of elephants are
greater than of other cattle when the animal is known to

be rare, hard to be caught, and harder still to tame?[1]   It is the same spirit of falsehood which magnifies the number of horse and foot possessed by the enemy; and with respect to the river, why, the wider it spreads the liker it becomes to a placid pool.   Rivers, as you know, that are confined between narrow banks and choked by narrow channels flow with torrent speed, while on the other hand the current slackens as the channel widens out.   Besides, all the danger is at the bank where the enemy waits to receive us as we disembark ; so that, be the breadth of the river what it may, the danger is all the same when we are in the act of landing.   But let us suppose that these stories are all true, is it then, I ask, the monstrous size of the elephants or the number of the enemy that you dread ? As for the elephants, we had an example of them before our eyes in the late battle when they charged more furiously upon their own ranks than upon ours, and when their vast bodies were cut and mangled by our bills and axes.   What matters it then whether they be the same number as Porus had, or be 3000, when we see that if one or two of them be wounded, the rest swerve aside and take to flight.   Then again, if it be no easy task to manage but a few of them, surely when so many thousands of them are crowded together, they cannot but hamper each other when their huge unwieldy bodies want room either to stand or run.   For myself, I have such a poor opinion of the animals that, though I had them, I did not bring them into the field, being fully convinced they occasion more danger to their own side than to the enemy.

"But it is the number, perhaps, of the horse and foot that excites your fears ! for you have been wont, you know, to fight only against small numbers, and will now for the first time have to withstand undisciplined multi-

---

[1] On the contrary, elephants are easy to tame. Arrian in his *Indica* (c. 13, 14) has described the manner both of trapping and taming them. The same methods are still employed, with only slight variations. See also Pliny, viii. 8-10; Diodôros, iii. 26 ; Ailianos, viii. 10 and 15, and x. 10 ; and Tzetzes, *Chiliad*, iv. 122.

tudes! The river Granicus is a witness of the courage of
the Macedonians unconquered in fighting against odds;[1]
so too is Cilicia deluged with the blood of the Persians,
and Arbela, where the plains are strewn with the bones of
your vanquished foes. It is too late, now that you have
depopulated Asia by your victories, to begin counting the
enemy's legions. When we were crossing the Hellespont,
it was then we should have thought about the smallness of
our numbers, for now Scythians follow us, Bactrian troops
are here to assist us, Dahans and Sogdians are serving in
our ranks. But it is not in such a throng I put my trust.
It is to your hands, Macedonians, I look. It is your
valour I take as the gage and surety of the deeds I mean
to perform.

"As long as it is with you I shall stand in battle, I
count not the number either of my own or the enemy's
army. Do ye only, I entreat, keep your minds full of
alacrity and confidence. We are not standing on the
threshold of our enterprise and our labours, but at their
very close. We have already reached the sunrise and
the ocean, and unless your sloth and cowardice prevent,
we shall thence return in triumph to our native land,
having conquered the earth to its remotest bounds. Act
not then like foolish husbandmen who, when their crops
are ripe, loose them out of hand from sheer indolence to
gather them. The prizes before you are greater than the
risks, for the country to be invaded not only teems with
wealth, but is at the same time feebly defended. So
then I lead you not so much to glory as to plunder.
You have earned the right to carry back to your own
country the riches which that sea casts upon its shores;
and it would ill become you if through fear you should
leave anything unattempted or unperformed. I conjure
you then by that glory of yours whereby ye soar above
the topmost pinnacle of human greatness—I beseech you

[1] There was no great disparity of numbers in the battle of the Graníkos between the Greeks and Persians, 35,000 on Alexander's side and 40,000 on the other.

by my services unto you, and yours unto me (a strife in which we still contend unconquered), that ye desert not your foster-son, your fellow-soldier, not to say your king, just at the moment when he is approaching the limits of the inhabited world.

"All things else you have done at my orders—for this one thing I shall hold myself to be your debtor. I, who never ordered you upon any service in which I did not place myself in the fore-front of the danger, I who have often with mine own buckler covered you in battle, now entreat you not to shatter the palm which is already in my grasp, and by which, if I may so speak without incurring the ill-will of heaven, I shall become the equal of Hercules and Father Bacchus. Grant this to my entreaties, and break at last your obstinate silence. Where is that familiar shout, the wonted token of your alacrity? Where are the cheerful looks of my Macedonians? I do not recognise you, soldiers, and, methinks, I seem not to be recognised by you. I have all along been knocking at deaf ears. I am trying to rouse hearts that are disloyal and crushed with craven fears."

When the soldiers, with their heads bent earthwards, still suppressed what they felt, "I must," he said, "have inadvertently given you some offence that you will not even look at me. Methinks I am in a solitude. No one answers me; no one so much as says me nay. Is it to strangers I am speaking? Am I claiming anything unreasonable? Why, it is your glory and your greatness we are asserting. Where are those whom but the other day I saw eagerly striving which should have the prerogative of receiving the person of their wounded king? I am deserted, forsaken, surrendered into the hands of the enemy. But I shall still persist in going forward, even though I should march alone. Expose me then to the dangers of rivers, to the rage of elephants, and to those nations whose very names fill you with terror. I shall find men that will follow me though I be deserted by you. The Scythians and Bactrians, once our foemen,

but now our soldiers—these will still be with me.[1]   Let
me tell you, I had die rather than be a commander on
sufferance.   Begone then to your homes, and go triumph-
ing because ye have forsaken your king![2]   For my part,
I shall here find a place, either for the victory of which
you despair, or for an honourable death."

*Chapter III.—Speech of Coenus on behalf of the army—
Alexander's displeasure at the refusal of the soldiers
to advance—He resolves to return—Raises altars as
memorials of his presence—Reaches the Acesines,
where Coenus dies—Reconciles Taxiles and Porus, and
then sails down stream*

But not even by this appeal could a single word be
elicited from any of the soldiers.   They waited for the
generals and chief captains to report to the king that the
men, exhausted with their wounds and incessant labours
in the field, did not refuse the duties of war, but were
simply unable to discharge them.   The officers, however,
paralysed with terror, kept their eyes steadfastly fixed on
the ground, and remained silent.   Then there arose, no
one knew how, first a sighing and then a sobbing, until,
little by little, their grief began to vent itself more freely
in streaming tears, so that even the king, whose anger
had been turned into pity, could not himself refrain from
tears, anxious though he was to suppress them.   At last,
when the whole assembly had abandoned itself to an
unrestrained passion of weeping, Coenus, on finding that
the others were reluctant to open their lips, made bold to

[1] So Caesar, when his soldiers,
terrified by the accounts they had
heard of the Germans, refused to
advance against them, said, that if
nobody else would go with him he
would set out with the Tenth Legion
alone (*Bell. Gall.* i. 40). Thirlwall
is of opinion that Alexander's threat
to throw himself on his Baktrian and
Skythian auxiliaries, and make the
expedition with them alone, most
likely misrepresents the tone which
he assumed.

[2] Cerealis addressed his men in
similar terms : " Go, tell Vespasian,
or Civilis and Classicus who are
nearer at hand, that you deserted
your leader on the field of battle"
(Tacitus, *H.* iv. 77).

step forward to the tribunal where the king stood, and signified that he had somewhat to say. When the soldiers saw him removing his helmet from his head—a custom observed in addressing the king—they earnestly besought him that he would plead the cause of the army.

"May the gods," he then said, "defend us from all disloyal thoughts ; and assuredly they do thus defend us. Your soldiers are now of the same mind towards you as they ever were in times past, being ready to go wherever you order them, ready to fight your battles, to risk their lives, and to give your name in keeping to after ages. So then, if you still persist in your purpose, all unarmed, naked and bloodless though we be, we either follow you, or go on before you, according to your pleasure. But if you desire to hear the complaints of your soldiers, which are not feigned, but wrung from them by the sorest necessity, vouchsafe, I entreat you, a favourable hearing to men who have most devotedly followed your authority and your fortunes, and are ready to follow you wherever you may go. Oh, sir! you have conquered, by the greatness of your deeds, not your enemies alone, but your own soldiers as well.

"We again have done and suffered up to the full measure of the capacity of mortal nature. We have traversed seas and lands, and know them better than do the inhabitants themselves. We are standing now almost on the earth's utmost verge, and yet you are preparing to go to a sphere altogether new—to go in quest of an India unknown even to the Indians themselves. You would fain root out from their hidden recesses and dens a race of men that herd with snakes and wild beasts, so that you may traverse as a conqueror more regions than the sun surveys. The thought is altogether worthy of a soul so lofty as thine, but it is above ours ; for while thy courage will be ever growing, our vigour is fast waning to its end.

"See how bloodless be our bodies, pierced with how many wounds, and gashed with how many scars! Our weapons are now blunt, our armour quite worn out. We have been driven to assume the Persian garb since that of our own country cannot be brought up to supply us. We have degenerated so far as to adopt a foreign costume. Among how many of us is there to be found a single coat of mail? Which of us has a horse? Cause it to be inquired how many have servants to follow them, how much of his booty each one has now left. We have conquered all the world, but are ourselves destitute of all things. Can you think of exposing such a noble army as this, all naked and defenceless, to the mercy of savage beasts, whose numbers, though purposely exaggerated by the barbarians, must yet, as I can gather from the lying report itself, be very considerable. If, however, you are bent on penetrating still farther into India, that part of it which lies towards the south is not so vast, and were this subdued you could then quickly find your way to that sea which nature has ordained to be the boundary of the inhabited world. Why do you make a long circuit in pursuit of glory when it is placed immediately within your reach, for even here the ocean is to be found. Unless, then, you wish to go wandering about, we have already reached the goal unto which your fortune leads you. I have preferred to speak on these matters in your presence, O King! rather than to discuss them with the soldiers in your absence, not that I have in view to gain thereby for myself the good graces of the army here assembled, but that you might learn their sentiments from my lips rather than be obliged to hear their murmurs and their groans." [1]

[1] " This speech, put into the mouth of Coenus, has a peculiar literary interest beyond the ordinary run of orations written for their leading characters by the rhetorical historians of antiquity. In the remaining works of the elder Seneca we have a *suasoria* or hortatory oration (see Mayor on Juvenal, i. 16) on this very subject, in which are arranged all the telling sentences that some of the most famous Roman rhetoricians could compose to suit the situation. The remarkable parallels found in this collection to the present speech of Curtius illustrates in a very striking way the artificial nature of these harangues, and show what a vast amount of labour this spirited and polished specimen probably took to produce. The corresponding speech in Arrian, v. 27, though less pointed than that in Curtius, is more natural and easy, and certainly far superior

When Coenus had made an end of speaking there arose from all parts of the audience assenting shouts, mingled with lamentations and confused voices, calling Alexander king, father, lord, and master. And now also the other officers, especially the seniors, who from their age possessed all the greater authority, and could with a better grace beg to be excused from any more service, united in making the same request. Alexander therefore found himself unable either to rebuke them for their stubbornness or to appease their angry mood. Being thus quite at a loss what to do, he leaped down from the tribunal and shut himself up in the royal pavilion, into which he forbade any one to be admitted except his ordinary attendants. For two days he indulged his anger, but on the third day he emerged from his seclusion, and ordered twelve altars of square stone to be erected as a monument of his expedition. He ordered also the fortifications around the camp to be drawn out wide, and couches of a larger size than was required for men of ordinary stature to be left, so that by making things appear in magnificent proportions he might astonish posterity by deceptive wonders.[1]

From this place he marched back the way he had come, and encamped near the river Acesines. There Coenus caught an illness, which carried him off.[2] The king was doubtless deeply grieved by his death, but yet he could not forbear remarking that it was but for the sake of a few days he had opened a long-winded speech as though he alone were destined to see Macedonia again. The fleet which he had ordered to be built was now riding in the stream ready for service. Memnon also had meanwhile brought from Thrace a reinforcement of 5000 cavalry, together with 7000 infantry sent by Harpalus.

to that put into the mouth of Alexander" (*Alexander in India*, p. 140, n. 5).

[1] See Note N, Alexander's Altars on the Hyphasis.

[2] Curtius is here in error as to the place of his death, for he died at the Hydaspês, as will be seen by a reference to Arrian, vi. 2. He is further in error, like Diodôros, in making the fleet start on its voyage from the Akesinês instead of from the Hydaspês.

He also brought 25,000 suits of armour inlaid with silver and gold, and these Alexander distributed to the troops, commanding the old suits to be burned.[1]   Designing now to make for the ocean with a thousand ships, he left Porus and Taxiles, the Indian kings who had been disagreeing and raking up old feuds, in friendly relations with each other, strengthened by a marriage alliance ; and as they had done their utmost to help him forward with the building of his fleet, he confirmed each in his sovereignty.   He built also two towns, one of which he called Nicaea, and the other Bucephala, dedicating the latter to the memory of the horse which he had lost.   Then leaving orders for the elephants and baggage to follow him by land, he sailed down the river, proceeding every day about 40 stadia, to allow the troops to land from time to time where they could conveniently be put ashore.[2]

[1] "It is recorded," said Colonel Chesney in his Simla lecture on Alexander, "that he sent to Greece for 20,000 fresh suits of armour. A suit of armour and arms probably weighed three-fourths of a maund (60 lbs.), and we may assume that with the arms a good many other articles were indented for at the same time.   Altogether we may take it that the requisition was for not less than from 20,000 to 30,000 mule loads — 30,000 laden mules to be despatched from Macedonia to the Satlej ! A large order. And this suggests another consideration. Alexander's army on the Satlej was 50,000 strong ; how about his lines of communication?   During the late Afghan war over 50,000 men crossed the frontier, yet I believe the general had never at any time more than 10,000 men in hand at the front ; the rest were swallowed up in holding obligatory posts and keeping up the line of communication.   Now if 40,000 men are needed for this purpose to keep 10,000 effective in the front, when the distance to be covered was only 200 miles, what would be the force required to secure the line of communication between Macedonia and the army halted on the banks of the Satlej ?   The answer is to be found in the system of war pursued by Alexander's Greek generals, and garrisons were left at certain points on the road ; and where complete submission was made, the enemy was left in possession of his country and converted into an ally.   But when the resistance was obstinate Alexander left no enemies behind."   As Alexander led into India 120,000 men, Colonel Chesney's estimate that he had only 50,000 at the Hyphasis (which he calls the Satlej) must surely be far below the mark.

[2] Yet Pliny (vi. 17) says that though Alexander sailed on the Indus never less than 600 stadia per day, he took more than five months to complete the navigation of it ! This would give the Indus a length of 12,000 miles !. Aristoboulos said the navigation occupied ten months, but we may strike off a month from this estimate.   The voyage began near the end of October 326 B.C. The distance from the starting-point to the sea by the course of the river is between eight and nine hundred British miles.

Chapter IV.—Alexander subdues various tribes on his way to the Indus—Disasters to his fleet at the meeting of the rivers—His campaign against the Sudracae and Malli—Assails their chief stronghold and is left standing alone on the wall

Thus he came at length into the country where the river Hydaspes falls into the Acesines, and thence flows down to the territories of the Sibi.[1] These people allege that their ancestors belonged to the army of Hercules, and that being left behind on account of sickness had possessed themselves of the seats which their posterity now occupied. They dressed themselves with the skins of wild beasts, and had clubs for their weapons. They showed besides many other traces of their origin, though in the course of time Greek manners and institutions had grown obsolete. He landed among them, and marching a distance of 250 stadia into the country beyond their borders, laid it waste, and took its capital town by an assault made against the walls all round. The nation, consisting of 40,000 foot-soldiers, had been drawn up along the bank of the river to oppose his landing, but he nevertheless crossed the stream, put the enemy to flight, and, having stormed the town, compelled all who were shut up within its walls to surrender. Those who were of military age were put to the sword, and the rest were sold as slaves.

He then laid siege to another town, but the defenders made so gallant a resistance that he was repulsed with the loss of many of his Macedonians.[2] He persevered, however, with the siege till the inhabitants, despairing of their safety, set fire to their houses, and cast themselves along with their wives and children into the flames. War then showed itself in a new form, for while the inhabitants were destroying their city by spreading the flames, the enemy were striving to save it by quenching

[1] See Note E*e*, The Sibi. [2] See Note F*f*, The Agalassians.

them, so completely does war invert natural relations. The citadel of the town had escaped damage, and Alexander accordingly left a garrison behind in it. He was himself conveyed by means of boats around the fortress, for the three largest rivers in India (if we except the Ganges) washed the line of its fortifications. The Indus on the north flows close up to it, and on the south the Acesines unites with the Hydaspes.[1]

But the meeting of the rivers makes the waters swell in great billows like those of the ocean, and the navigable way is compressed into a narrow channel by extensive mud-banks kept continually shifting by the force of the confluent waters. When the waves, therefore, in thick succession dashed against the vessels, beating both on their prows and sides, the sailors were obliged to take in sail; but partly from their own flurry, and partly from the force of the currents, they were unable to execute their orders in time, and before the eyes of all two of the large ships were engulphed in the stream. The smaller craft, however, though they also were unmanageable, were driven on shore without sustaining injury. The ship which had the king himself on board was caught in eddies of the greatest violence, and by their force was irresistibly driven athwart and whirled onward without answering the helm.

He had already stripped off his clothes preparatory to throwing himself into the river, while his friends were swimming about not far off ready to pick him up, but as it was evident that the danger was about equal whether he threw himself into the water or remained on board, the boatmen vied with each other in stretching to their oars, and made every exertion possible for human beings to force their vessel through the raging surges. It then seemed as though the waves were being cloven asunder,

[1] Curtius has here confounded the junction of the Hydaspes and Akesines with that of the Indus and the combined stream of the Panjâb rivers. The geography of the passage is inexplicable. Arrian has given a vivid description of the confluence, but does not indicate that Alexander's life was in danger from its perilous navigation.

and as though the whirling eddies were retreating, and the ship was thus at length rescued from their grasp. It did not, however, gain the shore in safety, but was stranded on the nearest shallows. One would suppose that a war had been waged against the river. Alexander there erected as many altars as there were rivers, and having offered sacrifices upon them marched onward, accomplishing a distance of thirty stadia.

Thence he came into the dominions of the Sudracae and the Malli, who hitherto had usually been at war with each other, but now drew together in presence of the common danger. Their army consisted of 90,000 foot-soldiers, all fit for active service, together with 10,000 cavalry and 900 war chariots. But when the Macedonians, who believed that they had by this time got past all their dangers, found that they had still on hand a fresh war, in which the most warlike nations in all India would be their antagonists, they were struck with an unexpected terror, and began again to upbraid the king in the language of sedition. "Though he had been driven," they said, "to give up the river Ganges and regions beyond it, he had not ended the war, but only shifted it. They were now exposed to fierce nations that with their blood they might open for him a way to the ocean. They were dragged onward outside the range of the constellations and the sun of their own zone, and forced to go to places which nature meant to be hidden from mortal eyes.[1] New enemies were for ever springing up with arms ever new, and though they put them all to rout and flight, what reward awaited them? What but mists and darkness and unbroken night hovering over the abyss of ocean? What but a sea teeming with

[1] This rhetorical passage will remind the readers of Virgil of his description of the zones (*Georg.* i. 231-251): "Five zones comprise the heaven . . . of which two, the frozen homes of green ice and black storms, stretch far away. . . . One pole is thrust down beneath the feet of murky Styx . . . where eternal night, wrapped in her pall of gloom, sits brooding in unending silence." The passage was probably, however, suggested by the lines of the sixth book of the *Aeneid*, 794-796: "He (Augustus Caesar) will stretch his sway beyond Garamantian and Indian. See, the land is lying outside the stars, outside the sun's yearly path."

multitudes of frightful monsters—stagnating waters in which expiring nature has given way in despair?"[1]

The king, troubled not by any fears for himself, but by the anxiety of the soldiers about their safety, called them together, and pointed out to them that those of whom they were afraid were weak and unwarlike; that after the conquest of these tribes there was nothing in their way, once they had traversed the distance now between them and the ocean, to prevent their coming to the end of the world, which would be also the end of their labours; that he had given way to their fears of the Ganges and of the numerous tribes beyond that river, and turned his arms to a quarter where the glory would be equal but the hazard less; that they were already in sight of the ocean, and were already fanned by breezes from the sea.[2] They should not then grudge him the glory to which he aspired. They would over-pass the limits reached by Hercules and Father Bacchus, and thus at a small cost bestow upon their king an immortality of fame. They should permit him to return from India with honour, and not to escape from it like a fugitive.

Every assemblage, and especially one of soldiers, is readily carried away by any chance impulse, and hence the measures for quelling a mutiny are less important than the circumstances in which it originates. Never before did so eager and joyous a shout ring out as was now sent forth by the army asking him to lead them forward, and expressing the hope that the gods would prosper his arms and make him equal in glory to those whom he was emulating. Alexander, elated by these acclamations, at once broke up his camp and advanced against the enemy, which was the strongest in point of numbers of all the Indian tribes. They were making active preparations for war, and had selected as their

---

[1] "Racine (*Alex.* v. i.), imitating the present passage, says: *des déserts que le ciel refuse d'éclairer, où la nature semble elle-même expirer*" (*Alex. in Ind.* p. 148).

[2] From which they were yet some 600 miles distant!

head a brave warrior of the nation of the Sudracae.[1] This experienced general had encamped at the foot of a mountain, and had ordered fires to be kindled over a wide circuit to make his army appear so much the more numerous.   He endeavoured also at times, but in vain, to alarm the Macedonians when at rest by making his men shout and howl in their own barbarous manner.

As soon as day dawned, the king, full of hope and confidence, ordered his soldiers, who were eager for action, to take their arms and march to battle.   The barbarians, however, fled all of a sudden, but whether through fear or dissensions that had arisen among them, there is no record to show.   At any rate, they escaped timeously to their mountain recesses, which were difficult of approach. The king pursued the fugitives, but to no purpose; however, he took their baggage.

Thence he came into the city of the Sudracae, into which most of the enemy had fled,[2] trusting for safety as much to their arms as to the strength of the fortifications. The king was now advancing to attack the place, when a soothsayer warned him not to undertake the siege, or at all events to postpone it, since the omens indicated that his life would be in danger.   The king fixing his eyes upon Demophon (for this was the name of the soothsayer), said: " If any one should in this manner interrupt thyself, while busied with thine art and inspecting entrails, wouldst thou not regard him as impertinent and troublesome ? "   " I certainly would so regard him," said Demophon.   Then rejoined Alexander, "Dost thou not think then that when I am occupied with such important matters, and not with the inspection of the entrails of

---

[1] Called the Oxydrakai by Arrian. See Note P. Curtius here differs from Diodôros, who says that the Syrakousai (Oxydrakai) and Malloi could not agree as to the choice of a leader, and ceased in consequence to keep the field together. Both these historians are silent as to the operations conducted by Alexander during his march from the junction of the Hydaspês and the Akesinês to the capital of the Malloi situated above the old junction of the united stream of these two rivers with the Hydraôtês.

[2] But according to Arrian, Strabo, and Plutarch, the city where Alexander was nearly wounded to death belonged to the Malloi.

cattle, there can be any interruption more unseasonable to me than a soothsayer enslaved by superstition?"[1] Without more loss of time than was required for returning the answer, he ordered the scaling-ladders to be applied to the wall, and while the others were hesitating to mount them, he himself scaled the ramparts.[2]

The parapet which ran round the rampart was narrow, and was not marked out along the coping with battlements and embrasures, but was built in an unbroken line of breastwork, which obstructed assailants in attempting to get over. The king then was clinging to the edge of the parapet, rather than standing upon it, warding off with his shield the darts that fell upon him from every side, for he was assailed by missiles from all the surrounding towers. Nor were the soldiers able to mount the wall under the storm of arrows discharged against them from above.[3] Still at last a sense of shame overcame their fear of the greatness of the danger, for they saw that by their hesitation the king would fall into the hands of his enemies. But their help was delayed by their hurry, for while every one strove to get soonest to the top of the wall, they were precipitated from the ladders which they overloaded till they broke, thus balking the king of his only hope. He was in consequence left standing in sight of his numerous army, like a man in a solitude, whom all the world has forsaken.

---

[1] Thirlwall, with good reason, regards this incident as a mere embellishment of the story. "It is certain," he says, "that even if Alexander believed in such things less than he appears to have done, he was too prudent to disclose his incredulity, and so throw away an instrument which a Greek general might so often find useful" (*Hist. of Greece*, vii. c. 54). The story is found in Diodôros also. If a fiction, it may have been suggested by the fact that Alexander on approaching Babylon, where he died, was warned by Chaldaean soothsayers not to enter that city. If true, Alexander had doubtless in his mind the words of Hector (*Iliad*, xii. 237-243), where he expresses his contempt for omens drawn from the flight of birds. Hannibal had a similar contempt, as appears from Cicero, *de Div.* ii.

[2] Curtius, like Plutarch, represents Alexander to have been wounded after he had scaled the *city* wall, and thence leaped down into the *city*. But this is a mistake. It was the wall of the *citadel* he scaled, and it was within the *citadel* he was wounded, as we learn both from Arrian and Diodôros.

[3] "Probably a piece of gratuitous padding put in by Curtius to heighten the effect of his picture. Nothing of the kind is found in Arrian or Diodôros" (*Alex. in India*, p. 151).

Chapter V.—Alexander is severely wounded by an arrow within the stronghold of the Sudracae—The arrow is extracted by Critobulus

By this time his left hand, with which he was shifting his buckler about, became tired with parrying the blows directed against him from all round, and his friends cried out to him that he should leap down, and were standing ready to catch him when he fell. But instead of taking this course, he did an act of daring past all belief and unheard of—an act notable as adding far more to his reputation for rashness than to his true glory. For with a headlong spring he flung himself into the city filled with his enemies, even though he could scarcely expect to die fighting, since before he could rise from the ground he was likely to be overpowered and taken prisoner. But, as luck would have it, he had flung his body with such nice poise that he alighted on his feet, which gave him the advantage of an erect attitude when he began fighting. Fortune had also so provided that he could not possibly be surrounded, for an aged tree which grew not far from the wall, had thrown out branches thickly covered with leaves, as if for the very purpose of sheltering the king. Against the huge bole of this tree he so planted himself that he could not be surrounded, and as he was thus protected in rear, he received on his buckler the darts with which he was assailed in front ; for single-handed though he was, not one of the many who set upon him ventured to come to close-quarters with him, and their missiles lodged more frequently in the branches of the tree than in his buckler.

What served him well at this juncture was the far-spread renown of his name, and next to that despair, which above everything nerves men to die gloriously. But as the numbers of the enemy were constantly increasing, his buckler was by this time loaded with darts, and his helmet shattered by stones, while his knees sank under him from the fatigue of his protracted exertions. On seeing this, they who stood nearest incautiously rushed upon him in contempt of the danger. Two of these he smote with his sword, and laid them dead at his feet, and after that no one could muster up courage enough to go near him. They only plied him with darts and arrows from a distance off.

But though thus exposed as a mark for every shot, he had no great difficulty in protecting himself while crouching on his knees, until an Indian let fly an arrow two cubits long (for the Indians, as remarked already, use arrows of this length), and pierced him through his armour a little above his right side. Struck down by this wound, from which the blood spirted in great jets, he let his weapon drop as if he were dying without strength enough left to let his right hand extract the arrow. The archer, accordingly, who had wounded him, exulting in his success, ran forward with eager haste to strip his body. But Alexander no sooner felt him lay hands on his person, than he became so exasperated by the supreme indignity, I imagine, of the outrage, that he recalled his swooning spirit, and with an upward thrust of his sword pierced the exposed side of his antagonist. Thus there lay dead around the king three of his assailants, while the others stood off like men stupefied.

Meanwhile he endeavoured to raise himself up with his buckler, that he might die sword in hand, before his last breath left him, but finding he had not strength enough for the effort, he grasped with his right hand some of the defending boughs, and tried to rise with their help. His strength was, however, inadequate even to support his body, and he fell down again upon his knees, waving his hand as a challenge to the enemy to meet him in close combat if any of them dared. At length Peucestas in a different quarter of the town beat off the men who were defending the wall, and following the king's traces came to where he was. Alexander on seeing him thought that he had come not to succour him in life, but to comfort him in his death, and giving way through sheer exhaustion, fell over on his shield.

Then came up Timaeus, and a little afterwards Leonnatus followed by Aristonus.[1] The Indians, on discovering that the king was within their walls, abandoned all other places and ran in crowds to where he was, and pressed hard upon those who defended him. Timaeus, one of such, after receiving many wounds and making a gallant struggle, fell. Peucestas again, though pierced with three javelin wounds, held up his buckler not for his own, but the king's protection. Leonnatus, while endeavouring to drive back the barbarians who were eagerly pressing forward, was severely wounded in the neck, and fell down in a swoon at the king's feet. Peucestas was also now quite exhausted with the loss of blood from his wounds and could no longer hold up his buckler. Thus all the hope now lay in Aristonus, but he also was desperately wounded, and could no longer sustain the onset of so many assailants. In the meantime the rumour that the king had fallen reached the Macedonians.

What would have terrified others only served to stimulate their ardour, for, heedless of every danger, they broke down the wall with their pickaxes, and where they had made an entrance burst into the city and massacred great numbers of the Indians, chiefly in the pursuit, no resistance being offered except by a mere handful. They spared neither old men, women, nor children, but held whomsoever they met to have been the person by whom the king had been wounded, and in this way they at length satiated their righteous indignation.

Clitarchus and Timagenes state that Ptolemy, who afterwards became a king, was present at this fighting, but Ptolemy himself, who would not of course gainsay his own glory, has recorded in his memoirs that he was away at the time, as the king had sent him on an expedition

[1] Timaeus and Aristonus are mentioned only by Curtius as among those who came first to Alexander's rescue. It is supposed that the Timaeus of Curtius is the same person as the Limnaios of Plutarch.

elsewhere. This instance shows how great was the carelessness of the authors who composed these old books of history, or, it may be, their credulity, which is just as great a dereliction of their duty. The king was carried into a tent, where the surgeons cut off the wooden shaft of the arrow which had pierced him, taking care not to stir its point. When his armour was taken off they discovered that the weapon was barbed, and that it could not be extracted without danger except by making an incision to open the wound. But here again they were afraid lest in operating they should be unable to staunch the flow of blood, for the weapon was large and had been driven home with such force that it had evidently pierced to the inwards.

Critobulus, who was famous for his surgical skill,[1] was nevertheless swayed by fear in a case so precarious, and dreaded to put his hand to the work lest his failure to effect a cure should recoil on his own head. The king observing him to weep, and to be showing signs of fear, and looking ghastly pale, said to him : " For what and how long are you waiting that you do not set to work as quickly as possible ? If die I must, free me at least from the pain I suffer. Are you afraid lest you should be held to account because I have received an incurable wound ? " Then Critobulus, at last overcoming, or perhaps dissembling his fear, begged Alexander to suffer himself to be held while he was extracting the point, since even a slight motion of his body would be of dangerous consequence. To this the king replied that there was no need of men to hold him, and then, agreeably to what had been enjoined him, he did not wince the least during the operation.[2]

When the wound had then been laid wide open and the point extracted, there followed such a copious discharge

<hr />

[1] Pliny (vii. 37) mentions a Critobulus who acquired great celebrity by extracting an arrow from the eye of Philip, Alexander's father. Arrian again says that some authors assigned the credit of the operation in Alexander's case to Kritodêmos, a physician of Kôs, but others to Perdikkas.

[2] So Marius in like circumstances forbade himself to be bound (Cicero, *Tusc. Disput.* ii. 22).

of blood that the king began to swoon, while a dark mist came over his eyes, and he lay extended as if he were dying. Every remedy was applied to staunch the blood, but all to no purpose, so that the king's friends, believing him to be dead, broke out into cries and lamentations. The bleeding did, however, at last stop, and the patient gradually recovered consciousness and began to recognise those who stood around him. All that day and the night which followed the army lay under arms around the royal tent. All of them confessed that their life depended on his single breath, and they could not be prevailed on to withdraw until they had ascertained that he had fallen into a quiet sleep. Thereupon they returned to the camp entertaining more assured hopes of his recovery.

Chapter VI.—Alexander recovers and shows himself to the army—His officers remonstrate with him for his recklessness in exposing his life to danger—His reply to their appeal

The king, who had now been kept for the space of seven days under treatment for his wound without its being as yet cicatrised, on hearing that a report of his death had gained a wide currency among the barbarians, caused two ships to be lashed together and his tent to be set up in the centre where it would be conspicuous to every one, so that he might therefrom show himself to those who believed him to be dead. By thus exposing himself to the view of the inhabitants he crushed the hope with which the false report had inspired his enemies. He then sailed down the river,[1] starting a good while before the rest of the fleet, lest the repose which his weak bodily condition still required should be disturbed by the noise of rowing. On the fourth day after he had embarked he reached a country deserted by its inhabitants, but fruitful

---

[1] The Hydraôtês or Râvi, which in those days joined the Akesinês below Multân.

in corn and well stocked with cattle. Here along with his soldiers he enjoyed a welcome season of rest.

Now it was a custom among the Macedonians that the king's especial friends and those who had the guard of his person watched before his tent during any occasional illness. This custom being now observed as usual, they all entered his chamber in a body. Alexander fearing they might be the bearers of some bad news, since they had all come together, enquired whether they had come to inform him that the enemy had that moment arrived. Then Craterus, who had been chosen by the others as their medium to let the king know the entreaties of his friends, addressed him in these terms: "Can you imagine," he began, "that we could be more alarmed by the enemy's approach, even if they were already within our lines, than we are concerned for your personal safety, by which, it seems, you set but little store? Were the united powers of the whole world to conspire against us, were they to cover the land all over with arms and men, to cover the seas with fleets, and lead ferocious wild beasts against us, we shall prove invincible to every foe when we have you to lead us. But which of the gods can ensure that this the stay and star of Macedonia will be long preserved to us when you are so forward to expose your person to manifest dangers, forgetting that you draw into peril the lives of so many of your countrymen? For which of us wishes to survive you, or even has it within his power? Under your conduct and command we have advanced so far that there is no one but yourself who can lead us back to our hearths and homes.

"No doubt while you were still contending with Darius for the sovereignty of Persia, one could not even think it strange (though no one wished it) that you were ever ready and eager to rush boldly into danger, for where the risk and the reward are fairly balanced, the gain is not only more ample in case of success, but the solace is greater in case of defeat. But that your very life should be paid as the price of an obscure village, which of your soldiers, nay, what inhabitant of any barbarous country that has heard of your greatness can tolerate such an idea? My soul is struck with horror when I think of the scene which was lately presented to our eyes.

"I cannot but tremble to relate that the hands of the greatest dastards would have polluted the spoils stripped from the invincible Alexander, had not fortune, looking with pity on us, interfered for your deliverance. We are no better than traitors, no better than deserters, all of us who were unable to keep up with you when you ran into danger; and should you therefore brand us all with dishonour, none of us will refuse to give satisfaction for that from the guilt of which he could not secure himself. Show us, we beseech you then, in some other way, how cheap you hold us. We are ready to go wherever you order. We solicit that for us you reserve obscure dangers and inglorious battles, while you save yourself for those occasions which give scope for your greatness. Glory won in a contest with inferior opponents soon becomes stale, and nothing can be more absurd than to let your valour be wasted where it cannot be displayed to view."

Ptolemy and others who were present addressed him in the same or similar terms, and all of them, as one man, besought him with tears that, sated as he was with glory, he would at last set some limits to that passion and have more regard for his own safety, on which that of the public depended. The affection and loyalty of his friends were so gratifying to the king that he embraced them one by one with more than his usual warmth, and requested them all to be seated.[1]

Then, in addressing them, he went far back in a review of his career and said: "I return you, most faithful and most dutiful subjects and friends, my most heartfelt thanks, not only because you at this time prefer my safety to

[1] Arrian, on the contrary, states, on the authority of Nearchos, that Alexander was annoyed by the remonstrances of his friends.

your own, but also because from the very outset of the war you have lost no opportunity of showing by every pledge and token your kindly feelings towards myself, so that I must confess my life has never been so dear to me as it is at present, and chiefly so, that I may long enjoy your companionship. At the same time, I must point out that those who are willing to lay down their lives for me do not look at the matter from my point of view, inasmuch as I judge myself to have deserved by my bravery your favourable inclinations towards me, for you may possibly be coveting to reap the fruit of my favour for a great length of time, perhaps even in perpetuity, but I measure myself not by the span of age, but by that of glory.

" Had I been contented with my paternal heritage, I might have spent my days within the bounds of Macedonia, in slothful ease, to an obscure and inglorious old age ; although even those who remain indolently at home are not masters of their own destiny, for while they consider a long life to be the supreme good, an untimely death often takes them by surprise. I, however, who do not count my years but by my victories, have already had a long career of life, if I reckon aright the gifts of fortune. Having begun to reign in Macedonia, I now hold the supremacy of Greece. I have subdued Thrace and the people of Illyria ; I give laws to the Triballi and the Maedi,[1] and am master of Asia from the shores of Hellespont as far south as the shores of the Indian Ocean. And now I am not far from the very ends of the earth, which when I have passed I purpose to open up to myself a new realm of nature—a new world. In the turning-point of a single hour I crossed over from Asia into the borders of Europe.[2] Having conquered both these continents in the ninth year of my reign, and in my twenty-eighth year, do you think I can pause in the task

[1] A Thracian tribe whose country is mentioned in Ptolemy's *Geography* as a *stratēgia*—that is, a province governed by a general of the army.

[2] That is when he crossed the Tanaïs (Jaxartês) to attack the Skythians. " Unus Pellaeo juveni non sufficit orbis."

of completing my glory, to which, and to which only, I have entirely devoted myself? No, I shall not fail in my duty to her, and wheresoever I shall be fighting I shall imagine myself on the world's theatre, with all mankind for spectators. I shall give celebrity to places before unnoted. I shall open up for all nations a way to regions which nature has hitherto kept far distant.

" If fortune shall so direct that in the midst of these enterprises my life be cut short, that would only add to my renown. I am sprung from such a stock that I am bound to prefer living much to living long.[1] Reflect, I pray you, that we have come to lands in the eyes of which the name of a woman is the most famed for valour. What cities did Semiramis build! What nations did she bring to subjection! What mighty works did she plan! We have not yet equalled the glorious achievements of a woman, and have we already had our fill of glory? No, I say. Let the gods, however, but favour us, and things still greater remain for us yet to do. But the countries we have not yet reached shall only become ours on condition that we consider nothing little in which there is room for great glory to be won. Do you but defend me against domestic treason and the plots of my own household,[2] and I will fearlessly face the dangers of battle and war.

" Philip was safer in the field of fight than in the theatre. He often escaped the hands of his enemies—he could not elude those of his subjects.[3] And if you examine how other kings also came by their end, you can count more that were slain by their own people than by their enemies. But now lastly, since an opportunity has presented itself to me of disclosing a matter which I have

---

[1] Referring to his descent from Achilleus, whose career was short but glorious.

[2] Alexander here refers to the plot of Hermoläos and the pages against his life.

[3] Philip was assassinated by Pausanias while entering the door of a theatre. The Elzevir editor aptly quotes an epigram on Henry IV. of France, to whom a saying was attributed *Duo protegit unus* :

" Gallorum Rex regna, inquis, duo protegit
    unus ;
    Protexêre tuum nec duo regna caput."

for a long time been turning over and over in my mind, I give you to understand that to me the greatest rewards of all my toils and achievements will be this, that my mother Olympias shall be deified as soon as she departs this life. If I be spared, I shall myself discharge that duty, but if death anticipate me, bear in memory that I have entrusted this office to you." With these words he dismissed his friends ; but for a good many days he remained in the same encampment.

Chapter VII.—The affair of Biton and Boxus at Baktra— Embassy from the Sudracae and Malli proffering sub- mission — Alexander entertains his army and the embassy at a sumptuous banquet — Single combat between a Macedonian and an Athenian champion

While these things were doing in India, the Greek soldiers who had been recently drafted by the king into settlements around Bactra disagreed among themselves and revolted, for the stronger faction, having killed some of their countrymen who remained loyal, had recourse to arms, and making themselves masters of the citadel of Bactra, which happened to be carelessly guarded, forced even the barbarians to join their party. Their leader was Athenodorus, who had also assumed the title of king, not so much from an ambition to reign as from a wish to return to his native country along with those who acknow- ledged his authority. Against his life one Biton, a citizen of the same Greek state as himself, but who hated him from envy, laid a plot, and having invited him to a banquet, had him assassinated during the festivities by the hands of a native of Margiana called Boxus. The day following Biton, in a general meeting which had been convoked, persuaded the majority that Athenodorus had without any provocation formed a plot to take away his life. Others, however, suspected there had been foul play on Biton's part, and by degrees this suspicion spread itself about among the rest.   The Greek soldiers, therefore, took up arms to put Biton to death should an opportunity present itself.

But the leading men appeased the anger of the multitude, and Biton being thus freed from his imminent danger, contrary to what he had anticipated, soon afterwards conspired against the very man to whom he owed his safety.   But when his treachery came to their knowledge they seized both Biton himself and Boxus.   The latter they ordered to be at once put to death, but Biton not till after he had undergone torture.   The instruments for this purpose were already being applied to his limbs when the soldiers, it is not known why, ran to their arms like so many madmen.   On hearing the uproar they made, the men who had orders to torture Biton desisted from their office, thinking that the object of the rioters, whom they had heard shouting, was to prevent them going on with their work.   Biton, stripped as he was, ran for protection to the Greeks, and the sight of the wretched man sentenced to death caused such a revulsion of their feelings that they ordered him to be set at liberty.   Having twice escaped punishment, he returned to his native country with the rest of those who left the colonies which the king had assigned to them.[1]   These things were done about Bactra and the borders of Scythia.

In the meantime a hundred ambassadors came to the king from the two nations we have before mentioned.[2] They all rode in chariots and were men of uncommon stature and of a very dignified bearing.   Their robes were of linen and embroidered with inwrought gold and purple.   They informed him that they surrendered into his hands themselves, their cities, and their territories, and that he was the first to whose authority and protection

---

[1] The incident is mentioned briefly by Diodôros (xvii. 99). The 3000 Greeks who left their colonies to return home suffered great hardships on the way, and were slain by the Macedonians after Alexander's death.

[2] The Sudracae and the Malli. They arrived while Alexander was still in camp near the confluence of the Hydraôtês with the Akesinês, where he had joined Hêphaistiôn and Nearchos.

they had intrusted their liberty which for so many ages they had preserved inviolate. The gods, they said, were the authors of their submission and not fear, seeing that they had submitted to his yoke while their strength was quite unbroken. The king at a meeting of his council accepted their proffer of submission and allegiance, and imposed on them the tribute which the two nations paid in instalments to the Arachosians.[1] He further ordered them to furnish him with 2500 horsemen, all which commands were faithfully carried out by the barbarians. After this he gave orders for the preparation of a splendid banquet to which he invited the ambassadors and the petty kings of the neighbouring tribes. Here a hundred couches of gold had been placed at a small distance from each other, and these were hung round with tapestry curtains which glittered with gold and purple. In a word he displayed at this entertainment all that was corrupt in the ancient luxury of the Persians as well as in the new-fangled fashions which had been adopted by the Macedonians, thus intermixing the vices of both nations.

At ·this banquet there was present Dioxippus the Athenian, a famous boxer,[2] who on account of his surprising strength was already well known to the king, and one even of his favourites. Some there were who from envy and malice used to carp at him between jest and earnest, remarking they had a full-fed good-for-nothing beast in their company, who when others went forth to fight would rub himself with oil and take exercise to get up his appetite. Now at the banquet a Macedonian called Horratus, who was by this time "flown with wine," began to taunt him in the usual style, and challenged him, if he

---

[1] A statement, as Thirlwall observes, hardly consistent either with the boasts of independence made by the two nations, or with their recorded actions.

[2] Athenaios (vi. 13) relates, on the authority of Aristoboulos, that this Dioxippos, the Athenian, whom he calls a *pankratiast*, when Alexander on a certain occasion was wounded, and the blood flowing, exclaimed: "This is ichor such as flows in the veins of the blessed gods." Ailianos in his *Hist. Var.* (x. 22) describes his combat with the Macedonian. Pliny (xxxv. 11) informs us that Dioxippos was painted as a victor in the Olympic *pancratium* by Aleimachus.

were a man, to fight him next day with his sword, after
which the king would judge of his temerity or of the
cowardice of Dioxippus. The terms of the challenge
were accepted by Dioxippus, who treated with contempt
the bravado of the insolent soldier. The king finding
next day that the two men were more than ever bent on
fighting, and that he could not dissuade them, allowed
them to do as they pleased. The soldiers came in crowds
to witness the affair, and among others Greeks who backed
up Dioxippus.[1]

The Macedonian came with the proper arms, carrying
in his left hand a brazen shield and the long spear called
the *sarissa*, and in his right a javelin. He wore also a
sword by his side as if he meant to fight with several
opponents at once. Dioxippus again entered the ring
shining with oil, wearing a garland about his brows,
having a scarlet cloak wrapped about his left arm, and
carrying in his right hand a stout knotty club. This
singular mode of equipment kept all the spectators for a
time in suspense, because it seemed not temerity but
downright madness for a naked man to engage with one
armed to the teeth. The Macedonian accordingly, not
doubting for a moment but that he could kill his adversary
from a distance, cast his javelin at him, but this Dioxippus
avoided by a slight bending of his body, and before the
other could shift the long pike to his right hand, sprang
upon him and broke the weapon in two by a stroke of
his club. The Macedonian, having thus lost two of his
weapons, prepared to draw his sword, but Dioxippus closed
with him before he was ready to wield it, and suddenly
tripping up his heels, knocked him down as with a blow
from a battering-ram. He then wrested his sword from
his grasp, planted his foot on his neck as he lay prostrate,

---

[1] It is uncertain whether the Macedonians were of the same blood as the Greeks. Their kings undoubtedly were, but Grote, influenced by his antipathy to Alexander, who had crushed the liberties of Greece, considered him little better than a barbarian, "who had at most put on some superficial varnish of Hellenic culture." See on this point Freeman's *Historical Essays*, vol. ii. pp. 192-201, 3rd ed.

and brandishing his club would have brained him with it, had he not been prevented by the king.

The result of the match was mortifying not only to the Macedonians, but even to Alexander himself, for he saw with vexation that the vaunted bravery of the Macedonians had fallen into contempt with the barbarians who attended the spectacle. This made the king lend his ear all too readily to the accusations of those who owed Dioxippus a grudge. So at a feast which he attended a few days afterwards a golden bowl was by a private arrangement secretly taken off the table, and the attendants went to the king to complain of the loss of the article which they themselves had hidden. It often enough happens that one who blushes at a false insinuation has less control of his countenance than one who is really guilty. Dioxippus could not bear the glances which were turned upon him as if he were the thief, and so when he had left the banquet he wrote a letter which he addressed to the king, and then killed himself with his sword. The king took his death much to heart, judging that the man had killed himself from sheer indignation, and not from remorse of conscience, especially since the intemperate joy of his enemies made it clear that he had been falsely accused.

Chapter VIII.—Alexander receives the submission of the Malli—Invades the Musicani and the Praesti, whose king Porticanus is slain—He next attacks King Sambus, many of whose cities surrendered—Musicanus having revolted is captured and executed—Ptolemy is wounded by a poisoned arrow in the kingdom of Sambus, but recovers—Alexander reaches Patala and sails down the Indus

The Indian ambassadors were dismissed to their several homes, but in a few days they returned with presents for Alexander which consisted of 300 horsemen, 1030 chariots each drawn by four horses, 1000 Indian bucklers, a great quantity of linen-cloth, 100 talents of steel,[1] some tame lions and tigers of extraordinary size, the skins also of very large lizards, and a quantity of tortoise shells.[2]   The king commanding Craterus to move forward in advance with his troops and to keep always near the river, down which he intended himself to sail, took ship along with his usual retinue, and dropping down stream came to the territories of the Malli.[3]   Thence he marched towards the Sabarcae,[4] a powerful Indian tribe where the form of government was democratic and not regal.   Their army consisted of 60,000 foot and 6000 cavalry attended by 500 chariots.

They had elected three generals renowned for their valour and military skill; but when those who lived near the river, the banks of which were most thickly studded with their villages,[5] saw the whole river as far as the eye could reach covered with ships, and saw besides the many thousands of men and their gleaming arms, they took fright at the strange spectacle and imagined that an army of the gods and a second Father Bacchus, a name famous in that country, were coming into their midst.   The shouts of the soldiers and the noise of the oars, together with the confused voices of the sailors encouraging each

---

[1] "The sword blades of India had a great fame over the East, and Indian steel, according to esteemed authorities, continued to be imported into Persia till days quite recent.   Its fame goes back to very old times.   Ktesias mentions two wonderful swords of such material that he got from the King of Persia and his mother.   It is perhaps the *ferrum candidum* of which the Malli and Oxydracae sent 100 talents' weight as a present to Alexander.   Indian iron and steel are mentioned in the *Periplus* as imports into the Abyssinian ports." See Yule's *Marco Polo*, i. p. 94.

[2] We learn from the *Periplus of the Erythraean Sea* that tortoise and other shells formed an important element in the ancient commerce of the East with the West.   For an account of Indian shells see *British*

India of the Edinburgh Cabinet Library, III. c. v. pp. 136-144.

[3] Alexander had, however, by this time taken their capital.   We learn from Arrian (*Indika*, c. 4) that their dominions extended to the junction of the Akesinês with the Indus.

[4] Lassen identifies this people with the *Sambastai* of Diodôros.   Orosius calls them the *Sabagrae*.   In Arrian the *Sambastai* appear as the *Abastanoi*, a name which transliterates the Sanskrit word *avasthâna*, which means, however, "a dwelling-place," and does not denote a people.   See note on Arrian, p. 155.

[5] Two other tribes are mentioned by Arrian as having sent deputies to Alexander while in camp near the confluence, the *Xathroi* and the *Ossadioi*, concerning whom see notes on Arrian, p. 156.

other, so filled their alarmed ears that they all ran off to the army and cried out to the soldiers that they would be mad to offer battle to the gods, that the number of ships carrying these invincible warriors was past all counting.[1] By these reports they created such a terror in the ranks of their own army that they sent ambassadors commissioned to surrender their whole nation to Alexander.

Having received their submission, he came on the fourth day after to other tribes which had as little inclination for fighting as their neighbours. Here therefore he built a town, which by his orders was called Alexandrea,[2] and then he entered the country of the people known as the Musicani.[3] While he was here he held an enquiry into the complaints advanced by the Parapamisadae against Terioltes,[4] whom he had made their satrap, and, finding many charges of extortion and tyranny proved against him, he sentenced him to death. On the other hand Oxyartes, the governor of the Bactriani, was not only acquitted, but, as he had claims upon Alexander's affections, was rewarded with an extension of the territory under his jurisdiction. Having thereafter reduced the Musicani, Alexander put a garrison into their capital, and marched thence into the country of the Praesti, another Indian tribe.[5] Their king was Porticanus, and he with a great body of his countrymen had shut himself up within a strongly-fortified city. Alexander, however, took it after a three days' siege. Porticanus, who had taken refuge within the citadel after the capture of the city, sent

---

[1] Their alarm would no doubt be increased by the sight of the many coloured flags of the vessels, as we may infer from the words of Pliny (xix. 1): "The first attempt at dyeing canvas with the costliest hues for dyeing wearing apparel was made in the fleets of Alexander the Great when he was navigating the river Indus, for then his generals and prefects had distinguished by differences of colour the ensigns of their vessels, and the natives along the shore were lost in amazement at the variety of their colours. It was with a purple sail Cleopatra came with Antony to Actium, and fled therefrom. This was the colour of the admiral's ensign."

[2] Chachar opposite Mithânkôt, a little below the great confluence. See Note on Arrian.

[3] See Note on Arrian, p. 156.

[4] Called Tyriaspès by Arrian. Oxyartes was Alexander's father-in-law.

[5] For the Praesti and Porticanus see Note to Arrian, p. 158.

deputies to the king to arrange about terms of capitulation. Before they reached him, however, two towers had fallen down with a dreadful crash, and the Macedonians having made their way through the ruins into the citadel, captured it and slew Porticanus, who with a few others had offered resistance.

Having demolished the citadel and sold all the prisoners, he marched into the territories of King Sambus, where he received the submission of numerous towns.[1] The strongest, however, of all the cities which belonged to this people, he took by making a passage into it underground. To the barbarians, who had no previous knowledge of this device for entering fortified places, it seemed as if a miracle had been wrought when they saw armed men rise out of the ground in the middle of their city almost without any trace of the mine by which they had entered being visible.[2] Clitarchus says that 80,000 Indians were slain in that part of the country, and that numerous prisoners were sold as slaves. The Musicani again rebelled, and Pithon being sent to crush them, brought the chief of the tribe, who was also the author of the insurrection, to the king, who ordered him to be crucified, and then returned to the river, where the fleet was waiting for him.

The fourth day thereafter he sailed down the river to a town that lay at the very extremity of the kingdom of Sambus. That prince had but lately surrendered himself to Alexander, but the people of the city refused to obey him, and had even closed their gates against him. The king, however, despising the paucity of their numbers, ordered 500 Agrianians to go close up to the walls and then to retire by little, in order to entice the enemy from the town, who would in that case certainly pursue under the belief that they were retreating. The Agrianians, after some skirmishing, suddenly showed their backs to the enemy as they had been ordered, and were hotly pur-

[1] See Note S.
[2] Aurengzêb captured Surât by a similar device, and to the great astonishment of the inhabitants.

sued by the barbarians, who fell in with other troops led by the king in person. The fighting was therefore renewed, with the result that out of the 3000 barbarians who were in the action, 600 were killed, 1000 taken prisoners, and the rest driven back into the city. But this victory did not end so happily as at first sight it promised to do, for the barbarians had used poisoned swords, and the wounded soon afterwards died; while the surgeons were at a loss to discover why a slight wound should be incurable, and followed by so violent a death. The barbarians had been in hopes that the king, who was known to be rash and reckless of his safety, might be in this way cut off, and in fact it was only by sheer good luck that he escaped untouched, fighting as he did among the very foremost.

Ptolemy was wounded in the left shoulder, slightly indeed, but yet dangerously on account of the poison, and his case caused the king especial anxiety. He was his own kinsman; some even believed that Philip was his father, and it is at all events certain that he was the son of one of that king's mistresses. He was a member of the royal body-guard, and the bravest of soldiers. At the same time, he was even greater and more illustrious in civil pursuits than in war itself. He lived in a plain style like men of common rank, was liberal in the extreme, easy too of access, and a man who gave himself none of the high airs so often assumed by courtiers. These qualities made it doubtful whether he was more loved by the king or by his countrymen. At all events, now that his life was in danger, he was for the first time made aware of the great affection entertained for him by the Macedonians, who by this time seem to have presaged the greatness to which he afterwards rose, for they showed as much solicitude for him as they did for Alexander himself. Alexander, again, though fatigued with fighting and anxiety, sat watching over Ptolemy, and when he wished to take some rest, did not leave the sick-room, but had his bed brought into it.

He had no sooner laid himself down than he fell into a profound sleep, from which, when he awoke, he told his attendants that in a vision he had seen a creature in the form of a serpent carrying in its mouth a plant, which it offered him as an antidote to the poison. He gave besides such a description of the colour of the plant as he was sure would enable any one falling in with it to recognise it. The plant was found soon afterwards, as many had gone to search for it, and was laid upon the wound by Alexander himself. The application at once removed the pain and speedily cicatrised the wound.[1] The barbarians finding themselves disappointed of their first hopes, surrendered themselves and their city.

Alexander marched thence into the Patalian territory. Its king was Moeres,[2] but he had abandoned the town and fled for safety to the mountains. Alexander then took possession of the place, and ravaged the surrounding country, from which he carried off a great booty of sheep and cattle, besides a great quantity of corn. After this, taking some natives acquainted with the river to pilot his way, he sailed down the stream to an island which had sprung up almost in the middle of the channel.[3]

Chapter IX.—Perils encountered on the voyage down the western arm of the Indus to the sea—Alexander returns from the mouth of the river to Patala

Here he was obliged to make a longer stay than he had anticipated, because the pilots, finding they were not strictly guarded, had absconded. He then sent out a party of his men to search for others. They returned without finding any, but his unquenchable ambition to

---

[1] According to Diodôros this happened in the neighbourhood of Harmatelia, for conjectures as to the position of which see Note T. Strabo says it happened in the country of the Oreitai.

[2] It has been thought this name may be constructed from *Maharâjah,* "great king." For identification of Patala see Note U.

[3] This island is called by Arrian Killouta, and by Plutarch Skilloustis. See Note on Arrian, p. 164.

see the ocean and reach the boundaries of the world, made him entrust his own life and the safety of so many gallant men to an unknown river without any guides possessed of the requisite local knowledge. They thus sailed on ignorant of everything on the way they had to pass. It was entirely left to haphazard and baseless conjecture how far off they were from the sea, what tribes dwelt along the banks, whether the river was placid at its mouth, and whether it was thereabouts of a depth sufficient for their war-ships. The only comfort in this rash adventure was a confident reliance on Alexander's uniform good fortune. The expedition had in this manner now proceeded a distance of 400 stadia, when the pilots brought to his notice that they began to feel sea-air, and that they believed the ocean was not now far off.

The king, elated by the news, exhorted the sailors to bend to their oars. The end of their labours, he said, for which they had always been hoping and praying, was close at hand; nothing was now wanting to complete their glory; nothing left to withstand their valour. They could now, without the hazard of fighting, without any bloodshed, make the whole world their own. Even nature herself could advance no farther, and within a short time they would see what was known to none but the immortal gods. He nevertheless sent a small party ashore in a boat in order to take some of the natives straggling about, from whom he hoped some correct information might be obtained. After all the huts near the shore had been searched, some natives at last were found hidden away in them. These, on being asked how far off the sea was, answered that they had never so much as heard of such a thing as the sea, but that on the third day they might come to water of a bitter taste which corrupted the fresh water. From this it was understood they meant the sea, whose nature they did not understand. The mariners therefore plied their oars with increased alacrity, and still more strenuously on the following day as they drew nearer to the fulfilment of their hopes.

S

On the third day they observed that the sea, coming up with a tide as yet gentle, began to mingle its brine with the fresh water of the river. Then they rowed out to another island that lay in the middle of the river, making, however, slower progress in rowing since the stream of the river was now beaten back by the force of the tide. They put in to the shore of the island, and such as landed ran hither and thither in quest of provisions, never dreaming of the mishap which was to overtake them from their ignorance of tides. It was now about the third hour of the day when the ocean, undergoing its periodic change, rose in flood-tide, and began to burst upon them and force back the current of the river, which being at first retarded, and then more violently repelled, was driven upward contrary to its natural direction with more than the impetuosity of rivers in flood rushing down precipitous beds. The men in general were ignorant of the nature of the sea, and so, when they saw it continually swelling higher, and overflowing the beach which before was dry, they looked upon this as something supernatural by which the gods signified their wrath against their rash presumption.

When the vessels were now fairly floated, and the whole squadron scattered in different directions, the men who had gone on shore ran back in consternation to the ships, confounded beyond measure by a calamity of a nature so unexpected. But amid the tumult their haste served only to mar their speed. Some were to be seen pushing the vessels with poles; others had taken their seats to row, but in doing so had meanwhile been preventing the proper adjustment of the oars. Others again, in hastening to sail out into the clear channel, without waiting for the requisite number of sailors and pilots, worked the vessels to little effect, crippled as these were and otherwise difficult to handle. At the same time several other vessels drifted away with the stream before those who were pell-mell crowding into them could all get on board, and in this case the crowding caused as much delay in hurrying off as did the scarcity of hands in the other vessels. From one side were shouted orders to stay, from another to put off, so that amid this confusion of contradictory orders nothing that was of any service could be seen or even heard. In such an emergency the pilots themselves were useless, since their commands could neither be heard for the uproar, nor executed by men so distracted with terror.

The ships accordingly ran foul of each other, broke away each other's oars, and bumped each other's sterns. A spectator could not have supposed that what he saw was the fleet of one and the same army, but rather two hostile fleets engaged in a sea-fight. Prows were dashed against poops, and vessels that damaged other vessels in front of them were themselves damaged in turn by vessels at their stern. The men, as was but natural, lost their temper, and from high words fell to blows. By this time the tide had overflowed all the level lands near the river's edge, leaving only sandheaps visible above the water like so many islands. To these numbers of the men swam for safety, neglecting through fear the safety of the vessels they quitted, some of which were riding in very deep water where depressions existed in the ground, while others were stranded on shoals where the waves had covered the more or less elevated parts of the channel. But now they were suddenly surprised with a new danger, still greater than the first, for the sea, which had begun to ebb, was rushing back whence it came with a strong current, and was rendering back the lands which just before had been deeply submerged. This pitched some of the stranded vessels upon their sterns, and caused others to fall upon their sides, and that too with such violence that the fields around them were strewn with baggage, arms, broken oars, and wreckage.

The soldiers, meanwhile, neither dared to trust themselves to the land nor to leave their ships, as they dreaded that some calamity, worse than before, might at any moment befall them. They could scarcely indeed believe what they saw and experienced, these shipwrecks upon dry land, and the presence of the sea in the river. Nor did their misfortunes end here, for as they did not know that the tide would soon afterwards bring back the sea and float their ships, they anticipated that they would be reduced by famine to the most dismal extremities. To add to their terror monstrous creatures of frightful aspect, which the sea had left behind it, were seen wandering about.

As night drew on the hopelessness of the situation oppressed even the king himself with harassing anxieties. But no care could ever daunt his indomitable spirit, and great as was his anxiety it did not prevent him from remaining all night on the watch and giving out his orders. He even sent some horsemen to the mouth of the river with instructions that when they saw the tide returning they should go before it and announce its approach. Meanwhile he caused the shattered vessels to be repaired, and those that were overturned to be set upright, at the same time ordering the men to be ready and on the alert when the land would be inundated by the return of the tide. The whole of that night had been spent by the king in watching and addressing words of encouragement to his men, when the horsemen came back at full gallop, with the tide following at their heels. It came at first with a gentle current which sufficed to set the ships afloat, but it soon gathered strength enough to set the whole fleet in motion. Then the soldiers and sailors, giving vent to their irrepressible joy at their unexpected deliverance, made the shores and banks resound with their exulting cheers. They asked each other wonderingly wherefrom so vast a sea had suddenly returned, whereto it had retired the day before, what was the nature of this strange element, which at one time was out of harmony with the natural laws of space, but at another was obedient to some fixed laws in respect of time?[1] The king conjecturing from what had happened

[1] See Note G*g*, Tides in Indian Rivers.

that the tide would return after sunrise, took advantage
of it, and starting at midnight sailed down the river
attended by a few ships, and having passed its mouth,
advanced into the sea a distance of 400 stadia, and thus
at last accomplished the object he had so much at heart.
Having then sacrificed to the tutelary gods of the sea and
of the places adjacent, he took the way back to his fleet.

*Chapter X.—Alexander goes homeward by land, leaving
     Nearchus to follow by sea and conduct the fleet to the
     head of the Persian Gulf—Disastrous march through
     Gedrosia—Alexander arrives in Carmania, where he
     holds Bacchic revels to celebrate his conquests*

He sailed thence up the river, and next day reached
a place of anchorage not far from a salt lake,[1] the peculiar
properties of which being unknown to his men, deceived
those who thoughtlessly bathed in its waters.   For scabs
broke out over their bodies, and the disease being con-
tagious, infected even others who had not bathed.   The
application of oil, however, cured the sores.   Then as the
country through which the army was to pass was dry and
waterless, Alexander sent on Leonnatus in advance to
dig wells, while he remained himself with the troops
where he was, waiting for the arrival of spring.   In the
meantime he built a good many cities,[2] and ordered
Nearchus and Onesicritus, who were experienced navi-
gators, to sail with the stoutest ships down to the ocean,
and proceeding as far as they could with safety to make
themselves acquainted with the nature of the sea.

---

[1] This lake, however, was discovered neither on this voyage nor on
this arm of the Indus, but during a
subsequent voyage which Alexander
made down the eastern arm.

[2] "No magnificent idea," says
Vincent, "is requisite to conceive the
building of cities in the East.   A fort
or citadel with a mud wall to mark
the circumference of the pettah or
town is all that falls to the share of
the founder.   The habitations are
raised in a few days or hours. . . .
The Soldan of Egypt insults Timour
by telling him : 'The cities of the
East are built of mud, and ephemeral ;
ours in Syria and Egypt are of stone,
and eternal.' "

Having done this, they might return to join him by sailing up either the same river or the Euphrates.[1]

The winter being now wellnigh over, he burned the useless ships, and marched homeward with his army by land. In the course of nine encampments he reached the land of the Arabites, and in nine more the land of the Cedrosii—a free people, who agreed to surrender after holding a council to consider the subject. As they surrendered voluntarily, nothing was exacted from them except a supply of provisions. On the fifth day thereafter he came to a river, which the natives called the Arabus, and beyond it he found the country barren and waterless. This he traversed, and so entered the dominions of the Oritae. Here he gave Hephaestion the great bulk of the army, and divided the rest of it, consisting of light-armed troops, between Ptolemy, Leonnatus, and himself. These three divisions plundered the Indians simultaneously, and carried off a large booty. Ptolemy devastated the maritime country, while the king himself and Leonnatus between them ravaged all the interior. Here too he built a city, which he peopled with Arachosians.[2] Thence he came to those Indians who inhabit the sea-coast, possessing a great extent of country, and holding no manner of intercourse even with their next neighbours.

This isolation from the rest of the world has brutalised their character, which even by nature is far from humane. They have long claw-like nails and long shaggy hair, for they cut the growth of neither. They live in huts constructed of shells and other offscourings of the sea. Their clothing consists of the skins of wild beasts, and

---

[1] Nearchos with the fleet rejoined the army at a point on the river, Pasitigris or Karun, near the modern village of Ahwaz, where was a bridge by which Alexander led his army from Persis to Sousa, where he arrived February 324 B.C.

[2] The Alexandreia of Diodôros, and probably also the Alexandreia which, as we learn from Pliny (vi. 25), was built by Leonnatos by Alexander's orders on the confines of the Arian nation. It may also be the fifteenth of the Alexandreias of Stephanos Byz., which he places in the country of the Arachosians next to India. It was perhaps, however, the *Portus Alexandri*, now Karâchi, where Nearchos was detained by the prevalence of the monsoon for twenty-four days.

they feed on fish dried in the sun, and on the flesh of sea monsters cast on the shore during stormy weather.[1] The Macedonians having by this time consumed all their provisions, suffered first from scarcity and at last from hunger, so that they were driven to search everywhere for the roots of the palm, which is the only tree that country produces. When even this kind of food failed them, they began to kill their beasts of burden, and did not spare even their horses. They were thus deprived of the means of carrying their baggage, and had to burn the rich spoils taken from their enemies, for the sake of which they had marched to the utmost extremities of the East.

A pestilence succeeded the famine, for the new juices of the unwholesome esculents on which they fed, super-added to the fatigue of marching and the strain of their mental anxiety, had spread various distempers among them, so that they were threatened with destruction whether they remained where they were or resumed their march. If they stayed famine would assail them, and if they advanced a still deadlier enemy, pestilence, would have them in its grasp. The plains were in consequence bestrewn with almost more bodies of the dying than of the dead. Even those who suffered least from the distemper could not keep pace with the main army, because every one believed that the faster he travelled he advanced the more surely to health and safety. The men, therefore, whose strength failed craved help from all and sundry, whether known to them or unknown. But there were no beasts of burden now by which they could be taken on, and the soldiers had enough to do to carry their arms, whilst at the same time the dreadful figure of the calamity impending over themselves was ever before their eyes. Being thus repeatedly appealed

---

[1] Hence their name *Ichthyophagoi*. They inhabited the maritime parts of the Oreitai and Gedrosians. In sailing along their coast Nearchos and his men suffered great hardships from scarcity of provisions. See Arrian's *Indika*, 24-31. Much may also be read of this people in Strabo, Pliny, Ailianos, and Agatharchides.

to, they could not so much as bear to cast back a look at their comrades, their pity for others being lost in their fears for themselves.

Those, on the other hand, who were thus forsaken, implored the king, in the name of the gods and by the rites of their common religion, to help them in their sore need, and when they found that they vainly importuned deaf ears, their despair turned to frantic rage, so that they fell to imprecations, wishing for those who refused to help them a similar death and similar friends. The king, feeling himself to be the cause of so great a calamity, was oppressed with grief and shame, and sent orders to Phrataphernes, the satrap of the Parthyaeans,[1] to forward him upon camels provisions ready cooked, and he also notified his wants to the governors of the adjacent provinces. In obedience to his orders the supplies were at once forwarded, and the army being thus rescued, from famine at least, reached eventually the frontiers of Cedrosia, a region which alone of all these parts produces everything in great abundance. Here, therefore, he halted for some time to refresh his harassed troops by an interval of repose.

Meanwhile he received a letter from Leonnatus reporting that he had defeated the Oritae, who had brought against him a force of 8000 foot and 300 horse. Word came also from Craterus that he had crushed an incipient rebellion, instigated by two Persian nobles, Ozines and Zariaspes, whom he had seized and placed under custody. On leaving this place Alexander appointed Sibyrtius to be governor of that province in succession to Memnon, who had lately been cut off by some malady, and he then marched into Carmania, which was governed by the satrap Aspastes, whom he suspected of having designed to make himself independent while he was a great distance off in India. Aspastes came to meet Alexander, who, dissembling his resentment, received him

---

[1] Arrian (vi. 27) says, however, that Phrataphernes brought the provisions spontaneously. Diodôros is at one with Curtius on the point.

graciously, and let him remain in office till he could inquire into the charges preferred against him. Then as the different governors, in compliance with his demands, had sent him a large supply of horses and draught cattle from their respective provinces, he accommodated all his men who wanted them with horses and waggons. He restored also their arms to their former splendour, for they were now not far from Persia, which was a rich country and in the enjoyment of profound peace.

So then Alexander, whose soul aspired to more than human greatness, since he had rivalled, as we said before, the glory which Father Bacchus had achieved by his conquest of India, resolved also to match his reputation by imitating the Bacchanalian procession which that divinity first invented, whether that was a triumph or merely some kind of frolic with which his Bacchanals amused themselves. To this end he ordered the streets through which he was to pass to be strewn with flowers and chaplets, and beakers and other capacious vessels brimming with wine to be placed at all the house doors. Then he ordered waggons to be made, each capable of holding many soldiers, and these to be decorated like tents, some with white canvas and others with costly tapestry.

The king headed the procession with his friends and the members of his select body-guard, wearing on their heads chaplets made of a variety of flowers. The strains of music were to be heard in every part of the procession, here the breathings of the flute, and there the warblings of the lyre. All the army followed, feasting and carousing as they rode in the waggons, which they had decorated as gaily as they possibly could, and had hung round with their choicest and showiest weapons. The king himself and the companions of his revelry rode in a chariot, which groaned under the weight of goblets of gold and large drinking cups made of the same precious metal. The army for seven days advanced in this bacchanalian fashion, so that it might have fallen an easy prey to the vanquished if they had but had a spark of spirit to attack it when in this drunken condition. Why, a thousand men only, if with some mettle in them and sober, could have captured the whole army in the midst of its triumph, besotted as it was with its seven days' drunken debauch.

But fortune, which assigns to every thing its fame and value in the world's estimation, turned into glory this gross military scandal; and the contemporaries of Alexander, as well as those who came after his time, regarded it as a wonderful achievement, that his soldiers, though drunk, passed in safety through nations hardly as yet sufficiently subdued, the barbarians taking, what was in reality a piece of great temerity, to be a display of well-grounded confidence.[1]   All this grand exhibition, however, had the executioner in its wake, for the satrap Aspastes, of whom we before made mention, was ordered to be put to death.[2] So true is it that cruelty is no obstacle to the indulgence of luxury, nor luxury to the indulgence of cruelty.

---

[1] This description is much over-drawn. Thirlwall thus remarks upon it : " We cannot wonder that, in the enjoyment of pleasures, from which they had been so long debarred, they abandoned themselves to some excesses, perhaps only following the example of their chiefs and of Alexander himself; " and this was probably the main ground of fact for the exaggeration of later writers.

[2] Arrian alludes to his execution in his *Indika*, c. 36.

DIODÔROS SICULUS

BIBLIOTHECA HISTORICA OF DIODÔROS SICULUS

SEVENTEENTH BOOK

Chapter LXXXIV. — Alexander at Massaga — His treachery towards the Indian mercenaries who had capitulated

When the capitulation on those terms had been ratified by oaths, the Queen [of Massaga], to show her admiration of Alexander's magnanimity, sent out to him most valuable presents, with an intimation that she would fulfil all the stipulations. Then the mercenaries at once, in accordance with the terms of the agreement, evacuated the city, and after retiring to a distance of eighty stadia, pitched their camp unmolested without thought of what was to happen. But Alexander, who was actuated by an implacable enmity against the mercenaries, and had kept his troops under arms ready for action, pursued the barbarians, and falling suddenly upon them, made a great slaughter of their ranks. The barbarians at first loudly protested that they were attacked in violation of sworn obligations, and invoked the gods whom he had desecrated by taking false oaths in their name. But Alexander with loud voice retorted that his covenant merely bound him to let them depart from the city, and was by no means a league of perpetual amity between them and the Macedonians. The mercenaries, undismayed by the greatness of their danger, drew their ranks together in form of a ring, within which they placed the women and children to guard them on all sides against their assailants. As they were now desperate, and by their audacity and feats of valour, made the conflict in which they closed hot work for the enemy, while the Macedonians held it a point of honour not to be outdone in courage by a horde of barbarians, great was the astonishment and alarm which the peril of the crisis created. For as the combatants were locked together fighting hand to hand, death and wounds were dealt round in every variety of form. Thus the Macedonians, when once their long spikes had shattered the shields of the barbarians, pierced their vitals with the steel points of these weapons, and on the other hand the mercenaries never hurled their javelins without deadly effect against the near mark presented by the dense ranks of the enemy. When many were thus wounded and not a few killed, the women, taking the arms of the fallen, fought side by side with the men, for the imminence of the danger and the great interests at stake forced them to do violence to their nature, and to take an active part in the defence. Accordingly some of them who had supplied themselves with arms, did their best to cover their husbands with their shields, while others who were without arms did much to impede the enemy by flinging themselves upon them and catching hold of their shields. The defenders, however, after fighting desperately along with their wives, were at last overpowered by superior numbers, and met a glorious death which they would have disdained to exchange for a life with dishonour.[1] Alexander spared the unwarlike and unarmed multitude, as well as the women that still survived, but took them away under charge of the cavalry.

[1] This happened at Mazaga, the capital of Assakênos. Plutarch, it will be seen, justly condemns Alexander for this gross violation of the compact into which he had entered with the Indian mercenaries.

Chapter LXXXV.—Alexander captures the rock Aornos

He took many other cities, and put to death all who offered resistance to his arms. He then advanced to the rock called Aornos, unto which such of the inhabitants as survived had fled for refuge, because it was a stronghold of incomparable security.[1] Heraklês, it is said, had in the days of old assaulted this rock, but had abandoned the siege on the occurrence of violent earthquakes and signs from heaven. Now, when this story came to Alexander's ears, it only whetted his eagerness to attack the stronghold, and match himself against the god in a contest for glory. The rock was 100 stadia in circuit, 16 stadia in height, and had a level surface, forming a complete circle. On its southern side it was washed by the Indus, the greatest of Indian rivers, but elsewhere it was all environed with deep ravines and inaccessible cliffs. When Alexander, who perceived the difficult nature of the ground, had given up all hope of taking the place by assault, there came to him an old man accompanied by his two sons. He was miserably poor, this man, and had lived a long time in that neighbourhood, inhabiting a cave with three lairs cut into the rock, which served as night-quarters for himself and his sons. He had thus a familiar knowledge of all that locality. This old man then, coming to the king, explained to him what his circumstances were, and undertook to guide his army up the difficult ascent, and take him to a position which commanded the barbarians in occupation of the rock. Alexander promised the man an ample recompense for this service, and in following his guidance seized in the first place the narrow pass which alone gave access to the rock, and, as there was no exit from it elsewhere, he so closely blocked up the enemy that no assistance could possibly reach them from any quarter. In the next place he set all his men to work to fill up with a mound the ravine which

[1] For its identification see Note F, Aornos.

lay at the root of the rock. Having thus got nearer the place, he pushed the siege with all possible vigour, making assaults for seven days and as many nights without intermission, the troops taking duty by turns. The advantage, however, lay at first with the barbarians, who fought from a higher position, and killed many who pressed the attack too recklessly. But when the mound had been completed, and catapults which shot bolts to a great distance and other engines of war had been brought to bear against them, and when it became manifest besides that the king would by no means abandon the siege, the Indians were struck with despair. Alexander, whose sagacity foresaw what would occur, withdrew the guard which he had left at the pass, thus giving the men on the rock, if they wished to retire, a free passage out. So then the barbarians, dismayed alike by the valour of the Macedonians and the king's fixed ambition to be master of the place, evacuated the rock by night.

Chapter LXXXVI.—Alexander crosses the Indus, and is hospitably received by Taxilês

Alexander having thus outwitted the Indians by these feints, obtained possession of the rock without risk being incurred. He then gave his guide the stipulated reward, and moved off with his army at the very time when Aphrikês, an Indian who had 20,000 soldiers and 15 elephants, was hovering about in that locality.[1] This man certain of his followers put to death, and, having brought his head to Alexander, procured for this service their own safety. The king took them into his own ranks, and got possession of the elephants, which were wandering at large about the country.

He then came to the river Indus, and, finding that the thirty-oared galleys which he ordered had been prepared, and the passage bridged, he gave his army a rest of thirty days to recruit their strength. Having then offered to

---

[1] Aphrikês is called Eryx by Curtius.

the gods sacrifices on a magnificent scale, he led his army over to the other side, where he met with an incident which took a strange and unexpected turn. For Taxilês being by this time dead, his son Môphis [1] had succeeded to the government. Now Môphis had before this not only sent word to Alexander, then in Sogdiana, that he would fight on his side against any Indians who might appear in arms against him, but at this juncture had also sent ambassadors to say that he surrendered his kingdom into his hands. So when Alexander was at a distance of forty stadia he set forth to meet him, attended by his friends, and his army drawn up in battle order and his elephants ranged in line. Alexander, seeing a great host advancing towards him drawn up as if for action, thought that the Indian had treacherously offered to surrender that he might thus fall upon the Macedonians before they could prepare for battle. He therefore ordered the trumpeters to sound to arms, and, having marshalled his troops, advanced to give the Indians battle. But Môphis, on seeing the commotion in the Macedonian ranks, and comprehending its cause, left his army, and riding forward with a few of his friends, corrected the mistake into which the Macedonians had fallen, and surrendered himself and his army to the king. Alexander, to mark his approbation of this conduct, gave back his kingdom to Môphis, and ever afterwards treated him as a friend and ally. He also changed his name to Taxilês. [2]

Chapter LXXXVII.—Alexander marches against Pôros —The appearance presented by the Indian army with its elephants

Such were the transactions of this year—that in which Chremês was archon at Athens, and in which the Romans

[1] More correctly *Omphis* as given by Curtius. See Biog. Appendix, *s.v.* Omphis.

[2] The father of Omphis had quite recently died, and Omphis did not assume the sovereignty at once on his decease, but waited till Alexander sanctioned his doing so. He then, as a matter of course, along with the sovereignty assumed also the dynastic title *Taxilês*.

appointed Publius Cornelius and Aulus Postumius consuls.[1] Thereafter Alexander, who had recruited his army by an interval of rest in the country of Taxilês, took the field against Pôros, the king of the neighbouring Indians, who had an army of more than 50,000 foot, about 3000 horse, above 1000 chariots, and 130 elephants. This king had made an alliance with another prince called Embisaros,[2] the ruler of an adjacent tribe, and who possessed an army which was but little inferior to his own. Alexander, on learning that this king was 400 stadia distant, resolved to attack Pôros before his ally could reach him. Pôros, being warned of the near approach of the enemy, at once drew up his troops in order of battle. His cavalry he distributed on the wings, and his elephants he placed in his front line at equi-distances, and so arranged as to strike the enemy with terror. In the intervals between the animals he stationed the rest of his soldiers, instructing them to succour the elephants and protect them from being assailed in flank by the enemy's missiles. The whole disposition

[1] Alexander's campaign, in which he conquered the country extending from the Hindu Kush to the Indus, took place in the year 327 B.C. In the year following he marched eastward through the Panjâb as far as the Hyphasis, conquering on his way Pôros and the Kathaians, and from the Hyphasis he retraced his way to the Hydaspês. He then sailed down that river, and then down the Akesinês into which it falls, until about the end of the year he reached the Indus. It will be seen from Arrian, v. 19, that the battle with Pôros was fought in the archonship of Hêgemôn at Athens, whose year of office, it is otherwise known, extended from the 28th of June 327 to the 17th of July 326 B.C. Hêgemôn was succeeded by Chremês, so that Diodôros antedates his archonship. He was archon after the defeat of Pôros and not before. With regard to the two consuls named, it does not appear that they ever held the consulship simultaneously. Publius Cornelius (Scipio Barbatus) was consul in 328 B.C. along with C. Plautius Decianus. In

the following year *Spurius* Postumius Albinus was master of the horse to the Dictator Claudius Marcellus, but I can find nowhere in the lists the name of *Aulus* Postumius as holding any office about that time. In Smith's *Classical Dictionary* the year 327 B.C. appears as the *annus mirabilis* of Alexander's life, for early in the spring he completes the conquest of Sogdiana and marries Roxana. Thereafter he returns to Baktra, then marches to invade India, and crossing the Hydaspês defeats Pôros. He then marches to the Hyphasis, and thence returns to the Hydaspês. In the autumn he sails down the Hydaspês to the Indus! See vol. iii. p. 1346 and vol. i. *s.v.* Alexander III. The events of two years are thus compressed into the space of a single year. Clinton's chronology, which is very confused for the period from 327 to 323, seems to have been followed.

[2] His name appears in Arrian more correctly as Abisares. He may be described as the King of Kashmîr.

of his army gave it very much the appearance of a city—
the elephants as they stood resembling its towers, and the
men-at-arms placed between them resembling the lines of
wall intervening between tower and tower. But Alexander,
having observed how the forces of the enemy had been
disposed, regulated thereby the formation of his own line.

Chapter LXXXVIII.—The defeat of Pôros

The Macedonian cavalry began the action, and
destroyed nearly all the chariots of the Indians. Upon
this the elephants, applying to good use their prodigious
size and strength, killed some of the enemy by trampling
them under their feet, and crushing their armour and
their bones, while upon others they inflicted a terrible
death, for they first lifted them aloft with their trunks,
which they had twined round their bodies, and then
dashed them down with great violence to the ground.
Many others they deprived in a moment of life by goring
them through and through with their tusks. But the
Macedonians heroically bore the brunt of this dreadful
onslaught, and having killed with their long pikes the
men stationed between the elephants, made the poise of
the battle equal. They next assailed the animals themselves with a storm of javelins, thus piercing them with
numerous wounds, which so tortured them that the Indians
mounted on their backs lacked sufficient strength to
control their movements, for the animals on heading to
their own ranks bore against them with an impetuosity
not to be repressed, and trampled their own friends under
their feet. Then ensued a great confusion, but Pôros,
who was mounted on the most powerful of all his
elephants, on seeing what had happened, gathered around
him forty of the animals that were still under control,
and falling upon the enemy with all the weight of the
elephants, made a great slaughter with his own hand, for
he far surpassed in bodily strength any soldier of his

army. In stature he measured five cubits, while his girth
was such that his breastplate was twice the size required
for a man of ordinary bulk. For this reason the javelins
he flung from his hand flew with all but the impetus of
shots from a catapult. The Macedonians who stood
opposed to him being terror-struck at his astonishing
prowess, Alexander sent to their assistance the archers
and the divisional light troops, with orders that every
man should make Pôros the object of his aim. The
soldiers lost no time in carrying out these orders. Their
bolts flew thick and fast, and as the Indian king at whom
they were all aimed presented a broad mark, none of
them failed to carry home. Pôros fought on with heroic
courage, but being drained of blood by the number of his
wounds, he fainted away, and leaning on his elephant for
support, was borne to the ground. A report having
spread that their king was dead, the remnant of the
Indian host fled from the field, but many of them were
slain in the flight.

*Chapter LXXXIX.—Losses sustained by each side in the
battle of the Hydaspês—Alexander orders a fleet to be
built on the Hydaspês.*

Alexander having gained this splendid victory, recalled
his soldiers from the field by sound of trumpet. In this
engagement more than 12,000 of the Indians fell, among
whom were two of the sons of Pôros, and his generals, and
the most distinguished of his other officers. More than
9000 men were taken prisoners, and eighty elephants
were captured. Pôros himself, who was still alive, was
given into the hands of the Indians to be cured of his
wounds. Of the Macedonians, there fell 280 horsemen and
more than 700 foot-soldiers. The king buried the dead,
and in proportion to their merits rewarded those who had
signalised themselves by their bravery in the action. He
then sacrificed to the Sun, as the deity who had given

him the conquest of the eastern parts of the world. As the mountainous country adjacent produced much well-grown fir, and not a little cedar and pine, besides an unlimited quantity of other kinds of timber fit for building ships, he prepared what ships he required. For he intended, after he had reached the limits of India and subdued all its inhabitants, to sail down stream to the ocean. He founded two cities, one beyond the river at the place where he crossed, and the other on the field where he had defeated Pôros.[1] The work of building the ships was quickly finished, owing to the great number of hands employed on it ; and he then appointed Pôros, who had recovered from his wounds, in consideration of the valour he had displayed, to be king of the country over which he had formerly ruled. He then gave his army thirty days to recruit in this region, which yielded an unstinted supply of all the necessaries of life.

Chapter XC.—Some account of the serpents, apes, and trees seen by the Macedonians in India

In the mountainous country which adjoined the scene of action there were found other peculiar products besides timber for shipbuilding, for it abounded with snakes of an extraordinary size, being sixteen cubits in length,[2] and with many kinds of apes, which also were remarkable for their size. The apes of themselves suggested what stratagem should be employed in hunting them, for they are prone to imitate whatever they see men doing, but yet are not easily overpowered by mere force, since they are possessed both of great strength of body and sharpness of wit. Some members, therefore, of the hunting party smear their eyes with honey, others in full view of their game put on their shoes, while others hang mirrors around their necks. Then, having affixed nooses to their

[1] Boukephala and Nikaia, for which see Note on Arrian, p. 110.

[2] See Note Z, Indian Serpents.

shoes, they leave these behind them, and in place of the honey they substitute gum, and at the same time attach hauling-ropes to the mirrors.   So when the apes try to do all that they had seen done by the men they find themselves powerless to do so, for their eyelids are glued together, their feet entangled in the nooses, and their bodies held fast by the ropes.   In these circumstances they fall an easy prey to the hunters.

Alexander having struck terror into the king called Embisaros, who had come too late to the assistance of Pôros, compelled him to do what he commanded.   Having then crossed the river with his army, he advanced through a country of surpassing fertility, for it had various kinds of trees which rose to a height of seventy cubits, and had such a girth that it took fully four men to clasp them round, while their shadow projected to a distance of 300 feet.   This region also was much infested with snakes.   These were small in size, and marked with diverse colours, for while some were like bronze-coloured wands, others had a thick hair-like mane, and with their sting inflicted a death of acute pain, for the sufferings of any one they bit were dreadful, and were accompanied with a flux of sweat which looked like blood.   On this account the Macedonians, being terribly plagued by their stings, suspended their couches from the trees, and kept awake the greater part of the night ; but when they had learned from the natives that a certain root was an antidote, its application relieved them from their sufferings.[1]

---

[1] This is the whip-snake which is thus described in *British India* of the Edinburgh Cabinet Library, vol. iii. pp. 121, 122: "The whip snake is common to the Concan, where it conceals itself among the foliage of trees, and darts at the cattle grazing below, generally aiming at the eye. A bull, which was thus wounded at Dazagon, tore up the ground with extreme fury, and died in half an hour, foaming at the mouth. The habit of the reptile is truly singular, for it seems to proceed neither from resentment nor from fear, nor yet from the impulse of appetite; but seems, 'more than any other known fact in natural history, to partake of that frightful and mysterious principle of evil, which tempts our species so often to tyrannize for mere wantonness of power.'"

Chapter XCI.—Alexander pursues Pôros, nephew of the great Pôros — Subdues the Adrestai and Kathaians and enters the kingdom of Sôpeithês—Peculiar customs of the natives of these parts

When he moved forward with his forces certain men came to inform him that Pôros, the king of the country, who was the nephew of that Pôros whom he had defeated, had quitted his kingdom and fled to the nation of the Gandaridai. Alexander, irritated at the news, despatched Hêphaistiôn into his country with a body of troops and ordered him to hand over the kingdom to the other Pôros who was on his side. He then marched in person against the Adrestai,[1] and having reduced some of their cities which offered resistance, and persuaded others to surrender, he invaded the country of the Kathaians, a people among whom the custom prevailed that widows should be burned along with their husbands, the barbarians having put in force a decree to this effect because an instance had occurred of a wife procuring her husband's death by poison.[2] The king laid siege to their greatest and strongest city and burned it to the ground, in revenge for the many dangers incurred in capturing it. While he was besieging another considerable city the Indians in a suppliant manner entreated his mercy and he spared them accordingly.

He next warred against the cities that were subject to the sway of Sôpeithês.[3] These were governed by laws in the highest degree salutary, for while in other respects their political system was one to admire, beauty was held among them in the highest estimation. For this reason a discrimination between the children born to them is made at the stage of infancy, when those that are perfect in their limbs and features, and have constitutions which

---

[1] The Adraïstai of Arrian. See Note on that author, p. 116.

[2] See Note I*i*, Suttee.

[3] More correctly Sôphytês. See Biog. Appendix, *s.v.*

promise a combination of strength and beauty, are allowed to be reared, while those that have any bodily defect are condemned to be destroyed as not worth the rearing.[1] They make their marriages also in accordance with this principle, for in selecting a bride they care nothing whether she has a dowry and a handsome fortune besides, but look only to her beauty and other advantages of the outward person. It follows that the inhabitants of these cities are generally held in higher estimation than the rest of their countrymen. Their king Sôpeithês, who was admired by all for his beauty and his stature, which exceeded four cubits, came forth from the city where his palace was, and on surrendering himself and his kingdom to Alexander was reinstated in his authority by the clemency of the conqueror. Sôpeithês with the utmost cordiality feasted the whole army in splendid style for several days.

FIG. 12.—SÔPHYTÊS.

Chapter XCII.—*Courage and ferocity of the dogs in the dominions of Sôpeithês*

Among the many valuable presents which he bestowed on Alexander were 150 dogs remarkable for their size and strength, and superior also in other points, and said to have been bred from tigresses.[2] Being desirous that Alexander should have proof of their mettle by seeing them at work, he placed a full-grown lion within an enclosure, and selecting two of the least valuable of the dogs included in the present, cast them to the lion. When these were likely to be vanquished by the wild beast he let loose other two dogs. Then when the four dogs together proved more than a match for the lion, a man who was sent into the ring with a knife cut away the right leg of one of the dogs. When the king loudly remonstrated, and his body-guards rushed forward and arrested the hand

---

[1] This was also a Spartan institution.   [2] See Note Bô.

of the Indian, Sôpeithês announced that he would give three dogs instead of the one which was mutilated. Then the huntsman, taking hold of the leg, cut it away quietly bit by bit. The dog, without uttering so much as a yell or a moan of pain, kept his fangs fixed in the bite, until all his blood being drained he drew his last breath on the body of the lion.

Chapter XCIII.—Submission of Phêgeus—Advance to the Hypanis—Description given by Phêgeus of the country beyond the Hypanis—Of the Praisians and their king Xandrames

During these transactions Hêphaistiôn, who had made large conquests of Indian territory with the expedition under his command, rejoined Alexander, who, after having praised that general for his valour and devotion to his service, then led his army into the dominions of Phêgeus.[1] Here, as the natives welcomed the presence of the Macedonians, and Phêgeus came out with many gifts to meet them, Alexander consented to let him retain his kingdom. Then having for two days enjoyed along with his army the noble hospitality of this prince, he advanced toward the Hypanis,[2] a river with a width of seven stadia, a depth of six fathoms, and a violent current which made its passage difficult. He had obtained from Phêgeus a description of the country beyond the Indus : First came a desert which it would take twelve days to traverse ; beyond this was the river called the Ganges which had a width of thirty-two stadia, and a greater depth than any other Indian river; beyond this again were situated the dominions of the nation of the Praisioi and the Gandaridai,[3] whose king, Xandrames, had

[1] More correctly *Phegelas* as given by Arrian. See Biog. Appendix, *s.v.*
[2] Usually called the Hyphasis. It is now the Beäs which joins the Satlej. The name of the Hyphasis was sometimes, however, applied to the united stream, but this is contrary to Sanskrit usage.
[3] See Notes C*c* and D*d*.

an army of 20,000 horse, 200,000 infantry, 2000 chariots, and 4000 elephants trained and equipped for war. Alexander, distrusting these statements, sent for Pôros and questioned him as to their accuracy. Pôros assured him of the correctness of the information, but added that the king of the Gandaridai was a man of quite worthless character, and held in no respect, as he was thought to be the son of a barber.[1] This man—the king's father—was of a comely person, and of him the queen had become deeply enamoured. The old king having been treacherously murdered by his wife, the succession had devolved on him who now reigned. Alexander, though sensible of the difficulties which would attend an expedition against the Gandaridai, had nevertheless no thought of swerving from the path of his ambition, but having in his favour the courage of the Macedonians and the responses of the oracles, he was buoyed up with the hope that he would conquer the barbarians, for had not the Pythian priestess pronounced him invincible, and had not Ammôn promised him the dominion of the whole world ?[2]

Chapter XCIV.—Miserable condition of the Macedonian army—Its refusal to advance beyond the Hypanis

He saw, however, that his soldiers were dispirited by interminable campaigns, and by their exposure for nearly eight years to toils and dangers reduced to a condition of the utmost misery, and he therefore conceived it was

---

[1] The Indian barber (*nápit*) belonged to the Sudra or servile caste. Besides the duties proper to his calling, he has other avocations, his services being often required for the performance of certain domestic ceremonies such as those connected with marriage, etc.

[2] "Kallisthenes adds (after the exaggerating style of tragedy) that when Apollo had deserted the oracle among the Branchidai, on the temple being plundered by the Branchidai (who espoused the party of the Persians in the time of Xerxes), and the spring had failed, it then reappeared *on the arrival of Alexander* ; that the ambassadors also of the Milesians carried back to Memphis numerous answers of the oracle respecting the descent of Alexander from Jupiter, and the future victory which he should obtain at Arbela, the death of Darius, and the political changes at Lacedaemon" (Strabo, XVII. i. 43). See also Introd. p. 28.

necessary for him to animate his troops for the expedition against the Gandaridai [1] by plying them with suitable arguments. For death had made severe ravages in his ranks, and all hope was gone that his wars would ever come to an end. Then their horses' hoofs had been worn off by ceaseless marches, and their weapons worn out by use. The Hellenic costumes again were by this time threadbare and could not be replaced, and hence the men were obliged to use cloth woven in barbaric looms wherewith to cut out such dresses for themselves as were worn by Indians. It also so happened that violent storms of rain burst from the clouds for the space of seventy days, accompanied with continual outbreaks of thunder and lightning. Alexander, considering this state of things an obstacle to his designs, placed all his hopes of gaining his ends on winning by benefactions the hearty support of his soldiers. Accordingly he allowed them to plunder the enemy's country where supplies of all sorts abounded, and on those days when the army was busily engaged in foraging he called together the soldiers' wives and children, and then promised to give the women an allowance of food month by month, and the children a donative according to the calculations of what their fathers received as the pay of their military rank. When the soldiers who had found a rich and ample booty returned to the camp, he gathered them all together, and in a well-weighed speech addressed the assembly on the subject of the expedition against the Gandaridai ; but when the Macedonians would by no means assent to his proposals he renounced his contemplated enterprise.

Chapter XCV.—Alexander erects altars and other memorials near the Hypanis, and returns to the Akesinês

He then resolved to set up marks to indicate the limits to which he had advanced ; so first of all he built

---

[1] Properly the *Gangaridai.*

altars to the twelve gods of 50 cubits in height.   Having
next enclosed an encampment thrice the size of the one he
occupied, he dug round it a trench 50 feet broad and 40
feet deep, and with the earth cast up from this trench
he erected a rampart of extraordinary dimensions.   He
further ordered quarters to be constructed as for foot-
soldiers, each containing two beds 5 cubits in length for
each man, and besides this accommodation, two stalls of
twice the ordinary size for each horseman.   Whatever
else was to be left behind was directed to be likewise
proportionately increased in size.   His object in all this
was not merely to make a camp as for heroes, but at the
same time to leave among the people of the country
tokens of mighty men to show with what enormous
bodily strength they were endowed.   When these works
were finished he retraced his steps with all his army to
the river Akesinês.[1]   On reaching it he found that the
boats had been built, and when he had rigged these out,
he ordered an additional number to be constructed.   At
this time there arrived from Greece allies and mercenaries
led by the generals in command of the allies, amounting
to more than 30,000 foot and not much less than 6000
cavalry.   Splendid full suits of armour besides were
brought for the infantry to the number of 25,000,[2] and
100 talents of medicinal drugs, all which he distributed
among the soldiers.   When the equipment of the fleet
was finished, and 200 boats without hatches and 800
tenders had been got ready, he proceeded to give names
to the cities which had been founded on the banks of the
river, calling one Nikaia in commemoration of his victory,
and the other Boukephala after his horse that perished
in the battle with Pôros.

[1] Diodôros should have said the *Hydaspês*.   [2] See Note on Curtius, p. 231.

Chapter XCVI.—Voyage to the Southern Ocean begun— Submission of the Siboi—The Agalassians attacked and conquered

Alexander now embarked with his friends, and started on the voyage to the Southern Ocean. The bulk of the army simultaneously marched along the banks of the river under the command of Krateros and Hêphaistiôn. On coming to the place where the Akesinês and Hydaspês join each other the king landed his troops, and led them against a people called the Siboi. These, it is said, were descended from the soldiers who, under Heraklês, attacked the rock Aornos, and after failing to capture it were settled by him in this part of the country. Alexander encamped near their capital, and thereupon the citizens who filled the highest offices came forth to meet him, and reminded him how they were connected by the ties of a common origin. They avowed themselves to be, in virtue of their kinship, ready and willing to do whatever he might require, and presented him also with magnificent gifts. Alexander was so gratified by their professions of goodwill that he permitted their cities to remain in the enjoyment of their freedom.[1] He then advanced his arms against their next neighbours ; and finding that the people called Agalassians[2] had mustered an army of 40,000 foot and 3000 horse, he gave them battle, and proving victorious put the greater number of them to the sword. The rest, who had fled for safety to the adjacent towns, which were soon captured, he condemned to slavery. The remainder of the inhabitants had been collected into one place, and he seized 20,000 of them, who had taken refuge in a large city, which he stormed. The Indians, however, having barricaded the narrow streets, fought with great vigour from the houses, so that Alexander in pressing the attack lost not a few Macedonians. This enraged him, and he set fire to the city,

---

[1] See Note E*e*, The Sibi.   [2] See Note F*f*, The Agalassians.

burning with it most of its defenders.[1] He gave quarter, however, to 3000 of the survivors, who had fled for refuge to the citadel and sued for mercy.

Chapter XCVII.—Disaster to the fleet at the confluence of the rivers

He again embarked with his friends, and sailed down stream as far as the confluence of the Indus with the two rivers already mentioned. These mighty streams met with tumultuous roar, and formed at their junction many formidable eddies, which destroyed whatever sailing craft were sucked into their vortex. The current besides was so swift and strong that it baffled all the skill of the pilots. Two ships of war foundered in consequence, and of the other vessels not a few were stranded. A furious surge broke over the admiral's ship itself—a mishap which nearly proved fatal to the king. Wherefore, as death itself stared him in the face, he stripped off his clothes, and in his naked condition clung to anything that offered a chance of safety. His friends were at the same time swimming alongside the ship, every one eager to receive the king in the event of its capsizing. The utmost confusion prevailed on board, the men contending with the force of the current, and the river baffling all human skill and endeavour, so that it was with the greatest difficulty Alexander made the shore, on which he was cast along with the vessels. For this unexpected deliverance he offered sacrifice to the gods for his escape from extreme peril after contending, like Achilles, with a river.[2]

[1] See Curtius, ix. 4.

[2] This happened at the junction of the Akesinês with the *Hydaspês* and not with the *Indus*, as here represented. For the contest of Achilles with the Simoeis and Skamander, see the twenty-first book of the *Iliad*.

Chapter XCVIII.—Combination of the Syrakousai and Malloi—Alexander, neglecting the warning of a soothsayer, attacks their stronghold, and scales the walls of its citadel

He undertook next an expedition against the Syrakousai[1] and the people called the Malloi, two populous and warlike nations. The inhabitants, he found, had mustered a force of 80,000 foot, 10,000 horse, and 700 chariots. Before Alexander's coming they had been at feud with each other, but on his approach had settled their differences, and cemented an alliance by intermarriage, each nation taking and giving in exchange 10,000 of their young women for wives.[2] They did not, however, combine their forces and take the field, for as a dispute had arisen about the leadership, they had drawn off into the adjoining towns. Alexander, while approaching the city that first came in his way, was pondering how he could lay siege to it and capture it at the very first assault, when one of the soothsayers, named Dêmophôn, came to him and said that he had been forewarned by certain omens that the king in besieging the place would be very dangerously wounded, and he therefore advised Alexander to let that city alone for the present, and meanwhile turn his attention to other enterprises. But the king sharply rebuked him for hampering the valour of men in the heat of action. He then made arrangements for the conduct of the siege, and he led himself the way to the city, which he was ambitious to reduce at once by a vigorous assault. The battering train was, however, late in coming up, and he was him-

[1] The Oxydrakai.

[2] " The two races (*Oxydrakai* and *Malloi*) were composed of widely different elements, for the name of one appears to have been derived from that of the Sudra caste ; and it is certain that the Brahmins were predominant in the other. We can easily understand why they did not intermarry, and were seldom at peace with each other, and that their mutual hostility was only suspended by the common danger which now threatened their independence."—Thirlwall's *Hist. of Greece*, vii. c. 54.

self the first to burst open a postern, and by this side entrance get into the city. He then cut down many of the defenders, put the rest to flight, and pursued them into the citadel. As the Macedonians were meanwhile detained fighting at the wall, he seized a ladder, and applying it to the rampart of the fortress, began to mount it, holding the while his shield above his head. He climbed up with such activity that he quickly reached the top, and surprised the barbarians who were stationed there on guard. The Indians did not venture to close with him, but assailed him from a distance off with darts and arrows, so that the king was sorely galled with the pelting storm of missiles. By this time the Macedonians had applied to the walls two scaling ladders, up which they were mounting, when both of them from being overcrowded broke down, precipitating every one to the ground.

Chapter XCIX.—Alexander left alone leaps down from the walls into the citadel, bravely defends himself, but is dangerously wounded—He is rescued by his friends, who capture the stronghold—The Greek colonists in Bactria revolt

The king being thus isolated from all help, performed a feat of marvellous audacity, which well deserves to be put on record. For, thinking it would be unworthy of his characteristic good fortune if he retired from the walls to his men leaving his purpose unaccomplished, he leaped down, arms and all, alone as he was, into the citadel. The Indians hastened up to assail him, but with undaunted courage he sustained the brunt of their onslaught. Protecting himself on his right hand by the shelter of a tree rooted by the wall, and on the left by the wall itself, he thus kept the Indians at bay, firmly fixed in his purpose to bear himself right gallantly like a king by whom such great things had been achieved, and ambitious to make the close of his life the most glorious of his whole career, for numerous were the blows which he received on his helmet, nor few were those which he caught on his shield.   At last, however, being hit by an arrow under the pap, he sank on his knee, overcome by the force of the blow.   The Indian who had shot the arrow immediately sprang forward, thinking lightly of the danger, but while he was fetching down a blow, Alexander smote him with his sword under the ribs, and, as the wound was mortal, the barbarian fell.   Then the king, grasping a branch within reach of his hand, and raising himself up with it, challenged any of the Indians who so wished to come forward and fight him.   Just at this crisis Peukestas, one of the hypaspists, who had mounted by a different ladder, was the first who succeeded in covering the king with his shield.   After him many others appeared on the scene, who terrified the barbarians and saved Alexander. The city was then stormed, and the Macedonians, in their rage for what the king had suffered, slew all whom they could anywhere find, and filled the city with dead bodies. While the king's attention was for many days absorbed with the curing of his wound, the Greek colonists of Bactria and Sogdiana, who had long felt it a great grievance to be settled among barbarians, when they heard at that time that the king had died of a wound, revolted from the Macedonians, and, having mustered to the number of 3000, set out on their return home.   They had many sufferings to endure on the way, and they were subsequently put to death by the Macedonians after Alexander's death.

Chapter C.—Alexander recovers from his wound—Combat between Koragos and Dioxippos—Dioxippos becomes victor

Alexander, on being cured of his wound, gave thank-offerings to the gods for his recovery, and entertained his

U

friends with great banquets. During the revels a note-worthy incident occurred. Among the invited guests was a Macedonian called Koragos,[1] who was remarkable for his great bodily strength and the number of his brave exploits in war. This man, in an access of drunken bravado, challenged to single combat the Athenian Dioxippos, a prize-fighter, who had been crowned at the public games for victories of the highest distinction. The guests present at the carousal naturally were in-terested in the match, and Dioxippos having accepted the challenge, the king fixed the day on which the combat should come off. At the time appointed for the match the people thronged in tens of thousands to witness the spectacle. The Macedonians, who were of the same race with Koragos, and the king himself joined in show-ing their eagerness for the success of their compatriot, while the Greeks were unanimous in backing up Dioxippos. The champions advanced into the lists, the Macedonian arrayed in costly armour, the Athenian naked, rubbed over with oil, and wearing a close-fitting skull-cap made of felt. As both men excited the wonder and admiration of the spectators by the massive strength of their limbs and their superlative prowess, the contest, it was antici-pated, would be of the nature of a fight between two gods; for the Macedonian, with his stalwart form and the dazzling splendour of his arms, which filled the beholders with amazement, was taken to be like Mars, while Dioxippos, by his prodigious strength, his practice in wrestling and carrying the characteristic club, showed like Heraklês. When they advanced to the attack the Macedonian from the proper distance discharged his javelin, but his antagonist, swerving a little aside, eluded the coming blow. Then the former again advanced with his long Macedonian pike levelled for the charge, but the other on seeing him approach sufficiently near, struck the pike with his club and shattered it to pieces. The Mace-donian, after being thus twice baffled, came on to the

[1] Called Horratas by Curtius.

next round intending now to use his sword, but when he was just on the point of drawing it, Dioxippos unexpectedly sprang forward, and with his left hand seized the hand that was drawing the sword, while with his right hand he pushed Koragos from where he stood, tripped up his legs, and hurled him to the ground.   Then Dioxippos, planting his foot on his foeman's neck and lifting up his club, directed his eyes towards the spectators.

Chapter CI.—The Macedonians plot against Dioxippos, who in consequence takes away his own life—Alexander's regret for his loss

The multitude having loudly applauded the victor for the supreme courage whereby, contrary to all expectation, he had won the day, the king ordered him to let his antagonist go, and then, dismissing the assembly, withdrew to his tent deeply mortified by the discomfiture of the Macedonian.   Then Dioxippos, letting the fallen man go, quitted the field with a famous victory and wearing fillets with which his countrymen had adorned his brows in gratitude for the honour which he had conferred on all Greeks in common.   Fortune, however, did not allow the victor any long time to enjoy his triumph, for the king became more and more alienated from him, and all Alexander's friends and all the Macedonians about the court were so envious of his worth and fame, that they laid a plot against him, and persuaded the chief steward of the royal household to hide away one of the golden wine-cups under his pillow.   So at their next banquet when the wine was served, they charged Dioxippos with theft on the pretence that the cup had been found in his possession, thus subjecting him to shame and disgrace.   From this he saw clearly that the Macedonians with one consent had set themselves against him, and he then rose from the banquet, and soon afterwards, when within his own chamber, wrote a letter to Alexander regarding the machinations which had been formed against him. This letter he entrusted to his own servants to deliver into the king's own hands. He then put an end to his life, and thus, by having inconsiderately accepted a challenge, terminated his career by an act of still greater folly. Many of those accordingly who blamed him for a want of sense, sarcastically remarked it was a misfortune to have great strength of body and but a modicum of brain. The king on perusal of the letter took the man's end much to heart, and in after times often regretted the loss of a man of his noble qualities. As he made no use of him in his lifetime, but felt the want of him when he was gone, and when regret was unavailing, he came to know the nobility of the man's nature from its contrast to the baseness of his calumniators.[1]

Chapter CII. — The Sambastai, Sodrai, and Massanoi submit to Alexander, who founds near the banks of the river a city called Alexandreia—He conquers the kingdoms of Mousikanos, Portikanos, and Sambos— The last effects his escape

Alexander having given orders to his army to march along the river in a line parallel with the course of the navigation, proceeded on his voyage down stream towards the ocean, and on reaching the dominions of the Sambastai,[2] landed to invade their country. They were a people inferior to none in India either for numbers or for bravery. They dwelt in cities in which the democratic form of government prevailed, and on hearing that the Macedonians were coming to attack them collected 60,000 foot soldiers, 6000 horse, and 500 chariots. But when the fleet bore in sight they were thrown into great alarm by the novelty of the appearance it presented and the unexpectedness of its presence, and, as they were at the same time disheartened by the reports which circulated

---

[1] For a notice of Dioxippos, see Note on Curtius, p. 249.

[2] For their identification, see Note on Curtius, p. 252.

about the Macedonians, they adopted the advice of their elders not to fight, and therefore sent on an embassy consisting of fifty of their foremost citizens, under the belief that they would be treated with all proper courtesy. The king having commended them for coming and expressed his readiness to make peace with them, was presented by the inhabitants with gifts of great magnificence, and was besides accorded heroic honours. He then moved on towards the tribes called Sodrai[1] and Massanoi,[2] who occupied the country on both sides of the river, and in these parts he founded near the river the city of Alexandreia,[3] in which he planted a colony of 10,000 men. He next reached the dominions of King Mousikanos, seized that potentate, and, having put him to death, subjugated his people.[4] He next invaded the territories under the sway of Portikanos, and took two cities at the first assault, which he permitted the soldiers to sack and then burned. Portikanos himself fled into a part of the country which offered means of defence, but in a battle he was defeated and slain. All the cities subject to his sceptre Alexander captured and razed to the ground, and by these severe measures spread consternation among the surrounding tribes.[5] He next plundered the kingdom of Sambos, and having enslaved and destroyed most of his cities, put upwards of 80,000 of the barbarians to the sword.[6] The nation called the Brahmanoi were involved in like calamities, but, as the rest sued for mercy, Alexander punished the most guilty and acquitted the rest of the offences charged against them. King Sambos escaped the danger with which he was menaced by taking flight with thirty elephants into the country beyond the Indus.

---

[1] See Note R for their identification.

[2] Cunningham inclines to believe that the *Massanoi* of Diodôros are the *Musarnoi* of Ptolemy, whose name, he says, still exists in the district of *Muzarka* to the west of the Indus below Mithankot. See his *Anc. Geog. of Ind.* p. 254.

[3] For its identification see Note R and Note on Arrian, p. 156.

[4] See Note on Arrian, p. 157, regarding the position of this country.

[5] Porticanos is called Oxykanos by Arrian. See Note on that author, p. 158.

[6] For the kingdom of Sambos see Note S.

Chapter CIII.—Harmatelia holds out against Alexander—In a battle with its inhabitants Ptolemy is wounded by a poisoned arrow, but is cured by an antidote revealed to Alexander in a dream

At the extremity of the country of the Brachmans there lay in the midst of difficult ground the city called Harmatelia,[1] and as the inhabitants presumed alike on their valour and the security of their position, Alexander despatched against them a few light-armed troops, who were directed to hang on the rear of the enemy, and to take to flight in case they were attacked. These men proceeded to attack the ramparts, but being only 500 strong were regarded with contempt. A body therefore of 3000 men under arms sallied out from the city against these troops, which pretending to be panic-struck, took to a precipitate flight. But the king with a few followers stood his ground against the barbarians who gave pursuit, and after a severe conflict slew some and took others prisoners. On the king's side, however, not a few received wounds which all but proved fatal, since the barbarians had anointed their steels with a deadly tincture, and had taken the field to bring the war to an issue in full reliance on its efficacy. This virulent tincture was prepared from snakes of a certain kind which were hunted by the natives, who on killing them exposed their carcases to the sun in order that the flesh might be decomposed by the burning heat of his rays. As this process went on the juices fell out in drops, and by this liquid the poison was secreted from the carcases of the snakes. Accordingly, when any one was wounded, his body at once became numb, and sharp pains soon succeeded, while the whole frame was shaken with tremblings and convulsions. The skin became cold and livid, and the stomach discharged bile. A foam, moreover, of a black colour issued from the wound and putrefied. At this stage the poison quickly

[1] See Note T.

spread to the vital parts of the body, and caused a death of fearful agony. Those, therefore, who had been severely wounded and those who had received nothing more than an accidental scratch suffered equally. While the wounded were perishing by such a horrible death, the king was not so much grieved for the others, but was in the deepest distress of mind on account of Ptolemy, who afterwards became a king, and for whom he had at that time a warm affection. Now at this crisis an incident occurred of a strange and marvellous nature, which concerned Ptolemy, and which some ascribed to the provident care of the gods for his safety. For as he was loved by all the soldiers for his bravery and his unbounded generosity, so in his hour of need he obtained the kindly help he required. For the king in his sleep saw a vision in which he appeared to see a serpent holding a plant in its mouth, and showing its nature and its powers, and the place where it grew. Then Alexander, when he awoke, had search made for the plant and discovered it. This he ground into a powder, which he not only laid as a plaster on Ptolemy's body, but also administered to him as a potion, and by this means restored him to health. When the valuable properties of the plant became known, the other patients to whom the remedy was applied recovered in like manner.[1] He then laid siege to the capital of the Harmatêlioi, a city both of great size and strength. As the inhabitants, however, came to meet him with the symbols of suppliants, and tendered their submission, he dismissed them without enacting any retributive penalty.

[1] See Note on Curtius, p. 256.

Chapter CIV.—Alexander sails down to the mouth of the Indus—Sails back to Tauala (Patala ?)—Starts on his march homewards, instructing Nearchos to explore the way with his fleet to the head of the Persian Gulf —Ravages the land of the Oritians and founds another Alexandreia

He then sailed down the stream with his friends to the ocean, and when he had there seen two islands he forthwith offered a sacrifice of great splendour to the gods, casting at the same time many large drinking-cups of gold, along with the libations they held, into the bosom of the deep. Having next erected altars to Têthys and Okeanos, he assumed that he had finished the expedition which he had undertaken. He then started on the return voyage, and in sailing up the river came to Tauala,[1] a city of great note, with a political constitution drawn on the same lines as the Spartan; for in this community the command in war was vested in two hereditary kings of two different houses, while a council of elders ruled the whole state with paramount authority. Alexander now burned all the vessels that were worn out, and gave the command of the rest that were still serviceable to Nearchos and some others of his friends, whom he instructed to coast along the shores of the ocean, and after having carefully explored whatever lay on their route, to rejoin him at the mouth of the river Euphrates. He himself with his army traversed a great extent of country, overcoming those who opposed him, and treating humanely those who offered their submission. He thus gained over without any danger being incurred the people called the Arbitai and the inhabitants of Kedrôsia. Then, after passing through an extensive waterless tract, of which no inconsiderable part was desert, he reached the borders of Oritis. Here he divided his army into three parts, giving Ptolemy the command of the first division,

[1] Evidently an error for *Patala*, for the identification of which see Note U.

and Leonnatos of the second, Ptolemy being commissioned to ravage and plunder the seaboard, and Leonnatos the interior, while the third division, under his own command, devastated the plains towards the hills and the hill country itself. While the fury of war was thus at one and the same time let loose over the whole land, conflagration, pillage, and massacre ran riot in every special locality. The soldiers accordingly soon appropriated a vast amount of booty, while the number of the inhabitants cut off by the sword amounted to many myriads. All the neighbours of these unfortunate tribes, appalled by the destruction which had overtaken them, submitted to the king. But Alexander, who was ambitious to found a city by the seaside, discovered a harbour sheltered from the violence of the waves, and which had a convenient site near it, and he built thereon the city of Alexandreia.[1]

Chapter CV.—How the Oritians bury their dead—The Ichthyophagoi described—Sufferings and losses of the army in the Gedrôsian desert—Relief sent by various satraps—Leonnatos is attacked by the Oritians

Alexander having stolen into the country of the Oritai by the passes, quickly reduced the whole of it to submission. The Oritai, while in other respects closely resembling the Indians, have one custom which is different, and altogether staggers belief. It has reference to their treatment of the dead. For when a man dies his relatives, naked and holding spears, carry away his body to the oak-coppices which grow in their country, and having there deposited it, and stripped it of the apparel and ornaments with which it is arrayed, they leave it to be devoured by wild beasts. When they have divided the garments which were worn by the deceased, they sacrifice to the heroes now in the under world, and give an entertainment to the members of his household.

[1] See Note on Curtius, p. 262.

Alexander next advanced towards Kedrôsia, following the route along the sea-coast. He encountered on the way an inhospitable and utterly savage tribe, for there the natives let their nails grow without ever cutting them from the day they are born to old age, allow their growth of hair to become matted, have complexions scorched with the heat of the sun, and are dressed with the skins of wild beasts. They subsist on the flesh of whales stranded on their shores. Their habitations they prepare by running up walls, and forming the roofs of the ribs of the whale, these supplying beams of a length of 18 cubits. For covering over the roofs they use instead of tiles the scales of fish.[1] Alexander, in passing through the country of these savages, was much distressed by the scarcity of provisions; but in the next country he entered he fared still worse, for it was desert and bare of everything useful to support life. As many perished from sheer want, the stout hearts of the Macedonians yielded to despondency, and Alexander was overwhelmed with no ordinary grief and anxiety; for it seemed a terrible thing that his men, who surpassed all mankind in bravery and in arms, should perish ingloriously in a desert land and in utter destitution. He therefore despatched messengers post-haste into Parthyaia,[2] and Drangianê,[3] and Areia,[4] and the other states bordering on the desert, enjoining them to send quickly to the passes of Karmania dromedaries and other beasts of burden laden with food and other necessaries. These messengers having rapidly performed the journey to the satraps of these provinces, caused ample supplies of provisions to be conveyed to the appointed place. Alexander had, however, before their arrival lost

---

[1] All these particulars are recorded at length in the *Indika* of Arrian, from c. 24 to c. 31.

[2] Generally called Parthia, then a small state.

[3] Drangianê, now the province of Seistan. The inhabitants Drangoi, and also Zarangoi. Drangianê was separated from Gedrôsia by the Baitian mountains, now called the Washati.

[4] Areia was a small province included in Ariana which embraced nearly the whole of ancient Persia. The name is connected with the Indian word *ârya*, "noble" or "excellent." It occupied the tract from Meshed to Herat.

many of his soldiers from his inability to relieve their
wants ; and afterwards, when he was on the march, some
of the Oritai, having attacked the troops commanded by
Leonnatos and slain a good many men, escaped scatheless
into their own country.[1]

*Chapter CVI.—Revels of Alexander and the army after
     escaping from the desert—Officials who had abused
     their authority called to account—Nearchos visits
     Alexander at Salmous, and recounts the incidents of
     his voyage*

When the desert had been crossed with all these pain-
ful experiences, he came to an inhabited region which
abounded with all things useful.   He here allowed his
army to recruit its exhausted powers, and then marched
forward for seven days with his soldiers splendidly dressed
as at a public assembly, while he celebrated a festival to
Dionysos, heading himself the procession of the revellers,
and, as he led the way, quaffing intoxicating draughts of
wine.   At the end of all this having come to learn that
many high-placed officials had transgressed all bounds
of law by an arbitrary and outrageous exercise of their
authority, he decided that not a few of his satraps and
generals stood in need of punishment.   As the odium in
which these leading men were held on account of their
scandalous disregard of the law was a matter of public
notoriety, many of them who held high posts of command
in the army, and whose conscience accused them of out-
rages and other violations of their duty, became seriously
alarmed.   Some whose troops consisted of mercenaries
revolted from the king, and others who had amassed
riches took to flight.   The king on hearing this wrote to
all the commanders and satraps throughout Asia that

---

[1] Arrian, however, relates in his
Indika (c. 23), that Leonnatos defeated the Oreitai and their allies in
a great battle in which all the leaders
and 6000 men were slain, while his
own loss was very trifling.

immediately after they had read his letter they should dismiss all the mercenaries.

When the king was just at this time staying in a sea-coast town called Salmous, and holding a dramatic exhibition, the officers of the expedition which had been directed to navigate the ocean along its shores put into harbour, and, proceeding straightway to the theatre, saluted Alexander, and gave him an account of their adventures. The Macedonians, delighted to see their old comrades once more among them, marked the event with loud and prolonged cheering, and all the theatre was in a transport of joy that could not be exceeded.[1] The voyagers described how the ocean was subject to the strange vicissitude of the ebbing and flowing of its waters, and that when it ebbed numerous islands were unexpectedly revealed to view at the projections of land along the coast, while at flood-tide all these lands just mentioned were again submerged, a full gale blowing meanwhile towards shore, and whitening with foam all the surface of the water. But the strangest part of their story was that they had encountered a great many whales, and these of an incredible size. They were in great dread of these monsters, and at first gave up all hopes of life, thinking they might at any moment be consigned, boats and all, to destruction ; but when, on recovering from their panic, they raised a simultaneous shout, which they increased by rattling their arms and sounding the trumpets, the creatures took alarm at the strange noise, and sank to the depths below.

[1] Arrian gives in his *Indika* (c. 33-35) full details of the journey of Nearchos from the coast to Alexander's camp, which lay a five days' march inland, and of the affecting interview between the king and his admiral, whom he had given up for lost. Arrian's narrative may be implicitly trusted, as it was based on the *Journal* of Nearchos, whose veracity is unimpeachable. The admiral did not appear in the theatre until his interview with Alexander had been concluded. Diodôros is clearly in error in placing Salmous on the coast.

Chapter CVII.—Kalanos, the Indian philosopher, immolates himself—Alexander marries the daughter of Darius

When the king had heard their story to the end, he ordered the leaders of the expedition to sail up to the mouth of the Euphrates. At the head of his army he traversed himself a great stretch of country, and arrived on the borders of Sousiana. About that time Kalanos, the Indian who had made great progress in philosophy, and was held in honour and esteem by Alexander, brought his life to an end in a most singular manner; for when he was three years over three score and ten, and up till then had never known what illness was, he resolved to depart this life as one who had received the full measure of happiness alike from nature and from fortune. He was now, however, afflicted with a malady which became daily more and more burdensome, and he therefore requested the king to prepare for him a great funeral pyre, and to order his servants to set fire to it as soon as he should ascend it. Alexander at first tried to divert him from his purpose, but when he found that all his remonstrances were unavailing, he consented to do him the service asked. Orders were accordingly given for doing the work, and when the pyre was ready the whole army attended to witness the extraordinary spectacle. Then Kalanos, following the rules prescribed by his philosophy, stepped with unflinching courage on to the summit of the pyre, and perished in the flames which consumed it. Some of the spectators condemned the man for his madness, others for the vanity shown in his act of hardihood, while some admired his high spirit and contempt of death. The king honoured him with a sumptuous funeral, and then proceeded to Sousa, where he married Stateira, the elder of the two daughters of Darius.

PLUTARCH

PLUTARCH'S LIFE OF ALEXANDER

Chapter LVIII.—Alexander at Nysa

. . . When the Macedonians were hesitating to attack the city called Nysa, because the river which ran past it was deep, "Unlucky man that I am," Alexander exclaimed, "why did I not learn to swim?" and so saying he prepared to ford the stream. After he had withdrawn from the assault, envoys arrived from the besieged with an offer to surrender. They were at first surprised to find him clad in his armour, and still stained with the dust and blood of battle. A cushion was then brought to him, which he requested the eldest of the envoys to take and be seated. This man was called Akouphis, and he was so much struck with the splendour and courtesy with which he was received that he asked what his countrymen must do to make him their friend. Alexander replied : "They must make you their governor, and send me a hundred of their best men." At this Akouphis laughed, and said : "Methinks, O King! I should rule better if, instead of the best, you took the worst."

Chapter LIX.—Interchange of civilities between Alexander and Taxilês—Alexander breaks his faith with Indian mercenaries, and hangs some Indian philosophers

Taxilês, it is said, ruled over a part of India which was as large as Egypt, afforded good pasturage, and had a very fertile soil. He was a shrewd man, and after he had embraced Alexander, said to him : " Why should we two, Alexander, fight with one another if you have come to take away from us neither our water nor our necessary food—the only things about which sensible men ever care to quarrel and fight. As for anything else, call it money or call it property, if I am richer than you, what I have is at your service ; but if I have less than you, I would not object to stand debtor to your bounty." Alexander was delighted with what he said, and, giving him his right hand in token of his friendship, exclaimed : " Perhaps you think from the friendly greetings we have exchanged our intercourse will be continued without a contest. There you are mistaken, for I will war to the knife with you in good offices, and will see to it that you do not overcome me in generosity." Alexander therefore, after having received many presents from Taxilês, and given him more in return, at last drank to his health, and accompanied the toast with the present of a thousand talents of coined money. This act of his greatly vexed his friends, but made him stand higher in favour with many of the barbarians. As the Indian mercenary troops, consisting, as they did, of the best soldiers to be found in the country, flocked to the cities which he attacked, and defended them with the greatest vigour, he thus incurred serious losses, and accordingly concluded a treaty of peace with them ; but afterwards, as they were going away, set upon them while they were on the road, and killed them all. This rests as a foul blot on his martial fame, for on all other occasions he observed the rules of civilised warfare as became a king.[1] The philosophers gave him no less trouble than the mercenaries, because they reviled the princes who declared for him and encouraged the free states to revolt from his authority. On this account he hanged many of them.[2]

[1] This incident occurred at Mazaga, the capital of Assakênos.

[2] The Brahmans of Sindh are here referred to.

Chapter LX. — The account of the battle with Pôros, as given by Alexander himself—Alexander's noble treatment of Pôros

How the war against Pôros was conducted he has described in his own letters. He tells us that the river Hydaspês ran between the two camps, and that Pôros with his elephants which he had posted with their heads towards the stream, constantly guarded the passage. Alexander himself, day after day, caused a great noise and disturbance to be made in his camp, in order that the barbarians might be gradually led to view his movements without alarm. At last, upon a dark and stormy night, he took a part of the infantry and a choice body of cavalry, marched to a considerable distance from the enemy, and crossed over to an island of no great size. Here he was exposed with his army to the rage of a violent thunderstorm, amid which rain fell down in torrents, and though he saw some of his men struck dead with the lightning, he nevertheless advanced from the island and reached the furthermost bank of the river. The Hydaspês was now flooded by the rains, and its raging current had chosen a new channel of great width, down which a great body of water was carried. In fording this new bed, he could with difficulty keep his footing, as the bottom was very slippery and uneven. It was here that Alexander is said to have exclaimed, "O Athenians! can you believe what dangers I undergo to earn your applause?" This particular rests on the authority of Onesikritos, for Alexander himself merely says that he and his men left their rafts, and under arms waded through the second torrent with the water up to their breasts. After crossing, he himself rode forward about twenty stadia in advance of the infantry, concluding that if the enemy attacked him with their cavalry only, he could easily rout them; but if they moved forward their entire force, he could bring his infantry into the field before fighting began. He was right in both conclusions, for he fell in with 1000 horse and 60 war-chariots of the enemy, and these he routed, capturing every chariot, and slaying 400 of the horsemen. Pôros thus perceived that Alexander himself had crossed the river, and he therefore advanced against him with all his army, except some troops which he left to guard his camp, in case the Macedonians should cross from the opposite bank to attack it. Alexander, dreading the elephants and the great numbers of the enemy, did not engage with them in front, but attacked them himself on the left wing, ordering Koinos to fall upon them on the right. Both wings were broken, and the enemy, driven from their position, thronged always towards the centre where the elephants were posted. The contest, which began early in the morning, was so obstinately maintained that it was fully the eighth hour of the day before the Indians renounced all attempts at further resistance. This description of the battle is given by the chief actor in it himself in his letters. Most historians are agreed that Pôros stood four cubits and a span high, and that his gigantic form was not less proportioned to the elephant which carried him, and which was his biggest, than was a rider of an ordinary size to his horse. This elephant showed wonderful sagacity and care for its royal master, for while it was still vigorous it defended him against his assailants and repulsed them, but when it perceived that he was ready to sink from the number of his wounds and bruises, fearing that he might fall off its back, it gently lowered itself to the ground, and as it knelt quietly extracted the darts from his body with its trunk. When Pôros was taken prisoner, Alexander asked him how he wished to be treated. "Like a king," answered Pôros. When Alexander further asked if he had anything else to request, "Every thing," rejoined Pôros, "is comprised in the words, like a king." Alexander then not only reinstated Pôros in his kingdom with the title of satrap, but added a large province to it, subduing the inhabitants whose form of government was the republican. This country, it is said, contained 15 tribes, 5000 considerable cities, and villages without number.[1] He subdued besides another district three times as large, over which he appointed Philippos, one of his friends, to be satrap.

Chapter LXI.—Death of Boukephalas, and Alexander's regret at his loss

After the battle with Pôros, Boukephalas died, not immediately, but some time afterwards, from wounds which he received in the engagement. This is the account which most historians give, but Onesikritos says that he died of old age and overwork, for he had reached his thirtieth year.[2] Alexander deeply regretted his loss, taking it as much to heart as if it had been that of a faithful friend and companion. He founded a city in his honour on the banks of the Hydaspês, and named it Boukephalia. It is also recorded that when he lost a pet dog called Peritas, which he had brought up, and of which he was very fond, he founded a city and called it by the name of this dog. Sôtiôn tells us that he had heard this from Potamôn of Lesbos.

---

[1] "When the Greek writers tell us that the district between the Hydaspes and the Hyphasis alone contained 5000 cities (!), none of which was less than that of Cos (Strabo, xv. p. 686), and that the dominions of Pôros, which were confined between the Hydaspes and the Acesines—a tract not more than 40 miles in width—contained 300 cities (id. p. 698), it is evident that the Greeks were misled by the exaggerated reports so common with all Orientals, and which were greedily swallowed by the historians of Alexander with a view of magnifying the exploits of the great conqueror."—Bunbury, *Hist. of Anc. Geog.* I. p. 453.

[2] See Note to Arrian, p. 112, and to Curtius, p. 212.

Chapter LXII.—The army refuses to advance to the Ganges —Alexander, preparing to retreat, erects altars which were afterwards held in veneration by the Praisian kings—The opinion of Androkottos

The battle with Pôros depressed the spirits of the Macedonians, and made them very unwilling to advance farther into India. For as it was with the utmost difficulty they had beaten him when the army he led amounted only to 20,000 infantry and 2000 cavalry, they now most resolutely opposed Alexander when he insisted that they should cross the Ganges.[1] This river, they heard, had a breadth of two-and-thirty stadia, and a depth of 100 fathoms, while its farther banks were covered all over with armed men, horses, and elephants. For the kings of the Gandaritai and the Praisiai[2] were reported to be waiting for him with an army of 80,000 horse, 200,000 foot, 8000 war chariots, and 6000 fighting elephants. Nor was this any exaggeration, for not long afterwards Androkottos,[3] who had by that time mounted the throne, presented Seleukos with 500 elephants, and overran and subdued the whole of India with an army of 600,000 men. Alexander at first in vexation and rage withdrew to his tent, and shutting himself up lay there feeling no gratitude towards those who had thwarted his purpose of crossing the Ganges ; but regarding a retreat as tantamount to a confession of defeat. But being swayed by the persuasions of his friends, and the entreaties of his soldiers who stood weeping and lamenting at the door of his tent, he at last relented, and prepared to retreat. He first, however, con-

---

[1] This seems an almost inexcusable mistake on Plutarch's part—his conducting Alexander as far as the Ganges ! The author of the *Periplûs* made the same egregious blunder. It is possible, however, to put a different construction on the expressions used by Plutarch, and to suppose that he wrote so carelessly that he did not mean what his words seem to imply.

[2] See Notes Cc and Dd for these people.

[3] More correctly Sandrakyptos, or Chandragupta. See Biog. Appendix, *s.v.* Sandrokottos.

trived many unfair devices to exalt his fame among the natives, as, for instance, causing arms for men and stalls and bridles for horses to be made much beyond the usual size, and these he left scattered about. He also erected altars for the gods which the kings of the Praisiai even to the present day hold in veneration, crossing the river to offer sacrifices upon them in the Hellenic fashion.[1] Androkottos himself, who was then but a youth, saw Alexander himself, and afterwards used to declare that Alexander could easily have taken possession of the whole country since the king was hated and despised by his subjects for the wickedness of his disposition and the meanness of his origin.[2]

Chapter LXIII.—Alexander starts on a voyage down stream, reducing tribes by the way — He is dangerously wounded in the capital of the Malloi—Extraction of the arrow from his wound—His recovery

After marching thence Alexander, who wished to see the outer ocean, ordered many rafts and vessels managed with oars to be built, and he then fell down the rivers in a leisurely manner. But the voyage was neither an idle one nor unattended with warlike operations, for at times he disembarked, and attacking the cities which adjoined the banks succeeded in subduing them all. But he very nearly lost his life when he was amongst the people called the Malloi, who were said to be the most warlike of all the Indians. For in besieging their city, after he had driven the defenders from the walls by volleys of missiles, he was the first man to ascend a scaling ladder and reach the summit of the wall.[3] Just then the ladder broke, so that he was left almost alone, and as the barbarians who were standing at the foot of the wall inside shot at him

[1] See Note N, Altars at the Hyphasis.
[2] See Biog. Appendix, *s.v.* Sandrokottos.

[3] This was the wall of the citadel, not of the city, as Plutarch represents.

from below, he was repeatedly hit with their missiles. He
therefore poised himself and leaped down into the midst
of his enemies, alighting by good chance on his feet. The
flashing of his arms as he brandished them made the
barbarians think that lightning or some supernatural
splendour played round his person, and they therefore
drew back and dispersed. But when they saw that he
was attended by two followers only, some of them
attacked him at close-quarters with swords and spears,
while one man, who stood a little farther off, shot an
arrow from his bow at full bent, and with such force that
it pierced through his corselet and lodged itself in the
bones of his breast.[1] As he staggered under the blow
and sank upon his knees, the barbarian ran up with his
drawn scimitar to despatch him. Peukestas and Limnaios[2]
placed themselves before Alexander to protect him ; both
of them were wounded, one of them mortally ; but
Peukestas, who survived, continued to make some resistance, while the king slew the Indian with his own hand.
Alexander was wounded in many places ; and at last
received a blow on his neck from a club, which forced
him to lean for support against the wall with his face
turned towards the enemy. The Macedonians, who by
this time had come up, crowded round him, and snatching
him up, now insensible to all around him, carried him off
to his tent. A rumour immediately ran through the
camp that he was dead, and his attendants having with
great difficulty sawed through the arrow, which had a
wooden shaft, were thus able after much trouble to take
off his corselet. They had next to extract the barbed
head of the arrow which was firmly fixed in one of his
ribs. This arrow-head is said to have measured three
fingers' breadths in width and four in length. Accordingly, when it was pulled out, he swooned away and was
brought very near the gates of death, but he at length

[1] This fact, attested by all the historians, confirms the truth of the
reports as to the great skill of the
Indians in archery.

[2] Called Timaeus by Curtius, p. 240.

revived.   When he was out of danger, but still very weak, having for a long time to follow the mode of life most conducive to the restoration of his health, he heard a disturbance outside his tent, and learning that the Macedonians were longing to see him he put on his cloak and went out to them.   After sacrificing to the gods, he again moved forward and subdued a great extent of country and many considerable cities that lay on his route.

Chapter LXIV.—Alexander's interview with the Indian gymnosophists

He captured ten of the gymnosophists who had been principally concerned in persuading Sabbas[1] to revolt, and had done much harm otherwise to the Macedonians. These men are thought to be great adepts in the art of returning brief and pithy answers, and Alexander proposed for their solution some hard questions, declaring that he would put to death first the one who did not answer correctly and then the others in order.[2]

He demanded of the first "Which he took to be the more numerous, the living or the dead?"   He answered, "The living, for the dead are not."

The second was asked, "Which breeds the largest animals, the sea or the land?"   He answered, "The land, for the sea is only a part of it."

[1] He is called Sambos by Arrian, and was the ruler of the mountainous region west of the Indus, having Sindimana for his capital, the city now called Sehwan.   See Biog. Appendix, s.v. Sambos.

[2] "He (Alexander) caused ten Indian philosophers, whom the Greeks called gymnosophists, and who were naked as apes, to be seized. He proposes to them questions worthy of the gallant Mercury of Visé, promising them with all seriousness that the one who answered worst would be hanged the first, after which the others would follow in their order.   This is like Nabuchodonosor, who absolutely wished to slay the Magians if they did not divine one of his dreams which he had forgotten, or the Calif of The Thousand and One Nights who was to strangle his wife when she came to the end of her stories.   But it is Plutarch who tells this silly story; we must respect it; he was a Greek" (Voltaire, Dict. Phil. s.v. Alexandre).   See also Note Hh, Indian Gymnosophists.

The third was asked, "Which is the cleverest of beasts?" He answered, "That with which man is not yet acquainted."

The fourth was asked, "For what reason he induced Sabbas to revolt?" He answered, "Because I wished him to live with honour or die with honour."

The fifth was asked, "Which he thought existed first, the day or the night?" He answered, "The day was first by one day." As the king appeared surprised at this solution, he added, "Impossible questions require impossible answers."

Alexander then turning to the sixth asked him "How a man could best make himself beloved?" He answered, "If a man being possessed of great power did not make himself to be feared."

Of the remaining three, one being asked "How a man could become a god?" replied, "By doing that which is impossible for a man to do."

The next being asked, "Which of the two was stronger, life or death?" he replied, "Life, because it bears so many evils."

The last being asked, "How long it was honourable for a man to live?" answered, "As long as he does not think it better to die than to live."

Upon this Alexander, turning to the judge, requested him to give his decision. He said they had answered each one worse than the other. "Since such is your judgment," Alexander then said, "you shall be yourself the first to be put to death." "Not so," said he, "O king, unless you are false to your word, for you said that he who gave the worst answer should be the first to die."

*Chapter LXV.—Onesikritos confers with the Indian gym-
nosophists Kalanos and Dandamis—Kalanos visits
Alexander and shows him a symbol of his empire*

The king then gave them presents and dismissed them
to their homes. He also sent Onesikritos to the most
renowned of these sages, who lived by themselves in
tranquil seclusion, to request that they would come to
him.[1] This Onesikritos was a philosopher who belonged
to the school of Diogenês the Cynic. He tells us that
one of these men called Kalanos ordered him with the
most overbearing insolence and rudeness to take off his
clothes, and listen naked to his discourse—otherwise he
would not enter into conversation with him even if he
came from Zeus himself. Dandamis, however, was of a
milder temper, and when he had been told about Sôkrates,
Pythagoras and Diogenês, he said they appeared to him
to have been men of genius, but from an excessive defer-
ence to the laws had subjected their lives too much to
their requirements. But other writers tell us that he said
nothing more than this, " For what purpose has Alexander
come all the way hither? " Taxilês, however, persuaded
Kalanos to visit Alexander. His real name was Sphinês,
but as he saluted those whom he met with " Kale," which
is the Indian equivalent of "Chairein" (that is, "All
hail"), he was called by the Greeks Kalanos. This
philosopher, we are told, showed Alexander a symbol of
his empire. He threw down on the ground a dry and
shrivelled hide and planted his foot on the edge of it.
But when it was trodden down in one place, it started up
everywhere else. He then walked all round it and showed
that the same thing took place wherever he trod, until at
length he stepped into the middle, and by doing so made
it all lie flat. This symbol was intended to show
Alexander that he should control his empire from its
centre, and not wander away to its distant extremities.

[1] The interviews of Onesikritos with the Indian philosophers took place earlier than is here stated—when Alexander was at Taxila.

*Chapter LXVI.—Alexander visits the island Skilloustis,
and sailing thence explores the sea—Sufferings of his
army on the march homeward, and extent of its losses
—Relief sent by the satraps*

Alexander's voyage down the rivers to the sea occupied seven months.   On reaching the ocean he sailed to
an island which he himself has called Skilloustis, but
which is generally known as Psiltoukis.[1]   On landing
there he sacrificed to the gods, exploring afterwards the
nature of the sea and the coast as far as he could
penetrate.   This done, he turned back, after praying to
the gods that no man might ever overpass the limits
which his expedition had reached.   He ordered his fleet

FIG. 13.—GREEK
WARSHIP.

to sail along the coast, keeping India
on the right hand ; and he appointed
Nearchos to the chief command, with
Onesikritos as the master pilot.   He
himself, returning by land with the
army, marched through the country
of the Oreitai, where he was reduced
to the sorest straits from the scarcity
of provisions, and lost such numbers of men that he hardly brought
back from India the fourth part of his military force, though
he entered it with 120,000 foot and 15,000 horse.   Many
perished from malignant distempers, wretched food, and
scorching heat, but most from sheer hunger, for their
march lay through an uncultivated region, inhabited only
by some miserable savages, the owners of a small and
inferior breed of sheep, accustomed to feed on sea-fish,
which gave to their flesh a rank and disagreeable flavour.[2]

[1] Called Killouta by Arrian. The
native name has not otherwise been
preserved.   The city which Pliny
calls Xylenopolis was probably situated in Killouta, and was the naval
station whence Nearchos started on

his voyage. The name means "city
of wood."

[2] Arrian relates in his *Indika* (c.
26) that Nearchos in the course of
his voyage, having landed at a place
on the Gedrôsian coast called Kalama,

With great difficulty, therefore, he traversed this desert region in sixty days, and reached Gedrôsia, where all the men were at once supplied with abundance of provisions, furnished by the satraps and kings of the nearest provinces.

Chapter LXVII.—Alexander and the army indulge in wild revelry on emerging from the desert

After he had given his forces some time to recruit, he led them in a joyous revel for seven days through Karmania. He himself sat at table with his companions mounted on a lofty oblong platform drawn by eight horses, and in that conspicuous position feasted continually both by day and by night. This carriage was followed by numberless others, some with purple hangings and embroidered canopies, and others screened with overarching green boughs always fresh gathered, conveying the rest of Alexander's friends and officers crowned with garlands and drinking wine. There was not a helmet, a shield, or a pike to be seen, but all along the road the soldiers were dipping cups, horns, and earthen vessels into great jars and flagons of wine, and drinking one another's healths, some as they went marching forward, and others as they sat by the way. Wherever they passed might be heard the music of the pipe and the flute and the voices of women singing and dancing and making merry. During this disorderly and dissolute march the soldiers after their cups indulged in ribald jests, as if the god Dionysos himself were present among them and accompanying their joyous procession.[1] Alexander, on reaching the capital of Gedrôsia, again halted to refresh his army, and entertained it with feasting and revelry.

received from the natives a present of sheep and fish. The admiral recorded that the mutton had a fishy taste like the flesh of sea-birds, because for want of grass the sheep were fed on fish.

[1] See Note on Curtius, p. 266.

JUSTIN

HISTORIAE PHILIPPICAE OF JUSTINUS

TWELFTH BOOK

Chapter VII.—Alexander visits Nysa and Mount Merus —Receives the submission of Queen Cleophis and captures the Rock (Aornos)

. . . After this he advanced towards India that he might make the ocean and the remotest East the limits of his empire. In order that the decorations of his army might be in keeping with this grandeur, he overlaid the trappings of the horses and the arms of his soldiers with silver. He then called the army his argyraspids, because the shields they carried were inwrought with silver. When he had reached the city of Nysa, and found that the inhabitants offered no resistance, he ordered their lives to be spared, from a sentiment of reverence towards Father Bacchus, by whom the city had been founded; at the same time congratulating himself that he had not only undertaken a military expedition like that god, but had even followed his very footsteps. He then led his army to view the sacred mountain, which the genial climate had mantled over with vine and ivy, just as if husbandmen had with industrious hands laboured to make it the perfection of beauty. Now the army on reaching the mountain, in a sudden access of devout emotion, began to howl in honour of the god, and to the amazement of the king ran unmolested all about the place, so that he perceived that by sparing the citizens he had not

Y

so much served their interests as those of his own army. Thence he marched to the Daedali mountains [1] and the dominions of Queen Cleophis,[2] who, after surrendering her kingdom, purchased its restoration by permitting the conqueror to share her bed, thus gaining by her fascinations what she had not gained by her valour. The offspring of this intercourse was a son, whom she called Alexander, the same who afterwards reigned as an Indian king. Queen Cleophis, because she had prostituted her chastity, was thereafter called by the Indians *the royal harlot.* When Alexander after traversing India had come to a rock of a wonderful size and ruggedness, unto which many of the people had fled for refuge,[3] he came to know that Hercules had been prevented from capturing that very rock by an earthquake. Being seized, therefore, with an ambitious desire of surpassing the deeds of Hercules, he made himself master of the rock with infinite toil and danger, and then received the submission of all the tribes in that part of the country.

Chapter VIII.—Alexander conquers Porus—Builds Nicaea and Boucephala, and reduces the Adrestae, Gesteani, Praesidae, and Gangaridae—Advances to the Cuphites (Beäs), beyond which the army refuses to follow him —He agrees to return, and leaves memorials of his progress

One of the Indian kings called Porus, a man remarkable alike for his personal strength and noble courage, on hearing the report about Alexander, began to prepare war against his coming. Accordingly, when hostilities broke out, he ordered his army to attack the Macedonians, from whom he demanded their king, as if he was his private enemy. Alexander lost no time in joining battle,

---

[1] See Note on Curtius, p. 194.
[2] The Queen of Mazaga, capital of the Assakenians. See Note D.
[3] The rock Aornos, identified with Mount Mahaban. See Note F.

but his horse being wounded at the first charge, he fell headlong to the ground, and was saved by his attendants who hastened up to his assistance. Porus again, when fainting from the number of his wounds, was taken prisoner. His defeat he took so much to heart that when he had received quarter from the victor, he neither wished to take food nor would allow his wounds to be attended to, and indeed could scarcely be induced to wish for life. Alexander, out of respect for his valour, restored him in safety to his sovereignty. There he built two cities, one which he called Nicaea, and the other Boucephala, after the name of his horse. Moving thence he conquered the Adrestae, the Gesteani, the Praesidae, and the Gangaridae,[1] after defeating their armies with great slaughter. When he reached the Cuphites,[2] where the enemy awaited him with 200,000 cavalry, his soldiers, worn out not less by the number of their victories than by their incessant toils, all besought him with tears to bring at last the war to a close—besought him to have some remembrance of his native country and the duty of returning to it—to have some consideration for the years of his soldiers, to whom scarcely so much of life now remained as would suffice them for returning home. Some pointed to their hoary hair, others to their wounds, others to their bodies withered with age or seamed with scars. None, they said, except themselves had brooked a continuous service under two kings, Philip and Alexander ; and now at last they entreated he would send them home where their bodies, wasted as they were to skeletons, might be buried in the tombs of their fathers,

---

[1] The Adrestae are the Adraïstai of Arrian. See Note on that author, p. 116. The Gesteani seem to be the Kathaians. The Praesidae must be the Prasians (though Saint-Martin would identify them with the Praesti of Curtius), and the Gangaridae the people of Lower Bengal.

[2] The river reached was the Hyphasis. How Justin came to call it the Cuphites it is difficult to understand.

Can he have had in his recollection the Kâbul river, called sometimes by the classical writers the *Kuphes*, with *Kuphet* as the stem for the oblique cases, and mistaken it for the river which arrested Alexander's progress ? Like Plutarch, he erroneously supposes that the Macedonian army was confronted with a great host encamped on the opposite bank of the river.

seeing it was from no want of will they failed to second his wishes, but from the incapacity of age. If, however, he would not spare his soldiers, he should at all events spare himself, and not wear out his good fortune by subjecting it to too severe a strain. Alexander was moved by these well-grounded entreaties, and, as if he had now reached the goal of victory, ordered a camp to be made of an unusual size and splendour, in order that the work, while calculated to terrify the enemy by its vastness, might be left to render himself an object of admiration to future ages. Never did the soldiers apply themselves with such alacrity to any work as they did to this ; and when it was finished they retraced their way to the parts whence they had come as joyfully as if they were returning from a field of victory.

Chapter IX.—Alexander sailing down the Panjâb rivers to the ocean, reduces the Hiacensanae, Silei, Ambri, and Sigambri—He is dangerously wounded in attacking one of their strongholds

From thence Alexander proceeded to the river Acesines[1] and sailed down stream towards the ocean. On his way he received the submission of the Hiacensanae[2] and the Silei[3] whom Hercules had founded. Sailing onward, he came to the Ambri and the Sigambri,[4] who opposed him with an army of 80,000 foot and 60,000 cavalry. Having defeated them, he led his army to their capital. On his observing from the wall, which he was himself the first to mount, that the city was left without defenders, he leaped down without any attendant into the level space at the foot of the wall. Then the enemy, noticing that he was alone, rushed together with loud shouts from all quarters

---

[1] *Hydaspes* he should have said.
[2] For the identification of this people, see Note F*f*.
[3] The *Silei* are probably the *Sibi*. See Note E*e*.

[4] By the *Ambri* must be meant the *Malli*, and by the *Sigambri* the *Oxydrakai*. The text must be corrupt.

of the city to finish, if possible, the wars that embroiled the world, by one man's death, and give the many nations he had attacked their revenge. Alexander made an obstinate resistance, and single-handed fought against thousands. It surpasses belief to tell how neither the multitude of his assailants, nor the ceaseless storm of their missiles, nor their savage yells made him quail, and how, alone as he was, he slew and put thousands to flight. When at last he saw that he was being overpowered by numbers, he placed his back against the stem of a tree which grew near the wall, and by this means protected himself till, after he had for a long time stood at bay, his danger became at length known to his friends, who forthwith leaped down from the wall to his assistance. Of these many were slain in the act of defending him, and the issue of the conflict remained doubtful till the walls were thrown down and the whole army came to his rescue. In this battle Alexander was pierced by an arrow under the pap, but even while he was fainting from the loss of blood he sank on his knee, and continued fighting till he slew the man by whom he had been wounded. The operation required for curing his wound threw him into a deadlier swoon than the wound itself had produced.

Chapter X.—Alexander reaches the city of King Ambigerus (Sambos ?)—Ptolemy is there wounded by a poisoned arrow—An antidote to the poison is revealed to Alexander in a dream—He sails down to the mouth of the Indus — Founds Barce — Leaves India and returns to Babylon

His safety was for a time despaired of, but having at last recovered he sent Polyperchon with part of the army to Babylon. Having himself embarked with a very select company of his friends, he made a voyage along the shores of the ocean. On his reaching the city of King

Ambigerus [1] the inhabitants who had heard that he was invulnerable by steel, armed their arrows with poison, which thus inflicted a double wound. With this deadly weapon they killed great numbers of the enemy and repulsed them from the walls. Among many others that were wounded was Ptolemy, but he was rescued from danger just when he appeared to be dying, as soon as he had swallowed a potion prepared from a particular herb which had been revealed to the king in a vision as being an antidote to the poison. The greater part of the army was saved by the same remedy. Alexander having taken the city by storm poured out a libation to the ocean, praying at the same time for a prosperous return to his own country. He was then carried down with the tide in his favour to the mouth of the river Indus. And then like a victor who had triumphantly driven his chariot round the goal, he fixed the frontiers of his empire, having advanced till the deserts at the world's end barred his farther progress by land, and till seas were no longer navigable. As a monument of his achievements he founded in those parts the city of Barce.[2] He erected altars also, and on departing left one of his friends to be governor of the maritime Indians. As he intended to march homewards by land, and had learned that his route would lie through arid wastes, he ordered wells to be dug at convenient places. Since these were found to yield a copious supply of water he effected his return to Babylon.

[1] This is supposed to be a corrupt reading for Ambiregis, in which case *Ambi* is a mistake for *Sambi*. We know that the incident referred to happened in the dominions of this king. In Orosius (iii. 19) the name is transcribed as *Ambiraren*.

[2] Nothing is known of this city, unless it be, as Cunningham thinks, the *Barbari* of Ptolemy, and the *Barbarike Emporium* of the author of the *Periplûs*. See his *Anc. Geog.* p. 295.

Chapter IV.—Seleucus Nicator subjugates the Bactrians and enters India—The history of Sandrocottus who was then King of India—Seleucus makes a treaty of peace with him and returns to the West

. . . Seleucus Nicator waged many wars in the east after the partition of Alexander's empire among his generals. He first took Babylon, and then with his forces augmented by victory subjugated the Bactrians. He then passed over into India, which after Alexander's death, as if the yoke of servitude had been shaken off from its neck, had put his prefects to death. Sandrocottus was the leader who achieved their freedom, but after his victory he forfeited by his tyranny all title to the name of liberator, for he oppressed with servitude the very people whom he had emancipated from foreign thraldom. He was born in humble life, but was prompted to aspire to royalty by an omen significant of an august destiny. For when by his insolent behaviour he had offended Nandrus,[1] and was ordered by that king to be put to death, he sought safety by a speedy flight. When he lay down overcome with

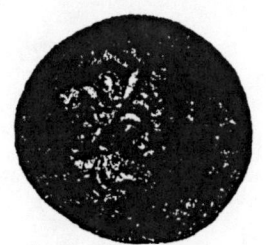

FIG. 14.—SELEUCUS NICATOR.

---

[1] *Nandrum* has been here substituted for the common reading *Alexandrum*, which Gutschmid (*Rhein. Mus.* 12, 261) has shown to be an error.

fatigue and had fallen into a deep sleep, a lion of enormous size approaching the slumberer licked with its tongue the sweat which oozed profusely from his body, and when he awoke, quietly took its departure. It was this prodigy which first inspired him with the hope of winning the throne, and so having collected a band of robbers, he instigated the Indians to overthrow the existing government. When he was thereafter preparing to attack Alexander's prefects, a wild elephant of monstrous size approached him, and kneeling submissively like a tame elephant received him on to its back and fought vigorously in front of the army. Sandrocottus having thus won the throne was reigning over India when Seleucus was laying the foundations of his future greatness. Seleucus having made a treaty with him and otherwise settled his affairs in the east, returned home to prosecute the war with Antigonus.

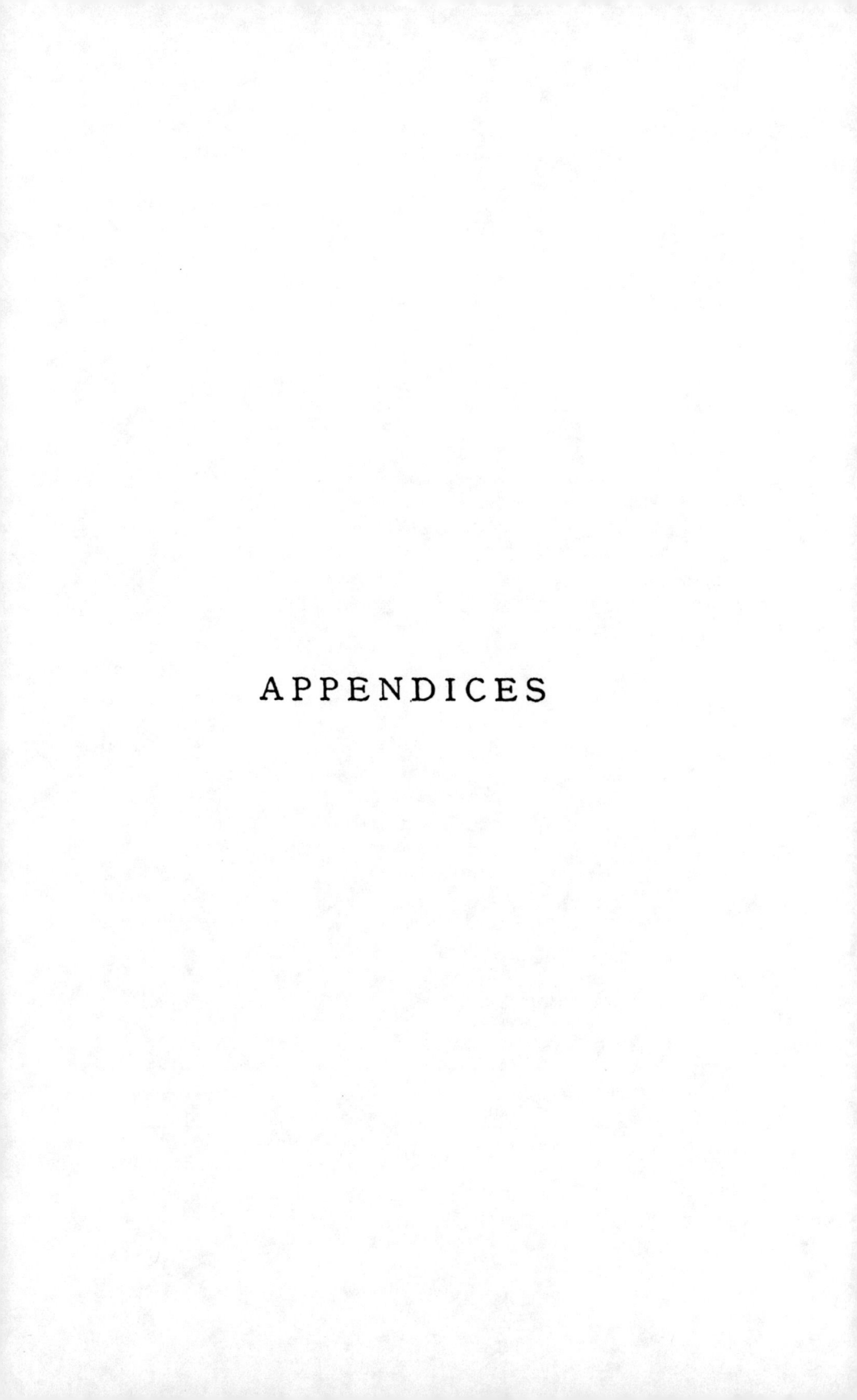

APPENDICES

NOTES A-L*l*

Alexander had founded this city at the foot of Paropanisos in the spring of 329 B.C., before he crossed into Baktria. For distinction's sake it was called Alexandreia "under Kaukasos," or "of the Paropamisadai." Its position has been a subject much discussed. Sir A. Burnes and Lassen fixed it at Bamiân, but to this there is the objection that Bamiân is situated in the midst of the mountains, and is reached from Kâbul after the main ridge of the Hindu-Kush has been crossed. A position which would suit better for the foundation of a permanent settlement is to be found in the rich and beautiful valley of the Koh-Dâman, which, as its name implies, extends up to the very foot of the great mountain rampart. Towards the northern edge of this valley lies the village of Charikar, whence the three roads that lead into Baktria diverge. In the neighbourhood of this commanding position is a place called Opiân or Houpiân, where vast ruins, first discovered by Masson, indicate the former presence of an important town. A link to connect this place with Alexandreia is supplied by Stephanos of Byzantium, who describes Alexandreia as "a city in Opianê, near India." From this we may infer that Opiân or Houpiân was the capital of a country of the same name, and that it formed the site of the city which Alexander founded under Kaukasos. This view has been advocated by Dr. H. Wilson and V. de Saint-Martin, and also by General Cunningham, who supports it by a reference to the famous itinerary preserved in Pliny (*N. H.* VI. xvii. 21), from Diognêtos and Baitôn, who recorded the distances of Alexander's marches. Alexandreia, it is there stated, was 50 miles distant from Ortospanum, and 237 from Peukolatis. As Ortospanum has been on sufficient grounds identified with Kâbul, and Peukolatis with Hashtnagar on the river Landaï, the question arises whether Houpiân is at the required distance from each of these places, and General Cunningham shows that such is the case, allowance being made for the rough methods employed in calculating such distances in ancient times. Bunbury inclines to accept this identification, but thinks that as Opianê is in Stephanos the name of a country, the evidence of the modern appellation (Houpiân) is of little weight in determining the position of the city. No mention of this Alexandreia occurs either in Ptolemy or the *Periplûs of the Erythraian Sea*, but it is mentioned in the *Mahâvanso* under the form Alasaddâ, or Alasandâ, as Hardy writes it. About the 7th century again of our aera, the Chinese pilgrim Hiouen Thsiang speaks of Houpiân (Hou-pi-na in Chinese transcription) as a large city in which the chief of the Vardaks resided. Its ruin may be dated from the aera of the Mohammedan conquest, for Baber in his *Memoirs* speaks of Houpiân as if it were merely the name of the Pass which opens on the valley of the Ghorbund. According to Hardy, Alasandâ was the birthplace of Menander (the Milinda of Sanskrit), the Graeco-Baktrian king. See Wilson's *Ar. Antiq.* pp. 179-182; V. de Saint-Martin, *Étude*, 21-26; Cunningham's *Anc. Geog. of India*, pp. 19-26; Bunbury's *Hist. of Anc. Geog.* i. 490-492; Weber's *Die Griechen in Indien*; and Hardy's *Manual of Buddhism*, p. 516.

Note B.—Nikaia

This is a Greek word meaning *victorious*, and may possibly be a translation of the indigenous name of the place. Wilson (*Ar. Antiq.* p. 183) takes this view, and fixes the site of Nikaia on the plain of Begrâm at a spot with ruins about some eighteen miles distant from Houpiân. The original name of the place may have been *Jayapura*, which means *the city of victory*. According to others, Nikaia is a transliteration of *Nichaia-gram*, a place said to be in Kafîristân—that is, in the upper part of the valleys which slope away from the Hindu-Kush and carry their waters to the Kâbul river on its left. A belief was at one time current that the Kafîrs of Bajour were descended from the Macedonians whom Alexander had left there when he passed through the country on his way to India. They had, it was said, many points of character in common with the Greeks. They were celebrated for their beauty and their European complexions. They worshipped idols, drank wine in silver cups or vases, used chairs and tables, and spoke a language unknown to their neighbours. Elphinstone during his Kâbul mission (in 1808) caused inquiries to be made as to the truth of these reports, which had greatly excited his curiosity. It was found that though they were in the main correct, yet the fact that the people had no certain traditions of their own as to their origin, while the languages spoken by the different tribes were all of them closely allied to Sanskrit, showed the theory of their Greek origin to be untenable. In the list which was furnished to the envoy of the names of their tribes and villages, Nisa is the only one in which any similarity to Nikaia can be traced. In Lassen's opinion, Nikaia was not built on the site of any previously existing town, but was first founded by Alexander, who named it the *victorious* in anticipation of the triumphs which awaited him in India. General Abbott identified it with Nangnihar, a place about four or five miles west of Jalâlâbâd, which he thought Curtius took to be the point where Alexander first entered Indian territory. General Cunningham again, like Ritter and Droysen, thinks that Nikaia must have been Kâbul, otherwise that important town, through which Alexander must have marched, would be passed over by his historians without mention. He cites in proof a passage from the *Dionysiakê* of Nonnus, in which Nikaia is described as a stone city situated near a lake. The lake, he says, is a remarkable feature which is peculiar in Northern India to Kâbul and Kâshmîr. The authority of Nonnus, however, on such a point is of no worth whatever. Wilson's view that Nikaia occupied the site of Bagrâm seems preferable to any other. It is the view also which Bunbury favours. (See his *History of Ancient Geography*, p. 439 *n.*)

NOTE C.—ASPASIOI ASSAKÊNOI

The Aspasioi are the people called by Strabo, in his list of the tribes which occupied the country between the Kôphês and the Indus, the Hippasioi. They are easily to be recognised under either of these names as the As'vaka who are mentioned in the *Mahâbhârata* along with the Gândhâra as the barbarous inhabitants of far distant regions in the north. The name of the As'vaka, derived from *as'va*, "a horse," means cavaliers, and indicates that their country was renowned in primitive times, as it is at the present day, for its superior breed of horses. The fact that the Greeks translated their name into Hippasioi (from ἵππος, a horse) shows that they must have been aware of its etymological signification. V. de Saint-Martin inclines to think that the name of the Hippasioi is partly preserved in that of the Pachaï, a considerable tribe located in the upper regions of the

Kôphês basin. It is more distinctly preserved in *Asip* or *Isap*, the Pukhto name of this tribe, called by Mohammedans the *Yusufzai.* The name of the Assakênoi, like that of the Aspasioi, represents the Sanskrit As'vaka, which in the popular dialect is changed into Assaka, and by the addition of the Persian plural termination into Assakan, a form which Arrian has all but exactly transcribed, and which appears without any change in the Assa-kanoi of Strabo and the Assacani of Curtius. They are now represented by the Aspîn of Chitral and the Yashkun of Gilgit. Some writers think, however, that the name of the Assakans or Asvakans is still extant in that of the Afghans, for the change of the sibilant into the rough aspirate is quite normal, and also that of *k* into *g*, a mute of its own order. Dr. Bellew, however, in his *Inquiry into the Ethnography of Afghanistan*, finds the source of the name in the Armenian Aghván, and says it seems clear from what he has explained that the name Afghân merely means "mountaineer," and is neither an ethnic term of distinct race nationality nor of earlier origin than the period of the Roman dominion in Asia Minor. See the *Inquiry*, pp. 196-208.

Note D.—Mazaga

The name of this place, which in Sanskrit would appear as Mâs'aka, has various forms in the classics—*Massaga* as in our author here, *Massaka* in his *Indika*, *Mazaga* in Curtius, and *Masoga* in Strabo, who says it was the capital of King Assakanos. The exact position of this important place has not yet been ascertained, but its name as that of an ancient site still remains in the country. The Emperor Baber states in his *Memoirs* that at the distance of two rapid marches from the town of Bajore (the capital of the province of the same name), lying to the west of the river Pañjkoré, there was a town called Masha-nagar on the river of Sévad (Swât). Rennell identified this name with the Massaga of Alexander's historians, and no doubt correctly. M. Court, who has given interesting information about the country of the Yuzafzaïs, which he collected among the inhabitants of the plains, learned from them that at twenty-four miles from Bajore there exists a ruined site known under the double name of Maskhine and Massangar (Massanagar). In the grammar again of Pânini, who was a native of Gândhâra, in which the Assakan territory was comprised, the word Mâs'akâvatî occurs, given as the name both of a river and a district. It may then fairly be presumed that Massaga was the capital of the Mâs'akâvatî district, and that the impetuous stream which, as we learn from Curtius, ran between steep banks and made access to Massaga difficult on the east side, was the Mâs'akâvatî of Pânini (*v.* Lassen, *Ind. Alt.* II. pp. 136-138; V. de Saint-Martin, *Étude*, pp. 35, 36; and Abbott, *Gradus ad Aornon*). Curtius (viii. 37, 38) describes with more minuteness than Arrian the nature of the engineering operations designed to make the attack against the walls practicable. He states that Assacanus, the king of the place, died before Alexander's arrival, and not after the siege had begun, as Arrian relates. He adds that Assacanus was succeeded by his mother (wife?), whose name was Cleophis, and who, according to Justin, bore a son whose paternity was ascribed to Alexander. In reference to this statement Dr. Bellew remarks that at the present day several of the chiefs and ruling families in the neighbouring states of Chitral and Badakhshan boast a lineal descent from Alexander the Great.

Note E.—Bazira

Some writers have taken Bazira to be Bajore, which lies mid-way between the river of Kunâr and the Landaï, but there is nothing beyond the similarity of the two names to recommend this view. As the Bazirians fled for refuge to the rock Aornos, which overhung the Indus, it is evident they could not have inhabited a place so remote from the rock as Bajore. Cunningham finds a more likely position for Bazira at Bâzâr, "a large village situated on the *Kalpan*, or Kâli-pâni river, and quite close to the town of *Rustam*, which is built on a very extensive old mound. . . . According to tradition this was the site of the original town of Bâzâr. The position is an important one, as it stands just midway between the Swât and the Indus rivers, and has therefore been from time immemorial the *entrepôt* of trade between the rich valley of Swât and the large towns on the Indus and Kâbul rivers. . . . This identification is much strengthened by the proximity of Mount *Dantalok*, which is most probably the same range of hills as the *Montes Daedali* of the Greeks." See his *Anc. Geog. of India*, pp. 65, 66.

Note F.—Aornos

The identification of this celebrated rock has been one of the most perplexing problems of Indian archaeology. The descriptions given of it by the classical writers are more or less discrepant, and their indications as to its position very vague and obscure.

It has thus been identified with various positions, against each of which objections of more or less weight may be urged, but the view of General Abbott, who has identified it with Mount Mahâban, has the balance of argument in its favour, and is now generally adopted. The rock, to judge from Arrian's description of it, must have been in reality a mountain of very considerable height, with a summit of tableland crowned here and there with steep precipices. Curtius, on the other hand, says that the rock, which was on all sides steep and rugged, did not rise to its pinnacle in slopes of ordinary height and of easy ascent, but that in shape it resembled the conical pillar of the racecourse, called the *meta*, which springs from a broad basis and gradually tapers till it terminates in a sharp point. Here Arrian, who drew his facts from Ptolemy, a prominent actor in capturing Aornos, is, as usual, a safer guide than Curtius, who wrote for effect, and often dealt unscrupulously with the facts of history. Arrian, again, is at variance with Diodôros in his estimate both of the circuit and of the height of the rock, for while with him it has a circuit of 200 stadia (about 23 miles) and a height of 11, Diodôros reduces the circuit by one-half and increases the height to 16 stadia. Curtius is silent on these points, but he mentions a circumstance of great importance which Arrian has failed to note, namely, that the roots of the rock were washed by the river Indus. That he is right here cannot be questioned, for the statement is corroborated both by Diodôros and by Strabo (xv. 687), while Arrian, who says nothing that can lead us to think that his view was different, supplies us with a proof that Aornos was close to the Indus, for he says of the city of Embolima, which we now know to have been on the Indus, that it was situated close to Aornos. The position thus indicated is about sixty miles above Attak, where the Indus escapes into the plains from a long and narrow mountain gorge which the ancients mistook for its source. Colonel Abbott in 1854 explored this neighbourhood, and came to the conclusion that Mount Mahâban, a hill which abuts precipitously on the western bank of the Indus about eight miles west from the site of Embolima, was Aornos. His arguments in support of this identification are given in his *Gradus ad Aornon*. His description of Mount Mahâban agrees in the main with that which Arrian has given of Aornos. "The rock Aornos," he says, "was the most remarkable feature of the country, as is the Mahâban. It was the refuge of all the neighbouring tribes. It was covered with forests. It had good soil sufficient for a thousand ploughs, and pure springs of water everywhere abounded. It was 4125 feet above the plain, and 14 miles in circuit. It was precipitous on the side of Embolima, yet not so steep but that 220 horse and the war-engines were taken to the summit. The summit was a plain where cavalry could act. It would be difficult to offer a more faithful description of the mount." "Why the historians," he adds, "should all call it the *rock* Aornos, it would be difficult to say. The side on which Alexander scaled the main summit had certainly the character of a rock, but the whole description of Arrian indicates a table mountain." Cunningham, in his *Ancient Geography of India*, advances some arguments against this identification, but they cannot be considered sufficiently cogent to warrant its rejection unless a better could be substituted. That which he proposes, however, is altogether untenable. What he suggests is that the hill-fortress of Râni-gat, situated immediately above the small village of Nogram, about sixteen miles north by west from Ohind, which he takes to be the site of Embolima, corresponds in all essential particulars, except in its elevation (under 1200 feet), with the description of Aornos as given by Arrian, Strabo, and Diodôros. Now if the elevation stated, which is some 6000 feet under what Arrian assigns to Aornos, was really the height of the rock, then the details of the operations by which it was captured are rendered partly unintelligible. Thus, why should Ptolemy, after ascending the rock to a certain distance, have kindled a fire to let Alexander, who remained at the base, know where he was? Can we not easily see with the naked eye from the foot to the top of a small hill only ten or eleven hundred feet high? More-over, we are informed that it took Alexander from daybreak till noon to reach the position occupied by Ptolemy. Can it be supposed that all that space of time was required for the ascent of a hill not much higher than Arthur's Seat, near Edinburgh? The highest mountain in Great Britain could be climbed in half the time. Another equally fatal objection to this theory is the distance of Râni-gat from the Indus. The roots of the rock were indubitably washed by that river, but Râni-gat is no less than sixteen miles distant from it. At the same time, if Râni-gat were Aornos, then Ohind cannot be Embolima, for Arrian says that Embolima was close to (ξύνεγγυς) Aornos. The identification of the rock with Raja Hodi's fort opposite Attak, first suggested by General Court and afterwards supported by the learned missionary Loewenthal, has in its favour the fact that the position is on the Indus, but it is otherwise untenable. It is uncertain whether the name Aornos is purely Greek or an attempt at the transliteration of the indigenous name. If purely Greek, then Dionysios Perieg. (l. 1150) is right in saying that men called the rock Aornis

z

because even swift-winged birds had difficulty in flying over it.
If indigenous, the name may be referred to *Aranai*, which, as Dr.
Bellew states, is a common Hindi name for hill ridges in these
parts. He identifies the rock as *Shàh Dum* or *Malka*, on the
heights of Mahâban, the stronghold of the Wahabi fanatics, at the
destruction of which he was present in 1864. See his *Inquiry*,
p. 68.

NOTE G.—NYSA

Arrian's narrative indicates neither in what part of the Kôphên
and Indus Dôâb Nysa was situated, nor at what time Alexander
made his expedition to the place. But we learn from Curtius
(viii. 10), Strabo (xv. 697), and Justin (xii. 7) that he was there
before he had as yet crossed the Choaspes and taken Massaga,
and Arrian says nothing from which it can be inferred that his
opinion was different. Nysa was therefore most probably the
city which Ptolemy calls Nagara or Dionysopolis, and which has
been identified with Nanghenhar (the Nagarahâra of Sanskrit), an
ancient capital, the ruins of which have been traced at a distance
of four or five miles west from Jalâlâbâd. This place was called
also Udyânapura, *i.e.* "the city of gardens," which the Greeks from
some resemblance in the sound translated into Dionysopolis, a
compound meaning "the city of Dionysos." At some distance
eastward from this site, but on the opposite bank of the river,
there is a mountain called Mar - Koh (*i.e.* snake-hill) which, if
Nysa be Nagara, may be regarded as the Mount Meros which
lay near it, and was ascended by Alexander. It has, however,
been assumed that, in Arrian's opinion, the expedition to Nysa
was not an early incident of the campaign in the Dôâb, but the
last of any importance after the capture of Aornos. The only
ground for this assumption is that his account of the expedition
to Nysa follows that of all the other transactions recorded to
have occurred west of the Indus. But the reason of this is not
far to seek. Arrian, on examining the accounts given by different
writers of the visit to Nysa and Meros, concluded that they were
for the most part apocryphal, and as he did not wish to mix up
romance with history, reserved the subject for separate treatment.
Abbott, who took it for granted that Arrian wished it to be
understood that Alexander visited Nysa after the capture of the
rock, looked for the site of that city nearer the Indus than the
plain of Jalâlâbâd; and found one to suit the requirements in the
neighbourhood of Mount Elum, called otherwise Râm Takht or
"the throne of Râm." This remarkable mountain, he says, rises
like some mighty pagoda to the height of nine or ten thousand

feet, and answers in many points to the descriptions given of Meros, being densely covered with forests, full of wild beasts and of a height at which, in that part of India, ivy, box, etc., flourish. At its roots are the following old towns with names all derivable from Bacchos: Lusa (Nysa), Lyocah (Lyaeus), Elye, Awân, Bimeeter (Bimêtêr), Bôkra (Bou-Kera), and Kerauna (Keraunos). Beneath the town of Lusa flows the river Burindu, which is occasionally unfordable during the spring. Abbott makes this remark about the river with reference to the statement in Plutarch that when Alexander sat down before Nysa, the Macedonians had some difficulty of advancing to the attack on account of the depth of the river that washed its walls. V. de Saint-Martin and Dr. Bellew identify Nysa with Nysatta, a village near the northern bank of the Kâbul river about six miles below Hashtnagar, but except some correspondence between the names, there seems little to recommend this view. Strabo has one or two passages concerning Nysa. "In Sophoclês," he says, "a person is introduced speaking the praises of Nysa, as a mountain sacred to Bacchos: 'Whence I beheld the famed Nysa, the resort of the Bacchanalian bands, which the horned Iacchos makes his most pleasant and beloved retreat, where no bird's clang is heard.' From such stories they gave the name Nysaians to some imaginary nation, and called their city Nysa, founded by Bacchos; a mountain above the city they called Mêros, alleging as a reason for imposing these names that the ivy and vine grow there, although the latter does not perfect its fruit, for the bunches of grapes drop off before maturity in consequence of excessive rains" (xv. 687). In a subsequent passage (697) he says: "After the river Kôphês follows the Indus. The country lying between these two rivers is occupied by the Astakênoi, Masianoi, Nysaioi, and the Hippasioi. Next is the territory of Assakanos, where is the city Masoga." Pliny also has one or two notices of Nysa. "Most writers," he says (*H. N.* vi. 21), "assume that the city Nysa and also the mountain Merus, consecrated to the god Bacchus, belong to India. This is the mountain whence arose the fable that Bacchus issued from the thigh (μηρός) of Jupiter. They also assign to India the country of the Aspagani so plentiful in vines, laurel, and box, and all kinds of fruitful trees that grow in Greece." In Book viii. 141, he says "that on Nysa, a mountain in India, there are lizards 24 feet in length, and in colour yellow or purple or blue."

· The legend that Dionysos was bred in the thigh of Zeus owes its origin to a figurative mode of expression, common among the Phoenicians and Hebrews, which was taken by the Greeks in a literal sense. See the Epistle to the Hebrews, vii. 10. The Kafîrs who now occupy the country through which Alexander first marched on his way from the Kaukasos to the Indus, are said by Elphinstone to drink wine to great excess, men and women alike. "They dance," he adds, "with great vehemence, using many gesticulations, and beating the ground with great force, to a music which is generally quick, but varied and wild. Such usages would certainly have struck the Macedonians as Bacchanalian." So certainly would such a spectacle as the following, described by Bishop Heber in his *Indian Journal*: "The two brothers Rama and Luchman, in a splendid palkee, were conducting the retreat of their army. The divine Hunimân, as naked and almost as hairy as the animal he represented, was gamboling before them, with a long tail tied round his waist, a mask to represent the head of a baboon, and two great pointed clubs in his hands. His army followed, a number of men with similar tails and masks, their bodies dyed with indigo, and also armed with clubs. I was never so forcibly struck with the identity of Rama and Bacchus. Here were before me Bacchus, his brother Ampelus, the Satyrs, smeared with wine-lees, and the great Pan commanding them." I may, in conclusion, subjoin a notice of Bacchos in India from Polyainos: "Dionysos marching against the Indians in order that the Indians might receive him did not equip his troops with armour that could be seen, but with soft raiment and fawn skins. The spears were wrapped round with ivy, and the thyrsus had a sharp point. In making signals he used cymbals and drums instead of the trumpet, and, by warming the enemy with wine, he turned them (from war) to dancing. These and all other Bacchic orgies were the stratagems of war by which Bacchos subjugated the Indians and all the rest of Asia. Dionysos, when in India, seeing that his army could not endure the burning heat, seized the three-peaked mountain of India. Of its peaks one is called Korasibiê, another Kondaskê, but the third he himself named Mêros in commemoration of his birth. Upon it were many fountains of water sweet of taste, abundance of game and fruit, and snows, which gave new vigour to the frame. The troops quartered there would take the barbarians of the plains by surprise, and put them to an easy rout by attacking them with missiles from their commanding position on the heights above. Dionysos having conquered the Indians, invaded Baktria, taking with him as auxiliaries the Indians themselves and the Amazons."

Note H.—Gold-digging Ants

Herodotos was the first writer who communicated to the Western nations the story of these ants. He relates it thus (iii. 102) : " There are other Indians bordering on the city of Kaspatyros and the country of Paktyike (Afghânistân) settled northward of the other Indians, who resemble the Baktrians in the way they live. They are the most warlike of the Indians, and are the men whom they send to procure the gold (paid in tribute to the King of Persia), for their country adjoins the desert of sand. In this desert then and in the sand there are ants, in size not quite so big as dogs, but larger than foxes. Some that were captured were taken thence, and are with the King of the Persians. These ants, forming their dwelling underground, heap up the sand as the ants in Greece do, and in the same manner; and are very like them in shape. The sand which they cast up is mixed with gold. The Indians therefore go to the desert to get this sand, each man having three camels . . . (c. 105). When the Indians arrive at the spot they fill their sacks with the sand, and return home with all possible speed. For the ants, as the Persians say, having readily discovered them by the smell, pursue them, and, as they are the swiftest of all animals, not one of the Indians could escape except by getting the start while the ants were assembling."

Nearchos (quoted by Strabo, xv. 705) says that he saw skins of the ants which dig up gold as large as the skins of leopards. Megasthenes also (as quoted in the same passage) says that among the Dardai, a populous nation of the Indians living towards the east and among the mountains, there was a mountain plain of about 3000 stadia in circumference, below which were mines containing gold, which ants not less in size than foxes dig up. In winter they dig holes and pile up the earth in heaps, like moles, at the pit-mouths. Pliny (xi. 31) repeats the story in these terms : "The horns of the Indian ant fixed up in the temple of Hercules at Erythrae were objects of great wonderment. These ants excavate gold from mines found in the country of those Northern Indians who are called the Dardae. They are of the colour of cats and of the size of Egyptian wolves. The Indians steal the gold which they dig up in winter during the hot season when the ants keep within their burrows to escape the stifling sultriness of the weather. The ants, however, aroused by the smell, sally out and frequently overtake and mangle the robbers, though they have the swiftest of camels to aid their flight." It is now understood that the gold-digging ants were neither, as the ancients supposed, an extraordinary kind of real ants, nor, as many learned men have since supposed, larger animals mistaken for ants, but Tibetan miners who, like their descendants of the present day, preferred working their mines in winter when the frozen soil stands well and is not likely to trouble them by falling in.   The Sanskrit word pîpilika denotes both an *ant* and a particular kind of *gold*.

The Dards consist now of several wild and predatory tribes which are settled on the north-west frontier of Kashmîr and by the banks of the Indus.   The gryphons who guarded the gold were Tibetan mastiffs, a breed of unmatched ferocity.   Gold is still found in these regions.

Note I.—Taxila

Pliny, in his *Natural History* (vi. 21), gives sixty miles as the distance from Peukolatis (Hashtnagar) to Taxila.   This would fix its site somewhere on the Haro river to the west of Hasan Abdâl, or just two days' march from the Indus.   But according to the itineraries of the Chinese pilgrims, Fa-Hian and Hwen Thsiang, Taxila lay at three days' journey to the east of the Indus, and as they made that journey, their authority on the point cannot be questioned.   Taxila, it may be therefore concluded, must have been situated in the immediate neighbourhood of Kâla-ka-Sarâi. Now at the distance of just one mile from this place, near the rock-seated village of Shah-Dheri, Cunningham discovered the ruins of a fortified city scattered over a wide space, extending about three miles from north to south, and two miles from east to west, and these ruins he took to be those of Taxila.   They lie about eight miles south-east of Hasan Abdâl, thirty-four miles west from the famous tope of Manikyâla, and twenty-four miles north-west from Rawal Pindi.   The most ancient part of these ruins, according to the belief of the natives, is a great mound rising to a height of sixty-eight feet above the bed of the stream, called the Tabrâ Nala, which flows past its east side.   Cunningham's identification has now been accepted by all archaeologists, and a Greek text hitherto neglected strikingly confirms its correctness.   This text is to be found in the Pseudo-Kallisthenes, and I here translate the remarks made upon it by Sylvain Lévi in a paper which he submitted last year to the Société Asiatique, and which will be found printed at pp. 236, 237 in the 15th volume of the 8th series of the *Journal* of that society: "The Pseudo-Kallisthenes dwells complacently on the sojourn of Alexander at Taxila and his conversations with the Brahmans. The Brahmans (III. xii. 9, 10) blame the conduct of Kalanos, who, in violation of the duties of his caste, went to live with the Macedonians. ' It has not pleased him,' say they, ' to drink the water of wisdom at the river Tiberoboam.' And further on (III. xiii. 12) they ask, ' How could Alexander be the master of all the world when he has not yet gone beyond the river Tiberoboam?' The Latin of Julius Valerius gives, in the first case, Tiberunco fluvio; in the second, Tyberohoam. The various readings of the Greek manuscripts, indicated by C. Müller in his edition (Didot, 1846), give Boroam, Baroam, Tiberio-potamos, and lastly (MS. A.) Tibernabon. The site fixed by Cunningham for the city of Taxila is distinctly traversed by a river called Tabrâ Nala, which divides into two the ancient city, and washes the foot of the citadel. The ease of confounding the Ϲ with λ in the manuscripts per-'mits the correction of Tibernabon into Tibernalon. The essential part of the name is, moreover, Tabrâ, *nala* being a designation common to small affluents. The resemblance of the two words Tabrânala and Tibernalos is at once apparent; the persistence of geographical names has nothing surprising in it, especially in India. The city of Takshas'ila ought then to be placed definitely on the banks of the Tabrânala (a small affluent of the Haro, which bends its course to the Indus, into which it falls twelve miles below Attock) in the position proposed by General Cunningham."

Taxila, as Alexander found it, was very populous, and possessed of almost incredible wealth. Pliny states that it was situated on a level where the hills sink down into the plain, while Strabo praises the soil as extremely fertile from the number of its springs and water-courses. The Chinese pilgrim, Hwen Thsiang, by whom it was visited in 630 A.D., and afterwards in 643, confirms what Strabo has reported. Taxila, which in Ptolemy's *Geography* appears as *Taxiala*, represents either the Sanskrit Takshas'ilâ, *i.e.* "hewn stone," or, more probably, Takshakas'ilâ, *i.e.* "Rock of Takshaka," the great Nâga King. Others, however, take it to represent the Pali Takkas'ila, *i.e.* the rock of the Takkas, a powerful tribe which anciently occupied the regions between the Indus and the Chenâb (v. *Journal of the Royal Asiatic Society*, vol. xx. p. 343). The famous As'ôka, the grandson of Chandragupta (Sandrokottos), resided in Taxila during the lifetime of his father, Vindusâra, as viceroy of the Panjâb. About the beginning of the second century B.C. Taxila appears to have formed part of the dominions of the Graeco-Baktrian king, Eukratides. In

126 B.C. it was wrested from the Greeks by the Sus or Abars, with whom it remained for about three-quarters of a century, when it was conquered by the Kushân tribe under the great Kanishka. In the year 42 A.D. it is said to have been visited by Apollonios of Tyana and his companion, the Assyrian Damis, who wrote a

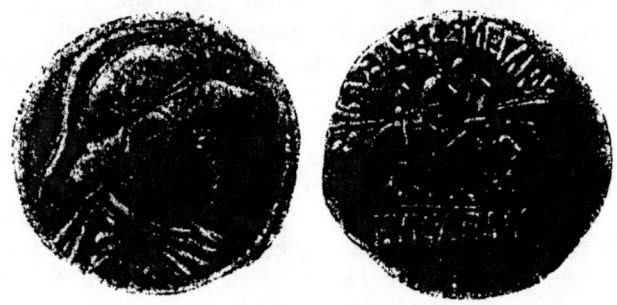

FIG. 15.—EUKRATIDES.

narrative of the journey, which Philostratos professes to have followed in his life of Apollonios. In 400 A.D. it was visited by Fa-Hian, who calls it Chu-sha-shi-lo, *i.e.* "the severed head," the usual name by which Taxila was known to the Buddhists of India (*v.* Cunningham's *Anc. Geog. of India*, pp. 104-121).

Note J.—Site of Alexander's Camp on the Hydaspês

It is a point of great importance to determine where the camp was situated which Alexander formed on reaching the Hydaspês, and which he made his headquarters till he effected the passage of the river. Without knowing this it cannot with certainty be decided at what point he made the passage or where he defeated Pôros, or where he founded the two cities, Nikaia and Boukephala, which he built after his victory. Such high authorities as Sir A. Burnes, General Court, and General Abbott have placed the camp at Jhîlam, but Lord Elphinstone and General Cunningham prefer Jalâlpûr, a place some thirty miles lower down the stream. These writers all drew their conclusions from personal knowledge of the localities concerned. Cunningham, who wrote later than the others, visited the Hydaspês in 1863, and in his *Geography of Ancient India* (pp. 157-179) gives an account of the scope and results of his investigations. He points out that Alexander in advancing from Taxila to the Hydaspês had two roads—one called the *upper*, which proceeded through a rich and fertile country, past Rawal Pindi, Manikyâla, and Rohtâs to Jhîlam, and another called the *lower*, which proceeded, with an inclination to southward, to Dudhiâl, and thence by Asanot and Vang to Jalâlpûr. He then shows from Strabo and Pliny that Alexander must have advanced by the *lower* road. According to Strabo (XV. i. 32), "the direction of Alexander's march, as far as the Hydaspês, was, for the most part, towards the south; after that, to the Hypanis, it was more towards the *east.*" Now, if Alexander had taken the route by Jhîlam he would have advanced in one continuous straight line, which is in direct opposition to the explicit statement of Strabo, which makes him deviate towards the south. Pliny again (vi. 21), quoting from Diognêtos and Baitôn, the *mensores* of Alexander, gives the distance from Taxila to the Hydaspês as 120 (Roman) miles. In comparing this distance with that from Shah-Dheri to Jhîlam and Jalâlpûr respectively, we must reject Jhîlam, which is no less than sixteen miles short of the recorded distance, while Jalâlpûr differs from it by less than two miles. The same author thinks that the camp probably extended for about six miles along the bank of the river from Shah Kabir, two miles to the north-east of Jalâlpûr, down to Syadpûr, four miles to the west-south-west. In this position the left flank of the camp would have been only six miles from the wooded promontory of Kotera, where he intended to steal his passage across the river. The breadth of the Hydaspês at Jalâlpûr is about a mile and a quarter.

Note K.—Battle with Pôros

To the accounts of this memorable battle given by Arrian and the four other writers translated in this volume, I here add the account of it given by Polyainos in his work *On the Stratagems of War* (II. ix. 22):

"Alexander, in his Indian expedition, advanced to the Hydaspes with intention to cross it, when Porus appeared with his army on the other side determined to dispute his passage. Alexander then marched towards the head of the river, and attempted to cross it there. Thither also Porus marched, and drew up his army on the opposite side. He then made the same effort lower down; there, too, Porus opposed him. Those frequent appearances of intention to cross it, without ever making one real attempt to effect it, the Indians ridiculed, and, concluding that he had no real design to pass the river, they became more negligent in attending his motions, when Alexander, by a rapid march gaining the banks, effected his purpose on barges, boats, and hides stuffed with straw, before the enemy had time to come up with him, who, deceived by so many feint attempts, yielded him at last an uninterrupted passage. In the battle against Porus, Alexander posted part of his cavalry in the right wing, and part he left as a body of reserve at a small distance on the plain. His left wing consisted of the phalanx and his elephants. Porus ordered his elephants to be formed against him, himself taking his station on an elephant at the head of his left wing. The elephants were drawn up within fifty yards of each other, and in those interstices was posted his infantry, so that his front exhibited the appearance of a great wall; the elephants looked like so many towers, and the infantry like the parapet between them. Alexander directed his infantry to attack the enemy in front, while himself at the head of the horse advanced against the cavalry. Against those movements Porus ably guarded. But the beasts could not be kept in their ranks, and, wherever they deserted them, the Macedonians in a compact body pouring in closed with the enemy, and attacked them both in front and flank. The body of reserve, in the meantime wheeling round and attacking their rear, completed the defeat" (*Shepherd's Translation*).

Grote, referring to this battle, remarks that "the day on which it was fought was the greatest day of Alexander's life, if we take together the splendour and difficulty of the military achievement and the generous treatment of his conquered opponent." Military critics cannot point to a single strategical error in the whole series of operations conducted by Alexander himself, or his generals acting under his orders, from the time he encamped on the bank of the Hydaspês till the overthrow and surrender of Pôros. At the same time the courage and skill with which the Indian king contended against the greatest soldier of antiquity, if not of all time, are worthy of the highest admiration, and present a striking contrast to the incompetent generalship and pusillanimity of Darius. "The Greeks," says General Chesney, "were loud in praises of the Indians; never in all their eight years of constant warfare had they met with such skilled and gallant soldiers, who, moreover, surpassed in stature and bearing all the other races of Asia. . . . The Indian village community flourished even at that distant period, and in the brave and manly race which fought so stoutly under Porus twenty-two centuries ago we may recognise all the fine qualities of the Punjabi agrarian people of the present day, the gallant men who fought us in our turn so stubbornly, now the most valuable component of the Indian empire, and the best soldiers of its Queen-Empress."

Note L.—The Kathaians

The Kathaioi, it would appear from the text, inhabited the regions lying to the east of the Hydraôtês. Some writers, however, as Strabo informs us (XV. i. 30), placed their country in the tract between the Hydaspês and Akesinês, but this view is manifestly wrong. They are described by ancient authors as one of the most powerful nations of India. Their very name indicates their warlike propensities and predominance, for if it is not identical with that of the military caste, *Kshatriya*, it is at least a modified form of that word. Arrian subsequently (vi. 15) mentions a tribe of independent Indians whose name is a still closer transliteration of *Kshatriya*, the *Xathroi*, whose territories lay between the Indus and the lower course of the Akesinês. Strabo (XV. i. 30) notices some of the peculiar manners and customs of the Kathaians, such as infanticide, and Sati. Lassen has pointed out that their name is connected with that of the Kattia, a nomadic race scattered at intervals through the plains of the Panjâb, but supposed to be the aborigines of the country and of Kolarian descent. Their name occurs in that of the province of Kâthiawâr, which now comprises the province of Gujerat.

Note M.—Sangala

Sir E. H. Bunbury, referring to the uncertainty of the identifications of the tribes and cities of the Panjâb mentioned by Alexander's historians, says : "While the general course of his march must have followed approximately the same line of route that has been frequented in all ages from the banks of the Indus to those of the Beas, his expeditions against the various warlike tribes that refused submission to his arms led him into frequent excursions to the right and left of his main direction. And with regard to these localities we have a general clue to guide us. The most important of these sites to determine would be that of Sangala, the capital of the Cathaeans, which, according to the narrative of Arrian, was situated between the Hydraotes and the Hyphasis. Hence it was placed by Burnes at Lahore, and by others at Umritsir. But on the other hand there are not wanting strong reasons for identifying Sangala with the Sakala of Indian writers, and this was certainly situated to the west of the Hydraotes, between that river and the Acesines" (*Hist. of Anc. Geog.* pp. 444, 445). This was the view of General Cunningham, who, taking *S'âkala* or *Sâkala* (the *Sagala* of Ptolemy's *Geography*) to be the name in Sanskrit of the place which the Greeks called *Sangala*, found

a site for it at Sânglawâla-Tiba, a small rocky hill with ruins upon
it and with a large swamp at its base, and situated between the
Râvi (Hydraôtês) and the Chenâb (Akesinês) at a distance of about
sixty miles to the west of Lahore. This was no doubt the site of
the S'âkala of Sanskrit writers and of the She-kie-lo of the Chinese
pilgrim Hwen Thsiang, who visited the place in 630 A.D. But
it cannot have been the site of the Sangala of the Greeks, for, in
the first place, according to the testimony of all the historians,
that city lay between the Hydraôtês and the Hyphasis, and was
attacked by Alexander after he had crossed the former river. To
meet this objection Cunningham assumes that Alexander must
have recrossed the Hydraôtês on hearing that the Kathaians had
risen in his rear. His thus turning aside from the direction of
his march to make his rear secure is quite consistent with his
usual practice, but the historians say nothing from which it can
possibly be inferred that on this occasion he made any retrograde
movement. But again philology as well as history is adverse
to this identification, for, as has lately been shown by M. Sylvain
Lévi (*Journal Asiatique*, series viii. vol. xv. pp. 237-239), *Sangala*,
in accordance with the rules of transcription, must be taken to
represent not *Sâkala*, but *Sâmkala*. Now, just as in Diodôros
and Curtius we find Sangala mentioned in connection with a king
called Sôphytês, so in an Appendix to Pânini's *Grammar*, called
the Gana-pâtha, *Sâmkala* is mentioned in connection with
Saubhuta, which, in accordance with the rules of transcription
and the Greek practice of designating Indian rulers after their
territories, is evidently the name of the country over which
Sôphytês ruled. This country, which was rich and prosperous, as
its very name implies, lay between the Hydraôtês and the
Hyphasis, probably in the district of Amritsar and towards the
hills. Arrian in his narrative of the campaign between these two
rivers makes no mention of Sôphytês, or, as he calls him,
Sôpeithes, but he afterwards refers to a king of this name whose
dominions lay between the Hydaspês and Akesinês. Strabo
was aware of the discrepancy of the accounts as to where the
dominions of the Kathaians and King Sôphytês were situated.

NOTE N.—ALEXANDER'S ALTARS ON THE HYPHASIS

These altars are mentioned by Pliny, who says (vi. 21) : " The
Hyphasis was the limit of the marches of Alexander, who, however, crossed it, and dedicated altars on the further bank."
Pliny stands alone in placing these altars on the left bank of
the river. The historians all place them on the right bank.

Philostratos states that Apollonios of Tyana on his journey into
India in the second century of our aera, found the altars still
subsisting and their inscriptions still legible. Plutarch affirms
that in his days they were held in much veneration by the
Praisians, whose kings, he says, were in the habit of crossing the
Ganges every year to offer sacrifices in the Grecian manner upon
them. It would, however, be unsafe to place much credit in
either of these statements. The altars have been sought for in
recent times, but not the slightest vestige of them has been
discovered. Masson and some other modern writers place them
on the Gharra (the united stream of the Vipas'â and the S'atadru
(or Satlej), but this view, while otherwise exposed to serious
objections, is upset by the fact alone that in ancient times the
two rivers united at a point forty miles below their present junction.
As Pliny (vi. 21) gives the distance from the Hyphasis to the
Hesidrus (Satlej) along the Royal Road at 169 miles, it is evident
that the altars must have been situated at a point high above
the junction of these two rivers. V. de Saint-Martin is inclined
to think that the altars may have been situated near a chain of
heights met with in ascending the Beiàs, and known locally under
the name of the *Sekandar-giri*, that is, "Alexander's mountain."
These heights are at no great distance from Râjagiri, a small and
obscure place, but supposed to represent Râjagriha mentioned
in the *Râmâyana* as the capital of a line of princes called the
As'vapati (or *Assapati* in Prakrit) who governed the Kekaya, or,
as Arrian calls them in his *Indika*, the Kêkeoi. Lassen, followed
by Saint-Martin, identified Sôpeithes as belonging to the line of
princes indicated. The identification has been superseded by a
better, but Saint-Martin's argument, as far as it concerns the
position of the altars, is not thereby affected. Sir E. H. Bunbury
considers that the point where Alexander erected the twelve
altars cannot be regarded as determined within even approximate
limits. It appears probable, he thinks, that they were situated at
some distance above the confluence of the two rivers, and not
very far from the point where the Beas emerges from the
mountain ranges. We learn indeed, he adds, that throughout
his advance Alexander kept as near as he could to the mountains;
partly from the idea that he would thus find the great rivers more
easily passable, as being nearer their sources; partly from an
exaggerated impression of the sterile and desert character of the
plains farther south (*Hist. of Anc. Geog.* p. 444).

Note O.—Voyage down the Hydaspês and Akesinês to the Indus

From the point of embarkation at Nikaia (Mong) to the confluence of the united streams of the Panjâb with the Indus, the distance in a straight line may be reckoned at about 300 miles. Alexander in descending to this confluence had no sooner left the dominions of Pôros than he was engaged in a constant succession of hostilities with the riparian tribes. He had no intention of leaving India as a fugitive. He must depart as a conqueror and master of all wherever he appeared. He had no wish, therefore, even had it been possible, to drop quietly down stream to the ocean. He must demand submission to his authority from all the tribes he might encounter on his way, and, if this were refused, enforce it at the sword's point. These tribes were the bravest of the brave in India—the very ancestors of the Rajputras, or Rajputs, whose splendid military qualities have spread their fame throughout the world. Such of these tribes as inhabited the fertile regions adjacent to the rivers seemed to have settled in towns and villages and to have practised agriculture, while those that tenanted the deserts which extended far eastward into the interior led a half-wandering pastoral life, and subsisted as much on the produce of rapine as on the produce of their flocks and herds. They were all proudly jealous of their independence, and owned no authority but that of their proper chiefs. Though they were separated into distinct tribes, which were almost perpetually at feud, they were still able when confronted with a common danger to combine into formidable confederacies. In all times they have opposed to invasion a vigorous and sometimes a desperate resistance (v. Saint-Martin, *Étude*, p. 113).

Note P.—The Malloi and Oxydrakai

The names of these two warlike tribes are very frequently conjoined in the narratives of the historians. In Sanskrit works they appear as the Mâlava and the Kshudraka, and a verse of the *Mahâbhârata* combines them in a single appellation, *Kshudraka-mâlava*. They are mentioned in combination by Pânini also as two Bahîka people of the north-west. Arrian (*Indika*, c. iv.) places the Oxydrakai on the Hydaspês *above* its confluence with the Akesinês. It is doubtful, however, that this was their real position. Bunbury inclines to think that they lay on the east or left bank of the Satlej — the province of Bahawalpur — and that they may very well have extended as far as the junction of the Satlej with the Indus and the neighbourhood of Uchh. General Cunningham, he adds, is alone in placing the Oxydracae to the north of the Malli. That author has, however, the *Indika* to support his view. Their name in the classics appears in various forms, Strabo and Stephanos Byz. calling them *Hydrakai*, Pliny *Sydracae*, and Diodôros *Syrakousai*. Strabo says they were reported to be the descendants of Bacchos because the vine grew in their country, and because their kings displayed great pomp in setting out on their warlike expeditions after the Bacchic manner (XV. i. 8). They are no doubt to be identified with the S'udras, whose name in early times did not denote a caste, as it did afterwards, but a tribe of aborigines, or, at all events, a tribe of non-Aryan origin. The final *ka* in the Greek form of their name is a common Sanskrit suffix to ethnic names given or withheld at random. The single combat between Dioxippos and a Macedonian bravo called Horratas took place after a great banquet at which Alexander entertained the envoys of the Oxydrakai.

The territory of the Malloi was of great extent, comprehending a part of the Doâb formed by the Akesinês and the Hydraôtês, and extending, according to Arrian (*Indika*, c. iv.), to the confluence of the Akesinês and the Indus. In the *Mahâbhârata* they figure as a great people, being there distinguished into the Eastern, Southern, and Western Mâlavas (*Mahâbh.* vi. 107). They are mentioned also in the inscription of Samudragupta (of the first half of the third century A.D.) among other peoples of the Panjâb who were subject to the King of Madhya-desha (*v.* V. de Saint-Martin, *Étude*, pp. 116-120). "These two races," says Thirlwall (*History of Greece*, vii. 40), "were composed of widely different elements; for the name of one appears to have been derived from that of the Sudra caste; and it is certain that the Brahmins were predominant in the other. We can easily understand why they did not intermarry and were seldom at peace with each other." The feud, however, may have been one of race rather than of caste, though no doubt the distinctions of caste originated in difference of race.

NOTE Q.—THE CAPITAL OF THE MALLOI

Diodôros and Curtius assign this city to the Oxydrakai, but erroneously. General Cunningham identifies it with Multân and takes it to be also the capital of the Malloi "to which many men from other cities had fled for safety." Arrian seems, however, to indicate that the two places were distinct. V. de Saint-Martin inclines to identify the Mallian capital with Harrâpa (the Harapa which Cunningham takes to be the city captured by Perdikkas). Multân is at present the capital of the province of the same name, which comprises pretty nearly the same territories as those occupied by the Malloi of the Greek historians. Multân is not situated on the Râvi now, but on the Chenâb, and at a distance of more than thirty miles *below* the junction of that river with the Râvi. This circumstance would be quite fatal to Cunningham's view if the junction had not shifted. But it has shifted, for in Alexander's time the rivers met about fifteen miles below Multân. "The old channel (Cunningham says) still exists and is duly entered in the large maps of the Multân division. It leaves the present bed at Sarai Siddhû and follows a winding course for thirty miles to the south-south-west, when it suddenly turns to the west for eighteen miles as far as Multân, and, after completely encircling the fortress, continues its westerly course for five miles below Multân. It then suddenly turns to the south-south-west for ten miles, and is finally lost in the low-lying lands of the bed of the Chenâb. Even to this day the Râvi clings to its ancient channel, and at all high floods the waters of the river still find their way to Multân by the old bed, as I myself have witnessed on two occasions. The date of the change is unknown, but was certainly subsequent to A.D. 713." From Arrian's narrative it would appear that Alexander occupied three days, one of which was spent in rest, in advancing from the city of the Brachmans to the city of the Malloi. The distance traversed would be thirty-four miles, if Cunningham's identification of the former city with Atâri and of the latter with Multân be correct. The city where Alexander was wounded appears from Arrian's account to have been at some distance from the Hydraôtês, and if so could not have been Multân.

Note R.—Alexander in Sindh

Arrian and the other historians of Alexander have treated very briefly and vaguely his campaign in the valley of the Indus. Hence it is difficult to trace the course of his operations as he descended from the great confluence at Uchh to Patala where the Indus bifurcates to form the Delta. The distance between these two points, if measured by the course of the river, may be estimated at nearly four hundred miles, yet we find, as Saint-Martin observes, that in the descent not a single distance is indicated, nor a single peculiar feature of the country described which might serve as a sign-post for the direction and guidance of our inquiries. It is at the same time difficult to reconcile the discrepancies found to exist in the accounts transmitted to us, and altogether the search for identities must here mainly concern itself with the names of tribes. In determining how these tribes were collocated it is necessary to take cognisance of the changes which have taken place in the course of the Indus since Alexander's time. Captain M'Murdo was the first to call attention (in 1834) to these changes, which were not confined to the terminal course of the river, but extended more than two hundred miles above the Delta. He proved that up to the seventh century of our aera the main stream of the Indus, instead of following its present channel, pursued a more direct course to the sea some sixty or seventy miles farther east than it now flows. The old channel, which leaves the present stream at some distance above Bhakar, passes the ruins of Alôr, and then proceeds directly towards the south nearly as far as Brâhmanâbâd, above which it divides into two channels, one rejoining the present course above Haidarâbâd, while the other pursues a south-easterly course towards the Ran of Kachh. The voyage down the lower part of the course took place during the season of the inundation when the plains were laid far and wide under water, and the current was rapid and violent. As the march followed mainly the line of the river the country would appear to the Macedonians extremely rich, fertile, and populous, while the sterility of the regions that lay beyond the reach of the inundations would seldom be brought under their cognisance. In descending the river they could not fail to notice the contrast presented by the plains on its opposite banks, those on the east exhibiting a uniform expanse without any visible boundary, while those on the west were hemmed in by a great mountain rampart which in running southwards gradually approached the Indus till the roots of the hills were laved by its waters. The inhabitants would strike them as being more swarthy in their complexion than the men of the Panjâb, from whom they differed also in their political predilections, as they preferred kingly government to republican independence, and allowed the Brahman to exercise a decisive influence over public life. The descent of the Indus by Alexander, as Bunbury remarks, may be considered as constituting a kind of aera in the geographical knowledge of the Greeks. It does not appear, he adds, that it was ever repeated ; and while subsequent researches added materially to the knowledge possessed by the Greeks of the valley of the Ganges and the more easterly provinces of India, their information concerning the great river Indus and the regions through which it flows continued to be derived almost exclusively from the voyage of

Alexander and the accounts transmitted by the contemporary historians.

After leaving the great confluence the first tribe Alexander reached were the *Sogdoi*, who appear as the *Sodrai* in Diodôros, who states that Alexander founded among them on the banks of the river a city called Alexandreia in which he placed 10,000 inhabitants. The Sogdoi have been identified with the *Sohda* Rajputs who now occupy the south-east district of Sindh about Amarkot, but who in former times held large possessions on the banks of the Indus to the northward of Alôr. This place, though now only a scene of ruins, was formerly, before it was deserted by the river, one of the largest and most flourishing cities in all Sindh. Saint-Martin takes it to have been the Sogdian capital, and thinks that the city which Alexander founded lay in its vicinity at Rôri, since right opposite to this place there rose in the middle of the river the rocky island of Bhakar, which presented every natural advantage for the site of a great fortress. Cunningham, however, would place the capital higher up stream, about midway between Alôr and Uchh, at a village which appears in old maps under the name of Sirwahi, and which may possibly represent the *Seori* of Sindh history and the *Sodrai* of Diodôros. In this neighbourhood lies the most frequented ghât for the crossing of the Indus towards the west *viâ* Gandâva and the Bolan Pass ; and as the ghâts always determine the roads, it was probably at this point of passage Krateros recrossed the Indus when he was despatched with the main body of the army and the elephants to return home through the countries in which that Pass lay. The name *Sodrai*, some think, represents the Sanskrit *S'ûdra* which designates the servile or lowest of the four castes. If this be so, the Sodrai may be regarded as a remnant of the primitive stock which peopled the country before the advent of the Aryans (*v.* Lassen, *Ind. Alt.* ii. p. 174 ; Saint-Martin, *Étude*, pp. 150-161 ; Cunningham, *Anc. Geog. of India*, pp. 249-256).

Note S.—Sindimana

Sambus is called Sabus by Curtius, who, without giving the name of his capital, informs us that Alexander captured it by mining and then marched to rejoin his fleet on the Indus. The Greek name of this capital, *Sindimana*, has led to its identification with Sehwân, a site of very high antiquity. The great mound which was once its citadel has been formed chiefly of ruined buildings accumulated in the course of ages on a scarped rock at the end of the Lakki range of hills. Its water supply is at present entirely derived from the Indus, which not only flows under the eastern front of the town, but also along the northern by a channel from the great Manchur Lake, which perhaps formerly extended up even to the city walls. The objection to this identification, that Sehwân's position on the Indus conflicts with the statement that Alexander had to march from Sindomana to reach that river, is removed by the fact that the Indus has changed its course since Alexander's time. Wilson derives the Greek Sindomana from what he calls a very allowable Sanskrit compound, *Sindu-mân*, "the possessor of Sindh." Cunningham, however, would refer the name to *Saindava-vanam* or *Sainduwân*, "the abode of the Saindavas." *v.* his *Anc. Geog. of India*, pp. 263-266, and also Saint-Martin's *Étude*, p. 166, where it is stated that the name of Sambus is probably connected with that of the tribe called Sammah, whose chiefs have at different epochs played a distinguished part in the valley of the Indus. In Hindu mythology *Samba* is the son of Krishna. According to Plutarch, it was somewhere in the dominions of Sabbas that Alexander had his interview with the ten Indian gymnosophists. Sehwân is the Sewistan of the Arabs. According to Burton (writing in 1857), it is a hot, filthy, and most unwholesome place, with a rascally population (of 6000) which includes many beggars and devotees. *v.* his *Sindh*, p. 8. The population has since increased to upwards of 160,000.

NOTE T.—CITY OF THE BRACHMANS—HARMATELIA

This city of the Brachmans Cunningham takes to have been Brâhmana, or Brâhmanâbâd, which was ninety miles distant by water from Marija Dand, the point where he supposes Alexander rejoined his fleet after the capture of Sindimana. Brâhmanâbâd was situated on the old channel of the Indus forty-seven miles to the north-east of Haidarâbâd or Nirankot, the Patala of ancient times. Shortly after the Mohammedan conquest it was supplanted by Mansûra, which either occupied its site or lay very near it, as, according to Ibn Haukal, the place was called in the Sindh language Bâmiwân. It was destroyed by an earthquake sometime before the beginning of the eleventh century. Its ruins were discovered at Bambhra-ka-thûl by Mr. Bellasis, whose excavations have shown conclusively the truth of the popular tradition which ascribed its downfall to an earthquake. Cunningham further thinks that Brâhmanâbâd was the *Harmatelia* of Diodôros—the place where Ptolemy was wounded by the poisoned arrow. Harmatelia (he says) is only a softer pronunciation of *Brâhma-thala* or Brahmana-sthala, just as Hermes, the phallic god of the Greeks, is the same as Brahmâ, the original phallic god of the Indians. He thinks that the king whom Justin (xii. 10) calls *Ambiger* was no other than Mousikanos, whose dominions extended as far south as the Delta, *Ambiger* being his family name and Mousikanos his dynastic title (*Geog.* pp. 267-269). Saint-Martin, on the other hand, recognises Harmatelia in a place variously designated by Arab writers *Armael*, *Armaïl*, *Armâbil*, and *Armatel*, but of which the position is unknown (*Étude*, pp. 167, 168). In his ancient map of India Colonel Yule, who takes the same view as Saint-Martin, identifies Harmatelia with Bela.

NOTE U.—PATALA

The situation of Patala has been a fertile theme of controversy. Arrian seems, no doubt, to give here a clear indication of its position in saying that it stood near where the Indus bifurcates; but as this point has from time to time shifted, the controversy has turned mainly on the question where this point is to be fixed. The river bifurcates at present at Mottâri, which lies twelve miles above Haidarâbâd, and it has been known to bifurcate a little above, and also a little below Thatha, at Bauna also, and at Trikul. As a matter of fact, these bifurcations no longer exist, except perhaps for a part of the year when the river is in flood and recurs to some of its old channels. It is not then surprising that various identifications have been proposed for Patala. It was placed at Brâhmanâbâd by M'Murdo, Wilson, and Lassen; at Thatha by Rennell, Vincent, Ritter, and the two brothers, James and Sir Alexander Burnes; and at Haidarâbâd, the Nirankot of Arab writers, by Droysen, Benfey, Burton, Saint-Martin, Cunningham, and Bunbury. The arguments in favour of Haidarâbâd seem to be quite conclusive. They will be found stated at length in Saint-Martin's *Étude* (pp. 168-191), and Cunningham's *Geography* (pp. 279-287). One of the most cogent is that the dimensions of the Delta, as given by the Greek writers, are only justified if the apex of the Delta is taken to have been in Alexander's time at or near Haidarâbâd. If the apex had then been as high up as Brâhmanâbâd, or as far down as Thatha, the size of the Delta would be as grossly exaggerated in the one case as it would be underrated in the other. The same conclusion is indicated in the information supplied to the late Dr. Wilson of Bombay by the Brahmans of Sehwân, that, according to their local legends, as recorded in their Sanskrit books,

Thatha was *Déval*, and Haidarâbâd *Nîran*, and more anciently *Patolpuri*. *Patala* was thought at one time to have been a transcription of the Sanskrit Pâtâla, *the nether world*, into which the sun descends at the end of his day's journey, and hence THE WEST; but a better etymology is the Sanskrit *potala*, "a station for ships," from *pôta*, "a vessel." The name of the Indian Delta was Patalênê. Haidarâbâd stands on a long flat-topped hill, and Patala, if this was its site, must have occupied a commanding position, the advantages of which, alike for strategy and commerce, Alexander would perceive at a glance. The main stream of the Indus now flows to the west of this position. In the second chapter of his *Indika* Arrian repeats the statement that the Indus enters the ocean by two mouths. Aristoboulos estimated the interval between them at 1000 stadia, but Nearchos at 1800. The interval from the west to the east arm measures at present 125 British miles. The sea-front of the Egyptian Delta with which the Greeks compared that of the Indus Delta is not less than 160 miles. The Prince of Patala was called *Moeris*.

NOTE V.—ALEXANDER'S MARCH THROUGH GEDRÔSIA-PURA

" No traveller," says Bunbury, referring to the interior of Mekran, "has as yet traversed its length from one end to the other in the direction followed by Alexander. So far as we can judge, he appears to have kept along a kind of plain or valley, which is found to run nearly parallel to the coast between the interior range of the Mushti (or Washati) hills and the lower ragged hills that bound the immediate neighbourhood of the sea-coast. This line of route has been followed in very recent times by Major Ross from Kedj to Bela, and seems to form a natural line of communication, keeping throughout about the required distance (60 or 70 miles) from the coast [the distance required for maintaining communication with the fleet]. . . . This line of march so far as is yet known does not appear to traverse any such frightful deserts *of sand* as those described by the historians of Alexander. Nor can the site of Pura . . . be determined with accuracy. It has been generally identified with Bunpoor (Banpûr), the most important place in Western Beloochistan, or with Pahra, a village in the same neighbourhood; but the resemblance of name is in this case of little value—*poor* signifying merely a town—while the remoteness of Bunpoor from the sea, and its position to the north of the central chain of mountains, which Alexander must therefore have traversed in order to reach it, present considerable difficulties in the way of this view" (*Hist. of*

Anc. Geog. pp. 519-520). Strabo, in his chapter on Ariana, narrates in graphic detail, like Arrian, the sufferings experienced by the Macedonians in passing through Gedrôsia. The summer, he says, was purposely chosen for leaving India, since rains then fall in Gedrôsia, filling the rivers and wells which fail in winter. Alexander kept at the utmost from the sea not more than 500 stadia in order to secure the coast for his fleet. The army was saved by eating dates and the marrow of the palm-tree, but many persons were suffocated by eating unripe dates.

To account for the surprising length of time (60 days) occupied on this march, which could not have exceeded 400 English miles, we must suppose that the troops were obliged to make frequent halts at places where water was procurable. Strabo says that it was found necessary on account of the watering-places to make marches of two, four, and even sometimes of six hundred stadia generally during the night. The land distances, like the sea distances of Nearchos, seem to have been grossly exaggerated. The march of Semiramis through this desert and that of Cyrus seem to be mythical. Alexander's loss in men during the march must have been exaggerated by the historians, as he brought the bulk of his army with him to Pura.

Note W.—Indian Sages

According to Megasthenes the Indian sages were divided into two sects, Brahmans and Sarmans. There was besides a third sect, described as quarrelsome, fond of wrangling, foolish and boastful. The Brahmans, he says, were held in higher esteem than the Sarmans because there was more agreement in their doctrines. Among the Sarmans the Hylobioi (*living in woods*) were held in most honour, and next to them the physicians, who are mendicants and also ascetics, like the class above them and the class below them, which consisted of sorcerers and fortune-tellers. Megasthenes has related at some length the nature of the opinions and practices of all these sects, and Duncker considers that in all essential points his accounts agree with the native authorities, though the view taken may be here and there too favourable, in some points too advanced, in others not sufficiently discriminating. " It is true," he says, " that the Brahmans and the initiated of the Enlightened (Buddhists), the S'ramanas, are confounded in the order of the sages; this is shown by the statement that any one could enter into this order. . . . In the description of the life of the ascetics and wandering sages, the Brahmans and Bhikshus (mendicants) are again confounded, and if the Greeks tell us that the severe sages of the forest were too proud to go to the court at the request of the king, the statement holds good according to the evidence of the Epos of the Brahmanic saints, and the Sutras of the great teachers among the Buddhists. In the examination of the doctrines of the Indian sages, Megasthenes distinguished the Brahmans and the Buddhists, inasmuch as he opposes the less-honoured sects to the first, and declares the Brahmans to be the most important. From his whole account it is clear that at his date, *i.e.* about the year 300 B.C., the Brahmans had distinctly the upper hand. But, according to him, the S'ramanas took the next place to the Brahmans among the less-honoured sects. Among the Buddhists S'ramana is the ordinary name for their clergy" (*Hist. of Antiq.* pp. 422-424).

Note X.—The Indian Month

Curtius apparently means that the Indians mark time, not by taking a month to be the period from full moon to next full moon, but from new moon to full moon. "The year of the Indians (says Duncker) was divided into 12 months of 30 days; the month was divided into two halves of 15 days each, and the day into 30 hours (*muhurta*). In order to bring this year of 360 days into harmony with the natural time, the Brahmans established a quinquennial cycle of 1860 lunar days. Three years had 12 months of 30 lunar days; the third and fifth year of the cycle had 13 months of the same number of days. The Brahmans do not seem to have perceived that by this arrangement the cycle contained almost four days in excess of the astronomical time, and indeed they were not very skilful astronomers" (*v.* his *History of Antiquity*, iv. 283, 284). According to Weber this system of calculating time was borrowed from the Babylonians, but Max Müller and learned Hindus hold it to be indigenous. The Indian name for the half of a lunar month is *paksha*. The half from new moon to full moon was called at first *pûrva* (fore), and afterwards *s'ukla* (bright); the other half was called *apara* (posterior), and afterwards *krishna* (dark). Le Clerc concludes his criticism of this passage thus : "Matthaeus Raderus endeavours to explain Curtius as if he designed to demonstrate that one month began and was understood to commence a little after the change to the full moon, and the next, from the time when she began to decrease to the next change. This, indeed, ought to be his meaning; but it is strangely expressed, when he tells us that the moon begins to show herself horned on the sixteenth day, when 'tis evident she does not appear so till about seven days after full moon. But before Raderus, Thomas Lydiat had tried to solve the matter otherways. However, Scaliger, in his *Prolegomena* to his *Canones Isagogicae*, p. 11, has plainly showed that Lydiat neither understood Curtius nor Curtius the author which he copied from. The ancient Persians counted 15 days to each of their months, and 24 of these months to the solar year, before the introduction of Mohammedism, as John Chardin evidently demonstrates in his *Itinerarium Persicum*, tome xi. p. 14, quarto " (*v.* Rooke's *Arrian*, p. 12).

NOTE Y.—BATTLE WITH PÓROS

Mr. Heitland has the following note on this passage : " Arrian (v. 16, sec. 2) tells us that Alexander was making a flanking movement (παρήλαυνεν) with the bulk of his cavalry to attack the enemy's left wing. He then goes on (sec. 3) : *Against the right wing he sent Koinos at the head of his own regiment of horse and that of Dêmêtrios, and ordered him, when the barbarians on seeing what a dense mass of cavalry was opposed to them, should be riding along to encounter it, to hang close upon their rear,*[1] a hard passage, it is true, but one which need not be unintelligible to any one who bears in mind that Alexander's movement was a flanking one, and reads with care the description of his attack in c. 16, sec. 4, and c. 17, sec. 1, 2. The situation is this : Alexander was not himself in position on the right wing, but put Coenus there with some of the cavalry, while he himself with the main body made the flanking movement. This he did with speed, so as to take the Indian horse in flank, before they had time to change their front and meet him. They tried to execute this movement, but had not time ; and while they were in the confusion thus brought about, Coenus fell upon what had been their front, but was now their disordered flank. Whether the Indian horse from their right wing was brought over to succour that on their left or not, does not affect the probable position of Coenus. The one difficulty in the way of this explanation is the presence, according to Arrian, 15, sec. 7, of the war-chariots in front of the Indian horse. But it seems easier to suppose that Coenus was able to elude these clumsy adversaries than that Alexander expected him to see from the Macedonian left the right moment for his own charge, and then wheel round the rear of the whole Indian army and execute his orders opportunely. Diodorus, xvii. 88, says : *The Macedonian cavalry began the action, and destroyed nearly all the chariots of the Indians.*[2] If this

---

[1] Quoted by Heitland in the original.   [2] *Ibid.*

refers, as I think it does, to the beginning of the main battle, the chief objection is removed" (*Alexander in India*, pp. 122, 123). This explanation is different from that offered by Moberly, as the reader will see by referring to my note on Arrian, p. 104, *n*. 2.

NOTE Z.—INDIAN SERPENTS

Diodôros gives the length of the serpents at sixteen cubits, or about twenty-four feet. Ailianos also gives this as their length. He says (xvii. 2): "Kleitarchos states that about India a serpent sixteen cubits long is produced, but mentions there is another kind which differs in appearance from the rest. They are many sizes shorter, and display to the eye a variety of colours, as if they were painted with pigments. Stripes extend from the head to the tail, and are of various colours, some tinted like bronze, some like silver, some like gold, while others are crimson. The same writer notices that their bite proves very quickly fatal." Arrian in his *Indika* (c. 15) states on the authority of Nearchos that there are serpents in India spotted and nimble in their movements, and that one was caught which measured about sixteen cubits, though the Indians alleged that the largest snakes were much larger. Nearchos adds that Alexander summoned to his camp all the Indians most expert in the healing art, and that these succeeded in curing snake-bites, to find a remedy for which quite baffled the skill of all the Greek physicians. Strabo relates (XV. i. 28), that Abisaros, as the ambassadors he sent to Alexander reported, kept two serpents, one of 80 cubits, and the other, according to Onesikritos, of 140 cubits in length; but Strabo no more believed in this land-serpent than we do in the sea-serpent, for he adds that Onesikritos might as well be called the master-fabulist as the master-pilot of Alexander. He afterwards says that Aristoboulos saw a snake nine cubits and a span long, and that he himself while in Egypt had seen another of the same length which had been brought from India. Megasthenes wrote that serpents in India grow to such a size that they swallow deer and oxen whole. He referred no doubt to the python. The python of the Sunderbuns about the mouths of the Ganges are known to swallow deer whole. The Elzevir editor of Curtius cites statements about the size of Indian serpents which leave the extravagant estimate of Oneskritos far behind. Thus Maximus Tyrius (*Dissert.* 38) says: "Taxiles showed Alexander various wonders, and among these was a very large animal sacred to Bacchus, to which the Indians every day immolated victims.   This animal was a serpent (*draco*), of such a size that it equalled five acres of land."

NOTE A*a*.—INDIAN PEACOCKS

The peacock (*mayûra*) abounds in India especially in the forests at the foot of the Himalayas.   Ailianos has several notices of it in his work on animals.   In Book v. 2 1, after he has described its habits, and the pride it takes in displaying its gorgeous plumage, he states that it was brought into Greece from the barbarians.   Being for a long time rare, it was exhibited at the beginning of each month to the men and women of Athens who were lovers of the beautiful.   The charge for admission to the spectacle was a considerable source of gain. The price of a pair (cock and hen) was a thousand drachmas (or about £40 of our money).   Alexander the Macedonian, on seeing these birds in India, was so struck with admiration of their beauty that he denounced the severest penalties against any one who should kill them.   In Book xvi. 2 he notes that the Indian peacocks are the largest to be anywhere found.   In xiii. 18 he says : " In the palace where the greatest of all the Indian kings resides, besides many things else which excite admiration, eclipsing the splendour alike of Memnonian Sousa and all the boasted magnificence of Ekbatana, there are reared in the Royal Park tame peacocks and tame pheasants. . . . Within that park are shady groves, grassy meads planted with trees, and bowers woven by the craft of skilful woodmen.   So genial withal is the climate, that the trees are ever green, and never show signs of age, nor even shed their leaves.   Some are native to the soil, while others which are brought with great care from foreign parts, contribute to enhance the beauty of the landscape.   Not the olive, however, which is neither indigenous to India, nor thrives if brought into it.   The park is therefore frequented by wild birds as well as by the tame.   They seek its groves from choice, and there build their nests and rear their young.   Parrots too are bred there, which, flitting to and fro, keep hovering around the king.   Notwithstanding they are so numerous, no Indian will eat them, for they regard them as sacred, while the Brahmans esteem them above all other birds, and with good reason, since the parrot alone with a clear utterance repeats the words of human speech."   In xi. 33 he tells a story about a peacock of extraordinary size and beauty, which had been sent from India as a present to the King of Egypt, who thereupon dedicated the bird to Jupiter, the guardian god of his capital city. His work has several other passages which refer to the peacock ; but as these have no bearing upon India we do not cite them. The bird was introduced into Greece long before Alexander's time, for Dêmos, the friend of Perikles, reared peacocks at Athens, which many people came from Lacedaemon and Thessaly to see, as we learn from Athenaios, ix. 12. It is said that peacocks were first introduced into Greece from Samos.

NOTE B*b*.—INDIAN DOGS

A breed of dogs, large, powerful, and of untamable ferocity, is still found in the parts of India here mentioned.[1] Pliny, speaking of these Indian dogs, ascribes their savage disposition to the cause mentioned by Diodôros, the tiger blood that runs in their veins. The Indians, he says (viii. 40), assert that these dogs are begotten from tigers, for which purpose the bitches when in heat are tied up amid the woods. They think that the whelps of the first and second brood are too ferocious, but they rear those of the third. Ailianos (viii. 1) varies this statement by saying that tigers are the offspring of the first and second connection, but dogs of the third. He then proceeds thus : " Dogs that boast a tiger paternity disdain to hunt deer or to enter into an encounter with a wild boar, but delight to assail the lion as if to show their high pedigree. So the Indians gave Alexander, the son of Philip, a proof of the strength and mettle of these dogs in the manner following : They let go a deer, but the dog never stirred ; then a boar, but he still remained impassive. Then they tried a bear, but even this failed to rouse him to action. At last they let go a lion. Then the dog fired with rage, as if he now saw a worthy antagonist, did not hesitate for a moment, but flew to encounter him, gripped him fast, and tried to strangle him. Then the Indian who provided this spectacle for the king, and who knew well the dog's capacity of endurance, ordered his tail to be cut off. It was accordingly cut off, but the dog took not the least heed. The Indian ordered next one of his legs to be cut off. This was done, but the dog held to his grip as tenaciously as at first, just as if the dismembered limb were not his own, but belonged to some one else. The remaining legs were then cut off in succession, but even all this did not in the least make him relax the vigour of his bite. Last of all, his head was severed from the rest of his body, but even then his teeth were seen hanging on by

---

[1] The *Râmâyana* (ii. 70. 21) mentions among the Kaikeyas, "the dogs bred in the palace, gifted with the strength of the tiger and of huge body" (Dunck. iv. p. 403).

the part he had first gripped, while the head dangled aloft still clinging to the lion, though the original biter no longer existed. Alexander was very painfully impressed by what he saw, being lost in admiration of the dog, since after giving proof of his mettle he perished in no cowardly fashion, but preferring to die rather than to let his courage give way. The Indian, seeing the king's vexation, gave him four dogs like the one that was killed. He was much gratified with the gift, and gave in return a suitable equivalent. Joy at the possession of the four dogs soon obliterated from the mind of Philip's son his sorrow for the other." The same author writes nearly to the same effect in the nineteenth chapter of his fourth book : " I reckon Indian dogs among wild beasts, for they are of surpassing strength and ferocity, and are the largest of all dogs. This dog despises other animals, but fights with the lion, withstands his attacks, returns his roaring with baying, and gives him bite for bite. In such an encounter the dog may be worsted, but not till he has often severely galled and wounded the lion. The lion is, however, at times worsted by the Indian dog and killed in the chase. If a dog once clutches a lion, he retains his hold so pertinaciously that if one should even cut off his leg with a knife he will not let go, however severe may be the pain he suffers, till death supervening compels him." Aristotle, in his *History of Animals* (viii. 28), refers to these Indian dogs and the story of their tigrine descent. Even an earlier mention of them is to be found in Xenophon (*Kyn.* c. 10). We may hence infer that their fame had spread to Greece long before Alexander's time. Marco Polo mentions a province in China where the people had a large breed of dogs so fierce and bold that two of them together would attack a lion—an animal with which that province abounded (Yule's ed. ii. pp. 108, 109).

Note Cc.—The Gangaridai

This people occupied the country about the mouths of the Ganges, and may best be described as the inhabitants of Lower Bengal. The likeness of their name to that of the Gandaridai, the people of Gandhâra, whose seats were in the neighbourhood of the Indus and the Kôphên or Kâbul river, has been the source of much confusion and error. Fortunately the notice of them in the *Indika* of Megasthenes has been preserved both by Pliny and Solinus, from whom we learn that they were a branch of the great race of the Calingae, that their capital was Parthalis (Bardwan?), and that their king had an army of 60,000 foot, 1000 horse, and

700 elephants, which was always ready for action (Pliny, vi. 18; Solin. 52). They are mentioned in Ptolemy's *Geography* as a people who dwelt about the mouth of the Ganges and whose capital was Gangê. The name of the *Gangaridai* has nothing corresponding with it in Sanskrit, nor can it be, as Lassen supposed, a designation first invented by the Greeks, for Phegelas used it in describing to Alexander the races that occupied the regions beyond the Hyphasis. According to Saint-Martin, their name is preserved in that of the Gonghrîs of S. Bihâr, with whom were connected the Gangayîs of North-Western and the Gangrâr of Eastern Bengal. These designations he takes to be but variations of the name which was originally common to them all. Wilford, in his article on the chronology of the Hindus (*Asiat. Res.* v. p. 269), says that "the greatest part of Bengal was known in Sanskrit under the name of Gancaradesa, or 'country of Gancara,' from which the Greeks made Gangari-das." But this view must be rejected on the same ground as Lassen's. The Gangaridai are mentioned by Virgil, *Georg.* iii. l. 27. As their king, at the time when Megasthenes recorded the strength of the army which he maintained, was subject to Magadha, we may infer that Sandrokottos treated the various potentates who submitted to his arms as Alexander treated Taxilês and Pôros, permitting them to retain as his vassals the power and dignity which they had previously enjoyed.

Note D*d*.—The Prasioi

The Sanskrit word *Prâchyâs* (plur. of *Prachya*, "eastern") denoted the inhabitants of the east country, that is, the country which lay to the east of the river Sarasvatî, now the Sursooty, which flows in a south-western direction from the mountains bounding the north-east part of the province of Delhi till it loses itself in the sands of the great desert. The Magadhas, it would seem, had, before Alexander's advent to India, extended their power as far as this river, and hence were called Prâchyâs by the people who lived to the west of it. They are called by Strabo, Arrian, and Pliny, *Prasioi, Prasii*; by Plutarch, *Praisioi*; by Nikolaös Damask., *Praiisioi*; by Diodôros, *Brêsioi*; by Curtius, *Pharrasii*; by Justin, *Praesides*. Ailianos in general writes *Praisioi* like Plutarch, but in one passage where he quotes Megasthenes, he transcribes the name with perfect accuracy in the adjective form as *Praxiakê*. General Cunningham does not agree in referring the name to *Prâchya*, as all the other modern writers do, but takes *Prasii* to be only the Greek form of *Palâsiya* or *Parâsiya*, a "man of *Palâsa* or *Parâsa*," a name of

Magadha of which Palibothra was the capital. This derivation, he says, is supported by the spelling of the name given by Curtius, who calls the people *Pharrasii*, an almost exact transcript of Parâsiya (see his *Ancient Geog. of India*, p. 454). His view, we think, is hardly destined to supplant the other. Ptolemy describes in his *Geography* a small kingdom with seven cities which he locates in the regions of the upper Ganges, and calls Prasiakê. Kanoge is one of these cities, but Palibothra is not in the number, appearing elsewhere as the capital of the Mandalai. One is at a loss to understand what considerations could have led Ptolemy to push the Prasians so far from their proper seats and transfer their capital to another people.

NOTE E*e*.—THE SIBI

The Sanskrit word *S'ivi* denotes a country, the inhabitants of which, *Sivayas*, may be the Sibi of Curtius and Diodôros. The Sibi inhabited a district between the Hydaspês and the Indus, and their capital stood at a distance of about thirty miles from the former river, and, as appears from Diodôros, above its confluence with the Akesinês. As they were clad with the skins of wild beasts and were armed with clubs, they reminded the Greeks of Herakles, who was similarly dressed and armed, and thence arose the legend that the Sibi were the descendants of the followers of that wandering hero. The truth, however, is that the Sibi represent one of the chief aboriginal tribes of the regions of the Indus. The Sanskrit poems and the Pauranik traditions give this great tribe its real name *S'ibi*, and represent it as one of the important branches of the race which originally peopled all the north-western region. According to Moorcroft, the inhabitants of the district of Bimber are called Chibs, while Baber in his *Memoirs* had mentioned a people so named as belonging to the same parts. Arrian does not expressly mention Alexander's expedition against the Sibi in his *History*, but in his *Indika* (c. 5) he thus refers to them: "So also when the Greeks came among the *Sibai*, an Indian tribe, and observed that they wore skins, they declared that the *Sibai* were descended from those who belonged to the expedition of Herakles, and had been left behind; for besides being dressed in skins, the *Sibai* carry a cudgel and brand on their oxen the representation of a club." In the ordinary texts of Curtius the *Sibi* appears as the *Sobii*, and in Justin as the *Silei*. They are mentioned in the *History* of Orosius (iii. 19), along with a people called Gessonae, who are evidently the people called by Diodôros the *Agalassi*.

Note Ff.—The Agalassians

Curtius does not give the name of the people whom Alexander proceeded to attack after he had received the submission of the Sibi, but it is supplied by Diodôros, who calls them Agalasseis. Saint-Martin says (*Étude*, p. 115) that they adjoined the eastern side of the Sibi and occupied the country below the junction of the Hydaspês and Akesinês. Though *Agalassi* is the most commonly received reading of their name, yet there are many variant readings of it, especially in the manuscripts and editions of Justin, where we find *Agesinae, Hiacensanae, Argesinae, Agini, Acensoni,* and *Gessonae.* The last form occurs also in the *History* of Orosius (iii. 19), where the people it designates are mentioned along with the Sibi. The original name to which these may be referred is probably *Arjunâyana.* This name occurs between that of the Mâlava (Malloi) and that of the Yaudheyas on the Pillar at Allahabad, whereon Samudragupta, who reigned towards the end of the 4th century A.D., inscribed the names of the countries and peoples included in his dominions. The Arjunâyana are mentioned also by the Scholiast of Pânini, and in the geographical list which Wilford compiled from the *Varâha Sanhita.* Arrian in his *Indika* (c. 4) calls the people situated at the junction of the Hydaspês and Akesinês the *Arispai* (*Ibid.* p. 116, and footnotes).

Note Gg.—Tides in Indian Rivers

Several Indian rivers present the tidal phenomenon called the *bore*, the most celebrated being those of the Brahmaputra, the Ganges, the Nerbada, and the Indus. The bore is sometimes many feet in height, and the noise it makes in contending against the descending stream frightful. The bore which rushes up the Hughli has a speed of about seventeen or eighteen miles per hour. A vivid description of the tide or bore of the Nerbada has been given by the author of the *Periplûs.* "India," he says (c. 45), "has everywhere an abundance of rivers, and her seas ebb and flow with tides of extraordinary strength, which increase both at new and full moon, and for three days after each, but fall off intermediately. About Barygaza (Bharoch) they are more violent than elsewhere; so that all of a sudden you see the depths laid bare and portions of the land turned into sea, and the sea where ships were sailing but just before turned without warning into dry land. The rivers, again, on the access of flood-tide rushing into their channels with the whole body of the sea, are driven upwards against their natural course for a great many miles with a force that is irresistible." In c. 46, after explaining how dangerous these tides are to ships navigating the Nerbada, he thus proceeds : " But at new moons, especially when they occur in conjunction with a night tide, the flood sets in with such extra-ordinary violence that on its beginning to advance, even though the sea be calm, its roar is heard by those living near the river's mouth, sounding like the tumult of battle heard in the distance, and soon after the sea with its hissing waves bursts over the bare shoals."

Note H*h*.—Indian Philosophers

Arrian has given the account here promised of the Indian sages, whom he calls *Sophists*, in the eleventh chapter of his *Indika*. They formed the highest and most honoured of the seven castes into which, he says, Indian society was divided. His account is, however, very meagre compared with that which Strabo, quoting from the same authority, Megasthenes, has given in the fifteenth book of his *Geography*. We may subjoin a notice of the more important points. The philosophers were of two kinds, the Brachmânes and the Garmanes (S'ramanas, i.e. *Buddhist ascetics*). The Brachmans were held in greater repute, as they agreed more exactly in their opinions. They lived in a grove outside the city, lay upon pallets of straw and on skins, abstained from animal food and sexual intercourse. After living thirty-seven years in this manner each individual retired to his own possessions, led a life of greater freedom, and married as many wives as he pleased. They discoursed much upon death, which they held to be for philosophers a birth into a real and happy life. They maintained that nothing which happens to a man is bad or good, opinions being merely dreams. On many points their notions coincided with those of the Greeks. They said, for instance, that the world was created and liable to destruction, that it was of a spheroidal figure, and that its Creator governed it and was diffused through all its parts. They invented fables also, after the manner of Plato, on the immortality of the soul, punishments in Hades, and similar topics. Of the S'ramanas the most honourable were the Hylobioi. These, as their name imports, lived in woods, where they subsisted on leaves and wild fruits. They were clothed with garments made of the bark of trees, and abstained from commerce with women and from wine. The kings held communication with them by messengers, and through them worshipped the divinity. Next in honour to the Hylobioi were the physicians, who cured diseases by diet rather than by medicinal remedies, which were chiefly unguents and cataplasms. See XV. i. 58-60.

Arrian, in the opening chapters of the seventh book of his *Anabasis*, gives an account of Alexander's dealings with the Gymnosophists of Taxila which agrees in substance with that given by Strabo (XV. i. 61-65) based on the authority both of Aristoboulos and Onesikritos, the latter of whom was sent by Alexander to converse with the gymnosophists. For the details see Biog. Appendix, *s.v.* Kalânos.

NOTE I*i.*—SUTTEE (Diod. Note 12).

But Diodôros, in a subsequent part of his history (xix. 33), relates that the law had been enacted because of the great prevalence of the practice of wives poisoning their husbands. In c. 34 he states that the two widows of Kêteus, an Indian general who fell in the great battle in Gabienê between Eumenes and Antigonos, contended for the honour of being burned on the funeral pile of their husband, and that the younger was selected for the distinction, because the elder, being at the time with child, was precluded by law from immolating herself. Strabo says (XV. i. 62) that Aristoboulos and other writers make mention of Indian wives burning themselves voluntarily with their husbands.

From this it would appear that this cruel practice, known as *Suttee* (Sansk. *sati*, "a devoted wife"), which was suppressed by the humanity of the Indian Government in the days of Lord Bentinck, was one of high antiquity, but Mr. R. C. Dutt, in his able and learned work on *Civilisation in Ancient India*, assigns a much later date to its origin. He says (vol. iii. 199) that the barbarous rite was introduced centuries after Manu, whose *Institutes*, he thinks, were compiled within a century or two before or after the Christian aera. In a subsequent passage (p. 332) he states that Suttee was originally a Scythian custom, and was probably introduced into India by the Scythian invaders who poured into India in the Buddhist age (from 242 B.C. to 500 A.D.), and formed ruling Hindu races later on. There can be no doubt that Suttee was a Scythian practice. Their kings were entombed with sacrifices both of beasts and of human beings of both sexes, as we see from what Herodôtos relates in the seventy-first chapter of his fourth book. Still the statement of Diodôros shows that several centuries before the Skythian invasions of India took place Suttee was an established institution among a race of the purest Aryan descent such as were the Kathaians—a people whose name shows they were Kshatriyas. The Hindus themselves believe that the custom was of the very highest antiquity, and that a text of the *Rig-veda* sanctioned its observance. It has been discovered, however, that the text in question has been falsified and mistranslated, and that in point of fact no mention is found of the custom in Sanskrit literature till the Pauranik period, the beginning of which Mr. Dutt assigns to the sixth century of our aera.

NOTE K*k*.—ANCIENT INDIAN COINS

The following remarks on the ancient coinage of India are extracted from two papers contributed by Mr. W. Theobald to the *Journal of the Asiatic Society of Bengal*, Nos. III. and IV. of 1890, under the title *Notes on some of the Symbols found on the Punch-marked Coins of Hindustan*:—" The punch-marked coins," he says, "though presenting neither kings' names, dates, nor inscriptions of any sort, are nevertheless very interesting not only from their being the earliest money coined in India, and of a purely indigenous character, but from their being stamped with a number of symbols, some of which we can with the utmost confidence declare to have originated in distant lands and in the remotest antiquity. The punch used to produce these coins differed from the ordinary dies which subsequently came into use in that they

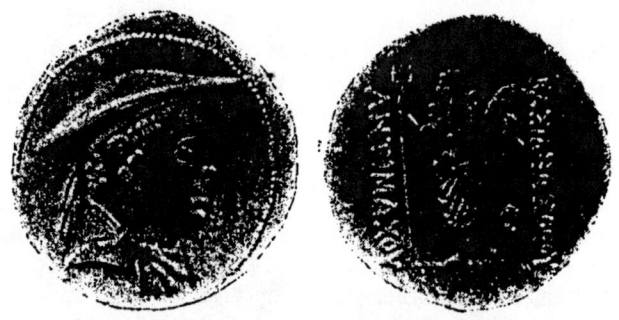

FIG. 16.—ANTIMACHOS.

covered only one of the many symbols usually seen on their pieces. Some of these coins were round and others of a rectangular form. The great bulk of these coins is silver (but some copper, and others gold). Some coins are formed of a copper blank thickly covered with silver before receiving the impression of the punches, and this contemporary sophistication of the currency is found to occur subsequently in various Indian coinages, in the Graeco-Bactrian of the Panjâb, the Hindu kings of Cabul, etc." Mr. Theobald thinks we may regard these pieces as a portion of those very coins (or identical in all respects) which the Brahman Chânakya, the adviser of Chandragupta, with the view of raising resources, converted, by recoining each *Kahapana* into eight, and amassed eighty kotis of *Kahapanas* (or Kârshâpanas). Mr. Theobald holds that the square coins, both silver and copper,

FIG. 17.—AGATHOKLÈS.

struck by the Greeks for their Indian possessions belong to no Greek national type whatever, but are obviously a novelty adopted in imitation of an indigenous currency already firmly established in the country. He adduces by way of proof the testimony of Curtius, where he states that Taxiles offered Alexander eighty talents of coined silver (*signati argenti*). What other, he asks, except these punch-marked coins could these pieces of coined silver have been? The name, he then adds, by which these coins are spoken of in the Buddhist *Sutras* about 200 B.C. was

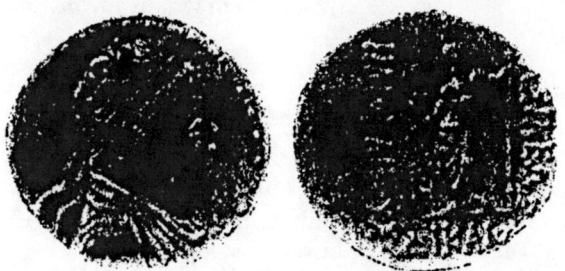

FIG. 18.—HELIOKLÈS.

" purana " = *old*, whence General Cunningham argues that the word *old*, as applied to the indigenous *Karsha*, was used to distinguish it from the new and more recent issues of the Greeks. Mr. Vincent A. Smith writes to the same effect. He considers the artistic coins to be of Greek origin, but holds that the idea of coining money, and the simple mechanical processes for rude coins, were not borrowed from the Greeks. It is, he thinks, impossible to prove that any given piece is older than Alexander, though some primitive coins may be older. The oldest Indian coins to which a date can be assigned are, in his opinion, those issued by Sôphytes, the contemporary of Alexander. The general adoption of Greek, or Graeko-Roman types of coinage, he assigns to the first century as a result of the Indo-Skythian

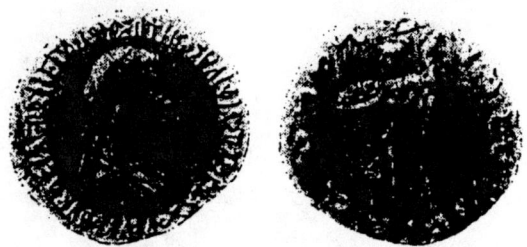

FIG. 19.—APOLLODOTOS.

invasions. Roman coins, it is well known, are found in all parts of India. In Indian writings the Roman *dênârius* appears in the form *dînâra*, and the Greek *drachmê* (which was about equivalent in value to the *denarius*) in the form *dramma*. The subject of the Indo-Greek coinage is discussed in A. v. Sallet's *Die Nachfolger Alexanders*.

NOTE LI.—AN AS'ÔKA INSCRIPTION

Transliteration.— . . . . yu Ichha
shavabhu . . . . shayama shamachaliyaṁ madava ti. Iyaṁ
vu mu . . .
Devânaṁ Piyeshâ ye dhaṁmavijaye she cha punâ ladhe Devânaṁ Pi . . . cha
shaveshu cha ateshu a shashu pi yojanashateshu ata Atiyoge
nâma Yona lâjâ palaṁ châ tenâ
Aṁtiyogenâ chatâli 4 lajâne Tulamaye nâma Aṁtekine nâma
Makâ nâ ma Alikyashudale nâma, nichaṁ Choda-Paṁdiyâ
avam Taṁbapaṁniyâ hevameva hevamevâ
Hidâlâjâ. Vis'a-Vaji-Yona-Kaṁbijeshu Nâbhake Nabhapaṁtishu
Boja-Pitinikyeshu
Adha-Puladeshu shavatâ Devânaṁ Piyashâ dhaṁmamânushathi
anuvataṁti.

Translation.—The following is considered of the highest importance by the God-beloved, namely Conquest by law; this Conquest, however, is made by the God-beloved as well here

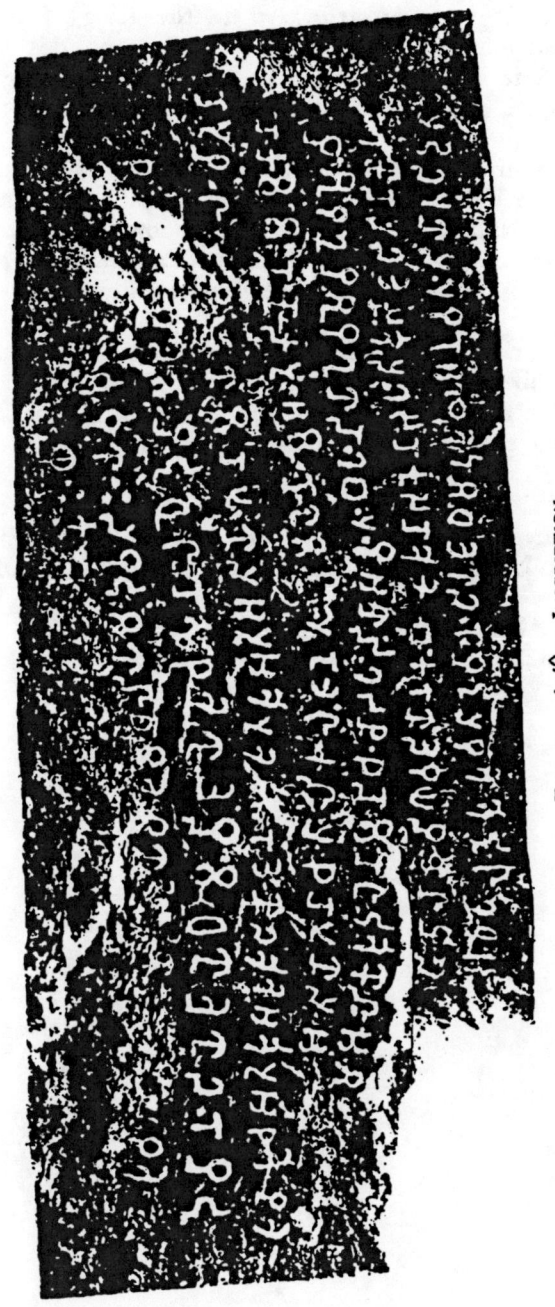

FIG. 20.—ASʹÓKA INSCRIPTION.

(*in his own kingdom*) as among all his neighbours, even as far
as six hundred yojanas (*leagues*), where the King of the Yonas
(*Greeks*), Antiyoka by name, dwells; and beyond this Antiyoka
where the four kings, Turamaya by name, Amtikina by name,
Maka by name, Alikasudara by name (dwell farther away) in the
south, where the Chodas and Paindas (*Pandyas*) (dwell), as far
as Tambapanini (*Ceylon*) (where) the Hida king (dwells). Among
the Vis'as, the Vajris (*Vrijis*), the Yonas (*Greeks*), the Kamboyas
(*Kabulis*), in Nâbhaka of the Nâbhitis, among the Bhojas, the
Pitinikas, the Andhras and the Puladas (*Pulindas*), the teaching
of the law of the God-beloved is universally followed.

This remarkable edict is found inscribed at four different
places: Shahbâzgarhi in Yusufzai, Mânsahra in Hazâra of the
Panjâb, Kâlsi above Dehra Dûn, and Girnâr in Kathiawâr.   In
the first two places the character employed is the Karoshtri,
that is, the Baktrian Pali, and in the other two the Indian Pali.
It is the Kâlsi inscription which is copied in the illustration.   By
the God-beloved (Piyeshâ or Piyadasi) is meant As'ôka himself.
The Grecian kings named in the inscription have already been
identified (p. 52), with the exception of Alikyashudale, who is
taken to be Alexander, King of Epeiros.   *v.* Senart's *Les Inscriptions de Piyadasi* and *Epigraphia Indica*, vol. ii.

BIOGRAPHICAL APPENDIX

ABISARES is called by Arrian the King of the Indian Mountaineers, and may perhaps be not improperly described as the King of Kâs'mîr. His name is derived from that of his kingdom, *Abhisâra*, which designated the mountainous country to the east of the Indus now known as *Hazâra*, a name in which some traces of the old seem to survive. After the fall of Mazaga, he sent troops across the Indus to aid the inhabitants in resisting Alexander. He sent embassies, however, to the conqueror both before and after the defeat of Pôros, whom he inclined to succour. Alexander allowed him to retain his kingdom, and when he died appointed his son to succeed him, as we learn from Curtius X. i.

AGGRAMMES.—*See* Xandrames.

ALKETAS was the brother of Perdikkas, who, after Alexander's death, assumed the regency of the empire. He was the son of Orontes, a Macedonian of the province of Orestis. He is first mentioned by Arrian as commander of one of the brigades which Alexander, towards the close of his Baktrian campaigns, despatched under Krateros into the country of the Paratakenians, who still held out against him. He is next mentioned in connection with the siege of Mazaga and Ora. When Alexander crossed the Hydaspês to encounter Pôros, Alketas remained behind in the camp with Krateros. After Alexander's death Alketas supported the cause of his brother, and by his orders put to death Kynanê, the half-sister of Alexander—a cruel act which his own troops resented. When Perdikkas was murdered in Egypt (321 B.C.) Alketas was at the time with Eumenes engaged against Krateros. He afterwards, however, joined his forces to those of Attalos; but being defeated in Pisidia, he slew himself to avoid falling into the hands of Antigonos.

AMBIGER, supposed to be a corrupt reading for Ambi-regis. —*See* under Sambus.

AMYNTAS, the son of Nikolaös, was appointed satrap of

Baktria in succession to Artabazos, who resigned the office on the ground of his advanced age. When Alexander left Baktria to invade India he left Amyntas in the province with a force of 10,000 foot and 3500 horse.

ANDROKOTTOS.—*See* Sandrokottos.

ANDROSTHENES, a native of Thasos, sailed with Nearchos, and was afterwards sent by Alexander to explore the Persian Gulf. He wrote an account of this voyage, and a work describing a coasting voyage to India.

ANTIGENES, an officer who served both under Philip and Alexander. In 340 B.C. he lost an eye at the siege of Perinthos. He was present in the battle with Pôros, and the divisions of the phalanx which he led on this occasion formed afterwards part of the large body of troops which Krateros led through the country of the Arachotians and Zarangians into Karmania. After the army reached Sousa he was for some time deprived of his command for having advanced some fraudulent claim. After Alexander's death he obtained the satrapy of Sousiana. In the wars between the generals he sided with Eumenes, whom he aided with the Argyraspids under his command. When Eumenes was defeated in 316 B.C. Antigenes fell into the hands of his enemy, Antigonos, who ordered him to be burned to death.

ANTIGONOS, called the One-eyed, was a Macedonian of Elimiôtis, and one of the generals of Alexander, but did not accompany him into India, as he had been appointed satrap of Phrygia. In the partition of the empire he received Phrygia, Lykia, and Pamphylia, and eventually made himself master of the whole of Asia Minor. He was slain in the battle of Ipsos 301 B.C. He was the father of Dêmêtrios Poliorkêtês, who founded a line of Macedonian kings.

ANTIGONOS GONATAS was one of the kings to whom As'ôka

FIG. 21.—ANTIGONOS GONATAS.

sent Buddhist missionaries. He was the son of Dêmêtrios Poliorkêtês, whom he succeeded as king of Macedonia in the year 283 B.C. His reign extended to forty-four years. His brother Antigonos Dôsôn reigned afterwards over Macedonia for

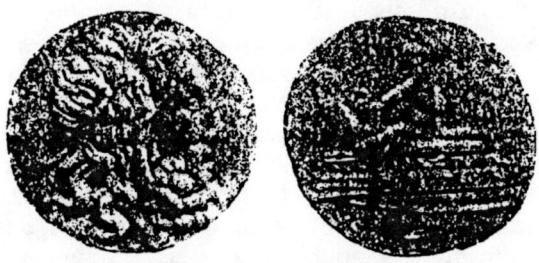

FIG. 22.—ANTIGONOS DÔSÔN.

nine years, from 229 to 220 B.C., in succession to Dêmêtrios II. the son of Gonatas.

ANTIOCHOS II., surnamed Theos, succeeded to the throne of Syria on the death of his father Antiochos I., who was the son of the famous Seleukos Nikator. During many years of his reign he was engaged in intermittent hostilities with Ptolemy Philadelphos the king of Egypt, who wrested from him Phoenicia and Hollow Syria. His power was further weakened by the revolt of

FIG. 23.—ANTIOCHOS II.

Arsakês, who established the Parthian empire (in 250 B.C.), and by the subsequent revolt of Theodotos, who made Baktria an independent kingdom. He was one of the kings of the West to whom Buddhist missionaries were sent by the Indian king As'ôka. His wife Laodikê caused him to be murdered in B.C. 246.

ANTIPATER.—This officer, who had great experience in war and civil affairs under Philip, was left regent of Macedonia when Alexander set out on his Asiatic expedition. Olympias, jealous of his power, was constantly engaged in intrigues against him, while she annoyed her son by filling her letters to him with complaints against his deputy. After the murder of Perdikkas in Egypt, Antipater succeeded him in the regency of the empire, and this he held till his death in 320 B.C.

APHRIKES, called Eryx by Curtius, was the same whom Arrian designates the *brother of Assakênos*, the king of Mazaga. He was put to death by his own followers.

APOLLONIOS, a native of Tyana in Kappadokia, was born in the year 4 B.C. He adopted the Pythagorean system of philosophy, and submitted himself to its ascetic discipline. He was credited with the possession of supernatural powers, and parallels have been drawn between his character and supposed miracles and those of Christ. He travelled in the East, and is said to have visited Taxila, the capital of Phraortes, an Indian prince, where he.met Iarchas, the chief of the Brahmans, and disputed with Indian gymnosophists. About a hundred years after his death an account of his life was written by Philostratos, which, notwithstanding that much of it is untrustworthy, is of great value for the investigation of Indian antiquity.

APOLLOPHANES was appointed satrap of the Oritians, but was deposed not long afterwards by Alexander for misgovernment.

ARIOBARZANES was the satrap of Persis. After the defeat of the Persians near Arbêla, he fled to secure the pass called the Persian Gates, which lay on the route to Persepolis. Alexander having gained the heights above his camp, the Persians took to flight, and Ariobarzanes made his escape with a few horsemen.

ARISTOBOULOS was a native of Kassandreia, a town on the isthmus which connects the peninsula of Pallênê with the mainland. He accompanied Alexander in his Asiatic expedition, and wrote a history of his wars, which was one of the principal sources used by Arrian in the composition of his *Anabasis*, and by Plutarch in his *Life of Alexander*. Arrian, in the preface to his great work, thus characterises the two authors whom he mainly followed: "Different authors have differed in their accounts of Alexander's life. . . . But I consider the narratives of Ptolemy and Aristoboulos to be more worthy of credit than the rest; Aristoboulos, because he attended Alexander in his expedition; and Ptolemy, not only for that reason, but also because he was afterwards himself a king, and for one in his position to have falsified facts would have been more disgraceful than for a man of humbler rank. Both of them, moreover, compiled their histories after Alexander was dead, when they were neither compelled, nor tempted by hope of reward, to misrepresent facts, and on this account they are the more worthy of credit." Lucian, nevertheless, accuses Aristoboulos of having invented marvellous stories of Alexander's prowess in battle; but it is thought that in the anecdote which he relates in this connection he has used by mistake the name of Aristoboulos for that of Onesikritos. *See* Lucian's *How History should be Written*, c. 12. It is said that Aristoboulos began the composition of his history when he was 84 years old, and that he lived to be 90.

ARISTONOUS was, like Alexander, a native of Pella, and was one of the seven or eight chief officers who formed his bodyguard, and had at all times access to his presence. According to Curtius he was one of the men who helped to save Alexander's life when he was assailed and wounded by the Mallians in their chief stronghold. On the death of Alexander he advocated the claims of Perdikkas to the supremacy. After the fall of Olympias, to whose cause he had attached himself, he was put to death by order of her antagonist, Kassander, in the year 316 B.C.

ARISTOTLE was born in 384 B.C. at Stageira, a seaport town near the isthmus which connects the peninsula terminating in Mount Athos with the mainland of Macedonia. When he was studying philosophy in Athens under Plato he received a letter from King Philip announcing the birth of his son Alexander. This letter has been preserved by Aulus Gellius in his *Noctes Atticae* (ix. 3):—"Philip to Aristotle greeting: know that a son has been born to me. I thank the gods, not so much for his birth, as that it has been his fortune to be born when you are in the prime of life; for I hope that being instructed and educated by you, he will prove himself worthy both of us and of the succession to so great a state." Thirteen years afterwards Philip summoned the great philosopher to his court, and entrusted him with the education of his son, which was conducted in quiet seclusion at Stageira, at a distance from Pella, the centre of political activity and court intrigue. Here Alexander remained for four years, at the end of which he was called to govern the kingdom during his father's temporary absence on an expedition against Byzantium. Along with him were educated other noble youths, Kassander, son of Antipater; Marsyas of Pella; Kallisthenes, who was related to Aristotle; Theophrastos, and probably also Nearchos, Ptolemy, and Harpalos. The course of instruction embraced poetry, eloquence, and philosophy, and, no doubt, also politics, though one of the leading aims of Alexander in after life, that of uniting all the nations under his sway into one kingdom without due regard to their individual peculiarities, was opposed to the views of his master. Alexander regarded Aristotle with sentiments of the deepest respect and affection, and rewarded him for his instructions with a munificence which has never been surpassed. Pliny mentions how liberally he supported the philosopher in his researches into natural science, especially in the department of zoology, ordering his vicegerents everywhere to supply him with specimens of all kinds of animals.   Unhappily the cordiality between them was interrupted when Kallisthenes began to express disapproval of the change in Alexander's conduct and policy. Aristotle died at the age of 63, about a year after the death of his pupil.

ARSAKÊS was the ruler of a small mountain kingdom which adjoined that of his brother Abisares, King of Kâs'mîr.

ARTABAZOS was a Persian satrap, who for some years maintained a war of rebellion against Artaxerxes III.   In the reign of Darius he distinguished himself by his fidelity to his sovereign. He took part in the battle of Gaugamela, and afterwards accompanied Darius in his flight.   Alexander, who approved of his fidelity to his master, rewarded him with the satrapy of Baktria. Ptolemy married one of his daughters and Eumenes another. He resigned his satrapy on account of his great age, and was succeeded by Kleitos.

ARTEMIDOROS was a Greek geographer who lived about 100 B.C.   His work on geography was abridged by Markianos.   Some fragments of the work, which was of high value, and of the abridgment, have been preserved by Strabo and other writers.

ASKLÊPIOS (AESCULAPIUS) was the god of the medical art.   His descendants were called Asklepiadai, and had their principal seats at Kôs and Knidos.   The Asklepiads were not only a fraternity of physicians, but an order of priests, who combined religion with the practice of their art.

AS'ÔKA was the son of Vindusâra and grandson of Chandragupta, called Sandrokottos by the Greeks.   He ascended the throne of Magadha in 270 B.C.   Having been converted to Buddhism, he established that faith as the state religion of his vast empire, which comprised the greater part of India.   He was zealous in promoting the spread of his creed, and even sent missionaries to expound its doctrines to the sovereigns of the West, Antiochos of Syria, Ptolemy of Egypt, Antigonos of Macedonia, Magas of Kyrênê and Alexander of Epiros.   His religious zeal, piety, and benevolence inspire all the many edicts he promulgated, which are still to be read cut on rocks, caves, and pillars.   The date of his death is uncertain, but is referred to the year 222 B.C.   His inscriptions are invaluable for the aid they contribute towards the solution of some of the most important and difficult problems with which the investigators of Indian antiquity have to deal. They throw light on many points of historical, chronological, and linguistic inquiry, as well as on others having reference to the social, political, and religious condition of the Indian people in the days when Buddhism first rose to the ascendant. An account of these inscriptions will be found in Lassen's *Alt. Ind.* ii. pp. 215-223.

ASSAGETES was, Lassen thinks, an Assakēnian chief. His name probably transliterates *As'vajit*; according to the same authority the word would mean "conquered by the horse."

ASSAKANOS, the King of Mazaga, the capital of the Assakēnians. According to Arrian he was slain during the siege of that stronghold by Alexander, but Curtius leads us to believe that he had died before the conqueror's advent.

ASTES, the chief of Peukelaôtis, submitted to Alexander when he entered India, but afterwards revolted and was slain by the troops under Hêphaistiôn.

ATHÊNAIOS was the author of the *Deipnosophists*, *i.e.* the *Banquet of the Learned*, or, perhaps, the *Contrivers of Feasts.* This work is described by a writer in Smith's *Classical Dictionary* as a vast collection of anecdotes, extracts from the writings of poets, historians, dramatists, philosophers, orators, and physicians, of facts in natural history, criticisms and discussions on almost every conceivable subject, especially on gastronomy. It contains numerous references to Alexander and the events of his time. Athênaios was a native of Naukratis, in Lower Egypt. He wrote in the earlier part of the third century of our aera.

ATHENODÔROS was the leader of the sedition of the Greek colonists settled in Baktria who were anxious to return to their native country.

ATTALOS.—Three persons of this name are mentioned in this work :

1. *Attalos*, one of the generals of King Philip, and uncle of Kleopatra, whom that king married in 337 B.C. At the nuptial festivities, Attalos requested the guests to pray to the gods that a legitimate heir to the throne might be the fruit of the marriage. This naturally gave great offence to Alexander and his mother, Olympias, who both in consequence withdrew from the kingdom. Attalos was in Asia at the time of Philip's death, and was instigated by Demosthenes to rebel against his successor. Alexander then caused him to be assassinated. It will be seen from what has been stated that the royal house of Macedonia practised polygamy.

2. *Attalos*, who commanded the Agrianians in the battles of Issos and Gaugamela.

3. *Attalos*, the son of Andromenes of Stymphalia, a district in Macedonia, or on its borders, was one of Alexander's chief officers. He was accused, along with his brothers, of complicity with Philôtas in his alleged conspiracy, but was honourably acquitted. In 328 B.C. he was left with other officers to hold Baktria in subjection, while Alexander himself marched against the Sogdians. In the campaign of 327 B.C. against the Assakênians and other tribes north of the Kabul River, Attalos served in the division of the army which Alexander commanded in person. He took part in the great battle in which the Assakênians were defeated, and in the siege of Ora. He fought also in the battle against Pôros. His division formed part of the troops which Krateros led by the route of the Bolan Pass into Karmania. After Alexander's death he supported Perdikkas, whose sister he had married. After the murder of Perdikkas he joined Alketas, his brother-in-law, but their united forces were defeated by Antigonos in Pisidia. Alketas was seized and imprisoned. His ultimate fate is unknown.

BAITÔN, one of the scientific men in Alexander's army, employed, like Diognêtos, in measuring the distances traversed in its marches, whence he was called Alexander's *bêmatistês*. He left a professional work, which, as we learn from Athênaios (x. p. 442) was entitled *Stages of Alexander's Marches*.

BALAKROS.—There were three officers of this name in Alexander's army. 1. The son of Nikanor, who was a Somatophylax, and was appointed satrap of Kilikia after the battle of Issos. He was slain in Pisidia in Alexander's lifetime. 2. The son of Amyntas was commander of the allies in succession to Antigonos, and commander, along with Peukestas, of the army which Alexander left in Egypt. 3. A commander of the javelin men who took part in the great battle with the Aspasians.

BARSINÊ, called also Stateira, was the elder daughter of Darius, and became the wife of Alexander at Sousa, 324 B.C. Within a year of Alexander's death she was treacherously murdered by Roxana.

BARZAËNTES, satrap of the Arachosians and Drangians, was one of the murderers of Darius. To escape Alexander he fled to India, but was given up by the inhabitants to Alexander, who ordered his death.

BÊSSOS, the satrap of Baktria, commanded the left wing of the Persian army at Arbêla, and was thus directly opposed to Alexander himself in that battle. After the battle he conspired against his unfortunate master, who was also his kinsman, and caused him to be assassinated lest he should fall into Alexander's hands—a result which would have frustrated his design of mounting the vacant throne. He fled across the Oxus, but was betrayed and delivered up to Alexander, who caused him to be tried before a council at Zariaspa, and after suffering mutilation to be executed.

CHANDRAGUPTA.—*See* Sandrokottos.

CHARÊS, or Cares, a native of Mytilênê in Lesbos, was an officer with Alexander who discharged the functions of court usher. He wrote a book (now lost) of anecdotes about Alexander's wars and private life, which is frequently quoted by Athênaios. Some fragments have also been preserved by Plutarch, Pliny, and Aulus Gellius.

CLEOPHIS, Queen of Mazaga, surrendered that city to Alexander, by whom she was kindly treated, and to whom she is said to have borne a son who became an Indian king. In Racine's tragedy, *Alexandre le Grand*, Cleophis, who figures as one of the *dramatis personae*, is made the sister of Taxilês.

DÊIMACHOS or DAIMACHOS was ambassador at the court of Allitrochades, the son and successor of Sandrokottos, and wrote a work on India in two books. He is pilloried by Strabo as the most mendacious of all writers about India.

DÊMÊTRIOS was one of the officers who formed Alexander's bodyguard. He was accused by Philôtas as being one of his accomplices in the conspiracy against the king's life, and was in consequence deprived of his post, to which Ptolemy was then preferred.

DÊMÊTRIOS, son of Pythonax, was one of the select band of cavalry called the *Companions*. He took part in the Indian campaigns.

DÊMÊTRIOS POLIORKÊTÊS, the son of Antigonos, became king of Macedonia in 294 B.C.

FIG. 24.—DÊMÊTRIOS POLIORKÊTÊS.

DIOSKORIDES, the famous writer on *Materia Medica*, was a native of Kilikia, and flourished, so far as can be conjectured, about the beginning of the second century of our aera.

EMBISAROS.—*See* Abisares.

EPIKTÊTOS, the famous philosopher, was a native of Hieropolis in Phrygia, and a freedman of Epaphroditus, the favourite of Nero. Arrian, who was one of his disciples, composed a short manual of his philosophy as taken down from his lectures, and known as the *Enchiridion*.

ERATOSTHENES was appointed by Ptolemy Euergetes (grandson of Alexander's Ptolemy) president of the Alexandrian Library, an office which he held for upwards of forty years. He may be considered as the founder of scientific geography, and in some measure also of systematic chronology. He was born at Kyrênê in 276 B.C., and educated in Athens, where he devoted himself to the study of learning and philosophy. He died in Alexandria in the year 196 B.C. His works, which were numerous and treated of a great variety of subjects, scientific and literary, have perished, with the exception of some fragments cited by other writers.

ERIGYIOS was by birth a Mitylenaian, and was an officer in Alexander's army. He commanded the cavalry of the allies both in the battle of Arbêla and when Alexander set out from Ekbatana in pursuit of Darius. He was slain fighting with Baktrian fugitives.

EUDÊMOS.—When Alexander heard in Karmania that Philip, who had been left in India as satrap, had been treacherously murdered by the mercenaries, he sent orders to Taxilês and Eudêmos to administer affairs till a new satrap should be appointed. Sometime after Alexander's death Eudêmos decoyed Pôros into his power and cut him off. He then left India either because Eumenes requiring his services in contending against Antigonos recalled him, or because he was unable to hold out against the native revolt headed by Sandrokottos. The troops and elephants which he took with him from India were of great service to Eumenes. After the fall of his chief Eudêmos was put to death by Antigonos.

EUMENES was a native of Kardia, a Greek colony situated in the Thracian Chersonese. He was private secretary to King Philip, and then to Alexander, whom he attended throughout his Asiatic expedition. It was one of his duties as royal secretary to keep a diary (*Ephêmerides*) in which the transactions of each day had to be recorded, and this work is quoted both by Arrian and Plutarch. He showed himself a man of consummate ability in the arts both of war and of politics. His alien origin, however, exposed him to the jealousy of the Macedonian officers. Hêphaistiôn in particular, Alexander's chief favourite, sought by every means to compass his overthrow. Eumenes, however, by his prudence and tact frustrated all attempts made to undermine his influence with the king who had a just appreciation of his merits. Though his labours were chiefly those of the closet, he was sometimes employed in the field, more especially on occasions of unusual emergency. When Alexander, on returning to Sousa, celebrated his own nuptials and those of his companions with oriental brides, he gave, as Arrian tells us (vi. 4), to Ptolemy, and Eumenes, the royal secretary, the daughters of Artabazos; to the former Artikama, and to the latter Artonis. After the king's death Eumenes obtained Kappadokia, Paphlagonia, and Pontos, and after some delay was established in the government of these provinces. After the death of Perdikkas, to whom he owed this service, he was requested by Olympias and Polysperchon to undertake the supreme command throughout Asia on behalf of the king. He had in consequence to contend against the faction opposed to the royal family which was headed by Antigonos, and supported by Ptolemy, Peithôn, Seleukos, and Nearchos. After coping successfully for a considerable time against this powerful confederacy, he was delivered up by his own troops to Antigonos, who, notwithstanding the remonstrances of Nearchos, ordered him to be put to death, 316 B.C.

GORGIAS, a commander of a division of the phalanx. He marched with Hêphaistiôn and Perdikkas by the Khaiber Pass to the Indus, and fought in the battle against Pôros.

HARPALOS was of princely birth, and nephew of King Philip. He was educated along with Alexander, whom he accompanied into Asia in the capacity of superintendent of his treasury. Having betrayed his trust he fled to Greece, but was recalled by Alexander, who overlooked his offence and reinstated him in his office. Alexander, on setting out from Ekbatana to pursue Darius, left Harpalos in that stronghold in charge of the vast treasures which had been transported thither from Sousa and other plundered capitals. Harpalos removed thence to Babylon, where he ruled as satrap while the king was in India. Here his licentiousness and extravagance exceeded all bounds. On hearing that Alexander had returned to Sousa, and was punishing with the utmost severity all officers who had misgoverned in his absence, he set out for the coast, taking with him the vast sum of 5000 talents and a large escort of troops. He crossed over to Attica, but the Athenians would not permit him to land until he had disbanded his followers. When he was admitted into the city he employed his wealth in bribing the orators to gain over the people to his cause in opposition to Alexander. He was, however, obliged to take to flight, and having landed with his treasures in the island of Crete, was there assassinated.

HÊKATAIOS, one of the earliest and most distinguished Greek historians and geographers, was a native of Milêtos, and lived about 520 B.C. He is the first Greek writer who distinctly mentions India. Some fragments of his works have been preserved.

HÊPHAISTIÔN was a native of Pella, and in his childhood appears to have been brought up with Alexander, who was of the same age as he, and not only continued to be his friend through life, but lavished upon him when removed by death the most extravagant honours. In the Egyptian expedition he commanded the fleet, and he distinguished himself in the battle of Arbêla, where he was wounded in the arm. When Philôtas was put to death the command of the horse guards was divided between him and Kleitos. He conducted important operations in Sogdiana and Baktria, and throughout all the subsequent campaigns until the army returned to Sousa. He was not possessed of any striking share of ability, and would certainly not have risen to eminence through his own unaided exertions. At Sousa Alexander gave him to wife Drypatis, one of the daughters of Darius, and the sister of Stateira, whom he himself married. Hêphaistiôn was soon afterwards cut off by fever at Ekbatana.

HERAKON, one of Alexander's officers, was appointed with two others to command the army in Media on the death of Parmenion. During Alexander's absence in the far east he committed many excesses, for which he was put to death on Alexander's return from India.

KALÂNOS was a gymnosophist of Taxila, who left India with Alexander, and burned himself alive on a funeral pile at Sousa. His real name, Plutarch says, was *Sphinês*; but the Greeks called him Kalânos, because, in saluting those he met, he used the word *kale!* equivalent to *hail!* The Sanskrit adjective *kalyâna* means salutary, lucky, well, etc. If we except Sandrokottos, Taxilês, and Pôros, there is no other Indian with whose history, opinions, and personal characteristics the classical writers have made us so well acquainted as with those of Kalânos. For this reason, as well as because it falls properly within the scope of my undertaking to do so, I shall here present translations of all the passages I can find which relate to him, and to another gymnosophist who was a man of a very different stamp called *Mandanes*, and sometimes, but improperly, *Dandamis*. Arrian (VII. i. 5—iii.) thus writes:—i. 5. I commend the Indian sages of whom it is related that certain of them who had been caught by Alexander walking about according to their wont in the open meadow, did nothing else in sight of himself and his army but stamp upon the ground on which they were stepping. When he asked them through interpreters what they meant by so doing, they replied thus: O King Alexander, each man possesses as much of the earth as what we have stepped on; but you, being a man like the rest of us, except that you wickedly disturb the peace of the world, have come so far from home to plague yourself and every one else, and yet ere long when you die you will possess just so much of the earth as will suffice to make a grave to cover your bones. ii. Alexander praised what they had said, but nevertheless continued to act in opposition to their advice. . . . When he arrived at Taxila and saw the Indian gymnosophists, he conceived a great desire that one of their number should live with him, because he admired their patience in enduring hardships. But the oldest of the philosophers, Dandamis by name, with whom the others lived as disciples, not only refused to go himself, but forbade the others to go. He is said to have replied that he was also a son of Zeus, if Alexander was such,[1] and that he wanted nothing that was Alexander's; for he was content with what he had, while he saw that the men with Alexander wandered over sea and land for no advantage, and were never coming to an end of their wanderings. He desired, therefore, nothing it was in Alexander's power to give: nor did he fear being excluded from anything he possessed; for while he lived, India would suffice for him, yielding him her fruits in due season, and when he died he would be delivered from the body an unsuitable companion. Alexander accordingly did not attempt to compel him to go with him, considering him free to please himself. But Megasthenes has stated that Kalânos, one of the philosophers of this place, was persuaded to go since he had no power of self-control, as the philosophers themselves allowed, who upbraided him because he had deserted the happiness among them, and went to serve another master than the deity. iii. I have thus written, because in a *History of Alexander* it was necessary to speak of Kalânos; for when he was in the

---

[1] Referring to the terms in which he was summoned to go to Alexander. He was to go to "the son of Zeus."

country of Persis he fell into delicate health, though he had never before had an illness. Accordingly, as he had no wish to lead the life of an invalid, he informed Alexander that, broken as he was in health, he thought it best to put an end to himself before he had experience of any malady that would oblige him to change his former mode of life. Alexander long and earnestly opposed his request; but when he saw that he was quite inflexible, and that if one mode of death was denied him he would find another, he ordered a funeral pyre to be piled up in accordance with the man's own directions, and ordered Ptolemy, the son of Lagos, one of the bodyguards, to superintend all the arrangements. Some say that a solemn procession of horses and men advanced before him, some of the men being armed, while others carried all kinds of incense for the pyre. Others again say that they carried gold and silver bowls and royal apparel; also, that a horse was provided for him because he was unable to walk from illness. He was, however, unable to mount the horse, and he was therefore carried on a litter crowned with a garland, after the manner of the Indians, and singing in the Indian tongue. The Indians say that what he sang were hymns to the gods and the praises of his countrymen, and that the horse which he was to have mounted—a Nêsaian steed of the royal stud—he presented to Lysimachos who attended him for instruction in philosophy. On others who attended him he bestowed the bowls and rugs which Alexander, to honour him, had ordered to be cast into the pyre. Then mounting the pile, he lay down upon it in a becoming manner in full view of the whole army. Alexander deemed the spectacle one which he could not with propriety witness, because the man to suffer was his friend; but to those who were present Kalânos caused astonishment in that he did not move any part of his body in the fire. As soon as the men charged with the duty set fire to the pile, the trumpets, Nearchos says, sounded by Alexander's order, and the whole army raised the war-shout as if advancing to battle. The elephants also swelled the noise with their shrill and warlike cry to do honour to Kalânos.

In a subsequent chapter (xviii.) Arrian records the following story of Kalânos: When he was going to the funeral pyre to die, he embraced all his other companions, but did not wish to draw near to Alexander to give him a parting embrace, saying he would meet him at Babylon and would there embrace him. This remark attracted no notice at the time; but afterwards, when Alexander died in Babylon, it came back to the memory of those who heard it, who then naturally took it to have been a prophecy of his death. Plutarch, in his *Life of Alexander*, has another notice of Kalânos besides that which the reader will find translated in chapter 65. In chapter 69 he thus writes: "It was here (in Persepolis) that Kalânos, on being for a short time afflicted with colic, desired to have his funeral pile erected. He was conveyed to it on horseback, and after he had prayed and sprinkled himself with a libation, and cut off part of his hair to cast into the fire, he ascended the pile, after taking leave of the Macedonians, and recommending them to devote that day to pleasure and hard drinking with the king, whom, said he, I shall shortly see in Babylon. Upon this he lay down on the pyre and covered himself up with his robes. When the flames approached he did not move, but remained in the same posture as when he lay down until the sacrifice was auspiciously consummated, according to the custom of the sages of his country. Many years afterwards another Indian in the presence of Caesar (Augustus) at Athens did the same thing. His tomb is shown till this day, and is called the *Indian's tomb.*—Alexander, on returning from the pyre, invited many of his friends and his generals to supper, where he proposed a drinking-bout, with a crown for the prize. Promachos, who drank most, reached four measures (14 quarts), and won the crown, which was worth a talent, but survived only for three days. The rest of the guests, Charês says, drank to such excess that forty-one of them died, the weather having turned excessively cold immediately after the debauch." The Indian who burned himself at Athens was called *Zarmanochegas*, as we learn from Strabo (XV. i. 73), who states, on the authority of Nikolaös of Damascus, that he came to Syria in the train of the ambassadors who were sent to Augustus Caesar by a great Indian king called Pôros. "These ambassadors," he says, "were accompanied by the person who burnt himself to death at Athens. This is the practice with persons in distress, who seek escape from existing calamities, and with others in prosperous circumstances, as was the case with this man. For as everything hitherto had succeeded with him, he thought it necessary to depart, lest some unexpected calamity should happen to him by continuing to live; with a smile, therefore, naked, anointed, and with the girdle round his waist, he leaped upon the pyre. On his tomb was this inscription: Zarmanochegas, an Indian, a native of Bargosa (*Barygaza, Baroch*), having immortalised himself according to the custom of his country, here lies." Lassen takes the name Zarmanochegas to represent the Sanskrit S'ramanachârya, *teacher of the S'ramanas,* from which it would appear he was a Buddhist priest. Strabo writes at greater length than our historians about the gymnosophists. In Book XV. i. 61 we have the following notices : " Aristoboulos says that he saw at Taxila two sophists, both Brachmans, of whom the elder had his head shaved, while the younger wore his hair ; disciples attended both. They spent their time generally in the market-place. They are honoured as public counsellors, and are free to take away without charge any article exposed for sale which they may choose. He who accosts them pours over them oil of jessamine in such quantities that it runs down from their eyes. They make cakes of honey and sesamum, of which large quantities are always for sale, and their food thus costs them nothing. At Alexander's table they ate standing, and, to give a sample of their endurance, withdrew to a spot not far off, where the elder, lying down with his back to the ground, endured the sun and the rains which had set in as spring had just begun. The other stood on one leg, holding up with both his hands a bar of wood 3 cubits long ; one leg being tired he rested his weight on the other, and did this throughout the day. The younger seemed to have far more self-command ; for though he followed the king a short distance, he soon returned to his home. The king sent after him, but the king, he said, should come to him if he wanted anything from him. The other accompanied the king to the end of his life. During his stay he changed his dress and altered his mode of life, saying, when reproached for so doing, that he had completed the forty years of discipline which he had vowed to observe. Alexander gave presents to his children. (63) Onesikritos says that he himself was sent to converse with these sages. . . . He found at the distance of twenty stadia from the city fifteen men standing in different attitudes, sitting or lying down naked, and continuing in these positions till the evening, when they went back to the city. What was hardest to bear was the heat of the sun, which was so powerful that no one else could bear without pain to walk barefooted on the ground at mid-day. (64) He conversed with Kalânos, one of these sages, who accompanied the king to Persia, and burned himself after the custom of his country on a pile of wood. Onesikritos found him lying upon stones, and drawing near to address him, informed him that he had been sent by the king, who had heard the fame of his wisdom. As the king would require an account of the interview, he was prepared to listen to his discourse if he did not object to converse with him. When Kalânos saw the cloak, head-dress, and shoes of his visitor, he laughed and said : " Formerly there was abundance of corn and barley in the world, as there is now of dust ; fountains then flowed with water, milk, honey, wine. and oil, but repletion and luxury made men turn proud and insolent. Zeus, indignant at this, destroyed all, and assigned to man a life of toil. When temperance and other virtues in consequence again appeared, then good things again abounded. But at present the condition of mankind tends to satiety and wantonness, and there is cause to fear lest the existing state of things should disappear." When he had finished he proposed to Onesikritos, if he wished to hear his discourse, to strip off his clothes, to lie down naked beside him on the same stones, and in that manner to hear what he had to say. While he was uncertain what to do, Mandanes, the oldest and wisest of the sages, reproached Kalânos for his insolence—the very vice which he had been condemning. Mandanes then called Onesikritos to him, and said, I commend the king, because, although he governs so vast an empire, he is yet desirous of acquiring wisdom, for he is the only philosopher in arms that I ever saw. . . . (65) "The tendency of his discourse," he said, "was this, that the best philosophy was that which liberated the mind from pleasure and grief; that grief differed from labour, in that the former was pernicious, the latter friendly, to men; for that men exercised their bodies with labour to strengthen the mental powers, whereby they would be able to end dissensions, and give every one good advice, both to the public and to private persons; that he should at present advise Taxilês to receive Alexander as a friend; for by entertaining a person better than himself he might be improved, while by entertaining a worse he might influence that person to be good. After this Mandanes inquired whether such doctrines were taught among the Greeks. Onesikritos answered that Pythagoras taught a like doctrine, and instructed his disciples to abstain from whatever had life; that Sôkrates and Diogenês, whose discourses he had heard, held the same views. Mandanes replied, that in other respects he thought them to be wise; but that they were mistaken in preferring custom to nature, else they would not be ashamed to go naked as he did, and to live on frugal fare, for, said he, that is the best house that requires least repairs. He states further that they employ themselves much on natural subjects, as forecasting the future, rain, drought, and diseases. On going into the city they disperse themselves in the market-places. . . . Every wealthy house, even to the women's apartments, is open to them. When they enter they converse with the inmates and share their meal. Disease of the body they regard as very disgraceful, and he who fears that it will attack him, prepares a pyre and lets the flames consume him. He anoints himself beforehand, and when he has placed himself upon the pile orders it to be lighted, and remains motionless while he is burning. (66) Nearchos gives

the following account of the sages: The Brachmans engage in
public affairs, and attend the kings as counsellors; the rest are
occupied in the study of nature. Kalânos belonged to the latter
class. Women study philosophy with them, and all lead an
ascetic life.

Athênaios in his *Gymnosophists* (x. p. 437) quotes, like Plutarch, from Charês, the account of the drinking bout which
followed the burning of Kalânos. He says that Alexander proposed the match on account of the bibulous propensities (*phil-
oinia*) of the Indians. Other references to Kalânos are to be
found in Ailianos, *V. H.* ii. 41 and v. 6; Lucian, *De M. Pereg.*
25; Cicero, *Disp. Tusc.* ii. 22, and *De Divin.* i. 23, 30. In the
romance *History of Alexander*, by the Pseudo-Kallisthenes, six
long chapters of Book iii. (11-17) are full of Kalânos, Mandanes,
and the Brachmans.

St. Ambrose wrote a work, *De Bragmanibus*, in which the
two gymnosophists are frequently mentioned.

KALLISTHENES was a native of Olynthos. He was brought
up and educated by Aristotle, to whom he was related, and at
whose recommendation he was permitted to accompany Alexander on his Asiatic expedition. He was deficient in tact and
prudence, and exasperated the king by the freedom with which
he censured him for adopting oriental customs, and especially
for requiring Macedonians to perform the ceremony of adoration.
When the plot of the pages to assassinate Alexander was discovered, Kallisthenes was charged with being an accessary.
According to Charês he was imprisoned for seven months, and
died in India; while Ptolemy states that he was tortured and
crucified. Besides other works, he wrote an account of Alexander's expedition, to which Strabo and Plutarch make a few
references, but it was a work of little if any value.

KANISHKA, a great Turanian conqueror, whose empire extended from Kabul to Agra and Gujrut. He was an ardent
Buddhist. The date of his coronation, 78 A.D., marks the beginning of the S'âkâbda aera.

KLEANDER, one of Alexander's officers. He was employed
to kill Parmenion, to whom he was next in command at Ekbatana.
He was himself put to death when he joined Alexander in Karmania, on account of his profligacy and oppression while in
Media.

KLEITOS was a Macedonian, and brother to Alexander's nurse.
He saved Alexander's life at the Granîkos. When the companion cavalry was divided into two bodies, the command of
one was given to Kleitos and of the other to Hêphaistiôn. In

328 B.C. he was appointed to succeed Artabazos in the satrapy of Baktria, but on the eve of his departure to take up this office he was killed by Alexander in a drunken brawl.

KOINOS was the son of Polemokrates, and the son-in-law of Parmenion. He was one of Alexander's ablest generals, and greatly distinguished himself on various occasions, and especially in the battle with Pôros. When Alexander had reached the Hyphasis and wished to proceed farther and reach the Ganges, Koinos had the courage to remonstrate, and the king was obliged to act on his advice. He died soon after of an illness, and was honoured with a splendid burial.

KÔPHAIOS.—A chief whose dominions lay to the west of the Indus and along the river Kôphên.

KORAGOS.—A Macedonian bravo called also Horratas.

KOSMAS INDIKOPLEUSTES.—An Egyptian monk who flourished towards the middle of the sixth century of our aera. In early life he was a merchant, and visited for traffic various countries, Aethiopia, Syria, Arabia, Persia, India, and many other places of the East. After he had taken to monastic life he wrote a work called *Christian Topography*, which is valuable for the geographical and historical information it contains. It has some notices concerning India, especially concerning its Christian communities.

KRATEROS, a Macedonian of Orestis, was one of Alexander's most distinguished generals, and next to Hêphaistiôn his greatest favourite. He was in command of infantry on the left wing at Issos, and of cavalry on the same wing at Gaugamela. He rose afterwards to be commander of one of the divisions of the phalanx. On the day of the battle with Pôros he was left with a part of the army in the camp, and did not cross the river till victory had declared for Alexander. He commanded the troops which were sent back from India by way of the Bolan Pass to Karmania. At Sousa he married Amastris, the niece of Darius, after which he led, along with Polysperchon, the discharged veterans back to Europe. In the division of the empire after Alexander's death Greece and Macedonia and other European provinces fell to the share of Antipater and Krateros, who divorced Amastris and married Phila, Antipater's daughter. In 321 B.C. Krateros fell in battle against Eumenes, who honoured his old comrade in the Indian wars with a magnificent funeral.

KYRSILOS, a native of Pharsalos, who accompanied Alexander to Asia and wrote an account of his exploits. He is mentioned by Strabo (XI. xiv. 12).

LEONNATOS, a native of Pella, was one of Alexander's most capable and distinguished officers. At the time of Philip's death he occupied one of the highest positions at court, being one of the select bodyguard called *sômatophylakes*, but under Alexander he was at first only an officer of the companion cavalry. After the battle of Issos he was sent to inform the wife of Darius of her husband's safety, and when Arrhybas, one of the bodyguards, died in Egypt, he was promoted to the vacant post. After this his name continually occurs among the names of those who were constantly about the king's person and stood highest in his confidence. On several occasions he showed the greatest courage, and at the siege of the Mallian stronghold he saved, along with Peukestas, the king's life. When the army marched back from India he was left to overawe the Oreitai, and to wait in their country till Nearchos should reach it with the fleet. He inflicted a crushing defeat on that people, who had assembled a large army after Alexander had left their borders. For this and other services he was rewarded at Sousa with a golden crown. In the division of the empire he received only the satrapy of the Lesser Phrygia, a share which by no means satisfied his ambition. Kleopatra, Alexander's sister, then offered him her hand on condition that he should assist her against Antipater, the regent of Macedonia. He consented, but when he passed over into that country he was slain in battle against the Greeks, who had revolted from Antipater, whose dominions he wished to appropriate in their integrity.

LYSIMACHOS was one of Alexander's great generals and one of his select bodyguards. He was born at Pella—the son of a Thessalian serf who by his flatteries had won the good graces of King Philip. Great personal strength and undaunted courage seem to have been the qualities by which Lysimachos gained his splendid position, for he was seldom entrusted by Alexander with any separate command of importance. He was present in the battle with Pôros, and was wounded at the siege of Sangala. In the division of the empire he obtained Thrace for his share, but his dominions after the battle of Issos, in which along with Seleukos, Ptolemy, and Kassander, he defeated Antigonos and his son Dêmêtrios, embraced for a time all Alexander's European possessions, in addition to Asia Minor. His third wife was Arsinoë, the daughter of Ptolemy, King of Egypt. In 281 B.C. he was defeated and slain by his old comrade in arms, Seleukos. He was then eighty years of age.

MEGASTHENÊS, the ambassador sent by Seleukos Nikator to

the court of Sandrokottos, and author of a work on India of the highest value. Though this work is lost, numerous fragments have been preserved by Strabo, Arrian, Pliny, and many other writers.

MELA, POMPONIUS, the first Roman author known to have composed a formal work on geography. It is supposed that he flourished under the Emperor Claudius.

MELEAGER was by birth a Macedonian, and served with distinction in Alexander's Asiatic campaigns, where he commanded one of the divisions of the phalanx. He was present in the great battles of the Granîkos, Issos, Gaugamela, and the Hydaspês. He was never entrusted, however, with any special or important command. He was a man of an insolent and factious disposition, and showed himself to be such in the discussions which arose between the generals after Alexander's death concerning the arrangements which should be made for the government of the empire. He led for a time the opposition against Perdikkas, but was afterwards for a short time associated with him in the regency. Two such colleagues could not long act in harmony. Perdikkas, who was an adept in the arts of dissimulation, lulled Meleager into fancied security, devised a cunning scheme for his overthrow, and having succeeded in this ordered him to be put to death.

MEMNÔN, the Rhodian, was the brother of Mentor, who stood high in the favour of Darius, and brother-in-law of Artabazos, the satrap of Lower Phrygia. On the death of his brother, Memnôn, who possessed great military skill and experience, succeeded to his authority, which extended over the coast of Asia Minor. He was the most formidable opponent Alexander encountered in Western Asia. Fortunately for him, Memnôn died in 333 B.C., when preparing to sail for Greece, where the Spartans were ready to join him and rise against the Macedonians.

MÔPHIS.—*See* TAXILÊS.

MOUSIKANOS was the ruler of a rich and fertile kingdom which lay along the banks of the Indus, in Upper Sindh. He submitted to Alexander without resistance, and was allowed to retain his sovereignty. The Brahmans, however, prevailed on him to revolt during Alexander's absence. He was captured by Peithôn and crucified by Alexander's orders.

MULLINUS is called by Curtius the king's secretary. Eumenes is probably meant. The name is not met with except in one passage in Curtius.

NEARCHOS.—Among all the great men associated with Alexander no one has left a reputation more noble and unsullied than that of Nearchos. The long and difficult voyage in unknown seas which he successfully accomplished ranks as one of the greatest achievements in the annals of navigation. He was free from the mad ambition to rule which gave rise to the deadly feuds between Alexander's other great generals, and stained the records of their lives with so many dark crimes. He was a native of Crete, but settled at Amphipolis, a Macedonian city near the Thracian border. He held a high position at the court of King Philip, where he attached himself to the party of the young prince, and was banished along with Ptolemy, Harpalos, and others, who had involved themselves in his intrigues. Alexander, on mounting the throne, recalled his former partisans, and did not neglect their interests. Nearchos accompanied him into Asia, where he was appointed governor of Lykia and other provinces south of the Tauros. This post he continued to hold for five years. He rejoined Alexander before he left Baktria to invade India, and in India he was appointed commander of the fleet which·was built on the Hydaspês. He conducted it down that river and the Akesinês and the Indus to Patala (now Haidarâbâd), a naval station at the apex of the Indus Delta. He arrived at that place about the time when the south-west monsoon usually sets in. Alexander, on returning to Patala from the excursions he made to the ocean, removed the fleet to Killouta, an island in the western branch of the Indus, which possessed a commodious haven. He then set out on his return to Persia, leaving the fleet with Nearchos, who had relieved Alexander's mind of a load of anxiety by voluntarily proffering his services to conduct the expedition by sea to the head of the Persian Gulf. When we consider, as Bunbury remarks, the total ignorance of the Greeks at this time concerning the Indian seas, and the imperfect character of their navigation, it is impossible not to admire the noble confidence with which Nearchos ventured to promise that he would bring the ships in safety to the shores of Persia, "if the sea were navigable and the thing feasible for mortal man." Nearchos wished to defer his departure till the monsoon had quite subsided, but as he was in danger of being attacked by the natives, who were no longer overawed by Alexander's presence, he set sail on the 21st of September, 325 B.C. He was forced, however, by the violence of the weather, when he had reached the mouth of the Indus, to take refuge in a sheltered bay at a station which he called Alexander's Haven, and which is now known as Karâchi, the great emporium of the trade of the Indus. After a detention here for twenty-four days, he resumed his voyage on the 23rd of October. Coasting the shore of the Arabies for 80 miles, he reached the mouth of the river Arabis (now the Purali), which divides the Arabies from the Oreitai. The coast of the latter people, which was 100 miles in extent, was navigated in eighteen days. At one of the landing-places the ships were supplied by Leonnatos with stores of corn, which lasted ten days. The navigation of the Mekrân coast which succeeded occupied twenty days, and the distance traversed was 480 miles English, though Nearchos in his journal has set it down at 10,000 stadia or 1250 miles. The expedition in this part of the voyage suffered great distress for want of provisions. The coast was barren, and its savage inhabitants, the Ichthyophagi,[1] had little else to subsist on than fish, which some of them ate raw.[2] The Karmanian coast, which succeeded, was not so distressingly barren, but was even, in certain favoured localities, extremely fertile and beautiful. Its length was 296 miles, and the time taken in its navigation was nineteen days, some of which, however, were spent at the mouth of the river Anamis (now the Minâb), whence Nearchos made a journey into the interior to apprise Alexander of the safety of his fleet. The coasts of Persis and Sousis were navigated in thirty-one days. Nearchos had intended to sail up the Tigris, but having passed its mouth unawares, continued sailing westward till he reached Diridôtis (Terêdon), an emporium in Babylonia on the Pallocopas branch of the Euphrates. He thence retraced his course to the Tigris, and ascended its stream till he reached a lake through which at that time it flowed and which received the river Pasitigris, the Ulaï of Scripture, and now the Karun. The fleet proceeded up this river till it met the army near a bridge on the highway from Persis to Sousa. It anchored at the bridge on the 24th of February, 324 B.C., so that the whole voyage was performed in 146 days. Nearchos received appropriate rewards for the splendid service he had so successfully performed. Alexander was sending him away on another great maritime expedition when the illness which carried off the great

---

[1] According to Dr. Bellew this name is the Greek equivalent of the Persian Mâhîkhorân, "fish - eaters," still surviving in the modern Makrân. [Since the above note was written the cause of Eastern learning and research has suffered a grievous loss by the death of this distinguished Orientalist, whose work on the Ethnology of Afghanistan will prove a lasting monument to his fame. The work discusses inter alia the ethnic affinities of the various races with which Alexander came into contact during his Asiatic expedition.]

[2] Major E. Mockler, the political agent of Makrân, contributed some years ago to the Journal of the Royal Asiatic Society a valuable paper on the identification of places on this coast mentioned by Arrian, Ptolemy, and Marcian, in which he corrected some errors into which the commentators on these authors had fallen.

conqueror broke up the enterprise. In the discussions which followed regarding the succession to the throne, Nearchos unsuccessfully advocated the claims of Heraklês, the son of Alexander by Barsinê, who was the daughter of Artabazos and the widow of Memnôn the Rhodian. He acquiesced, however, in the arrangements made by the other generals, and was content with receiving his former government, even though he was to hold it subject to the authority of Antigonos. He accompanied his superior when he marched against Eumenes, and interceded for the life of the latter when he fell into the hands of his enemies. Nothing is known of his history after the year 314 B.C., when he was selected by Antigonos to assist his son Dêmêtrios with his counsels when left for the first time in command of an army.

NIKANOR, the son of Parmenion, was commander of the hypaspists or footguards in the Asiatic expedition. He was present in the three great battles against the troops of Darius, and died of disease before the charge of conspiracy was preferred against his brother Philôtas.

OLYMPIAS, the mother of Alexander, was a passionate, ambitious, and intriguing woman. She was put to death by order of Kassander, the son of the regent Antipater, in 316 B.C., thus surviving her son seven years.

OMPHIS.—*See* Taxilês.

ONESIKRITOS was a Greek historical writer who accompanied Alexander on his Asiatic expedition. He professed the philosophy of Diogenes the Cynic, and on this account was sent by Alexander to converse with the gymnosophists of Taxila. He was the pilot of Alexander's ship and of the fleet in sailing down the Indus, and afterwards during the voyage to the head of the Persian Gulf. The history written by Onesikritos, which embraced the whole life of Alexander, fell into discredit owing to the manner in which he intermingled fact with fiction. His work was, however, too much undervalued. He was the first author who mentions the island of Taprobanê (Ceylon). In his later years he attached himself to the fortunes of Lysimachos of Thrace.

OROSIUS was a Spanish ecclesiastic of the fifth century, who wrote a history of the world from the creation down to the year A.D. 417.

OXYARTES, a Baktrian, the father of Alexander's queen Roxana, was one of the chiefs who accompanied Bessos on his retreat across the Oxus into Sogdiana. Alexander, after marrying his daughter, appointed him satrap of the land of the Paropamisidai, and his successors allowed him to retain that government. It is not known how long he lived, but it is supposed that he was dead when Seleukos undertook his Indian expedition, as his dominions were among those which were surrendered to Sandrokottos.

OXYKANOS, called Portikanos by Strabo and Diodôros, ruled a territory which adjoined that of Mousikanos, but its exact position or boundaries cannot be ascertained.

PANINI, the celebrated Indian grammarian, was a native of Salâtura, in Gandhâra. His date is generally referred to the fourth century B.C., but this is still a matter of controversy.

PARMÊNION was the most experienced and most trusted general who accompanied Alexander into Asia. He commanded the left wing of the Macedonian army in the three great battles against Darius. He was left in command in Media, and so did not accompany the expedition into India. His assassination has left an indelible stain on Alexander's character.

PATROKLÊS was a general who held under Seleukos and Antiochos an important government over some eastern provinces of the Syrian empire. He collected much valuable information regarding the little-known parts which adjoined his province. His work, embodying this information, is frequently quoted by Strabo.

PAUSANIAS was the author of an *Itinerary of Greece*, full of valuable topographical and antiquarian information. He wrote in the age of the Antonines.

PEITHÔN.—Three officers of this name accompanied Alexander into Asia—first, Peithôn, the son of Sôsiklês, who was wounded and taken prisoner by the Skythians under Spitamenes, and is not subsequently mentioned; second, Peithôn, the son of Krateuas, who, like Ptolemy, was a native of Eördaia, and a member of the select bodyguard; third, Peithôn, the son of Agênôr, who, like the preceding, rendered distinguished services in the Indian campaigns. The historians have recorded nothing of their previous achievements, and when they come to mention those performed in India, do not always make it clear to which of the two they mean to ascribe them.

PEITHÔN, the son of Krateuas, after Alexander's death proposed that Perdikkas and Leonnatos should be appointed joint regents of the empire, and for this service was rewarded with the satrapy of Media. After the assassination of Perdikkas he was himself, through the influence of Ptolemy, raised to the regency in conjunction with Arrhidaios, but was soon compelled to resign and retire to his Median government. He assisted Antigonos to overthrow Eumenes; but Antigonos, having subsequently suspected him of entertaining treasonable designs, brought him to trial before a council, and ordered him to be put to death in 316 B.C.

PEITHÔN, the son of Agênôr, took an active part in the wars against the Malloi and Mousikanos while holding the command of one of the divisions of the footguards. He was appointed satrap of Sindh from the great confluence downward to the sea-coast, and was left behind in his province when Alexander took his departure from India. After the death of Alexander he was confirmed in his government, but, it would appear, was ousted from it by Pôros. After the fall of Eumenes he received from Antigonos, whose side he had favoured, the satrapy of Babylon. While serving with Dêmêtrios, the son of Antigonos, he was slain in the battle of Gaza, in which the young prince rashly and against his advice engaged Ptolemy. This battle was fought in 312 B.C.

PERDIKKAS—one of Alexander's greatest generals—was a native of the Macedonian province of Orestis, and descended, according to Curtius, from a royal house. Under Philip he held one of the highest offices at court, being a sômatophylax, and under Alexander he held the same position along with the command of a division of the phalanx, but afterwards of a division of the companion cavalry. He distinguished himself at the siege of Thebes, where he was severely wounded, and in the three great battles against the armies of Darius. In the Persian, Sogdian, and Indian campaigns he was frequently entrusted with separate commands of great importance, and at Sousa was rewarded for his services with a crown of gold and with the hand of the daughter of the Median satrap. He was present with Alexander during his fatal illness; and it is said that the king when expiring took off the royal signet-ring from his finger and gave it to him, as if to indicate him as his successor. In the deliberations which followed to settle the succession, Perdikkas took a prominent part, and, with the consent of most of the other generals, was appointed to act as regent of the empire on behalf of Roxana's yet unborn child, which, it was hoped, might prove to be a son. His selfish ambition, however, and acts of cruelty soon created violent discontent, and a combination was formed against him by Antigonos, whom he attempted to bring to trial for misgovernment, but who effected his escape to Macedonia, and persuaded Antipater, Krateros, and Ptolemy to take up arms on his behalf. He was slain by his own troops in Egypt, whither he had proceeded in the hope of being able to crush Ptolemy before taking measures against the other confederates. Perdikkas was crafty, cruel, and arrogant, without magnanimity, and, indeed, without any virtue except personal courage and capacity as a general.

PEUKESTAS, a native of Mieza in Macedonia, was one of Alexander's great officers, and had the honour of carrying before him in battle the sacred shield taken down from the temple of Athêna at Ilion. He is first mentioned as one of the officers appointed to command a trireme on the Hydaspês. He had a chief share in saving Alexander's life in the citadel of the Mallian capital, and for this service was rewarded by being appointed a *sômatophylax* and afterwards satrap of Persia. After being presented at Sousa with a golden crown, he proceeded to take possession of his government, when he adopted the Persian dress and Persian customs, thus pleasing his subjects as well as Alexander himself. He was in attendance on the king during his last illness, but does not appear to have taken any leading part in the discussions held after his death regarding the succession. He was, however, permitted to retain his government. He took an active part in the war conducted by Eumenes against Antigonos. He was vain and fond of display, and his treachery towards Eumenes, whom he helped to betray into the hands of his enemies, has left a dark stain on his character.

PHEGELAS, or, as he is called by Diodôros, Phêgeus, was chief of a territory which lay between the Hydraôtes and the Hyphasis. With regard to the name, M. Sylvain Lévi gives preference to the form *Phegelas*, and states his reason thus: "The *e* answers to the *a* of Sanskrit, the *g* to the *g* or to the *j*. *Phegeus* does not border on a known form; Phegelas, on the contrary, answers directly to the Sanskrit *Bhagala*—the name of a royal race of Kshatriyas which the Gana-pâtha classes under the rubric Bâhu, etc., with the name even of Taxilês, Âmbhi." (*Journal Asiatique* for 1890, p. 239.)

PHILIPPOS, the son of Machatas, was one of Alexander's officers. In 327 B.C. he was appointed satrap of India. After Alexander left India he was assassinated in a conspiracy formed against him·by the mercenaries under his command.

PHRATAPHERNES was, under Darius, governor of Parthia and Hyrkania. He accompanied that sovereign in his flight from Arbêla, but after his death submitted to Alexander, who reinstated him in his satrapy. He joined Alexander in India after Pôros had been defeated, but seems to have soon afterwards returned to his satrapy, whence he sent supplies to the Macedonian army when pursuing its distressing march through Gedrôsia. The successors of Alexander allowed him to retain his satrapy.

POLYAINOS, a Macedonian, who flourished about the middle of the second century of our aera, and was the author of a work on the stratagems of war, which is still extant.

POLYKLEITOS was a native of Larissa, who wrote a history of Alexander. Most of the extracts preserved from this work refer to the geography of the countries which Alexander conquered.

POLYSPERCHON, or POLYPERCHON, was one of the oldest· officers of a high rank in Alexander's service. After the battle of Issos he was promoted to the command of a division of the phalanx in succession to Ptolemy, the son of Seleukos, who fell in that battle. In Baktria he offended Alexander by casting ridicule on the ceremony of prostration, and was thus for a time in disgrace. He was present at the passage of the Hydaspês, and also in the descent of the Indus, and was then sent with Krateros to conduct the veterans from India to Karmania by way of the Bolan Pass. He was not in Babylon at the time of Alexander's death, and hence was passed over in the allotment of the provinces made after that event. When war, however, broke out between Antipater and Perdikkas, the former committed to his hands the chief command in Macedonia and Greece during his absence in Asia. The veteran general showed himself worthy of the trust reposed in him, and received the reward of his services at Antipater's death, who appointed him, in preference to his own son, Kassander, to be his successor in the regency. After many vicissitudes of fortune, and disgracing his name by his treachery towards Phôkiôn, and his causing Heraklês, the son of Alexander, whose cause he had espoused, to be murdered, he disappears from history after the year 303 B.C.

PÔROS was the most powerful king in the Panjâb at the time of Alexander's invasion. He was then at enmity with Omphis, the king of Taxila, but in alliance with Abisarês, the king of Kâs'mîr. After his defeat and submission to the conqueror, he was confirmed in his kingdom, the limits of which were afterwards considerably extended. All that is known of his history will be found in the translations, if read along with the notice below, of Sandrokottos, except that after Alexander's death he made himself master of Sindh, from which he ousted Peithôn. The name of Pôros, which is formed from *Paura* or *Paurava*, with the Greek termination *os* added, shows that he belonged to a family of the Lunar race. Bohlen, however, takes the name to be a corruption of the Sanskrit *Paurusha*, which means "heroic."

PORTIKANOS.—*See* Oxykanos.

PTOLEMY, called the son of Lagos, is supposed to have been in reality the son of Philip, as his mother Arsinoê was the concubine of that king, and was pregnant when married to Lagos. Of all Alexander's generals Ptolemy was the one who approached him nearest in a capacity both for war and government, while he did not fall short of him in magnanimity of disposition. He was banished from Macedonia by Philip, who discovered that he was promoting with others a marriage between Alexander and the daughter of Pixodaros, the king of Karia. He rendered important services in the war against Darius; and when Dêmêtrios, a member of the select bodyguard, was arrested on suspicion of being concerned in the conspiracy of Philôtas, Ptolemy was promoted to fill his place. It was he who obtained information of the plot of Hermolaos, and by revealing it was probably the means of saving the king's life. In the battle with the Aspasians, Ptolemy slew their leader with his own hand, and in the campaigns in India he was on several occasions entrusted with separate commands of great importance. The story of Alexander's dream, which led to the discovery of a plant by which Ptolemy was cured of a dangerous wound inflicted by a poisoned arrow, must be apocryphal, since Arrian, who had Ptolemy's own memoirs of the expedition constantly before him, is silent on the subject. At Sousa he received in marriage a daughter of Artabazos. After Alexander's death he obtained Egypt as his share of the empire, and raised that country to a high pitch of prosperity. He reigned for no less than forty years. The dynasty which he founded, after subsisting for nearly two hundred years, ended with the death of Kleopatra.

PTOLEMY III. ascended the throne of Egypt in 247 B.C. in succession to his father Ptolemy Philadelphos. In the early part of his reign he overran Syria, and having thence turned his arms

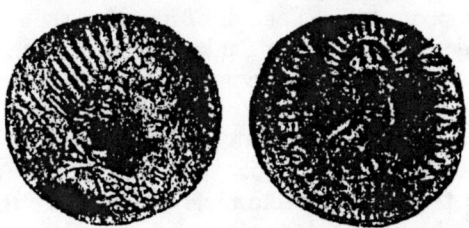

FIG. 25.—PTOLEMY III.

eastward, advanced as far as Babylon and Sousa, and received the submission of all the upper provinces of Asia as far as the borders of Baktria and India. On returning to his kingdom he carried back with him the statues of the Egyptian deities which Kambyses had removed to the East, and restored them to their proper temples, an act which won for him the gratitude of the Egyptians and the title by which he is generally known, Euergetês, *i.e.* Benefactor. Like his father he distinguished himself by his munificent patronage of literature and science. He was one of the kings to whom Buddhist missionaries were sent by the Indian king As'ôka. He died in the year 222 B.C.

PTOLEMY PHYSKON, king of Egypt, succeeded his brother Ptolemy VI., surnamed Philomêter.

RÔXANA, the daughter of the Baktrian chief Oxyartes, was considered by the Macedonians the most beautiful woman in Asia, next to the wife of Darius. Alexander, who found her charms irresistible, made her his wife, and she bore him a post-humous son, called Alexander Aigos, who was admitted to a share of the sovereignty under the regency of Perdikkas. Before his birth she had enticed Alexander's other widow, Barsinê or Stateira, to Babylon, and caused her to be murdered. She subsequently fell, with her son, into the power of Kassander, who placed them both in Amphipolis, where in 311 B.C. they were both murdered by their keeper, Glaukias.

SAMBUS was the satrap of a mountainous country adjoining the kingdom of Mousikanos, with whom he was at feud. His capital, called Sindimana, has been identified with Sehwân, a city on the Indus, for which see Note S. Sambus fled on Alexander's approach, not to evade submission, but because he learned that his enemy, Mousikanos, had been received into the conqueror's favour.

SANDROKOTTOS (CHANDRAGUPTA).—Sandrokottos, with the exception perhaps of his grandson, As'ôka, was the greatest ruler ancient India produced. Though of humble origin, he overthrew the Macedonian power in the Panjâb, conquered the kingdom of Magadha, and founded a wide empire such as no Indian king had before possessed. He is also memorable on another account. Those learned men who about a century ago took up the study of Sanskrit, established his identity with the Chandragupta who is mentioned in the Buddhist Chronicle of Ceylon as the founder of the Mauryan dynasty of Magadha, and by fixing the date of his accession to the throne of that kingdom, supplied the chronology of ancient India with its first properly-ascertained aera, and thus brought it into line with the chronology of general history.

. Besides the notices of this great sovereign in the writings we have translated, the following occur elsewhere in the classics :— Appian (*Syriakê*, c. 55), speaking of Seleukos, says : " And

having crossed the Indus, he warred with Androkottos, the king
of the Indians, who dwelt about that river, until he entered into
an alliance and a marriage affinity with him." Strabo (II. i. 9)
says : "Both of these men were sent to Palimbothra, Megasthenes
to Sandrokottos, and Dêimachos to Allitrochades, his son," and
in XV. i. 36 repeats the statement as concerns Megasthenes. In
XV. i. 53 we read: "Megasthenes, who was in the camp of
Sandrokottos, which consisted of 400,000 men, did not witness
on any day thefts reported which exceeded the sum of 200
drachmai, and this among a people who have no written laws,
who are ignorant even of writing, and regulate everything by
memory." Lastly, in XV. i. 57 we read: "Similar to this is the
account of the Enotokoitai, of the wild men, and of other
monsters. The wild men could not be brought to Sandrokottos,
for they died by abstaining from food." Arrian in his *Indika*
(c. 5) says: "But even Megasthenes, as far as appears, did not
travel over much of India, though no doubt he saw more of it
than those who came with Alexander, the son of Philip, for, as
he says, he had interviews with Sandrokottos, the greatest king of
the Indians, and with Pôros, who was still greater than he."[1]
Lastly, Athênaios mentions him in his *Deipnosophists* (c. 18 d):
"Phylarchos says that among the presents which Sandrokoptos,
the king of the Indians, sent to Seleukos were certain powerful
aphrodisiacs." It will be observed that Athênaios transcribes the
name of the Indian king more correctly than any of the other
authors.

These detached notices, combined with those which appear
in the translations, we may now gather together into a connected and consistent narrative. Sandrokottos was of obscure
birth, and, from the remark of Plutarch that in his early years he
had seen Alexander, we may infer that he was a native of the
Panjâb. It was at one time thought that he had in some way
offended the conqueror, and that to escape the effects of his displeasure, he had fled for protection to the court of Magadha.
But this belief must now be given up, as it was based on a
corrupt passage in Justin, which, by the restoration of the correct
reading, shows that it was not Alexander whom he had offended,
but Nandrus or Xandrames, the Magadha king. We do not
know what induced Sandrokottos to leave his home and take
service under the latter monarch, but we incline to attribute it to
a sentiment of patriotism forbidding him to seek office or advance-

---

[1] A slight emendation of the reading (suggested by Schwanbeck) restores
the passage to sense, making Arrian
say that Sandrokottos was greater
even than Pôros.

ment under a power which had crushed the liberties of his country. What the nature of his offence against Nandrus was does not appear, but he so dreaded his resentment that he quitted his dominions and returned home to the Panjâb. He found it, although Alexander had now been six years dead, still under Greek vassalage, and ruled as formerly in civil matters by Omphis of Taxila and the great Pôros, while the military administration had passed into the hands of Eudêmos. Soon after his arrival, however, the order of things was violently disturbed. Eudêmos having decoyed Pôros into his power, treacherously murdered him,[1] but had no sooner done so than he was recalled to the west to succour Eumenes in his war against Antigonos. As he took with him 3000 foot, 500 horse, and 125 elephants, he denuded the province of the main strength of the force by which it was held in subjection, and his departure was fatal to Greek power. The Indians, who longed for freedom, and were no doubt greatly incensed by the murder of Pôros, rose in revolt. Sandrokottos, who headed this movement, having collected a band of insurgents, overthrew the existing government, expelled the remainder of the Greek garrison, and finally installed himself in the sovereignty of the Panjâb and of all the lower valley of the Indus. The insurgents, whom he led to victory, are called by Justin *robbers*; but we must not thence infer that he was a bandit leader, who, by taking advantage of an opportune crisis, rose to power by the help of desperadoes whose crimes had banished them from society. His adherents were, in point of fact, chiefly the *Arattâ* of the Panjâb, who were always called *robbers*, and are denounced as such in the *Mahâbhârata*. The Kathaians, who so stoutly resisted Alexander at Sangala, were included under this designation, which means *Kingless*, and implies that they lived under republican institutions. The stories told by the same author of the lion which licked the sweat from Sandrokottos when asleep, and of the elephant which volunteered to carry him into battle, and thus gave presages of his future greatness, reflect the true spirit of oriental romance, and were no doubt derived from native traditions which somehow found their way to the west. They remind one of Joseph's dreams, in which he saw the sheaves and then the heavenly bodies falling down in obeisance before him.

Sandrokottos while in Magadha had seen that the king was held in such odium and contempt by his subjects that, as Plutarch

---

[1] It seems that Pôros, after Alexander's death, had possessed himself of the satrapy of the Lower Indus, held till then by Peithôn son of Agênôr.

tells us, he used often afterwards to speak of the ease with which Alexander might have possessed himself of the whole country. He accordingly had no sooner settled the affairs of the Panjâb than he prepared to invade the dominions of his former master. The success which he anticipated followed his arms. He overthrew with ease the unpopular despot, and having received the submission of Magadha, extended his conquests far beyond its eastern limits. He was thus able to combine into one great empire the regions both of the Indus and the Ganges. He established the seat of government at Palibothra, the capital of Magadha, a great city advantageously situated at the confluence of the Erannoboas or Sôn with the Ganges, and on the site now occupied by Pâtnâ, beneath which, at a depth of from 12 to 15 feet, its ruins lie entombed.

While Sandrokottos was thus, with a genius like that of Akbar, welding the states of India into unity, the successors of Alexander were too much engrossed with their internecine wars to concern themselves with his doings; but when they had for a time composed their differences, Seleukos Nikator, the king of Syria, advanced eastward to recover the Indian conquests of Alexander. The date of this expedition cannot be fixed with precision, but it was probably made in the year 305 B.C., or about ten years after Sandrokottos had ascended the throne of Palibothra. The records of it are unfortunately lost. . It seems that he was allowed to cross the Indus without opposition, but it is not known how far he advanced into the country. We do not even know whether the hostile armies came into actual conflict, but we may conjecture that the sight of the vast and formidable host brought into the field by his antagonist, who was an experienced commander of the stamp of Pôros, led him to think discretion would be the better part of valour, and to prefer entering into negotiations rather than to risk the chance of defeat. At all events he concluded a treaty by which he not only resigned his claims to the Greek conquests beyond the Indus, but ceded to the Indian king considerable districts extending westward from that river to the southern slopes of the Hindu-Kush. The compact was cemented by a matrimonial alliance, the Syrian king giving his daughter in marriage to Sandrokottos. Friendly relations seem to have subsisted ever afterwards between the two sovereigns.

Seleukos sent as his ambassador to the Indian court his friend and companion Megasthenes. This was a fortunate choice, for while there Megasthenes, who was an acute observer and of an inquisitive turn of mind, composed a work on India, in which he gave a faithful account of what fell under his own observation, as well as of what facts he could gather from trustworthy reports. That work, now lost, was the source whence Strabo and other classical authors derived most of their information regarding India. In such of the fragments thus preserved as relate to Sandrokottos, we find an admirable picture of his system of government, of his personal habits, and of the regulations of his court. He did not live to old age, but died in 291 B.C., before he had reached his fifty-fifth year.

When we turn to the Buddhist accounts of Chandragupta we find them tally so closely in all main points with the Greek accounts of Sandrokottos that no doubt can be left that the two names which are so nearly similar denote but one and the same person. As he was the founder of the dynasty to which the pious As'ôka, the Constantine of the Buddhist faith, belonged, the Buddhist writers assign to him an honourable pedigree which connected him even with the royal house whence Buddha himself sprang. His father, they tell us, reigned over a small kingdom situated in a valley among the Himalayas, and called Maurya, from the great number of its peacocks (*Mayûra*). He was killed in resisting an invasion of his enemies, but his queen escaped to Pataliputra, where she gave birth to a son whom she exposed in the neighbourhood of a cattle shed. The child, like Oedipûs, was found by a shepherd, who called him *Chandragupta* (*Moon protected*), and charged himself with his maintenance. There resided at that time in Pataliputra a Brahman who had come from the great city of Taxila in the Panjâb, and whose name was Chânakya. To him King Dhanananda had given an insult which could be expiated by nothing short of his destruction. While the Brahman was casting about for means whereby he could clear his score with the offender, Chandragupta, now a boy, fell under his cognisance. Having discovered that he was of royal descent, and foreseen from his conduct among his companions that in after life he would be capable of great achievements, he bought him from the shepherd and gave him a training adapted to make him a fit instrument for the execution of his designs. When Chandragupta had grown up, his master put under his command a body of troops kept secretly in his pay, and attempted a rebellion, which proved abortive. Chandragupta fled to the desert, but having ere long collected a fresh force he invaded Magadha from the border, that is, from the side of the Panjâb. He captured city after city till the capital itself fell into his hands. The king was slain, and Chandragupta ascended the vacant throne.

Another form of the native tradition assigns his paternity to Dhanananda (the last of the eight Nanda kings, who ruled in succession over Magadha), though not by his queen, but by a woman of low caste—a sudra called Mura. The Brahmans made this base-born scion of the royal house the instrument of their rebellious designs, and with the help of a northern prince, to whom they offered an accession of territory, raised him to the throne while he was yet a youth, and put Nanda and his eight sons to death. They did not make good their promise to their ally, but rid themselves of him by assassination. His son Malaya-ketu marched with a large army, in which were Yavanas (Greeks), to revenge his death, but returned without success to his country. It has been supposed that this expedition may have been the same as that of Seleukos.

The Nanda dynasty which was supplanted by the Mauryan in 315 B.C. had succeeded to that of Sisunâga in 370 B.C. Its last member, whom the Greeks call *Xandrames* and Curtius *Agrammes*, is variously named in native writings *Dhanananda*, *Nanda Mahâpadma*, and *Hiranyagupta*. Xandramas (of which Agrammes seems to be a distorted form) transliterates the Sanskrit *Chandramas*, which means *Moon-god*. A Hindu play—the Mudrâ Râkshasa—produced early in the Mahommedan period refers to the revolution by which Chânakya raised Chandragupta to power, but is of no historical value. Chandragupta was succeeded by his son Vindusâra, who is called by Strabo *Allitrochades*, and by Athênaios (xiv. 67),[1] *Amitrochates*, a form which transliterates the Sanskrit *Amitraghâta*, a title by which he was frequently designated, and which means *enemy-slayer*. He was succeeded by his son As'ôka in 270 B.C.

SELEUKOS NIKATOR, one of Alexander's great generals who made himself king of Syria, was the son of Antiochos, an officer of high rank in the service of King Philip. Seleukos was distinguished for his great personal strength and courage, and when he accompanied Alexander into Asia held a command in the companion cavalry. He crossed the Hydaspês with Alexander himself, and took an important part in the great battle which followed. At Sousa he was rewarded for his eminent services with the hand of Apama, an Asiatic princess, the daughter of Spitamenes. In the dissensions which broke out after Alexander's death among his generals, Seleukos sided with Perdikkas and

[1] The passage states that Amitrochates, the king of the Indians, wrote to Antiochos asking that king to buy and send him sweet wine, dried figs, and a sophist; and that Antiochos replied: We shall send you the figs and the wine, but in Greece the laws forbid a sophist to be sold. Athênaios quotes Hêgêsander as his authority.

the cavalry against Meleager and the infantry, and was in consequence made Chiliarch of the companions, one of the highest
offices, and one which Perdikkas himself had previously held.
He accompanied Perdikkas into Egypt, but he there put himself
at the head of the mutineers by whom his patron was assassinated.
At the second partition of the provinces made at Triparadeisos
321 B.C. he obtained the Babylonian satrapy, and established
himself in Babylon. He assisted Antigonos in the war against
Eumenes, but afterwards contended against him in alliance with
Ptolemy. During an interval when hostilities were suspended
between himself and his rivals, Seleukos undertook an expedition
into India to regain the conquests of Alexander over which Sandrokottos had established his authority. We do not know how
far he advanced into India, but he probably again crossed the
Hydaspês, which he had crossed twenty years before along with
the great conqueror himself. The result of the expedition was a
treaty by which Seleukos ceded to Sandrokottos his Indian provinces and the regions west of the Indus as far as the range of
Paropanisos, in exchange for 500 elephants, and a marriage
alliance by which the daughter of Seleukos became the bride of
the Indian king. Immediately either before or after this expedition, Seleukos in 306 B.C., following the examples of Antigonos
and Ptolemy, formally assumed the regal title and diadem. In
the battle of Ipsos 301 B.C., where Seleukos, in league with
Ptolemy, Lysimachos, and Kassander, fought against Antigonos,
the cavalry and elephants which the Syrian king brought into the
field were mainly instrumental in securing the victory. The
empire of Seleukos then became the most extensive of those
which had been formed out of Alexander's conquests, extending
from Phoenicia to Baktria and Sogdiana. After being engaged in
other wars, Seleukos crossed the Hellespont with an army with a
view to seize the crown of Macedonia, but was assassinated at
Lysimachia by Ptolemy Keraunos in the beginning of the year
280 B.C. in the thirty-second year of his reign.

SISIKOTTOS was an Indian who had deserted his countrymen
and taken service under Bessos. After the conquest of Baktria
he took service under Alexander, who, no doubt, obtained from
him much valuable information regarding India and its affairs.
After the capture of the rock Aornos, Sisikottos was left in command of the garrison which Alexander established there. He
afterwards sent messengers to inform Alexander that the Assakênians had revolted from him.

SITALKES was a leader of Thracian light-armed troops in
Alexander's service. He was left under Parmenion in Media,

and on Alexander's return from India was put to death for misgovernment.

SOLINUS was the author of a compendium of geography extracted mostly from the *Natural History* of Pliny. He lived about the middle of the third century A.D.

SÔPHEITES or SÔPEITHÊS was, according to Curtius and Diodôros, king of a territory situated to the west of the Hyphasis. According to Arrian his dominions (or those of a king of the same name) lay along the banks of the Hydaspês, and, as we learn from Strabo, embraced the salt range of mountains called *Oromenus* by Pliny. With regard to the name, Lassen took it to represent the Sanskrit *As'vapati*, "lord of horses." M. Sylvain Lévi, however, thinks this a fanciful identification of the two names, erring against Greek and against Sanskrit. He then says : "A drachma of Indian silver coined towards the end of the fourth century B.C. in imitation of Greek money bears the inscription ΣΩΦΥΤΟΥ. The form Sophytes is, then, the only one to be considered. The laws of transcription established by numerous examples give the equivalents : ω = ô or *aw*, φ = *bh*. Sophytes then leads back to Sobûtha or Saubh. The Gana-pâtha knows precisely a country of the name of Saubhûta. Pânini (IV. ii. 67 *sqq.*) shows by examples how local names are formed. . . . The name of Sâmkala, etc., is formed in this way. M. Bhandarkar has already recognised in the city of Sâmkala the famous fortress of Sangala, . . . but the Indian *savant* has not overcome the old prejudice which, regardless of the laws of transcription, identifies Sangala with S'âkala, capital of the Madras (Lassen, *Ind. Alt.* i. 801). . . . The identification firmly fixed of Sophytes and Saubhûta dissipates henceforward all doubts. Among the names classed in the Gana-pâtha under the rubric Sâmkala, etc., is found *Subhûta*, which gives, in virtue of the rule stated, *Saubhûta* as the name of a locality. Everything concurs in proving the correctness of our identification."

SPHINÊS.—*See* Kalânos.

SPITAKES is supposed to be the same as the Pittakos mentioned by Polyainos. He was slain fighting on the side of Pôros in the battle of the Hydaspês. His territories lay near that river.

SPITAMENES, the most formidable and persistent of all the chiefs who opposed Alexander in the regions of the Oxus and Jaxartes.

STASANÔR, a distinguished officer in Alexander's army, was a native of Soloi in Cyprus. For services rendered during the Baktrian campaign he was appointed satrap of Areia and afterwards of Drangiana. In the first partition of the provinces after

Alexander's death he was confirmed in his satrapy; but in the partition made at Triparadeisos he received the more important government of Baktria and Sogdiana. He ruled his subjects with justice and moderation. He is not heard of in history after 316 B.C.

STATEIRA or BARSINÊ, the daughter of Darius and wife of Alexander, was murdered after his death by Roxana with the consent of the regent Perdikkas.

STEPHANOS of Byzantium was the author of a geographical lexicon, in which the names of some Indian towns occur. His date is uncertain, but may be referred to the sixth or seventh century of our aera.

STRABO, the great geographer, was a native of Amasea in Pontos. He lived in the reign of Augustus, and during the first five years at least of Tiberius.

SIBYRTIOS was appointed by Alexander on returning from India satrap of Karmania, and afterwards of Arachosia and Gedrosia in succession to Thoas. He was confirmed in his government in accordance with the first and the second partition of the provinces. He incurred the displeasure of Eumenes, and thereby secured the patronage of Antigonos. Megasthenes was his friend, and at one time resided with him.

TAURÔN was an officer in Alexander's army, who distinguished himself in the battle with Pôros.

TAXILÊS, whose personal name was Omphis, ruled a fertile territory between the Indus and Hydaspês, which had for its capital the great and flourishing city of Taxila. He was at feud with his neighbour, King Pôros, and this probably determined him to send an embassy to Alexander while he was yet in Baktria, in the hopes of forming an alliance with him which would enable him to crush his powerful rival. He waited on Alexander before he had crossed the Indus, and when he reached Taxila entertained him and his army with the most liberal hospitality. After the defeat and submission of Pôros, Alexander effected a reconciliation between the two princes. Taxilês gave all the assistance in his power to help forward the construction and equipment of the fleet by which Alexander intended to convey a portion of his troops down the Hydaspês and the Indus to the ocean. For this service he was rewarded with an accession of territory. After the death of Alexander he was allowed to retain his power, which had been increased after the murder of the satrap Philip. Subsequently to the year 321 B.C. Eudêmos seems to have exercised supreme authority in his province. We know nothing regarding Taxilês after that date. M. Sylvain Lévi shows that the personal name of Taxilês is incorrectly given by Diodôros as *Mophis* instead of *Omphis*, which is the form in Curtius. He gives the reason thus : " The study of the words transcribed from the Indian languages into Greek proves that the *o* corresponds to an *â* or to an *o* in Sanskrit, while the φ is the regular transcription of *bh*. Mophis gives therefore a Sanskrit *Mobhi* or *Mâbhi*; neither the one nor the other is met with in the texts ; they are both strangers to the language as well as to the history of India. But *Âmbhi* presents itself in the Gana-pâtha, a genuine appendix to the *Grammar* of Pânini." He then shows that *Âmbhi* has been obtained from *Ambhas* in accordance with an established rule, and thus proceeds : " A double con-clusion unfolds itself—1st, The dynasty which was reigning at Taks'as'ilâ at the time of the Greek invasion was a family of Kshatriya descended from Ambhas, and designated by the patronymic Âmbhi ; 2nd, The dynasty Âmbhi has disappeared with the Greek rule soon after the death of Alexander. The revolt of India has swept away without doubt these allies of the stranger. Before the end of the fourth century B.C., Chandragupta, founder of the Mauryan dynasty and king of the Prasyas, joined to his dominions the kingdoms of the basin of the Indus. Taks'as'ilâ became the residence of a Mauryan governor. The part played by the Âmbhi does not appear to have been con-siderable enough to preserve their memory long ; the mention of them in the *Gana-pâtha* is the only known testimony to their existence. The *Gana-pâtha*, and, at the same time, the *Grammar* of Pânini, which is inseparable from it, are then *very probably contemporary with the Macedonian invasion.*" He adds as a footnote, " The mention of the Yavanas (Greeks) and of the Yavanâni (Greek writing) excludes the hypothesis of priority" (See *Journal Asiatique* for 1890, pp. 234-236).

TERIOLTES, called also TYRIASPES, was appointed satrap of the Paropamisadai, but was deposed, or, according to Curtius, put to death for misgovernment. His satrapy Alexander then gave to his father-in-law Oxyartes.

TLEPOLEMOS was appointed satrap of Karmania by Alexander on his return from India.

TYRIASPES.—*See* Terioltes.

VINDUSÂRA, the son of Sandrokottos.—*See* Sandrokottos.

XANDRAMES, king of Magadha.—*See* Sandrokottos.

INDICES

I. GENERAL INDEX

2 E

II. INDEX OF AUTHORITIES QUOTED OR REFERRED TO

THE END

Printed by R. & R. CLARK, *Edinburgh.*

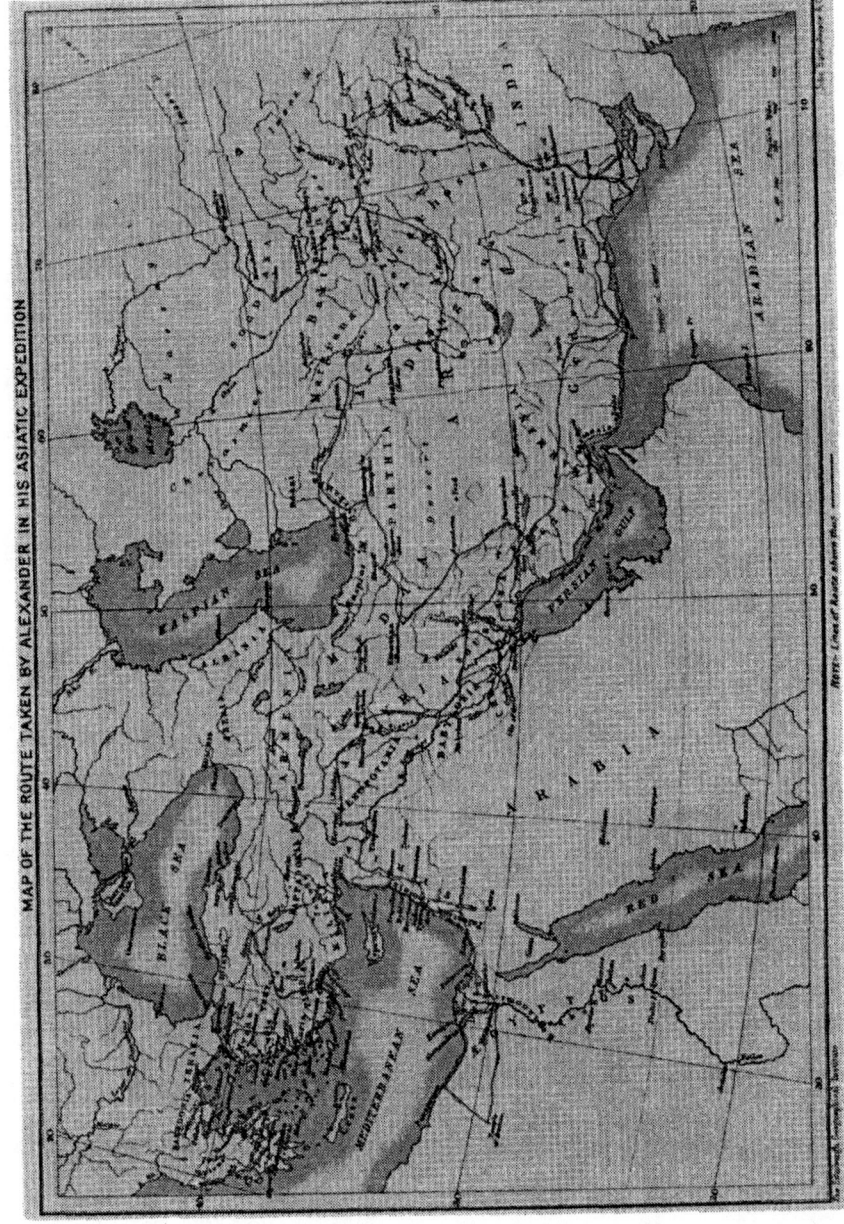

MAP OF THE ROUTE TAKEN BY ALEXANDER IN HIS ASIATIC EXPEDITION

NOTE: Line of Route shown thus ——————

Printed in the United States
114837LV00002B/192/A

9 780766 189201